casenote™
Legal Briefs
CONSTITUTIONAL LAW

Adaptable to courses utilizing **Sullivan** and **Gunther's** casebook on Constitutional Law

NORMAN S. GOLDENBERG, SENIOR EDITOR
PETER TENEN, MANAGING EDITOR

ALSO AVAILABLE!
CONSTITUTIONAL LAW OUTLINE
This Casenote Legal Briefs volume is now cross-referenced to the new **Casenote Law Outline** on Constitutional Law by Prof. Gary Goodpaster

STAFF WRITERS

ROBERTA E. SAND
DAVID TREBILCOCK
CLAUDIA NORBY
MATT HARDY
RALPH ARMIJO
RICHARD A. LOVICH
HOWARD MATTHEWS
JIM KNIGHT
JERRY SMILOWITZ
C. JEAN RYAN
HOWART SCOTT LEVIANT

ASPEN LAW AND BUSINESS
Aspen Publishers, Inc.
New York - Gaithersburg

FORMAT FOR THE CASENOTE LEGAL BRIEF

PARTY ID: Quick identification of the relationship between the parties. ◄──

PALSGRAF v. LONG ISLAND R.R. CO.
──► *Injured bystander (P) v. Railroad company (D)*
N.Y. Ct. App., 248 N.Y. 339, 162 N.E. 99 (1928).

NATURE OF CASE: This section identifies the form of action (e.g., breach of contract, negligence, battery), the type of proceeding (e.g., demurrer, appeal from trial court's jury instructions) or the relief sought (e.g., damages, injunction, criminal sanctions).

NATURE OF CASE: Appeal from judgment affirming verdict for plaintiff seeking damages for personal injury.

FACT SUMMARY: This is included to refresh the student's memory and can be used as a quick reminder of the facts.

FACT SUMMARY: Helen Palsgraf (P) was injured on R.R.'s (D) train platform when R.R.'s (D) guard helped a passenger aboard a moving train, causing his package to fall on the tracks. The package contained fireworks which exploded, creating a shock that tipped a scale onto Palsgraf (P).

CONCISE RULE OF LAW: Summarizes the general principle of law that the case illustrates. It may be used for instant recall of the court's holding and for classroom discussion or home review.

CONCISE RULE OF LAW: The risk reasonably to be perceived defines the duty to be obeyed.

FACTS: This section contains all relevant facts of the case, including the contentions of the parties and the lower court holdings. It is written in a logical order to give the student a clear understanding of the case. The plaintiff and defendant are identified by their proper names throughout and are always labeled with a (P) or (D).

FACTS: Helen Palsgraf (P) purchased a ticket to Rockaway Beach from R.R. (D) and was waiting on the train platform. As she waited, two men ran to catch a train that was pulling out from the platform. The first man jumped aboard, but the second man, who appeared as if he might fall, was helped aboard by the guard on the train who had kept the door open so they could jump aboard. A guard on the platform also helped by pushing him onto the train. The man was carrying a package wrapped in newspaper. In the process, the man dropped his package, which fell on the tracks. The package contained fireworks and exploded. The shock of the explosion was apparently of great enough strength to tip over some scales at the other end of the platform, which fell on Palsgraf (P) and injured her. A jury awarded her damages, and R.R. (D) appealed.

ISSUE: The issue is a concise question that brings out the essence of the opinion as it relates to the section of the casebook in which the case appears. Both substantive and procedural issues are included if relevant to the decision.

ISSUE: Does the risk reasonably to be perceived define the duty to be obeyed?

HOLDING AND DECISION: This section offers a clear and in-depth discussion of the rule of the case and the court's rationale. It is written in easy-to-understand language and answers the issue(s) presented by applying the law to the facts of the case. When relevant, it includes a thorough discussion of the exceptions to the case as listed by the court, any major cites to other cases on point, and the names of the judges who wrote the decisions.

HOLDING AND DECISION: (Cardozo, C.J.) Yes. The risk reasonably to be perceived defines the duty to be obeyed. If there is no foreseeable hazard to the injured party as the result of a seemingly innocent act, the act does not become a tort because it happened to be a wrong as to another. If the wrong was not willful, the plaintiff must show that the act as to her had such great and apparent possibilities of danger as to entitle her to protection. Negligence in the abstract is not enough upon which to base liability. Negligence is a relative concept, evolving out of the common law doctrine of trespass on the case. To establish liability, the defendant must owe a legal duty of reasonable care to the injured party. A cause of action in tort will lie where harm, though unintended, could have been averted or avoided by observance of such a duty. The scope of the duty is limited by the range of danger that a reasonable person could foresee. In this case, there was nothing to suggest from the appearance of the parcel or otherwise that the parcel contained fireworks. The guard could not reasonably have had any warning of a threat to Palsgraf (P), and R.R. (D) therefore cannot be held liable. Judgment is reversed in favor of R.R. (D).

DISSENT: (Andrews, J.) The concept that there is no negligence unless R.R. (D) owes a legal duty to take care as to Palsgraf (P) herself is too narrow. Everyone owes to the world at large the duty of refraining from those acts that may unreasonably threaten the safety of others. If the guard's action was negligent as to those nearby, it was also negligent as to those outside what might be termed the "danger zone." For Palsgraf (P) to recover, R.R.'s (D) negligence must have been the proximate cause of her injury, a question of fact for the jury.

CONCURRENCE / DISSENT: All concurrences and dissents are briefed whenever they are included by the casebook editor.

EDITOR'S ANALYSIS: This last paragraph gives the student a broad understanding of where the case "fits in" with other cases in the section of the book and with the entire course. It is a hornbook-style discussion indicating whether the case is a majority or minority opinion and comparing the principal case with other cases in the casebook. It may also provide analysis from restatements, uniform codes, and law review articles. The editor's analysis will prove to be invaluable to classroom discussion.

EDITOR'S ANALYSIS: The majority defined the limit of the defendant's liability in terms of the danger that a reasonable person in defendant's situation would have perceived. The dissent argued that the limitation should not be placed on liability, but rather on damages. Judge Andrews suggested that only injuries that would not have happened but for R.R.'s (D) negligence should be compensable. Both the majority and dissent recognized the policy-driven need to limit liability for negligent acts, seeking, in the words of Judge Andrews, to define a framework "that will be practical and in keeping with the general understanding of mankind." The Restatement (Second) of Torts has accepted Judge Cardozo's view..

CROSS-REFERENCE TO OUTLINE: Wherever possible, following each case is a cross-reference linking the subject matter of the issue to the appropriate place in the *Casenote Law Outline*, which provides further information on the subject.

[For more information on foreseeability, see Casenote Law Outline on Torts, Chapter 8, § II. 2., Proximate Cause.]

QUICKNOTES

FORESEEABILITY - The reasonable anticipation that damage is a likely result from certain acts or omissions.

QUICKNOTES: Conveniently defines legal terms found in the case and summarizes the nature of any statutes, codes, or rules referred to in the text.

NEGLIGENCE - Failure to exercise that degree of care which a person of ordinary prudence would exercise under similiar circumstances.

PROXIMATE CAUSE - Something which in natural and continuous sequence, unbroken by any new intervening cause, produces an event, and without which injury would not have occurred.

NOTE TO STUDENT

OUR GOAL. It is the goal of Casenotes Publishing Company, Inc. to create and distribute the finest, clearest and most accurate legal briefs available. To this end, we are constantly seeking new ideas, comments and constructive criticism. As a user of *Casenote Legal Briefs,* your suggestions will be highly valued. With all correspondence, please include your complete name, address, and telephone number, including area code and zip code.

THE TOTAL STUDY SYSTEM. *Casenote Legal Briefs* are just one part of the *Casenotes* TOTAL STUDY SYSTEM. Most briefs are (wherever possible) cross-referenced to the appropriate *Casenote Law Outline,* which will elaborate on the issue at hand. By purchasing a Law Outline together with your Legal Brief, you will have both parts of the *Casenotes* TOTAL STUDY SYSTEM. (See the advertising in the front of this book for a list of Law Outlines currently available.)

A NOTE ABOUT LANGUAGE. Please note that the language used in *Casenote Legal Briefs* in reference to minority groups and women reflects terminology used within the historical context of the time in which the respective courts wrote the opinions. We at Casenotes Publishing Co., Inc. are well aware of and very sensitive to the desires of all people to be treated with dignity and to be referred to as they prefer. Because such preferences change from time to time, and because the language of the courts reflects the time period in which opinions were written, our case briefs will not necessarily reflect contemporary references. We appreciate your understanding and invite your comments.

A NOTE REGARDING NEW EDITIONS. As of our press date, this *Casenote Legal Brief* is current and includes briefs of all cases in the current version of the casebook, divided into chapters that correspond to that edition of the casebook. However, occasionally a new edition of the casebook comes out in the interim, and sometimes the casebook author will make changes in the sequence of the cases in the chapters, add or delete cases, or change the chapter titles. Should you be using this Legal Brief in conjunction with a casebook that was issued later than this book, you can receive all of the newer cases, which are available free from us, by sending in the "Supplement Request Form" in this section of the book (please follow all instructions on that form). The Supplement(s) will contain all the missing cases, and will bring your *Casenote Legal Brief* up to date.

EDITOR'S NOTE. *Casenote Legal Briefs* are intended to supplement the student's casebook, not replace it. There is no substitute for the student's own mastery of this important learning and study technique. If used properly, *Casenote Legal Briefs* are an effective law study aid that will serve to reinforce the student's understanding of the cases.

Free access to briefs online!

Download the cases you want to include in your notes or outlines with full cut and paste abilities. Please fill out this form to be given access. No photocopies of this form will be accepted.

① **Name:** _____   **Phone:** (____) _____

Address: _____   **Apt.:**_____

City: _____   **State:**_____   **Zip Code:** _____

Law School: _____   **Year (circle one):**   1st   2nd   3rd

② **Cut out the UPC found on the lower left hand corner on the back cover of this book. Staple the UPC inside this box. Only the original UPC from this book will be accepted. (No photocopies or store stickers are allowed.)**

Attach UPC inside this box.

③ **E-mail:** _____ **(Print LEGIBLY or you may not get access!)**

④ **Title (course subject) of this book:** _____

⑤ **Adaptable to which casebook author:** _____

⑥ **Mail the completed form to:**   Law School Sales Associate
Aspen Law and Business
1185 Avenue of the Americas
New York, NY 10036

I understand that online access is granted solely to the purchaser of this book for the academic year in which it was purchased. Any other usage is not authorized and will result in immediate termination of access. Sharing of codes is strictly prohibited.

_____
Signature

Upon receipt of this completed form, you will be e-mailed codes so that you may access the briefs found in this book at **www.casenotes.com**.

SUPPLEMENT REQUEST FORM

At the time this book was printed, a brief was included for every major case in the casebook and for every existing supplement to the casebook. However, if a new supplement to the casebook (or a new edition of the casebook) has been published since this publication was printed and if that casebook supplement (or new edition of the casebook) was available for sale at the time you purchased this Casenote Legal Briefs book, we will be pleased to provide you the new cases contained therein AT NO CHARGE when you send us a stamped, self-addressed envelope.

TO OBTAIN YOUR FREE SUPPLEMENT MATERIAL, **YOU MUST FOLLOW THE INSTRUCTIONS BELOW PRECISELY** OR YOUR REQUEST WILL NOT BE ACKNOWLEDGED!

1. Please check if there is in fact an existing supplement and, if so, that the cases are not already included in your Casenote Legal Briefs. Check the main table of cases as well as the supplement table of cases, if any.

2. **REMOVE THIS ENTIRE PAGE FROM THE BOOK.** You MUST send this ORIGINAL page to receive your supplement. This page acts as your proof of purchase and contains the reference number necessary to fill your supplement request properly. No photocopy of this page or written request will be honored or answered. Any request from which the reference number has been removed, altered or obliterated will not be honored.

3. Prepare a STAMPED self-addressed envelope for return mailing. Be sure to use a FULL SIZE (9 X 12) ENVELOPE (MANILA TYPE) so that the supplement will fit and AFFIX ENOUGH POSTAGE TO COVER 3 OZ. **ANY SUPPLEMENT REQUEST NOT ACCOMPANIED BY A STAMPED SELF-ADDRESSED ENVELOPE WILL ABSOLUTELY NOT BE FILLED OR ACKNOWLEDGED.**

4. MULTIPLE SUPPLEMENT REQUESTS: If you are ordering more than one supplement, we suggest that you enclose a stamped, self-addressed envelope for each supplement requested. If you enclose only one envelope for a multiple request, your order may not be filled immediately should any supplement which you requested still be in production. In other words, your order will be held by us until it can be filled completely.

5. Casenotes prints two kinds of supplements. A "New Edition" supplement is issued when a new edition of your casebook is published. A "New Edition" supplement gives you all major cases found in the new edition of the casebook which did not appear in the previous edition. A regular "supplement" is issued when a paperback supplement to your casebook is published. If the box at the lower right is stamped, then the "New Edition" supplement was provided to your bookstore and is *not* available from Casenotes; however, Casenotes will still send you any regular "supplements" which have been printed either before or after the new edition of your casebook appeared and which, according to the reference number at the top of this page, have not been included in this book. If the box is not stamped, Casenotes will send you any supplements, "New Edition" and/or regular, needed to completely update your Casenote Legal Briefs.

★☞ *NOTE:* REQUESTS FOR SUPPLEMENTS WILL NOT BE FILLED UNLESS THESE INSTRUCTIONS ARE COMPLIED WITH!

6. Fill in the following information:

Full title of CASEBOOK __**CONSTITUTIONAL LAW**__

CASEBOOK author's name ____**SULLIVAN**____

Copyright year of new edition or new paperback supplement

Name and location of bookstore where this Casenote Legal Brief was purchased _____

Name and location of law school you attend _____

Any comments regarding Casenote Legal Briefs _____

NOTE: IF THIS BOX IS STAMPED, NO NEW EDITION SUPPLEMENT CAN BE OBTAINED BY MAIL.

PUBLISHED BY CASENOTES PUBLISHING CO., INC. 1640 5th ST, SUITE 208 SANTA MONICA, CA 90401

PLEASE PRINT
NAME _____ **PHONE** _____ **DATE** _____
ADDRESS/CITY/STATE/ZIP _____

Announcing the First *Totally Integrated* Law Study System

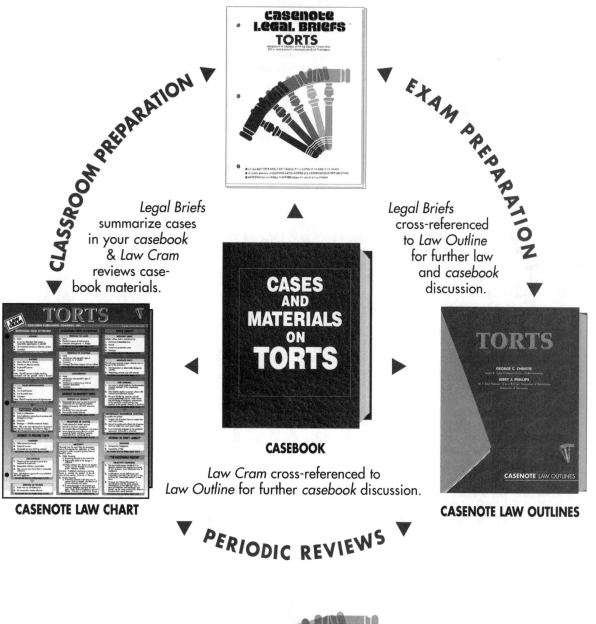

CASENOTE LEGAL BRIEFS

CLASSROOM PREPARATION

EXAM PREPARATION

Legal Briefs summarize cases in your *casebook* & *Law Cram* reviews casebook materials.

Legal Briefs cross-referenced to *Law Outline* for further law and *casebook* discussion.

CASEBOOK

Law Cram cross-referenced to *Law Outline* for further *casebook* discussion.

CASENOTE LAW CHART

CASENOTE LAW OUTLINES

PERIODIC REVIEWS

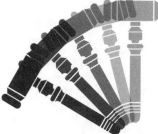

CASENOTES PUBLISHING COMPANY INC.

"Preparation is nine-tenths of the law..."

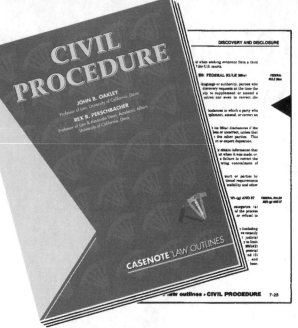

RENOWNED AUTHORS: *Every* **Casenote Law Outline** *is written by highly respected, nationally recognized professors.*

KEYED TO **CASENOTE LEGAL BRIEF** *BOOKS: In most cases,* **Casenote Law Outlines** *work in conjunction with the* **Casenote Legal Briefs** *so that you can see how each case in your textbook relates to the entire subject area. In addition,* **Casenote Law Outlines** *are cross-referenced to most major casebooks.*

ADMINISTRATIVE LAW (2002)
Charles H. Koch, Jr., Dudley W. Woodbridge Professor of Law, College of William and Mary
Sidney A. Shapiro, John M. Rounds Professor of Law, University of Kansas

CIVIL PROCEDURE (2001)
John B. Oakley, Professor of Law, University of California, Davis School of Law
Rex R. Perschbacher, Professor and Dean of University of California, Davis School of Law

COMMERCIAL LAW (see SALES • SECURED TRANSACTIONS • NEGOTIABLE INSTRUMENTS & PAYMENT SYSTEMS)

CONFLICT OF LAWS (1996)
Luther L. McDougal, III, W.R. Irby Professor of Law, Tulane University
Robert L. Felix, James P. Mozingo, III, Professor of Law, University of South Carolina

CONSTITUTIONAL LAW (2000)
Gary Goodpaster, Professor of Law, University of California, Davis School of Law

CONTRACTS (2001)
Daniel Wm. Fessler, Professor of Law, University of California, Davis School of Law

CORPORATIONS (2000)
Lewis D. Solomon, Arthur Selwin Miller Research Professor of Law, George Washington University
Daniel Wm. Fessler, Professor of Law, University of California, Davis School of Law
Arthur E. Wilmarth, Jr., Associate Professor of Law, George Washington University

CRIMINAL LAW (2002)
Joshua Dressler, Professor of Law, Ohio State University College of Law

CRIMINAL PROCEDURE (2001)
Joshua Dressler, Professor of Law, Ohio State University College of Law

ESTATE & GIFT TAX (2000)
Joseph M. Dodge, W.H. Francis Professor of Law, University of Texas at Austin

EVIDENCE (2000)
Kenneth Graham, Jr., Professor of Law, University of California, Los Angeles School of Law

FEDERAL COURTS (1997)
Howard P. Fink, Isadore and Ida Topper Professor of Law, Ohio State University College of Law
Linda S. Mullenix, Bernard J. Ward Centennial Professor of Law, University of Texas

FEDERAL INCOME TAXATION (2002)
Joseph M. Dodge, W.H. Francis Professor of Law, University of Texas at Austin

LEGAL RESEARCH (2001)
Nancy L. Schultz, Professor of Law, Chapman University
Louis J. Sirico, Jr., Professor of Law, Villanova University

NEGOTIABLE INSTRUMENTS & PAYMENT SYSTEMS (1995)
Donald B. King, Professor of Law, Saint Louis University
Peter Winship, James Cleo Thompson, Sr. Trustee Professor, Southern Methodist University

PROPERTY (2001)
Sheldon F. Kurtz, Percy Bordwell Professor of Law, University of Iowa
Patricia Cain, Professor of Law, University of Iowa

SALES (2001)
Robert E. Scott, Dean and Lewis F. Powell, Jr. Professor of Law, University of Virginia
Donald B. King, Professor of Law, Saint Louis University

SECURED TRANSACTIONS (2002)
Donald B. King, Professor of Law, Saint Louis University

TORTS (2001)
George C. Christie, James B. Duke Professor of Law, Duke University
Jerry J. Phillips, W.P. Toms Professor of Law, University of Tennessee

WILLS, TRUSTS, & ESTATES (2002)
William M. McGovern, Professor of Law, University of California, Los Angeles School of Law

CASENOTE LEGAL BRIEFS

CASENOTES PUBLISHING CO. INC. ● 1640 FIFTH STREET, SUITE 208 ● SANTA MONICA, CA 90401 ● (310) 395-6500

E-Mail Address - info@casenotes.com
Website - www.casenotes.com

PLEASE PURCHASE FROM YOUR LOCAL BOOKSTORE. IF UNAVAILABLE, YOU MAY ORDER DIRECT FROM ASPEN'S WEBSITE.

ABBREVIATIONS FOR BRIEFING

The following list of abbreviations will assist you in the process of briefing and provide an illustration of the technique of formulating functional personal abbreviations for commonly encountered words, phrases, and concepts.

acceptance	acp
affirmed	aff
answer	ans
assumption of risk	a/r
attorney	atty
beyond a reasonable doubt	b/r/d
bona fide purchaser	BFP
breach of contract	br/k
cause of action	c/a
common law	c/l
Constitution	Con
constitutional	con
contract	K
contributory negligence	c/n
cross	x
cross-complaint	x/c
cross-examination	x/ex
cruel and unusual punishment	c/u/p
defendant	D
dismissed	dis
double jeopardy	d/j
due process	d/p
equal protection	e/p
equity	eq
evidence	ev
exclude	exc
exclusionary rule	exc/r
felony	f/m
freedom of speech	f/s
good faith	g/f
habeas corpus	h/c
hearsay	hr
husband	H
in loco parentis	ILP
injunction	inj
inter vivos	I/v
joint tenancy	j/t
judgment	judgt
jurisdiction	jur
last clear chance	LCC
long-arm statute	LAS
majority view	maj
meeting of minds	MOM
minority view	min
Miranda warnings	Mir/w
Miranda rule	Mir/r
negligence	neg
notice	mtc
nuisance	nus
obligation	ob
obscene	obs

offer	O
offeree	OE
offeror	OR
ordinance	ord
pain and suffering	p/s
parol evidence	p/e
plaintiff	P
prima facie	p/f
probable cause	p/c
proximate cause	px/c
real property	r/p
reasonable doubt	r/d
reasonable man	r/m
rebuttable presumption	rb/p
remanded	rem
res ipsa loquitur	RIL
respondent superior	r/s
Restatement	RS
reversed	rev
Rule Against Perpetuities	RAP
search and seizure	s/s
search warrant	s/w
self-defense	s/d
specific performance	s/p
statute of limitations	S/L
statute of frauds	S/F
statute	S
summary judgment	s/j
tenancy in common	t/c
tenancy at will	t/w
tenant	t
third party	TP
third party beneficiary	TPB
transferred intent	TI
unconscionable	uncon
unconstitutional	unconst
undue influence	u/e
Uniform Commercial Code	UCC
unilateral	uni
vendee	VE
vendor	VR
versus	v
void for vagueness	VFV
weight of the evidence	w/e
weight of authority	w/a
wife	W
with	w/
within	w/I
without prejudice	w/o/p
without	w/o
wrongful death	wr/d

GLOSSARY

COMMON LATIN WORDS AND PHRASES ENCOUNTERED IN LAW

A FORTIORI: Because one fact exists or has been proven, therefore a second fact that is related to the first fact must also exist.

A PRIORI: From the cause to the effect. A term of logic used to denote that when one generally accepted truth is shown to be a cause, another particular effect must necessarily follow.

AB INITIO: From the beginning; a condition which has existed throughout, as in a marriage which was void ab initio.

ACTUS REUS: The wrongful act; in criminal law, such action sufficient to trigger criminal liability.

AD VALOREM: According to value; an ad valorem tax is imposed upon an item located within the taxing jurisdiction calculated by the value of such item.

AMICUS CURIAE: Friend of the court. Its most common usage takes the form of an amicus curiae brief, filed by a person who is not a party to an action but is nonetheless allowed to offer an argument supporting his legal interests.

ARGUENDO: In arguing. A statement, possibly hypothetical, made for the purpose of argument, is one made arguendo.

BILL QUIA TIMET: A bill to quiet title (establish ownership) to real property.

BONA FIDE: True, honest, or genuine. May refer to a person's legal position based on good faith or lacking notice of fraud (such as a bona fide purchaser for value) or to the authenticity of a particular document (such as a bona fide last will and testament).

CAUSA MORTIS: With approaching death in mind. A gift causa mortis is a gift given by a party who feels certain that death is imminent.

CAVEAT EMPTOR: Let the buyer beware. This maxim is reflected in the rule of law that a buyer purchases at his own risk because it is his responsibility to examine, judge, test, and otherwise inspect what he is buying.

CERTIORARI: A writ of review. Petitions for review of a case by the United States Supreme Court are most often done by means of a writ of certiorari.

CONTRA: On the other hand. Opposite. Contrary to.

CORAM NOBIS: Before us; writs of error directed to the court that originally rendered the judgment.

CORAM VOBIS: Before you; writs of error directed by an appellate court to a lower court to correct a factual error.

CORPUS DELICTI: The body of the crime; the requisite elements of a crime amounting to objective proof that a crime has been committed.

CUM TESTAMENTO ANNEXO, ADMINISTRATOR (ADMINISTRATOR C.T.A.): With will annexed; an administrator c.t.a. settles an estate pursuant to a will in which he is not appointed.

DE BONIS NON, ADMINISTRATOR (ADMINISTRATOR D.B.N.): Of goods not administered; an administrator d.b.n. settles a partially settled estate.

DE FACTO: In fact; in reality; actually. Existing in fact but not officially approved or engendered.

DE JURE: By right; lawful. Describes a condition that is legitimate "as a matter of law," in contrast to the term "de facto," which connotes something existing in fact but not legally sanctioned or authorized. For example, de facto segregation refers to segregation brought about by housing patterns, etc., whereas de jure segregation refers to segregation created by law.

DE MINIMUS: Of minimal importance; insignificant; a trifle; not worth bothering about.

DE NOVO: Anew; a second time; afresh. A trial de novo is a new trial held at the appellate level as if the case originated there and the trial at a lower level had not taken place.

DICTA: Generally used as an abbreviated form of obiter dicta, a term describing those portions of a judicial opinion incidental or not necessary to resolution of the specific question before the court. Such nonessential statements and remarks are not considered to be binding precedent.

DUCES TECUM: Refers to a particular type of writ or subpoena requesting a party or organization to produce certain documents in their possession.

EN BANC: Full bench. Where a court sits with all justices present rather than the usual quorum.

EX PARTE: For one side or one party only. An ex parte proceeding is one undertaken for the benefit of only one party, without notice to, or an appearance by, an adverse party.

EX POST FACTO: After the fact. An ex post facto law is a law that retroactively changes the consequences of a prior act.

EX REL.: Abbreviated form of the term ex relatione, meaning, upon relation or information. When the state brings an action in which it has no interest against an individual at the instigation of one who has a private interest in the matter.

FORUM NON CONVENIENS: Inconvenient forum. Although a court may have jurisdiction over the case, the action should be tried in a more conveniently located court, one to which parties and witnesses may more easily travel, for example.

GUARDIAN AD LITEM: A guardian of an infant as to litigation, appointed to represent the infant and pursue his/her rights.

HABEAS CORPUS: You have the body. The modern writ of habeas corpus is a writ directing that a person (body) being detained (such as a prisoner) be brought before the court so that the legality of his detention can be judicially ascertained.

IN CAMERA: In private, in chambers. When a hearing is held before a judge in his chambers or when all spectators are excluded from the courtroom.

IN FORMA PAUPERIS: In the manner of a pauper. A party who proceeds in forma pauperis because of his poverty is one who is allowed to bring suit without liability for costs.

INFRA: Below, under. A word referring the reader to a later part of a book. (The opposite of supra.)

IN LOCO PARENTIS: In the place of a parent.

IN PARI DELICTO: Equally wrong; a court of equity will not grant requested relief to an applicant who is in pari delicto, or as much at fault in the transactions giving rise to the controversy as is the opponent of the applicant.

IN PARI MATERIA: On like subject matter or upon the same matter. Statutes relating to the same person or things are said to be in pari materia. It is a general rule of statutory construction that such statutes should be construed together, i.e., looked at as if they together constituted one law.

IN PERSONAM: Against the person. Jurisdiction over the person of an individual.

IN RE: In the matter of. Used to designate a proceeding involving an estate or other property.

IN REM: A term that signifies an action against the res, or thing. An action in rem is basically one that is taken directly against property, as distinguished from an action in personam, i.e., against the person.

INTER ALIA: Among other things. Used to show that the whole of a statement, pleading, list, statute, etc., has not been set forth in its entirety.

INTER PARTES: Between the parties. May refer to contracts, conveyances or other transactions having legal significance.

INTER VIVOS: Between the living. An inter vivos gift is a gift made by a living grantor, as distinguished from bequests contained in a will, which pass upon the death of the testator.

IPSO FACTO: By the mere fact itself.

JUS: Law or the entire body of law.

LEX LOCI: The law of the place; the notion that the rights of parties to a legal proceeding are governed by the law of the place where those rights arose.

MALUM IN SE: Evil or wrong in and of itself; inherently wrong. This term describes an act that is wrong by its very nature, as opposed to one which would not be wrong but for the fact that there is a specific legal prohibition against it (malum prohibitum).

MALUM PROHIBITUM: Wrong because prohibited, but not inherently evil. Used to describe something that is wrong because it is expressly forbidden by law but that is not in and of itself evil, e.g., speeding.

MANDAMUS: We command. A writ directing an official to take a certain action.

MENS REA: A guilty mind; a criminal intent. A term used to signify the mental state that accompanies a crime or other prohibited act. Some crimes require only a general mens rea (general intent to do the prohibited act), but others, like assault with intent to murder, require the existence of a specific mens rea.

MODUS OPERANDI: Method of operating; generally refers to the manner or style of a criminal in committing crimes, admissible in appropriate cases as evidence of the identity of a defendant.

NEXUS: A connection to.

NISI PRIUS: A court of first impression. A nisi prius court is one where issues of fact are tried before a judge or jury.

N.O.V. (NON OBSTANTE VEREDICTO): Notwithstanding the verdict. A judgment n.o.v. is a judgment given in favor of one party despite the fact that a verdict was returned in favor of the other party, the justification being that the verdict either had no reasonable support in fact or was contrary to law.

NUNC PRO TUNC: Now for then. This phrase refers to actions that may be taken and will then have full retroactive effect.

PENDENTE LITE: Pending the suit; pending litigation underway.

PER CAPITA: By head; beneficiaries of an estate, if they take in equal shares, take per capita.

PER CURIAM: By the court; signifies an opinion ostensibly written "by the whole court" and with no identified author.

PER SE: By itself, in itself; inherently.

PER STIRPES: By representation. Used primarily in the law of wills to describe the method of distribution where a person, generally because of death, is unable to take that which is left to him by the will of another, and therefore his heirs divide such property between them rather than take under the will individually.

PRIMA FACIE: On its face, at first sight. A prima facie case is one that is sufficient on its face, meaning that the evidence supporting it is adequate to establish the case until contradicted or overcome by other evidence.

PRO TANTO: For so much; as far as it goes. Often used in eminent domain cases when a property owner receives partial payment for his land without prejudice to his right to bring suit for the full amount he claims his land to be worth.

QUANTUM MERUIT: As much as he deserves. Refers to recovery based on the doctrine of unjust enrichment in those cases in which a party has rendered valuable services or furnished materials that were accepted and enjoyed by another under circumstances that would reasonably notify the recipient that the rendering party expected to be paid. In essence, the law implies a contract to pay the reasonable value of the services or materials furnished.

QUASI: Almost like; as if; nearly. This term is essentially used to signify that one subject or thing is almost analogous to another but that material differences between them do exist. For example, a quasi-criminal proceeding is one that is not strictly criminal but shares enough of the same characteristics to require some of the same safeguards (e.g., procedural due process must be followed in a parol hearing).

QUID PRO QUO: Something for something. In contract law, the consideration, something of value, passed between the parties to render the contract binding.

RES GESTAE: Things done; in evidence law, this principle justifies the admission of a statement that would otherwise be hearsay when it is made so closely to the event in question as to be said to be a part of it, or with such spontaneity as not to have the possibility of falsehood.

RES IPSA LOQUITUR: The thing speaks for itself. This doctrine gives rise to a rebuttable presumption of negligence when the instrumentality causing the injury was within the exclusive control of the defendant, and the injury was one that does not normally occur unless a person has been negligent.

RES JUDICATA: A matter adjudged. Doctrine which provides that once a court of competent jurisdiction has rendered a final judgment or decree on the merits, that judgment or decree is conclusive upon the parties to the case and prevents them from engaging in any other litigation on the points and issues determined therein.

RESPONDEAT SUPERIOR: Let the master reply. This doctrine holds the master liable for the wrongful acts of his servant (or the principal for his agent) in those cases in which the servant (or agent) was acting within the scope of his authority at the time of the injury.

STARE DECISIS: To stand by or adhere to that which has been decided. The common law doctrine of stare decisis attempts to give security and certainty to the law by following the policy that once a principle of law as applicable to a certain set of facts has been set forth in a decision, it forms a precedent which will subsequently be followed, even though a different decision might be made were it the first time the question had arisen. Of course, stare decisis is not an inviolable principle and is departed from in instances where there is good cause (e.g., considerations of public policy led the Supreme Court to disregard prior decisions sanctioning segregation).

SUPRA: Above. A word referring a reader to an earlier part of a book.

ULTRA VIRES: Beyond the power. This phrase is most commonly used to refer to actions taken by a corporation that are beyond the power or legal authority of the corporation.

ADDENDUM OF FRENCH DERIVATIVES

IN PAIS: Not pursuant to legal proceedings.

CHATTEL: Tangible personal property.

CY PRES: Doctrine permitting courts to apply trust funds to purposes not expressed in the trust but necessary to carry out the settlor's intent.

PER AUTRE VIE: For another's life; in property law, an estate may be granted that will terminate upon the death of someone other than the grantee.

PROFIT A PRENDRE: A license to remove minerals or other produce from land.

VOIR DIRE: Process of questioning jurors as to their predispositions about the case or parties to a proceeding in order to identify those jurors displaying bias or prejudice.

NOTES

TABLE OF CASES

Continued on next page.

NOTES

TABLE OF CASES (Continued)

CHAPTER 1
THE NATURE AND SOURCES OF THE SUPREME COURT'S AUTHORITY

QUICK REFERENCE RULES OF LAW

1. **Judicial Review: The Bases and Implications of Marbury v. Madison.** The Supreme Court has the power, implied from Article VI, § 2 of the Constitution, to review acts of Congress and if they are found repugnant to the Constitution, to declare them void. (Marbury v. Madison)

   [For more information on judicial review, see Casenote Law Outline on Constitutional Law, Chapter 1, § II, The Doctrine of Judicial Review and Its Consequences.]

2. **The Nonjusticiability of Political Questions.** The fact that a suit seeks protection of a political right does not mean it necessarily presents a political question. (Baker v. Carr)

   [For more information on the political question doctrine, see Casenote Law Outline on Constitutional Law, Chapter 1, § III, Constitutional Limits on Federal Judicial Review.]

3. **The Nonjusticiability of Political Questions.** An action is nonjusticiable where there is a textually demonstrable constitutional commitment of the issue to a coordinate branch of government or a lack of judicially discoverable and manageable standards for resolving it. (Nixon v. United States)

   [For more information on judicial review, see Casenote Law Outline on Constitutional Law, Chapter 1, § III, Constitutional Limits on Federal Judicial Review.]

4. **Advisory Opinions, Standing, Mootness and Ripeness.** To establish standing, a plaintiff must show injury-in-fact, causation, and redressability, and Congress may not create a right of standing based on a generalized grievance against government. (Lujan v. Defenders of Wildlife)

   [For more information on standing, see Casenote Law Outline on Constitutional Law, Chapter 1, § III, Constitutional Limits on Federal Judicial Review.]

5. **Advisory Opinions, Standing, Mootness and Ripeness.** Although the Supreme Court derives its appellate jurisdiction from the Constitution, the Constitution also gives Congress the express power to make exceptions to that appellate jurisdiction. (Ex Parte McCardle)

   [For more information on jurisdiction stripping statutes, see Casenote Law Outline on Constitutional Law, Chapter 1, § II, The Doctrine of Judicial Review and Its Consequences.]

6. **Advisory Opinions, Standing, Mootness and Ripeness.** The question of standing (whether the litigant is entitled to have the court decide the merits of the dispute or of particular issues) has two limitations: 1) when the asserted harm is a "generalized grievance" shared substantially by all or a large class of citizens, that harm alone does not normally warrant exercise of jurisdiction; and 2) even when plaintiff presents "a case or controversy," generally he still must assert his own legal rights and interests, and cannot rest his claim to relief on the legal rights or interests of third parties. (Warth v. Seldin)

   [For more information on standing and causation, see Casenote Law Outline on Constitutional Law, Chapter 1, § III, Constitutional Limits on Federal Judicial Review.]

MARBURY v. MADISON
Justice (P) v. Secretary of State (D)
5 U.S. (1 Cranch) 137 (1803).

NATURE OF CASE: Writ of mandamus to compel delivery of commission.

FACT SUMMARY: President Jefferson's Secretary of State, Madison (D), refused to deliver a commission granted to Marbury (P) by former President Adams.

CONCISE RULE OF LAW: The Supreme Court has the power, implied from Article VI, § 2 of the Constitution, to review acts of Congress and if they are found repugnant to the Constitution, to declare them void.

FACTS: On March 2, 1801, the outgoing President of the United States, John Adams, named forty-two justices of the peace for the District of Columbia under the Organic Act passed the same day by Congress. William Marbury (P) was one of the justices named. The commissions of Marbury (P) and other named justices were signed by Adams on his last day in office, March 3, and signed and sealed by the Acting Secretary of State, John Marshall. However, the formal commissions were not delivered by the end of the day. The new President, Thomas Jefferson, treated those appointments that were not formalized by delivery of the papers of commission prior to Adams leaving office as a nullity. Marbury (P) and other affected colleagues brought this writ of mandamus to the Supreme Court to compel Jefferson's Secretary of State, James Madison (D), to deliver the commissions. John Marshall, the current Chief Justice of the Supreme Court, delivered the opinion.

ISSUE: Does the Constitution give the Supreme Court the authority to review acts of Congress and declare them, if repugnant to the Constitution, to be void?

HOLDING AND DECISION: (Marshall, C. J.) Yes. The Supreme Court has the power, implied from Article VI, § 2 of the Constitution, to review acts of Congress and if they are found repugnant to the Constitution, to declare them void. The government of the United States is a government of laws, not of men. The President, bound by these laws, is given certain political powers by the Constitution which he may use at his discretion. To aid him in his duties, he is authorized to appoint certain officers to carry out his orders. Their acts as officers are his acts and are never subject to examination by the courts. However, where these officers are given by law specific duties on which individual rights depend, any individual injured by breach of such duty may resort to his country's laws for a remedy. Here, Marbury (P) had a right to the commission, and Madison's (D) refusal to deliver it violated that right. The present case is clearly one for mandamus. However, should the Supreme Court be the court to issue it? The Judiciary Act of 1789 established and authorized United States courts to issue writs of mandamus to courts or persons holding office under U.S. authority. Secretary of State Madison (D) comes within the Act. If the Supreme Court is powerless to issue the writ of mandamus to him, it must be because the Act is unconstitutional. Article III of the Constitution provides that the Supreme Court shall have original jurisdiction in all cases affecting ambassadors, other public ministers and consuls, and where a state is a party. In all other cases, the Supreme Court shall have appellate jurisdiction. Marbury (P) urged that since Article III contains no restrictive words, the power to assign original jurisdiction to the courts remains in the legislature. But if Congress is allowed to distribute the original and appellate jurisdiction of the Supreme Court, as in the Judiciary Act, then the constitutional grant of Article III is form without substance. But no clause in the Constitution is presumed to be without effect. For the Court to issue a mandamus, it must be an exercise of appellate jurisdiction. The grant of appellate jurisdiction is the power to revise and correct proceedings already instituted; it does not create the cause. To issue a writ of mandamus ordering an executive officer to deliver a paper is to create the original action for that paper. This would be an unconstitutional exercise of original jurisdiction beyond the power of the court. It is the province and duty of the judicial department to say what the law is. And any law, including acts of the legislature, which is repugnant to the Constitution is void. Mandamus denied.

EDITOR'S ANALYSIS: Judicial review of legislative acts was a controversial subject even before the Constitution was ratified and adopted. Alexander Hamilton upheld the theory of judicial review in the Federalist Papers. He argued that the judiciary, being the most vulnerable branch of the government, was designed to be an intermediary between the people and the legislature. Since the interpretation of laws was the responsibility of the judiciary, and the Constitution the supreme law of the land, any conflict between legislative acts and the Constitution were to be resolved by the court in favor of the Constitution. But other authorities have attacked this position. In the case of *Eakin v. Raub*, Justice Gibson dissented, stating that the judiciary's function was limited to interpreting the laws and should not extend to scrutinizing the legislature's authority to enact them. Judge Learned Hand felt that judicial review was inconsistent with the separation of powers. But history has supported the authority of judicial review of legislative acts. The United States survives on a tripartite government. Theoretically, the three branches should be strong enough to check and balance the others. To limit the judiciary to the passive task of interpretation would be to limit its strength in the tripartite structure. Marbury served to buttress the judiciary branch making it equal to the executive and legislative branches.

[For more information on judicial review, see Casenote Law Outline on Constitutional Law, Chapter 1, § II, The Doctrine of Judicial Review and Its Consequences.]

QUICKNOTES

APPELLATE JURISDICTION - The power of a higher court to review the decisions of lower courts.

JUDICIAL REVIEW - The authority of the courts to review decisions, actions or omissions committed by another agency or branch of government.

ORIGINAL JURISDICTION - The power of a court to hear an action upon its commencement.

WRIT OF MANDAMUS - A court order issued commanding a public or private entity, or an official thereof, to perform a duty required by law.

BAKER v. CARR

Resident (P) v. State (D)

396 U.S. 186 (1962).

NATURE OF CASE: Action seeking a declaration of the unconstitutionality of a state law and injunctive relief.

FACT SUMMARY: Baker (P) alleged that because of population changes since 1901, the 1901 State Apportionment Act was obsolete and unconstitutional, and that the state legislature refused to reapportion itself.

CONCISE RULE OF LAW: The fact that a suit seeks protection of a political right does not mean it necessarily presents a political question.

FACTS: Between 1901 and 1961, Tennessee's population had grown substantially and had been redistributed. Baker (P) alleged that because of the population changes and the state legislature's failure to reapportion voting districts by itself, the 1901 Apportionment Act was unconstitutional and obsolete. Baker (P) also alleged that because of the makeup of the legislature resulting from the 1901 Act, redress in the form of a state constitutional amendment was difficult or impossible.

ISSUE: Does a constitutional challenge to a state apportionment act present a political question?

HOLDING AND DECISION: (Brennan, J.) No. The fact that a suit seeks protection of a political right does not mean it necessarily presents a political question. The primary reason that political questions have been held to be nonjusticiable is the separation of powers. An analysis of any case held to involve a political question will reveal: (1) a history of the issue's management by another governmental branch; (2) a lack of judicially manageable standards for resolving it; (3) the impossibility of deciding the case without an initial policy determination calling for nonjudicial discretion; (4) the impossibility of resolving it without expressing lack of respect due other government branches; (5) an unusual need for unquestioning adherence to a political decision already made; or (6) the potentiality of embarrassment from a variety of announcements by different governmental departments on one question. The mere fact that a suit seeks protection of a political right does not mean that it involves a political question. The Court cannot reject as involving a political question a real controversy as to whether a certain action exceeded constitutional limits. Here Baker (P) alleges that a state's actions violate his right to equal protection. None of the above-mentioned characteristics of a political question are present. Further, the nonjusticiability of claims arising under the Guaranty Clause can have no bearing on the justiciability of the equal protection claim presented here. The judgment of dismissal is reversed, and the case is remanded.

DISSENT: (Frankfurter, J.) A long line of cases has held that the Guaranty Clause is not enforceable through the courts. The present case involves all of the elements that have made the Guaranty Clause cases nonjusticiable. The Equal Protection Clause provides no clearer guide for judicial examination of apportionment statutes than would the Guaranty Clause. What is actually asked here is for the Court to choose among competing theories of representation, and ultimately, among competing political philosophies, to establish an appropriate frame of government for Tennessee. To find the Court's power to make such a choice in the broad guarantee of the Equal Protection Clause is to rewrite the Constitution.

EDITOR'S ANALYSIS: *Baker v. Carr* is the most important case on political questions. Traditionally, the Court refused to review cases arising from state apportionment statutes, since they were all said to present political questions. In *Colegrove v. Green*, 328 U.S. 549, it was contended that the fact that apportioned districts were not of approximate equality in population rendered the state apportionment act unconstitutional. The Court held that a political question was presented and so the case was nonjusticiable. However, in *Gomillion v. Lightfoot*, 364 U.S. 339, the Court showed some willingness to enter the area of apportionment. There a statute apportioned a district with the obvious purpose of excluding black votes. The Court held that a justiciable violation of equal protection had been alleged. In distinguishing *Colegrove*, it stated that there the complaint alleged only a dilution of the strength of the appellants' votes as a result of legislative inaction over a number of years, whereas in *Gomillion*, the petitioners complained that affirmative legislative action had deprived them of their votes.

[For more information on the political question doctrine, see Casenote Law Outline on Constitutional Law, Chapter 1, § III, Constitutional Limits on Federal Judicial Review.]

QUICKNOTES

JUSTICIABILITY - An actual controversy that is capable of determination by the court.

POLITICAL QUESTION - An issue that is more appropriately left to the determination of another governmental branch and which the court declines to hear.

NIXON v. UNITED STATES

Former judge (P) v. Federal government (D)

506 U.S. 224 (1993).

NATURE OF CASE: Appeal of conviction upon impeachment for high crimes and misdemeanors.

FACT SUMMARY: Nixon (P), a former judge, alleged that a Senate impeachment rule pursuant to which he was impeached was unconstitutional because it prohibited the full Senate from taking part in the impeachment evidentiary hearings.

CONCISE RULE OF LAW: An action is nonjusticiable where there is a textually demonstrable constitutional commitment of the issue to a coordinate branch of government or a lack of judicially discoverable and manageable standards for resolving it.

FACTS: Nixon (P), a former federal district court judge in Mississippi, was convicted of making false statements to a grand jury and sent to prison. He was subsequently accused in a bill of impeachment of high crimes and misdemeanors by the House of Representatives and convicted by the Senate under Senate Rule XI. That rule delegated to a Senate committee the task of hearing the testimony of witnesses in the impeachment trial. Nixon (P) filed suit, arguing that the rule was unconstitutional because it delegated the duty to try him to a committee, prohibiting the full Senate from taking part in the trial in violation of the Impeachment Trial Clause. The district court held the claim nonjusticiable and the court of appeals affirmed. The U.S. Supreme Court granted review.

ISSUE: Is an action nonjusticiable where there is constitutional commitment of the issue to a coordinate branch of government or a lack of judicially discoverable and manageable standards for resolving it?

HOLDING AND DECISION: (Rehnquist, C.J.) Yes. An action is nonjusticiable where there is a textually demonstrable constitutional commitment of the issue to a coordinate branch of government or a lack of judicially discoverable and manageable standards for resolving it. Article I, § 3, clause 6 of the Constitution provides: "The Senate shall have the sole Power to try all Impeachments." Because it is subject to a variety of definitions, the use of the word "try" cannot be interpreted as an implied limitation on the method by which the Senate might proceed in trying impeachments. Various reasons support finding the impeachment procedure nonjusticiable. The imposition of the requirements that the members be under oath and that there be a two-thirds vote to convict suggests that the framers did not intend to impose limitations by the use of the word "try." The use of the word "sole" also suggests that the framers intended to commit the issue exclusively to the Senate. The framers provided for both the impeachment trial and a separate criminal trial to avoid bias and insure independent judgment. Further, judicial review would be inconsistent with the framers' creation of impeachment as the only check on the judicial branch by the legislature. Finally, judicial review of the process could potentially expose the country"s political life to periods of chaos. Affirmed.

CONCURRENCE: (Stevens, J.) The central fact that the framers decided to assign the impeachment power to the legislative branch is far more significant than the inferences to be drawn of the use of "try" and "sole."

CONCURRENCE: (White, J.) The framers intended the use of the word "sole" to be a limitation on potential interference by the House and not on review by the judiciary. Further, to say that the use of the word "try" does not present a judicially manageable standard is insupportable where one would intuitively expect that the framers used the word in its legal sense.

CONCURRENCE: (Souter, J.) Not all judicial interference with the impeachment process is inappropriate, and such could be necessary if the Senate were to act in a manner seriously threatening the integrity of its results.

EDITOR'S ANALYSIS: In political question cases the Court is in large part concerned with the respect it owes to the legislative branch. This concern takes on different forms depending on the aspect of the doctrine at issue. The "textually demonstrable commitment of the issue to a coordinate political department" aspect is primarily a separation of powers question. The "lack of judicially discoverable and manageable standards" aspect is a question of Court's competence or ability to resolve the issue even if it is not committed to another branch.

[For more information on judicial review, see Casenote Law Outline on Constitutional Law, Chapter 1, § III, Constitutional Limits on Federal Judicial Review.]

QUICKNOTES

IMPEACHMENT - Criminal proceeding against a public officer.

LUJAN v. DEFENDERS OF WILDLIFE
Secretary of the Interior (D) v. Environmental organizations (P)
504 U.S. 555 (1992).

NATURE OF CASE: Appeal of injunction requiring the Secretary of the Interior to promulgate a regulation.

FACT SUMMARY: Defenders of Wildlife (P) sued for an injunction ordering the Secretary of the Interior (D) to apply the Endangered Species Act to actions taken in foreign countries.

CONCISE RULE OF LAW: To establish standing, a plaintiff must show injury-in-fact, causation, and redressability, and Congress may not create a right of standing based on a generalized grievance against government.

FACTS: Endangered Species Act § 7(a)(2) required federal agencies to consult with the Interior Department (D) to ensure that federal actions do not jeopardize endangered species. Interior (D) reinterpreted § 7(a)(2) to apply only in the United States or at sea. Defenders of Wildlife (P) sued for an injunction requiring Secretary of the Interior Lujan (D) to issue a regulation restoring the interpretation that § 7(a)(2) applies worldwide. To support standing, two of the Department's (D) members, who claimed to have observed certain endangered animals on trips to Egypt and Sri Lanka, averred that they would suffer harm from federal programs overseeing and funding projects in Egypt and Sri Lanka which threatened the animals. They also presented three novel standing theories whereby anyone anywhere with a vocational, educational, or aesthetic interest in an endangered species or "contiguous ecosystem" harmed by a federal activity would have standing. They also cited the "citizen suit" provision of the Act which grants "any person" the right to sue to enforce any of its provisions. The Secretary (D) moved for summary judgment, claiming Defenders (P) lacked standing. The district court instead issued Defenders (P) the injunction it sought. The court of appeals affirmed, and the Secretary (D) appealed.

ISSUE: Can Congress create a right of standing based on a generalized grievance against government, allowing a plaintiff to establish standing without showing injury-in-fact, causation, and redressability?

HOLDING AND DECISION: (Scalia, J.) No. To establish standing a plaintiff must show injury-in-fact, causation, and redressability. Congress may not create a right of standing based on a generalized grievance against government. Defenders (P) failed to establish injury-in-fact. "Someday" future intentions to observe animals do not establish "actual or imminent" injury. The novel theories establish harm to the ecosystem or animals but fail to establish injury to a plaintiff. It is pure speculation that anyone anywhere is harmed by a single project affecting some portion of a species without a specific connection. They also failed to establish redressability. Other agencies, not being parties, would not be bound by an injunction. Moreover, there was no evidence Egypt, Sri Lanka, or any other country would reduce a project or harm to endangered species if minimal U.S. support were stopped. The Act's "citizen-suit" provision is unconstitutional. Under Article III federal courts may not hear cases where the plaintiff merely has a generalized grievance against government. Congress may not give power to the courts which the Constitution says the courts do not have. Congress may create rights which establish injury-in-fact to satisfy Article III, but those rights must be individualized or there is no "case or controversy." Reversed.

CONCURRENCE: (Kennedy, J.) The Court must be sensitive to Congress' ability to create new standing rights. At a minimum, though, Congress must identify the injury it wishes to vindicate and relate the injury to a class of persons who can sue. The "citizen-suit" provision fails to do either.

CONCURRENCE: (Stevens, J.) Section 7(a)(2) was not intended to apply worldwide, so Defenders (P) lost on the merits, but it did have standing. If they genuinely wish to observe the animals in their habitat, they are injured when the animals are threatened. This injury is redressable. Federal agencies cannot ignore a judgment of this Court that an act of Congress applies to them. In passing § 7(a)(2), Congress decided that consultation impacts projects and endangered species, so the Court must make the same assumption.

DISSENT: (Blackmun, J.) On summary judgment, a plaintiff need show only a genuine issue of material fact as to standing. A reasonable fact finder could find members of Defenders (P), based on their professional backgrounds, return to Egypt and Sri Lanka likely. Requiring "concrete plans," such as buying plane tickets, proves nothing. Many environmental injuries cause harm far from the challenged activity. The funding agencies would be bound by an injunction based on their involvement in this case. Congress imposes procedural restraints on executive power. Surely the courts do not violate separation of powers by enforcing these procedures at the mandate of Congress.

EDITOR'S ANALYSIS: The precedential value of Lujan is questionable. Only four justices found that the plaintiffs had not established redressability. Only three justices agreed that there was no injury-in-fact and that the "citizen-suit" provision was invalid.

[For more information on standing, see Casenote Law Outline on Constitutional Law, Chapter 1, § III, Constitutional Limits on Federal Judicial Review.]

QUICKNOTES

CAUSATION - The aggregate effect of preceding events that bring about a tortious result; the causal connection between the actions of a tortfeasor and the injury that follows.

GENERALIZED GRIEVANCE - It refers to a class of actions that does not have standing because it does not represent a controversy for the particular plaintiff but is something that effects the general public.

INJURY IN FACT - An injury that gives rise to standing to sue.

REDRESSABILITY - Requirement that in order for a court to hear a case there must be an injury that is redressible or capable of being remedied.

STANDING TO SUE - Plaintiff must allege that he has a legally predictable interest at stake in the litigation.

EX PARTE McCARDLE

Federal government (P) v. Newspaper editor (D)

74 U.S. (7 Wall.) 506 (1869).

NATURE OF CASE: Appeal from denial of habeas corpus.

FACT SUMMARY: McCardle (D) appealed from a denial of habeas corpus to the Supreme Court, but Congress passed an act forbidding the Court jurisdiction.

CONCISE RULE OF LAW: Although the Supreme Court derives its appellate jurisdiction from the Constitution, the Constitution also gives Congress the express power to make exceptions to that appellate jurisdiction.

FACTS: After the Civil War, Congress imposed military government on many former Confederate states under authority of the Civil War Reconstruction Acts. McCardle (D), a Mississippi newspaper editor, was held in military custody on charges of publishing libelous and incendiary articles. McCardle (D) brought a habeas corpus writ based on a Congressional Act passed on February 5, 1867. The Act authorized federal courts to grant habeas corpus to persons held in violation of Constitutional rights, and also gave authority for appeals to the Supreme Court. The circuit court denied McCardle's (D) habeas corpus writ, but the Supreme Court sustained jurisdiction for an appeal on the merits. However, after arguments were heard, Congress passed an act on March 27, 1868, that repealed that much of the 1867 Act that allowed an appeal to the Supreme Court from the circuit court and the exercise by the Supreme Court of jurisdiction on any such appeals, past or present.

ISSUE: Does Congress have the power, under the Constitution, to make exceptions to the appellate jurisdiction of the Supreme Court?

HOLDING AND DECISION: (Chase, C. J.) Yes. Although the Supreme Court derives its appellate jurisdiction from the Constitution, the Constitution also gives Congress the express power to make exceptions to that appellate jurisdiction. The appellate jurisdiction of the Supreme Court is not derived from acts of Congress, but is conferred by the Constitution with such exceptions and regulations as Congress shall make. And though Congress has affirmatively described in the Act of 1789 the regulations governing the exercise of the Supreme Court's appellate jurisdiction, with the implication that any exercise of that jurisdiction not within the purview of the Act would be negated, the exception to the appellate jurisdiction in the present case is not to be inferred from such affirmations. The exceptions in this case are express. That part of the 1867 Act giving the court appellate jurisdiction in habeas corpus cases is expressly repealed. The effect is to take away the court's jurisdiction, dismissing the cause. When a legislative act is repealed, it is as if it had never existed except to transactions past and closed. Thus, no judgment can be rendered in a suit after repeal of the act under which it was brought. But this does not deny forever the court's appellate power in habeas corpus cases. The Act of 1868 affects only such appeals from circuit courts brought under the Act of 1867.

EDITOR'S ANALYSIS: McCardle is clearly an example of judicial restraint. The authority of Congress to control the jurisdiction of the Supreme Court is not unlimited. This was proved in *Marbury v. Madison,* 5 U.S. (1 Cranch) 137 (1803), where the Court, faced with an extension by Congress of its original jurisdiction as granted under the Constitution, refused to accept the constitutionality of the congressional act. While this specifically limited the Supreme Court's original jurisdiction, it provided Marshall with the ideal arena to assert the doctrine of judicial review. But in *McCardle,* the Court backed away from confrontation with Congress due to current day political crises that followed the Civil War. Thereafter, the Court sought to limit congressional power by the power of judicial review announced in *Marbury.* The Court held on several occasions that certain congressional attempts to delimit its jurisdiction were unconstitutional attempts to invade the judicial province. Such congressional actions were considered a violation of the separation of powers. Today, it is doubtful that McCardle would be sustained.

[For more information on jurisdiction stripping statutes, see Casenote Law Outline on Constitutional Law, Chapter 1, § II, The Doctrine of Judicial Review and Its Consequences.]

QUICKNOTES

APPELLATE JURISDICTION - The power of a higher court to review the decisions of lower courts.

ORIGINAL JURISDICTION - The power of a court to hear an action upon its commencement.

WARTH v. SELDIN
Residents (P) v. Municipality/public officials (D)
422 U.S. 490 (1975).

NATURE OF CASE: Appeal from dismissal of complaint on grounds of lack of standing.

FACT SUMMARY: Various organizations and individuals challenged the town of Penfield's (D) zoning ordinance which allegedly excluded persons of low and moderate income from living in the town.

CONCISE RULE OF LAW: The question of standing (whether the litigant is entitled to have the court decide the merits of the dispute or of particular issues) has two limitations: 1) when the asserted harm is a "generalized grievance" shared substantially by all or a large class of citizens, that harm alone does not normally warrant exercise of jurisdiction; and 2) even when plaintiff presents "a case or controversy," generally he still must assert his own legal rights and interests, and cannot rest his claim to relief on the legal rights or interests of third parties.

FACTS: Warth (P) and other individuals and various organizations resident in the Rochester, New York, metropolitan area, sued the town of Penfield (D), adjacent to Rochester, and the members (D) of its zoning, planning, and town boards. Warth (P) claimed that the town's zoning ordinance effectively excluded persons of low and moderate income from living in Penfield (D) in violation of the First, Ninth, and Fourteenth Amendments, and federal statutes. The district court, the court of appeals affirming, dismissed the complaint for lack of standing. Warth (P) appealed.

ISSUE: Does the question of standing (whether the litigant is entitled to have the court decide the merits of the dispute or of particular issues) have any limitations?

HOLDING AND DECISION: (Powell, J.) Yes. The question of standing (whether the litigant is entitled to have the court decide the merits of the dispute or of particular issues) has two limitations: 1) when the asserted harm is a "general grievance" shared substantially by all or a large class of citizens, that harm alone does not normally warrant exercise of jurisdiction; and 2) even when plaintiff presents a "case or controversy," generally he must still assert his own legal rights and interests, and cannot rest in his claim to relief on the legal rights or interest of third parties. As for the claims of the individual petitioners who asserted standing as persons of low or moderate income and as members of minority groups, the fact that they shared attributes common to persons who may have been excluded from Penfield (D) was an insufficient fact from which to conclude that they themselves had been excluded, or that Penfield (D) has violated their rights. There has been no personal injury alleged. They have not

alleged that their inability to find housing in Penfield (D) reasonably resulted from Penfield's (D) alleged constitutional and statutory violations, or that if the court affords relief, their inability will be removed. As for the petitioners who assert standing on the basis of their Rochester taxpayer status on grounds that Penfield's (D) failure to offer lower cost housing places the burden on Rochester, their asserted injury is conjectural and lacks any apparent line of causation between Penfield's (D) actions and the alleged injury. Any increase in Rochester taxes results from decisions of Rochester officials, non-parties, not from Penfield's (D) actions. The Rochester individuals assert no personal right, but the rights of third parties. The only relationship existing between them and the excluded prospective Penfield residents is an incidental congruity of interest. As for the petitioning associations, Metro-Act (P), Home Builders (P), and Housing Council (P), an association may have standing to seek relief from injury or as its members' representative, but it must allege that they, or any one member, are suffering immediate or threatened injury. Metro-Act (P), as to its claim of standing as a Rochester taxpayer and as a representative of members who are Rochester taxpayers or lower income persons, lacks standing for the same reasons as do those same individuals previously discussed. As to Metro-Act's (P) claim based on its representing the 9% of its members who are Penfield (D) residents, the harm was indirect, and thus Metro-Act (P) was only raising the rights of third parties. As for Home Builders (P), it can only have standing if it alleged facts sufficient to make out a case or controversy had the members themselves brought suit, but its claim that various members lost business opportunities and profits by not being able to build is not a common claim, and requires individual proof of injury and damages. Finally, Housing Council (P), which includes 17 groups involved in development of lower cost housing fails for the same reasons as did Home Builders (P). Affirmed.

DISSENT: (Brennan, J.) It was a "glaring defect" to view each set of plaintiffs as if it was bringing a separate lawsuit. The interests were intertwined. The facts which the Court says must be alleged in order to get into court reverts to a form of fact-pleading, long dispensed with in federal court.

EDITOR'S ANALYSIS: Note that had any party alleged that a zoning ordinance of the town was blocking a pending construction project, the question as to whether all administrative remedies had first been exhausted would have arisen. The standing question is whether the constitutional or statutory provision on which the claim rests properly can be understood to grant persons in the plaintiff's position a right to judicial relief. An additional limitation on standing is whether the interest sought to be protected by the complainant is arguably within the zone of interests to be protected or regulated by this statute or constitutional guarantee in question, 397 U.S. 150, 153 (1970).

[For more information on standing and causation, see Casenote Law Outline on Constitutional Law, Chapter 1, § III, Constitutional Limits on Federal Judicial Review.]

QUICKNOTES

STANDING - Whether a party possesses the right to commence suit against another party by having a personal stake in the resolution of the controversy.

GENERALIZED GRIEVANCE - It refers to a class of actions that does not have standing because it does not represent a controversy for the particular plaintiff but is something that effects the general public.

NOTES:

CHAPTER 2
NATIONAL POWERS AND LOCAL ACTIVITIES:
ORIGINS AND RECURRENT THEMES

QUICK REFERENCE RULES OF LAW

1. **National Powers and Local Activities.** (1) Certain federal powers, giving Congress the discretion and power to choose and enact the means to perform the duties imposed upon it, are to be implied from the Necessary and Proper Clause. (2) The federal Constitution and the laws made pursuant to it are supreme and control the Constitutions and the laws of the states. (McCulloch v. Maryland)

    [For more information on the Necessary and Proper Clause, see Casenote Law Outline on Constitutional Law, Chapter 2, § I, Federal-State Relations in General.]

2. **National Powers and Local Activities.** States may not limit the terms of members of Congress. (U.S. Term Limits, Inc. v. Thornton)

    [For more information on federal-state relations, see Casenote Law Outline on Constitutional Law, Chapter 2, § I, Federal-State Relations in General.]

McCULLOCH v. MARYLAND
Bank cashier (D) v. State (P)
17 U.S. (4 Wheat,) 316 (1819).

NATURE OF CASE: Action arising out of violation of a state statute.

FACT SUMMARY: McCulloch (D), the cashier of the Baltimore branch of the U.S. Bank, issued bank notes in violation of a Maryland (P) statute providing that no bank, without authority from the state, could issue bank notes except on stamped paper issued by the state.

CONCISE RULE OF LAW: (1) Certain federal powers, giving Congress the discretion and power to choose and enact the means to perform the duties imposed upon it, are to be implied from the Necessary and Proper Clause. (2) The federal Constitution and the laws made pursuant to it are supreme and control the Constitutions and the laws of the states.

FACTS: A Maryland (P) statute prohibited any bank operating in the state without state authority from issuing bank notes except upon stamped paper issued by the state. The law specified the fees payable for the paper, and provided for penalties for violators. An act of Congress established a U.S. Bank. McCulloch (D), the U.S. Bank's cashier for its Baltimore branch, issued bank notes without complying with the Maryland (P) law.

ISSUE: (1) Does Congress have the power to incorporate a bank? (2) Does a state have the power to impose fees on the operation of an institution created by Congress pursuant to its constitutional powers?

HOLDING AND DECISION: (Marshall, C.J.) (1) Yes. Certain federal powers, giving Congress the discretion and power to choose and enact the means to perform the duties imposed upon it, are to be implied from the Necessary and Proper Clause. It's true that this government is one of enumerated powers. However, the Constitution does not exclude incidental or implied powers. It does not require that everything be granted expressly and minutely described. To have so required would have entirely changed the character of the Constitution and made it into a legal code. The enumerated powers given to the government imply the ordinary means of execution. The power of creating a corporation may be implied as incidental to other powers, or used as a means of executing them. The Necessary and Proper Clause gives Congress the power to make "all laws which shall be necessary and proper, for carrying into execution" the powers vested by the Constitution in the U.S. Government. Maryland (P) argues that the word "necessary" limits the right to pass laws for the execution of the granted powers to those which are indispensable. However, in common usage, "necessary" frequently means convenient, useful, essential. Considering the word's common usage, its usage in another part of the Constitution (Article 1,

§ 10), and its inclusion among the powers given to Congress, rather than among the limitations upon Congress, it cannot be held to restrain Congress. The sound construction of the Constitution must allow Congress the discretion to choose the means to perform the duties imposed upon it. As long as the end is legitimate and within the scope of the Constitution, any means which are appropriate, are plainly adapted to that end, and which are not prohibited by the Constitution, but are consistent with its spirit, are constitutional. A bank is a convenient, useful, and essential instrument for handling national finances. Hence, it is within Congress's power to enact a law incorporating a U.S. bank. (2) No. The federal Constitution and the laws made pursuant to it are supreme and control the Constitutions and the laws of the states. The federal Constitution and the laws made in pursuance thereof are supreme. They control the Constitutions and laws of the states and cannot be controlled by them. Maryland (P) is incorrect in its contention that the powers of the federal government are delegated by the states which alone are truly sovereign. The Constitution derives its authority from the people, not from the states. Here, Maryland's (P) statute in effect taxes the operation of the U.S. Bank, a bank properly created within Congress' power. The power to tax involves the power to destroy. Here it is in opposition to the supreme congressional power to create a bank. Also, when a state taxes an organization created by the U.S. Government, it acts upon an institution created by people over whom it claims no control. The states have no power, by taxation or otherwise, to impede, burden, or in any manner control the operations of constitutional laws enacted by Congress. The Maryland (P) statute is, therefore, unconstitutional and void.

EDITOR'S ANALYSIS: Federalism is the basis of the Constitution's response to the problem of governing large geographical areas with diverse local needs. The success of federalism depends upon maintaining the balance between the need for the supremacy and sovereignty of the federal government and the interest in maintaining independent state government and curtailing national intrusion into intrastate affairs. The U.S. federal structure allocates powers between the nation and the states by enumerating the powers delegated to the national government and acknowledging the retention by the states of the remainder. The Articles of Confederation followed a similar scheme. The Constitution expanded the enumerated national powers to remedy weaknesses of the Articles. The move from the Articles to the Constitution was a shift from a central government with less powers to one with more powers.

[For more information on the Necessary and Proper Clause, see Casenote Law Outline on Constitutional Law, Chapter 2, § I, Federal-State Relations in General.]

QUICKNOTES

FEDERALISM - A scheme of government whereby the power to govern is divided between a central and localized governments.

U.S. TERM LIMITS, INC. v. THORNTON
Proponents of term limits (D) v. League of Women Voters (P)
514 U.S. 779 (1995).

NATURE OF CASE: Review of summary judgment striking down state term limits.

FACT SUMMARY: Arkansas' (D) congressional term limitation law was challenged as unconstitutional.

CONCISE RULE OF LAW: States may not limit the terms of members of Congress.

FACTS: In 1992, Arkansas (D) adopted by initiative a state constitutional amendment limiting the tenure of both state and federal elected officials. With respect to the United States congressional and senatorial delegations, the amendment provided that an incumbent could not have his name placed on a ballot after a set number of terms. The League of Women Voters (P) challenged this provision as contrary to the Constitution. The Arkansas Supreme Court held the amendment unconstitutional, and the Supreme Court granted review.

ISSUE: May states limit the terms of members of Congress?

HOLDING AND DECISION: (Stevens, J.) No. States may not limit the terms of members of Congress. The qualifications for sitting in the U.S. Congress are stated in Article I of the Constitution. The Supreme Court has already held that Congress itself cannot add to, subtract from, or otherwise change these qualifications. The issue here is whether the states can do so. First, states do not have a Tenth Amendment power in this area. The Tenth Amendment reserved to the states those powers that predated the Constitution and were not delegated to the federal government. State governments never had any powers over national elections prior to the Constitution, because there were none. Consequently, the Tenth Amendment gives the states no powers here. Second, the historical record is quite clear that the notion of term limits was vigorously debated prior to adoption of the Constitution, and to add such a requirement now would violate the framers' intent. Finally, to allow states to impose term limits would violate a fundamental principle of our system of representative democracy, to wit, that people should be free to choose whom they please to govern them. For these reasons, term limits violate the Constitution. U.S. Term Limits, Inc. (D), however, contends that the amendment in question does not truly limit terms but only restricts ballot access. The Constitution allows states to regulate the time, manner and place of elections. U.S. Term Limits (D) contends that the amendment constitutes such a regulation. It does not. The amendment tries to do indirectly what it cannot do in a direct manner, and this sort of form over substance argument will not be endorsed by the Court. Affirmed.

CONCURRENCE: (Kennedy, J.) The federal character of congressional elections flows from the political reality that our national government is republican in form and that national citizenship has privileges and immunities protected from state abridgement by the force of the Constitution itself.

DISSENT: (Thomas, J.) Nothing in the Constitution deprives the people of each state of the power to prescribe eligibility requirements for congressional candidates; it is silent in that area. Where the Constitution is silent, it raises no bar to action by the states or the people. The Court's analysis is wrong on several counts. The Tenth Amendment protects not only those powers preexisting the Constitution. All power flows from consent of the people; when the people have spoken, as they did here, and the Constitution does not countermand the will of the people, the Tenth Amendment applies. Also, the Qualifications Clause is a bare recitation of the minimum qualifications necessary to hold office; it says nothing to the effect than these are the only qualifications that can be imposed. Finally, the Court incorrectly equates limitations on ballot access with limits on tenure.

EDITOR'S ANALYSIS: The present case is a good illustration of two different and competing theories of constitutional interpretation. The majority's approach can be called "structural." While the Constitution did not specifically prohibit term limits, the Court invalidated them as contrary to our governmental structure. Justice Thomas, in his dissent, took a strict constructionist/literalist approach, looking to the text and nothing more.

[For more information on federal-state relations, see Casenote Law Outline on Constitutional Law, Chapter 2, § I, Federal-State Relations in General.]

QUICKNOTES

TENTH AMENDMENT - The Tenth Amendment to the United States Constitution reserves those powers therein, not expressly delegated to the federal government or prohibited to the states, to the states or to the people.

3

CHAPTER 3
THE COMMERCE POWER

QUICK REFERENCE RULES OF LAW

1. **The Decline of Limits on the Commerce Power from 1937 to 1995.** Under the Commerce Clause, Congress has the power to regulate any activity, even intrastate production, if the activity has an appreciable effect, either direct or indirect, on interstate commerce. (NLRB v. Jones & Laughlin Steel Corp.)

   [For more information on the affection doctrine, see Casenote Law Outline on Constitutional Law, Chapter 3, § I, The Principal Congressional Legislative Powers.]

2. **The Decline of Limits on the Commerce Power from 1937 to 1995.** Congress has the power to regulate the hours and wages of workers who are engaged in the production of goods destined for interstate commerce and can prohibit the shipment in interstate commerce of goods manufactured in violation of the wage and hour provisions. (United States v. Darby)

   [For more information on congressional plenary power over interstate commerce, see Casenote Law Outline on Constitutional Law, Chapter 3, § I, The Principal Congressional Legislative Powers.]

3. **New Limits on the Commerce Power since 1995.** The 1990 federal Gun-Free School Zones Act exceeded Congress's Commerce Clause regulatory powers. (United States v. Lopez)

   [For more information on congressional power, see Casenote Law Outline on Constitutional Law, Chapter 3, § I, The Principal Congressional Legislative Powers.]

4. **New Limits on the Commerce Power since 1995.** Commerce Clause regulation of intrastate activity may only be upheld where the activity being regulated is economic in nature. (United States v. Morrison)

5. **State Autonomy Limits on Congressional Power.** The federal government may not order a state government to enact particular legislation. (New York v. United States)

   [For more information on the commerce power, see Casenote Law Outline on Constitutional Law, Chapter 3, § I, The Principal Congressional Legislative Powers.]

6. **State Autonomy Limits on Congressional Power.** The federal government may not compel the states to enact or administer a federal regulatory program. (Printz v. United States)

   [For more information on federal-state relations, see Casenote Law Outline on Constitutional Law, Chapter 2, § I, Federal-State Relations in General.]

NATIONAL LABOR RELATIONS BOARD v. JONES & LAUGHLIN STEEL CORP.

Federal agency (P) v. Steel company (D)
301 U.S. 1 (1937).

NATURE OF CASE: Action alleging unfair labor practice under the National Labor Relations Act.

FACT SUMMARY: Jones & Laughlin Steel Corp. (D), a manufacturing company with subsidiaries in several states and nationwide sales, was charged with an unfair labor practice under the National Labor Relations Act. In defense, Jones & Laughlin (D) claimed that the Act was an unconstitutional attempt to regulate intrastate production.

CONCISE RULE OF LAW: Under the Commerce Clause, Congress has the power to regulate any activity, even intrastate production, if the activity has an appreciable effect, either direct or indirect, on interstate commerce.

FACTS: Pursuant to a complaint filed by a labor union, the National Labor Relations Board (P) found that Jones and Laughlin Steel (D) had engaged in "unfair labor practices." The Board (P) issued a cease and desist order to Jones & Laughlin (D) to stop using discriminatory and coercive practices to prevent union organization at two steel plants in and around Pittsburgh. The company refused to comply, and the Board (P) went to court for judicial enforcement of its order under the authority of the National Labor Relations Act of 1935. Jones & Laughlin (D) contended that the order was an unconstitutional exercise of the Board's (P) authority since the plants were not engaged in interstate commerce, being totally manufacturing facilities. The court of appeals upheld the company's position and refused enforcement of the order on the ground that the order "lay beyond the range of federal power."

ISSUE: Do the manufacturing portions of a large, integrated multi state corporation fall within the constitutional meaning of the term "activities affecting commerce" so as to allow federal regulation thereof?

HOLDING AND DECISION: (Hughes, C. J.) Yes. Under the Commerce Clause, Congress has the power to regulate any activity, even intrastate production, if the activity has an appreciable effect, either direct or indirect, on interstate commerce. The act of the Board (P) in ordering Jones & Laughlin (D) to cease interfering with its employees' rights of self-organization and collective bargaining, is an exercise of the congressional power to regulate interstate commerce. The definitions in the Act restrict the Board's (P) actions to protecting interstate commerce in the constitutional sense, and the Board (P) is given the power to determine if the practice in question affects commerce in such a way as to be subject to federal control. Congress has the power to protect interstate commerce by all appropriate types of legislation, and the controlling question is the effect on interstate commerce, not the source of the interference. Although such legislation may result in the regulation of acts that are intrastate in character, Congress still has the power to regulate if the intrastate acts bear such a close and substantial relation to interstate commerce that control is appropriate for the protection of commerce. Congress is forbidden only from regulating acts that have a remote and indirect effect on interstate commerce. Here, even though the application of the National Labor Relations Act results in the regulation of labor practices at Jones & Laughlin's (D) manufacturing plants, the circumstances indicate the required substantial effect on interstate commerce. If production were interrupted at one of the plants due to a labor dispute, the extensive nationwide operations of Jones & Laughlin (D) indicate that there would necessarily be an immediate effect on interstate commerce. Therefore, the National Labor Relations Act as applied to the facts of this case is a proper exercise of Congress' power to regulate interstate commerce.

DISSENT: (McReynolds, J.) The majority reasons that there is an effect on interstate commerce in the following manner: if the employer discharges a few employees for union activities, this will create discontent among the remaining employees which will lead to a strike which may result in reduced production which may decrease the volume of goods in interstate commerce. This is obviously only a remote and indirect effect on interstate commerce and not subject to federal regulation. Manufacture and production are purely local activities, even if the raw materials come from another state and the finished goods are shipped across state lines.

EDITOR'S ANALYSIS: With this case the Supreme Court retreated from its strict geographical definition of interstate commerce and the direct/indirect approach which it used in Schecter and Carter. Jones & Laughlin states that under the Commerce Clause Congress has the power to regulate any activity which has a significant effect on interstate commerce, regardless of whether that effect is direct or indirect. This new concept is often called the "affectation doctrine." Although the Court cited prior cases in its opinion and said it was not creating new law, Jones & Laughlin is, in effect, a reversal of the Schecter line of cases. The Court now bases its opinions on a combination of the Commerce Clause and the Necessary and Proper Clause — power to regulate interstate commerce extends to control over intrastate activities when necessary and appropriate to make regulation of interstate commerce effective.

[For more information on the affection doctrine, see Casenote Law Outline on Constitutional Law, Chapter 3, § I, The Principal Congressional Legislative Powers.]

QUICKNOTES

INTRASTATE - Any activity that takes place entirely within a single state and thus does not trigger regulation under the commerce clause.

UNITED STATES v. DARBY

Federal government (P) v. Lumber manufacturer (D)
312 U.S. 100 (1941).

NATURE OF CASE: Criminal prosecution for violation of Fair Labor Standards Act.

FACT SUMMARY: Darby (D) was a lumber manufacturer, some of whose goods were later shipped in interstate commerce. He was indicted for violation of the wage and hour provisions of the Fair Labor Standards Act, and defended on the ground that as an intrastate producer he was not subject to federal regulation.

CONCISE RULE OF LAW: Congress has the power to regulate the hours and wages of workers who are engaged in the production of goods destined for interstate commerce and can prohibit the shipment in interstate commerce of goods manufactured in violation of the wage and hour provisions.

FACTS: Darby (D) was a manufacturer of finished lumber, and a large part of the lumber he produced was shipped in interstate commerce. The purpose of the Fair Labor Standards Act was to prevent the shipment in interstate commerce of certain products produced under substandard labor conditions. The Act set up minimum wages and maximum hours and punished the shipment in interstate commerce of goods produced in violation of the wage/hour requirements and also punished the employment of persons in violation of those requirements. Darby (D) was arrested for both shipment of goods in violation of the Act and employment of workers in violation of the Act. The trial court dismissed the indictment on the ground that the Act was an unconstitutional regulation of manufacturing within the states.

ISSUE: Does Congress have the power to prohibit shipment in interstate commerce of goods produced in violation of the wage/hour provisions of the Labor Standards Act and the power to prohibit employment of workers involved in the production of goods for interstate shipment in violation of the wage/hour provisions of the Labor Standards Act?

HOLDING AND DECISION: (Stone, J.) Yes. Congress has the power to regulate the hours and wages of workers who are engaged in the production of goods destined for interstate commerce and can prohibit the shipment in interstate commerce of goods manufactured in violation of the wage and hour provisions. Both prohibitions are a constitutional exercise of Congress' commerce power. Although manufacturing itself is not interstate commerce, the shipment of goods across state lines is interstate commerce and the prohibition of such shipment is a regulation of commerce. Congress has plenary power to exclude from interstate commerce any article which it determines to be injurious to public welfare, subject only to the specific prohibitions

of the Constitution. In the Fair Labor Standards Act, Congress has determined that the shipment of goods produced under substandard labor conditions is injurious to commerce, and therefore has the power to prohibit the shipment of such goods, independent of the indirect effect of such prohibition on the states. The prohibition of employment of workers engaged in the production of goods for interstate commerce at substandard conditions is also sustainable, independent of the power to exclude the shipment of the goods so produced. The power over interstate commerce is not confined to the regulation of commerce among the states, but includes regulation of intrastate activities which so affect interstate commerce as to make regulation of them an appropriate means to the end of regulating interstate commerce. Here, Congress has determined that the employment of workers in substandard conditions is a form of unfair competition injurious to interstate commerce, since the goods so produced will be lower priced than the goods produced under adequate conditions. Such a form of competition would hasten the spread of substandard conditions and produce a dislocation of commerce and the destruction of many businesses. Since Congress has the power to suppress this form of unfair competition, and the Act is an appropriate means to that end, the wage/hour provisions are within Congress' power. It is irrelevant that only part of the goods produced will be shipped in interstate commerce; Congress has power to regulate the whole factory even though only a part of the products will have an effect on interstate commerce.

EDITOR'S ANALYSIS: Darby, like the preceding case of Jones & Laughlin, is an example of the application of the affectation doctrine. It had long been the law that Congress had the power to exclude from interstate commerce harmful objects or immoral activities, such as mismarked goods or lottery tickets. This case extends the power to exclude articles produced under conditions which Congress considered harmful to the national welfare. Even though production of lumber was an entirely intrastate activity, it was a part of an economic process that led to the eventual sale of lumber across state limits, affecting interstate commerce. The federal commerce power extends to purely intrastate transactions; the effect on commerce, not the location of the regulated act, is the basis for the exercise of the federal power. This case overruled the earlier case of *Hammer v. Dagenhart*, 247 U.S. 251 (1918), which held unconstitutional an attempt by Congress to exclude articles made by child labor from interstate commerce.

[For more information on congressional plenary power over interstate commerce, see Casenote Law Outline on Constitutional Law, Chapter 3, § I, The Principal Congressional Legislative Powers.]

QUICKNOTES

PLENARY - Unlimited and open; as broad as a given situation may require.

UNITED STATES v. LOPEZ
Federal government (P) v. Student (D)
514 U.S. 549 (1995).

NATURE OF CASE: Appeal from order reversing federal firearms law violation conviction.

FACT SUMMARY: Lopez (D) was convicted under the 1990 federal Gun-Free School Zones Act, which prohibited guns near schools.

CONCISE RULE OF LAW: The 1990 federal Gun-Free School Zones Act exceeded Congress's Commerce Clause regulatory powers.

FACTS: The 1990 federal Gun-Free School Zones Act made it a federal offense for a student to carry a gun onto campus. Lopez (D) was charged and convicted under the Act. On appeal, he contended that the Act was beyond Congress's powers under the Commerce Clause. The Fifth Circuit agreed and reversed. The Supreme Court granted review.

ISSUE: Did the 1990 Federal Gun-Free School Zones Act exceed Congress's Commerce Clause regulatory power?

HOLDING AND DECISION: (Rehnquist, C.J.) Yes. The 1990 federal Gun-Free School Zones Act exceeded Congress's Commerce Clause regulatory powers. It must be remembered that the federal government is one of limited, enumerated powers. For Congress to legislate, it must do so under an express constitutional provision. Since the 1930s, the Commerce Clause has been the source of most of Congress' legislative power. However, this clause is not a general grant of police power. A law passed under this Clause must relate to: 1) a channel of interstate commerce; 2) an instrumentality of interstate commerce; or 3) an activity having a substantial effect on interstate commerce. In this case, the regulated activity, carrying a gun to school, has no such effect. It is a purely local matter. Granted, if one is willing to accept a lengthy series of interferences and assumptions, such an activity may affect interstate commerce. Any activity can do so. However, if the concept of limited federal government is to have any meaning, Congress's legislative power must be cut off somewhere. That somewhere is the point at which a regulated activity does not substantially affect interstate commerce, and that point has been passed here. Affirmed.

CONCURRENCE: (Kennedy, J.) It is only with great care that this Court should intervene in matters relating to the Commerce Clause, as it is a matter best left to the political sectors of government. However, when an exercise of power under the Clause unduly upsets the balance of power between the states and the national government, as does the law at issue here, it is proper for the Court to intervene.

CONCURRENCE: (Thomas, J.) The substantial effects test is a New Deal innovation which goes far beyond the original intent of the Framers, who had a much narrower view of what was regulatable commerce. In fact, it grants Congress something approaching a general police power, a result clearly at odds with the Tenth Amendment.

DISSENT: (Stevens, J.) The education of our youth has a major impact on the national economy and is a proper subject for Commerce Clause regulation.

DISSENT: (Souter, J.) The Court's approach today constitutes a step backward towards the excessive judicial activism that characterized judicial review of congressional enactments during the first third of this century.

DISSENT: (Breyer, J.) In determining whether a regulated activity has a significant impact on interstate commerce, it is necessary to consider not a single example of the regulated activity, but rather the cumulative effects of all similar instances of that conduct. Here, it is clear that the cumulative impact of the possession of weapons by students on campus will, over time, have a significant impact on the national economy.

EDITOR'S ANALYSIS: Since 1937, the scope of congressional regulatory power under the Commerce Clause has grown enormously. By the 1960s, Congress' power under the Clause had increased to a level approaching a general police power. The present case represents the first significant break in this pattern and may signal a states' rights trend.

[For more information on congressional power, see ***Casenote Law Outline on Constitutional Law, Chapter 3, § I, The Principal Congressional Legislative Powers.]***

QUICKNOTES

COMMERCE CLAUSE - Article 1, section 8, clause 3 of the United States Constitution, granting Congress the power to regulate commerce with foreign countries and between the states.

ENUMERATED POWERS - Specific powers mentioned in, and granted by, the constitution; e.g. the taxing power.

POLICE POWER - The power of a government to impose restrictions on the rights of private persons, as long as those restrictions are reasonably related to the promotion and protection of public health, morals, safety, and the general welfare.

REGULATORY POWER – Power granted pursuant to statute granting a particular government agency ro body the authoirity to giovern a particular area.

UNITED STATES v. MORRISON
Federal government (P) v. Students (D)
529 U.S. 598 (2000).

NATURE OF CASE: Suit alleging sexual assault in violation of the Violence Against Women Act.

FACT SUMMARY: Brzonkala (P) brought suit against two football-playing male students (D) and Virginia Polytechnic University under the Violence Against Women Act.

CONCISE RULE OF LAW: Commerce Clause regulation of intrastate activity may be upheld only where the activity being regulated is economic in nature.

FACTS: Brzonkala (P), a student at Virginia Polytechnic Institute, complained that football-playing students Morrison (D) and Crawford (D) assaulted and repeatedly raped her. Virginia Tech's Judicial Committee found insufficient evidence to punish Crawford (D), but found Morrison (D) guilty of sexual assault and sentenced him to immediate suspension for two semesters. The school's vice president set this aside as excessive punishment. Brzonkala (P) then dropped out of the university and brought suit against the school and the male students (D) under the Violence Against Women Act, 42 U.S.C. § 13981, providing a federal cause of action of a crime of violence motivated by gender.

ISSUE: May Commerce Clause regulation of intrastate activity be upheld only where the activity being regulated is economic in nature?

HOLDING AND DECISION: (Rehnquist, C.J.) Yes. Commerce Clause regulation of intrastate activity may only be upheld where the activity being regulated is economic in nature. The Court considered whether either the Commerce Clause or the Fourteenth Amendment authorized Congress to create this new cause of action. There are three main categories of activity Congress may regulate under its Commerce Clause power: (1) the use of channels of interstate commerce; (2) regulation or protection of the instrumentalities of interstate commerce or persons or things in interstate commerce, though the threat may come from intrastate activities; and (3) the power to regulate those activities having a substantial relation to interstate commerce. Brzonkala (P) argued that § 13981 falls under the third category. In Lopez, this Court concluded that those cases in which federal regulation of intrastate activity (based on the activity's substantial effects on interstate commerce) has been sustained have included some type of economic endeavor. Gender motivated crimes of violence are not economic activities. While § 13981 is supported by numerous findings regarding the serious impact that gender-motivated violence has on victims and their families, the existence of congressional findings is not sufficient in itself to sustain the constitutionality of Commerce Clause legislation. Whether a particular activity affects interstate commerce sufficiently to come under the constitutional power of

Congress to regulate is a judicial question. The Court also rejects the argument that Congress may regulate noneconomic, violent criminal conduct based solely on that conduct's aggregate effect on interstate commerce. The regulation and punishment of intrastate violence that is not directed at the instrumentalities of interstate commerce is reserved to the states. Brzonkala (P) also argued that § 5 of the Fourteenth Amendment authorized the statutory cause of action. This argument is based on the assertion that there is pervasive bias in various state justice systems against victims of gender-motivated violence. While sex discrimination is one of the objects of the Fourteenth Amendment, the amendment only prohibits state action.

CONCURRENCE: (Thomas, J.) The notion of a substantial effects test is inconsistent with Congress' powers and early Commerce Clause jurisprudence, perpetuating the federal government's (P) view that the Commerce Clause has no limits.

DISSENT: (Souter, J.) Congress has the power to legislate with regard to activities that in the aggregate have a substantial effect on interstate commerce. The fact of the substantial effect is a question for Congress in the first instance and not the courts. Here Congress assembled a mountain of data demonstrating the effects of violence against women on interstate commerce.

DISSENT: (Breyer, J.) Congress, in enacting the statute, followed procedures that work to protect the federalism issues at stake. After considering alternatives, Congress developed the federal law with the intent of compensating for documented deficiencies in state legal systems, and tailored federal law to prevent its use in areas traditionally reserved to the states. This law represents the result of state and federal efforts to cooperate in order to resolve a national problem.

EDITOR'S ANALYSIS: The primary issue here is that the federal government is seeking to regulate areas traditionally regulated exclusively by the states. The majority concludes that the regulation and punishment of intrastate violence that is not directed to the instrumentalities of interstate commerce is the exclusive jurisdiction of local government. What the dissent argues here is that Congress in this case has amassed substantial findings to demonstrate that such intrastate violence does have an effect on the instrumentalities of commerce.

QUICKNOTES

COMMERCE CLAUSE - Article 1, section 8, clause 3 of the United States Constitution, granting Congress the power to regulate commerce with foreign countries and between the states.

INTRASTATE ACTS - For purposes of Commerce Clause analysis, refers to activities constituting commerce within a state, as opposed to interstate commerce.

NEW YORK v. UNITED STATES

State (P) v. Federal government (D)

505 U.S. 144 (1992).

NATURE OF CASE: Appeal of dismissal of suit for declaratory judgment.

FACT SUMMARY: New York (P) sought a declaration that the Low-Level Radioactive Waste Policy Amendments Act (1985 Act) was unconstitutional.

CONCISE RULE OF LAW: The federal government may not order a state government to enact particular legislation.

FACTS: Three states had disposal sites for radioactive waste. After study and negotiation, the National Governors' Association (NGA) devised a plan which became the 1985 Act. The 1985 Act set deadlines for every state to join a regional waste compact, develop in-state disposal, or find another way to dispose of its own waste. The 1985 Act assured the sited states they would not have the entire nation's waste burden, and gave the other 47 states seven more years of access to active sites. The 1985 Act provided three incentives for state compliance: (1) Congress authorized sited states to impose a surcharge, part of which would go into federal escrow, with funds to be returned to complying states; (2) Congress empowered sited states to deny access to states not in compliance; and (3) any state not in compliance by 1992 had to either take title to all waste generated in their state or else become liable to in-state waste generators for all damages. As of 1990 New York (P) had not joined a regional waste compact. Unable to settle on an in-state site, New York (P) sought to invalidate the 1985 Act as violative of state sovereignty principles of the Tenth Amendment. The sited states intervened as defendants. The district court dismissed, the court of appeals affirmed, and New York (P) appealed.

ISSUE: May the federal government order a state government to enact particular legislation?

HOLDING AND DECISION: (O'Connor, J.) No. The federal government may not order a state government to enact particular legislation. The federal government may provide incentives for states to regulate in a certain way by tying funding to acceptance of a federal plan or by giving states a choice between enacting a federal plan or having state law preempted by federal law. Here, the first incentive is a congressional exercise of Commerce Clause power (allowing sited states to impose a surcharge on interstate commerce and imposing a federal tax on that surcharge) combined with an exercise of Spending Clause power (making return of surcharges contingent on compliance with the federal plan). The second incentive is a routine exercise of the commerce power. If a state chooses not to follow the federal plan, generators of waste within that state become subject to federal regulation authorizing states with waste sites to deny access. The

burden would fall on the waste generators, not on the state, and the state would not be forced to spend funds or accede to federal direction. The third incentive, however, crossed the line to coercion. Whether a state "chooses" to take title to waste or to accept liability for disposal, the burden of not enacting the federal plan falls on the state. The strength of the federal interest is irrelevant. Federal courts may issue directives to state officials, but the Constitution expressly grants that authority. Such authority is outside Congress' enumerated powers and, for that reason, also infringes on state sovereignty reserved by the Tenth Amendment. While the 1985 Act was a creation of and compromise among the states, the states may not constitutionally consent to give up their sovereignty. Affirmed as to the first two incentives, reversed as to the third.

DISSENT: (White, J.) The Acts were the product of cooperative federalism. The states bargained among themselves to solve an imminent crisis and achieve compromises for Congress to sanction. New York (P) reaped the benefits of the 1985 Act, an agreement which it helped formulate, and should not be able to sue now. The majority wrongly finds that states cannot consent to relinquish some sovereignty. Tenth Amendment restrictions on the commerce power are procedural limits, designed to prevent federal destruction of state governments, not to protect substantive areas of state autonomy.

CONCURRENCE AND DISSENT: (Stevens, J.) The notion that Congress may not order states to implement federal legislation is incorrect and unsound. The federal government regulates state railroads, schools, prisons, and elections, and in time of war, Congress undoubtedly could command states to supply soldiers.

EDITOR'S ANALYSIS: Under the Articles of Confederation, the federal government could act only by ordering states to enact legislation. The Framers decided that the federal government needed power to regulate citizens directly and so drafted the Constitution. The Court interpreted the Framers' decision as a rejection of federal power to order states to enact legislation.

[For more information on the commerce power, see Casenote Law Outline on Constitutional Law, Chapter 3, § I, The Principal Congressional Legislative Powers.]

QUICKNOTES

ENUMERATED POWERS - Specific powers mentioned in, and granted by, the constitution, e.g. the taxing power.

STATE SOVEREIGNTY - The absolute power of self-government possessed by a state.

PRINTZ v. UNITED STATES

Law enforcement officer (P) v. Federal government (D)

521 U.S. 898, 117 S. Ct. 2365 (1997).

NATURE OF CASE: Review of judgment dismissing constitutional challenge to federal legislation.

FACT SUMMARY: A provision in the Brady Handgun Violence Prevention Act which compelled local officials to enforce the Act was challenged as unconstitutional.

CONCISE RULE OF LAW: The federal government may not compel the states to enact or administer a federal regulatory program.

FACTS: Congress enacted the Brady Handgun Violence Prevention Act. The law instituted a waiting period in the purchase of handguns. It also directed local law enforcement to conduct a background check on prospective handgun purchasers. This provision of the law was challenged by Printz (P) and other law enforcement officers (P) as unconstitutional. The Ninth Circuit upheld the law, and the Supreme Court granted review.

ISSUE: May the federal government compel the states to enact or administer a federal regulatory program?

HOLDING AND DECISION: (Scalia, J.) No. The federal government may not compel the states to enact or administer a federal regulatory program. Under our federal system of government, states are autonomous, sovereign entities, not mere instrumentalities of the federal government. The federal government may not recruit states to enforce its laws absent an express constitutional authorization for such command. Also, as a general matter, under the Constitution it is the responsibility of the president and the Executive Branch of government to enforce federal law. Congress cannot strip the president of this power. The present legislation tries to do this very thing. As there is no express constitutional grant of power to Congress to compel state compliance in its regulatory scheme at issue here, the measure is unconstitutional. Reversed.

CONCURRENCE: (O'Connor, J.) The Court appropriately refrains from deciding whether purely ministerial reporting requirements would fall under the rule stated here.

DISSENT: (Stevens, J.) If the Constitution empowers Congress to respond to a problem, there is nothing in the Constitution that forbids Congress to enlist state officers when necessary to make the response effective.

DISSENT: (Breyer, J.) Congress's approach in enforcing its law in this instance is hardly unique. The federal systems of many European nations involve local enforcement of federal law.

EDITOR'S ANALYSIS: One of the big issues of the 1990s has been federalism. States, reversing a trend of over half a century, have in the last decade been taking back some of the power that the federal government has assumed. The Tenth Amendment has come back from the dead, and the Court has shown a reluctance to give unlimited scope to the Commerce Clause as a basis for federal power. The present action is an example of the current emphasis on state's rights.

[For more information on federal-state relations, see Casenote Law Outline on Constitutional Law, Chapter 2, § I, Federal-State Relations in General.]

QUICKNOTES

BRADY ACT (THE BRADY HANDGUN VIOLENCE PREVENTION ACT) - A law enacted by Congress in 1993 which would provide for a waiting period before the purchase of a handgun, and for the establishment of a national instant criminal background check system to be contacted by firearms dealers before the transfer of any firearm.

COMMERCE POWER - The power delegated to Congress by the Constitution to regulate interstate commerce.

TENTH AMENDMENT - The Tenth Amendment to the United States Constitution reserves those powers therein, not expressly delegated to the federal government or prohibited to the states, to the states or to the people.

NOTES

CHAPTER 4
FEDERALISM-BASED RESTRAINTS ON OTHER NATIONAL POWERS IN THE 1787 CONSTITUTION

QUICK REFERENCE RULES OF LAW

1. **The Taxing Power as a Regulatory Tool.** A law passed by Congress under the pretext of executing its powers, but which is for the accomplishment of objects not within congressional power, is unconstitutional. (Child Labor Tax Case [Bailey v. Drexel Furniture Co.])

   [For more information on the taxing power of congress, see Casenote Law Outline on Constitutional Law, Chapter 3, § I, The Principal Congressional Legislative Powers.]

2. **The Spending Power as a Regulatory Device.** Congress may not, under the pretext of exercising the taxing power, accomplish prohibited ends, such as the regulation of matters of purely state concern and clearly beyond its national powers. (United States v. Butler)

   [For more information on the spending power of Congress, see Casenote Law Outline on ConstitutionalLaw, Chapter 3, I, The Principal Congressional Legislative Powers.]

3. **The Spending Power as a Regulatory Device.** Congress may withhold federal highway funds to states with a minimum drinking age of less than 21 years. (South Dakota v. Dole)

   [For more information on the spending power, see Casenote Law Outline on Constitutional Law, Chapter 3, § I, The Principal Congressional Legislative Powers.]

4. **War, Foreign Affairs, and Federalism.** The war power includes the power to remedy the evils which have arisen due to the war and does not necessarily end with the cessation of hostilities. (Woods v. Cloyd W. Miller Co.)

   [For more information on the domestic war power, see Casenote Law Outline on Constitutional Law, Chapter 3, § I, The Principal Congressional Legislative Powers.]

5. **Treaties, Foreign Affairs, and Federalism.** Congress can constitutionally enact a statute under Article I, § 8 to enforce a treaty created under Article II, § 2, even if the statute by itself is unconstitutional. (Missouri v. Holland)

   [For more information on the congressional treaty power, see Casenote Law Outline on Constitutional Law, Chapter 3, § I, The Principal Congressional Legislative Powers.]

CHILD LABOR TAX CASE [BAILEY v. DREXEL FURNITURE CO.]

Collector of Internal Revenue (D) v. Furniture company (P)

259 U.S. 20 (1922).

NATURE OF CASE: Action attacking the constitutionality of the Child Labor Tax Law.

FACT SUMMARY: The Child Labor Tax Law imposes a tax upon persons employing children under certain ages.

CONCISE RULE OF LAW: A law passed by Congress under the pretext of executing its powers, but which is for the accomplishment of objects not within congressional power, is unconstitutional.

FACTS: The Child Labor Act provides that any company employing children in violation of its provisions shall pay a tax equal to one-tenth of its net profits. The Act provides that mines and quarries shall not employ children under the age of 16; mills, canneries, and factories shall not employ children under the age of 14; and children under the age of 16 shall not work more than eight hours a day, more than six days a week, or before 6 a.m. or after 7 p.m. Anyone employing children believing them to be of the proper age is relieved of liability. Both the I.R.S. and the Labor Department are given the authority to enter and inspect any mine, quarry, mill, cannery, or factory. Drexel Furniture Co. (P) received notice from Bailey (D), the U.S. Collector of Internal Revenue, that it had been assessed $6,312.79 for having employed in its factory a boy under the age of 14. Drexel (P) paid the tax under protest and after rejection of its claim for a refund, brought this suit.

ISSUE: Is a congressional act which provides detailed specifications for the regulation of child labor and which imposes a heavy tax upon violators constitutional?

HOLDING AND DECISION: No. A law passed by Congress under the pretext of executing its powers, but which is for the accomplishment of objects not within congressional power, is unconstitutional. The principle announced by Marshall in McCullough v. Maryland is applicable here. "Should Congress, under the pretext of executing its powers, pass laws for the accomplishment of objects not entrusted to the government, it would be the painful duty of this tribunal . . . to say that such an act was not the law of the land." The Child Labor Tax Law concerns the regulation of the employment of children in the states, an exclusively state function under the Constitution. It provides a heavy extraction for a departure from a detailed and specified course of conduct in business. The amount of the tax is not to be proportioned to the degree or the frequency of the violation. Moreover, only employers who knew that the children were under age will be taxed. Scienter is associated with penalties, not taxes. Further, factories, etc., are to be subject to inspection by the Secretary of Labor as well as the I.R.S., the department normally charged with tax collection. In light of these features, "A court must be blind not to see that the so-called tax is imposed to stop the employment of children within the age limits prescribed." It is true that taxes imposed with the primary motive of obtaining revenue may have an incidental motive of discouraging the taxed activity. These taxes do not lose their character as taxes because of the incidental motives. But there is a point in the extension of the penalizing features of the tax when it loses its character as a tax and becomes a mere penalty with the characteristics of regulation and punishment. Such is the case with the Child Labor Tax Law, and for these reasons it is invalid.

EDITOR'S ANALYSIS: The taxing and spending powers have close functional and doctrinal ties to the commerce power, since the manner in which taxes are imposed can have significant regulatory impacts. As with commerce laws, taxing measures have been used to deal with "police" as well as economic problems. The court in Drexel noted the clear analogy between that case and Hammer, the child labor case. Regulations through taxing have been resorted to when the need for legislation seemed great and the direct regulatory authority through the Commerce Clause was "under constitutional clouds," such as in the cases of child labor and of New Deal legislation in the 1930s.

[For more information on the taxing power of congress, see Casenote Law Outline on Constitutional Law, Chapter 3, § I, The Principal Congressional Legislative Powers.]

QUICKNOTES

SCIENTER - Knowledge of certain facts; often refers to "guilty knowledge," which implicates liability.

TAXING POWER - The ability Congress to determine and collect taxes; used primarily to raise revenue, but also to effect policy and regulate and deter certain activities.

UNITED STATES v. BUTLER
Federal government (D) v. Receivers (P)
297 U.S. 1 (1936).

NATURE OF CASE: Action challenging the constitutionality of the Agricultural Adjustment Act of 1933.

FACT SUMMARY: The Agricultural Adjustment Act of 1933 stated that there was a national economic emergency arising from the low price of agricultural products in comparison with other commodities. To remedy this situation, a tax would be collected from processors of an agricultural product. The revenue raised would be paid to farmers who curtailed their production of that product.

CONCISE RULE OF LAW: Congress may not, under the pretext of exercising the taxing power, accomplish prohibited ends, such as the regulation of matters of purely state concern and clearly beyond its national powers.

FACTS: The Agricultural Adjustment Act of 1933 declared that a national economic emergency had arisen due to the disparity between the prices of agricultural and other commodities, resulting in the destruction of farmers' purchasing power. To remedy this situation, a tax would be collected from processors of agricultural products. The revenue raised thereby would be paid to farmers who voluntarily curtailed their production of those crops used by the processors. The Secretary of Agriculture was to determine the crops to which the Act's plan would apply. In July 1933, the Secretary determined that the Act's plan should be applied to cotton. A tax claim was presented to Butler (P) as receivers of the Hoosal Mills Corp., as cotton processors. The district court held the tax to be valid.

ISSUE: Is a tax on the processing of agricultural products valid where the revenue raised by the tax is to be paid to farmers who voluntarily curtail their production of crops?

HOLDING AND DECISION: (Roberts, J.) No. Congress may not, under the pretext of exercising the taxing power, accomplish prohibited ends, such as the regulation of matters of purely state concern and clearly beyond its national powers. First, Butler (P) has standing to question the validity of the tax because it is but a part of the unconstitutional plan of the Agricultural Adjustment Act. A tax, as the term is used by the Constitution, is an exaction for the support of the government. It has never been thought to mean the expropriation of money from one group for the benefit of another, as is attempted by the Act in question here. The Act is unconstitutional in that it invades the rights of the states. It is a statutory plan to regulate and control agriculture production, a matter beyond the power of the federal government. The government, in attempting to defend the Act, places great reliance on the fact that the Act's plan is voluntary. However, the farmer who chooses not to comply with the plan loses benefits. "The power to confer or withhold unlimited benefits is the power to coerce or destroy." Even if the plan were truly voluntary, it would not be valid. "At best, it is a scheme for purchasing with federal funds submission to federal regulation of a subject reserved to the states." Contracts for the reduction of acreage and the control of production are not within Congress' power. Congress has no power to enforce the ends sought by this Act onto the farmer. Hence, it may not indirectly accomplish those ends by taxing and spending to enforce them. If this Act is valid, Congress could exercise its power to regulate all industry. It could extract money from one branch of an industry and pay it to another branch. Congress may not, under the pretext of exercising the taxing power, accomplish prohibited ends.

DISSENT: (Stone, J.) Courts are to be concerned only with the power to enact statutes, not with their wisdom. The constitutional power of Congress to tax the processing of agricultural products is not questioned. The present tax is held to be invalid because the use to which its proceeds are to be put is disapproved. The tax is held to be invalid because it is a step in a plan to regulate agricultural production. The Court states that state powers are infringed by the expenditure of the proceeds of the tax to compensate farmers for the curtailment of their crop production. Such a limitation is contradictory and destructive of the power to appropriate for the public welfare, and is incapable of practical application. Congress' spending power is not subordinate to its legislative powers. This independent grant of power presupposes freedom of selection among diverse ends and aims and the capacity to impose such conditions as will render the choice effective. It is contradictory to say that there is a power to spend for the national welfare, while rejecting any power to impose conditions reasonably adapted to the end which justifies the expenditure. "If appropriation in aid of a program of curtailment is constitutional, and it is not denied that it is, payment to farmers on condition that they reduce their crop acreage is constitutional."

EDITOR'S ANALYSIS: The Butler decision contributed greatly to the pressure that produced the court-packing plan a few months later. It is called the landmark case in the area of federal regulation of local matters through taxation. However, if the tax and the appropriation provisions had not been so closely tied together, it is doubtful that the court would have invalidated the tax. The tax appeared to have a valid revenue-raising purpose, and once separated from the taxing provisions, there would have been no one with standing to attack the appropriation.

[For more information on the spending power of Congress, see Case note Law Outline on Constitutional Law, Chapter 3, § I, The Principal Congressional Legislative Powers.]

QUICKNOTES

COURT PACKING PLAN - An attempt to alter the composition of a court to maximize concurrence with the appointing officer's views.

SPENDING POWER - The ability of Congress to spend money in order to provide for the general welfare of the citizens of the United States.

SOUTH DAKOTA v. DOLE
State (P) v. Federal government (D)
483 U.S. 203 (1987).

NATURE OF CASE: Appeal from decisions upholding federal highway funding requirement.

FACT SUMMARY: Congress passed a law withholding federal highway funds to states with a minimum drinking age of less than 21 years.

CONCISE RULE OF LAW: Congress may withhold federal highway funds to states with a minimum drinking age of less than 21 years.

FACTS: In 1984, Congress enacted 20 U.S.C. § 138, which directed the Secretary of Transportation to withhold 5% of federal highway funds to states with a drinking age of less than 21 years of age. This was based on the perception that border states with drinking ages of less than 21 encouraged drinking and driving. South Dakota (P) sought a declaration that the law was unconstitutional. The district and circuit courts upheld the law, and the Supreme Court granted review.

ISSUE: May Congress withhold federal highway funds to states with a minimum drinking age of less than 21 years?

HOLDING AND DECISION: (Rehnquist, C.J.) Yes. Congress may withhold federal highway funds to states with a minimum drinking age of less than 21 years. It is well recognized that Congress may use its spending power to induce cooperation by states in areas which it cannot necessarily regulate directly. Therefore, even if Congress could not directly legislate state drinking ages, it can use the threat of withheld funds to achieve its regulatory goal. South Dakota (P) argued that alcohol is a special case, as the Twenty-First Amendment specifically leaves the regulation of drinking to the states. However, this leads the analysis back to its point of origin, namely, that Congress can indirectly regulate through its spending power. That is all it has done here. Affirmed.

DISSENT: (O'Connor, J.) Section 158 cannot be justified as reasonably related to the federal highway system. It is an attempt to regulate alcoholic beverages, something Congress may not do.

EDITOR'S ANALYSIS: It is not uncommon for Congress to attempt to regulate "with a carrot" rather than by direct regulation. The present case is one such action. Probably the most controversial area where this has been subject to constitutional consideration is in the area of abortions. Cases such as *Maher v. Roe*, 432 U.S. 464 (1977) and *Rust v. Sullivan*, 500 U.S. 173 (1991) have established Congress' right in this area.

[For more information on the spending power, see Casenote Law Outline on Constitutional Law, Chapter 3, § I, The Principal Congressional Legislative Powers.]

QUICKNOTES

GENERAL WELFARE - Governmental interest or concern for the public's health, safety, morals, and well-being.

SPENDING POWER - The power delegated to Congress by the Constitution to spend money in providing for the nation's welfare.

NOTES:

WOODS v. CLOYD W. MILLER CO.

Federal government (P) v. Landlord (D)

333 U.S. 138 (1948).

NATURE OF CASE: Action seeking an injunction of violations of the Housing and Rental Act of 1947.

FACT SUMMARY: Miller Co. (D) demanded of its tenants 40% and 60% rent increases in violation of the Housing and Rental Act of 1947. On December 31, 1946, the presidential proclamation terminated hostilities and inaugurated "peace in fact." The war had caused severe housing shortages.

CONCISE RULE OF LAW: The war power includes the power to remedy the evils which have arisen due to the war and does not necessarily end with the cessation of hostilities.

FACTS: Due to the housing shortage which still existed as a result of World War II, Congress enacted the Housing and Rental Act of 1947, which imposed rent controls of the same nature that existed during the War. In defiance of the Act, the Miller Co. (D) set rental increases of 40% to 60% in one of the projects it managed. The company then sought to enjoin enforcement of the Act against it for these violations, contending the war was over. While the President had declared a cessation of hostilities on December 31, 1946, the war was technically still going on, since no final peace accords had been achieved with all parties. The company further argued that since Congress had made no reference to its war powers when enacting the legislation, that Clause could not be used to justify the Act.

ISSUE: Does Congress have the power pursuant to the war power to attempt to remedy situations which were caused by the War and have continued to exist after hostilities have ceased?

HOLDING AND DECISION: (Douglas, J.) Yes. The war power includes the power to remedy the evils which have arisen due to the war and does not necessarily end with the cessation of hostilities. The war power includes the power to remedy evils which have arisen due to a war, and, "whatever may be the consequences when war is officially terminated, the war power does not necessarily end with the cessation of hostilities." The war power is adequate to support the preservation of rights created by wartime legislation. And it has an even broader sweep. In *Hamilton v. Kentucky Distilleries Co.* and *Ruppert v. Caffey*, prohibition laws enacted after the World War II armistice were sustained as exercises of the war power because they conserved labor and increased efficiency of production in the critical days of demobilization and helped conserve the supply of grains and cereals depleted by the war. Following these cases, the war power sustains the Housing and Rental Act. The legislative history of the Act makes it clear that the housing shortage resulting from the war has not been eliminated. The legislative history also makes it clear that Congress is invoking

the war power to sustain the Act. "The question of the constitutionality of action taken by Congress does not depend on its recitals of the power which it undertakes to exercise."

CONCURRENCE: (Jackson, J.) The United States is still technically in a state of war. Hence the war power is a valid ground for federal rent control. "I would not be willing to hold that war powers last as long as the effects and consequences of war, for if so they are permanent."

EDITOR'S ANALYSIS: Article I, § 8 gives Congress the power to declare war, to raise and support armies, to provide and maintain a navy, to make rules for the government and regulation of the land and naval forces, and to provide for organizing, arming, disciplining, and calling forth the militia. Under this power, Congress' enactment of comprehensive legislation regulating the national economy during a war has been sustained. The Emergency Price Control Act of 1942 was sustained as applying to rents in *Bowies v. Willingham*, 321 U.S. 503 (1944) and as to prices in *Yakus v. U.S.*, 321 U.S. 414 (1944). The Renegotiation Act was sustained in *Lichter v. U.S.*, 334 U.S. 742 (1948). It provided for recapture of excessive profits realized on war contracts where the ultimate source of payment was the U.S. government.

[For more information on the domestic war power, see Casenote Law Outline on Constitutional Law, Chapter 3, § I, The Principal Congressional Legislative Powers.]

QUICKNOTES

WAR POWER CLAUSE - Article I, § 8 of the United States Constitution granting Congress the power to declare war.

NOTES:

MISSOURI v. HOLLAND

State (P) v. Federal game warden (D)

252 U.S. 416 (1920).

NATURE OF CASE: An action in equity to enjoin the enforcement of the Migratory Bird Treaty Act.

FACT SUMMARY: Missouri (P) claimed that the Bird Treaty Act was an unconstitutional interference with the rights reserved to the states by the Tenth Amendment.

CONCISE RULE OF LAW: Congress can constitutionally enact a statute under Article I, § 8 to enforce a treaty created under Article II, § 2, even if the statute by itself is unconstitutional.

FACTS: On December 8, 1916, the United States entered into a treaty with Great Britain to protect birds that migrated between Canada and the United States. Congress passed a statute to enforce the Migratory Bird Treaty which allowed the Secretary of Agriculture to formulate regulations to enforce the treaty. The State of Missouri (P) filed a bill in equity to prevent Holland (D), the game warden of the United States, from enforcing the treaty. Missouri (P) claimed that the statute was an unconstitutional interference with the rights reserved to the states by the Tenth Amendment and that it had a pecuniary interest as owner of the wild birds which were being interfered with. Before the treaty had been entered into, Congress had attempted to regulate the killing of migratory birds within the states and that statute, standing by itself, had been declared unconstitutional. The United States contended that Congress had the power to enact the statute to enforce the treaty and that the statute and treaty were the supreme law of the land.

ISSUE: Can Congress validly enact a statute to enforce a treaty if the statute standing by itself would be unconstitutional because it interfered with the rights reserved to the states by the Tenth Amendment?

HOLDING AND DECISION: (Holmes, J.) Yes. Congress can constitutionally enact a statute under Article I, § 8 to enforce a treaty created under Article II, § 2, even if the statute by itself is unconstitutional. Article II, § 2 grants the President the power to make treaties and Article VI, § 2 declares that treaties shall be part of the supreme law of the land. If a treaty is a valid one, Article I, § 8, gives Congress the power to enact legislation that is a necessary and proper means to enforce the treaty. While acts of Congress are the supreme law of the land only when they are made in pursuance of the Constitution, treaties are valid when made under the authority of the United States. The Court stated that there were qualifications to the treaty-making power, but felt that the qualifications must be determined by looking at the facts of each case. There are situations that require national action which an act of Congress could not deal with, but which a treaty enforced with a congressional act could. Because Missouri (P) did not have the power to adequately control the problem connected with the migratory birds (nor did any other state acting alone), this was a situation which required national action. Therefore, even though Missouri (P) would have been able to establish regulations pertaining to the birds if Congress had not already done so, Congress could establish regulations in conjunction with the treaty without infringing on the rights reserved to the states by the Tenth Amendment. The Court rejected Missouri's (P) claim that it had a pecuniary interest as an owner when the birds were in the state. There is no ownership until there is possession and the birds never came into the possession of the State of Missouri (P). Congress can, therefore, constitutionally enact a statute under Article I, § 8 to enforce a treaty even if the statute by itself would be unconstitutional.

EDITOR'S ANALYSIS: Many people were upset with the decision in this case because they feared that the Court had interpreted the treaty power so broadly that all constitutional limitations could be overridden by the use of treaties and accompanying congressional legislation. In 1954, the Bricker Amendment was narrowly defeated, which required that a treaty could only become effective as internal law in the United States through legislation which would be valid in the absence of the treaty. This would have, in effect, overruled the decision in this case, because the congressional act was not valid when standing by itself. Several other similar proposals were made during the following three years, which also failed.

[For more information on the congressional treaty power, see Casenote Law Outline on Constitutional Law, Chapter 3, § I, The Principal Congressional Legislative Powers.]

QUICKNOTES

PECUNIARY - Monetary, relating to money.

TENTH AMENDMENT - The Tenth Amendment to the United States Constitution reserves those powers therein, not expressly delegated to the federal government or prohibited to the states, to the states or to the people.

TREATY - An agreement made between two or more independent nations; once a treaty is made into law, it becomes applicable to the states under Article IV, § 2 of the constitution.

5

CHAPTER 5
FEDERAL LIMITS ON STATE POWER TO REGULATE THE NATIONAL ECONOMY

QUICK REFERENCE RULES OF LAW

1. **Early Development.** If a state law conflicts with a congressional act regulating commerce, the congressional act is controlling. (Gibbons v. Ogden)

   [For more information on the congressional commerce power, see Casenote Law Outline on Constitutional Law, Chapter 3, § I, The Principal Congressional Legislative Powers.]

2. **Early Development.** If Congress has not exercised its power over commerce in a certain area, the states may regulate that area as long as such regulations do not conflict with the Commerce Clause in its dormant stage. (Willson v. Black-Bird Creek Marsh Co.)

   [For more information on concurrent state and federal power, see Casenote Law Outline on Constitutional Law, Chapter 2, § I, Federal-State Relations in General.]

3. **Early Development.** The states may regulate those areas of interstate commerce which are local in nature and do not demand one national system of regulation by Congress. (Cooley v. Board of Wardens)

   [For more information on the national-local rule, see Casenote Law Outline on Constitutional Law, Chapter 6, § I, The Dormant or "Negative" Commerce Clause.]

4. **The Modern Court's Approach.** State laws which are basically protectionist in nature unduly burden interstate commerce and thus are unconstitutional. (Philadelphia v. New Jersey)

   [For more information on state discriminatory effects on interstate commerce, see Casenote Law Outline on Constitutional Law, Chapter 6, § I, The Dormant or "Negative" Commerce Clause.]

5. **The Modern Court's Approach.** A locality may not discriminate against interstate commerce, even to protect the health and safety of its people if reasonable alternatives exist which do not discriminate and are adequate to conserve legitimate local interests. (Dean Milk Co. v. Madison)

   [For more information on state discriminatory effects on interstate commerce, see Casenote Law Outline on Constitutional Law, Chapter 6, § I, The Dormant or "Negative" Commerce Clause.]

6. **Laws Protectionist in Purpose or Effect.** Restrictions, imposed for the avowed purpose and with the practical effect of curtailing the volume of interstate commerce to aid local economic interests, will not be sustained. (H.P. Hood & Sons v. Du Mond)

   [For more information on the anti-embargo rule, see Casenote Law Outline on Constitutional Law, Chapter 6, § I, The Dormant or "Negative" Commerce Clause.]

7. **Facially Neutral Laws and Pike Balancing.** In deciding whether a state law places an unreasonable burden on interstate commerce, and hence cannot be sustained, the Court must balance the nature and extent of the burden which would be imposed by the statute against the merits and purposes to be derived from the state regulation. (Southern Pacific Co. v. Arizona)

   [For more information on state safety regulations on commerce, see Casenote Law Outline on Constitutional Law, Chapter 6, § I, The Dormant or "Negative" Commerce Clause.]

8. **Facially Neutral Laws and Pike Balancing.** A state safety regulation will be unconstitutional if its asserted safety purpose is outweighed by its degree of interference with interstate commerce. (Kassel v. Consolidated Freightways Corp.)

   [For more information on state safety regulation burdening interstate commerce, see Casenote Law Outline on Constitutional Law, Chapter 6, § I, The Dormant or "Negative" Commerce Clause.]

9. **The "Market Participant" Exception to the Dormant Commerce Clause.** If a state imposes burdens on commerce within a market in which it is a participant, but which have a substantial regulatory effect outside of that particular market, they are per se invalid under the Federal Commerce Clause. (South-Central Timber Development, Inc. v. Wunnicke)

   [For more information on market participant exception, see Casenote Law Outline on Constitutional Law, Chapter 6, § I, The Dormant or "Negative" Commerce Clause.]

10. **The Privileges and Immunities Clause of Article IV.** The Privileges and Immunities Clause applies to municipal ordinances which discriminate on the basis of municipal residence. (United Building & Construction Trades Council v. Mayor and Council of Camden)

    [For more information on preemption doctrine, see Casenote Law Outline on Constitutional Law, Chapter 2, § I, Federal-State Relations in General.]

11. **Preemption of State Authority.** In passing the Atomic Energy Act of 1954, Congress preempted state regulation of the radiological safety aspects involved in the construction and operation of nuclear plants but intended for the states to retain their traditional responsibility in the field of regulating electrical utilities for determining questions of need, reliability, cost, and other related state concerns. (Pacific Gas & Elec. Co. v. State Energy Resources Conservation & Development Comm'n)

GIBBONS v. OGDEN

Ship operator (D) v. Ship operator (P)

22 U.S. (9 Wheat.) 1 (1824).

NATURE OF CASE: Action seeking an injunction to protect an exclusive right to operate ships between New York City and New Jersey.

FACT SUMMARY: Ogden (P), after acquiring a monopoly right from the State of New York to operate ships between New York City and New Jersey, sought to enjoin Gibbons (D) from operating his ships, licensed by the federal government, between the same points.

CONCISE RULE OF LAW: If a state law conflicts with a congressional act regulating commerce, the congressional act is controlling.

FACTS: In 1803, the New York legislature granted an exclusive right to Robert Livingston and Robert Fulton to operate ships powered by fire or steam in New York waters for twenty years which was subsequently extended for another ten years. Ogden (P) obtained an assignment from Livingston and Fulton to operate his ships between Elizabethtown, New Jersey, and New York City. Gibbons (D) was also running two boats between these points and his boats had been enrolled and licensed under the laws of the United States for a Vessels to be employed in the coasting trade. Ogden (P) obtained an injunction stopping Gibbons (D) from operating his ships between the points for which Ogden (P) had received an exclusive right to operate his own ships. The case was appealed to the Supreme Court. Ogden (P) claimed that the federal government did not have exclusive jurisdiction over commerce, but that the states had retained power by which they could regulate commerce within their own states and that the exclusive right to operate his ships only concerned intrastate commerce. Gibbons (D) contended that Congress had exclusive power to regulate interstate commerce and that Now York had attempted to regulate interstate commerce by granting the exclusive right and enforcing it with the injunction.

ISSUE: If a state law conflicts with a congressional act regulating commerce, is the congressional act controlling?

HOLDING AND DECISION: (Marshall, J.) Yes. If a state law conflicts with a congressional act regulating commerce, the congressional act is controlling. Congress has the power to regulate navigation within the limits of every state and, therefore, the regulations which Congress passed controlling navigation within the boundaries of New York were valid. Ogden (P) argued that the states through the Tenth Amendment have the power to regulate commerce with foreign nations and among the states because the power which the states gave up to Congress to regulate commerce wasn't absolute and the residue of that power remained with the states. But Congress was given all the power to regulate interstate commerce, although it is possible for the states to pass regulations which may affect some activity associated with interstate commerce. In that case, states must base such regulations on some other source of power than the commerce power (such as the police power of the state). Regardless of the source of the state power, any time a state regulation conflicts with a federal regulation, the state regulation must yield to the federal law. Since in this case the law of New York conflicted with a federal regulation dealing with interstate commerce, the New York law is not valid. Accordingly, the Court dismissed Ogden's (P) suit to obtain an injunction against Gibbons (D).

EDITOR'S ANALYSIS: The federal commerce power is concurrent with state power over commerce within the state. Hence, the Court has been asked many times to define the line between federal and state power to regulate commerce. During the early history of the United States, the court was not often called upon to determine the scope of federal power under the Commerce Clause. Instead, the early cases generally involved some state action which was claimed to discriminate against or burden interstate commerce. Hence, the Commerce Clause operated as a restraint upon state powers. Most of these cases did not involve any exercise of the commerce power by Congress at all. Large-scale regulatory action by Congress began with the Interstate Commerce Act in 1887 and the Sherman Anti-trust Act in 1890. Challenges to these statutes initiated the major modern confrontations between the Court and congressional authority regarding commerce.

[For more information on the congressional commerce power, see Casenote Law Outline on Constitutional Law, Chapter 3, § I, The Principal Congressional Legislative Powers.]

QUICKNOTES

COMMERCE POWER - The power delegated to Congress by the Constitution to regulate interstate commerce.

INJUNCTION - A court order requiring a person to do or prohibiting that person from doing, a specific act.

WILLSON v. BLACK-BIRD CREEK MARSH CO.
Sloop owner (D) v. Dam owner (P)
27 U.S. (2 Pet.) 245 (1829).

NATURE OF CASE: Action to collect damages for the destruction of a dam.

FACT SUMMARY: Willson (D) damaged the Black-Bird Creek Marsh Company's (P) dam.

CONCISE RULE OF LAW: If Congress has not exercised its power over commerce in a certain area, the states may regulate that area as long as such regulations do not conflict with the Commerce Clause in its dormant stage.

FACTS: The Black-Bird Creek Marsh Company (P) was authorized by a Delaware law to build a dam on Black-Bird Creek which flowed into the Delaware River, and also to "bank the marsh and lowland" in the same area. The dam blocked the navigation of the creek and Willson (D), the owner of a sloop licensed under the federal navigation laws, broke through the Company's (P) dam in order to pass through the creek. The Company (P) brought an action in the state court for damages and was successful. Willson (D) claimed that the law authorizing the dam violated the Commerce Clause as the creek was navigable and the sloop was licensed under the federal navigation laws. The Company (P) argued that the state law was passed under the police power of the state in order to clean up a health hazard and there was no legislation by Congress which dealt with the same subject matter as the Delaware law with which the state law could conflict.

ISSUE: Can a state pass legislation concerning interstate commerce if Congress has not passed any regulations concerning the specific area dealt with by the state legislation?

HOLDING AND DECISION: (Marshall, J.) Yes. If Congress has not exercised its power over commerce in a certain area, the states may regulate that area as long as such regulations do not conflict with the Commerce Clause in its dormant stage. The Court held that a state can adopt means which increase the value of property and improve the health of the citizens of the state as long as such regulations don't conflict with powers of the federal government. If Congress had passed any act under its power to regulate commerce which dealt with small navigable creeks such as the one involved in this case, any state law which conflicted with such regulations would be void. However, Congress had not passed such regulations, and so, to be held invalid, the state law would have to conflict with the Commerce Clause in its dormant stage. The Court did not think that the Delaware law was repugnant to the power to regulate commerce in its dormant state, nor was it in conflict with any law passed on the subject. The judgment of the lower court was affirmed.

EDITOR'S ANALYSIS: Some writers feel that Chief Justice Marshall had changed his views which he set forth in the *Gibbons v. Ogden*, (22 U.S. (9 Wheat.) 1 (1824) case in which he held that the power to regulate interstate commerce rested solely with Congress. It isn't known whether Marshall regarded the Delaware legislative action as a health law and, therefore, not a regulation of interstate commerce, or whether he simply decided this case on its own facts without regard to the doctrines of exclusive congressional control over interstate commerce. The controversy in this case does not appear to have involved anybody other than the two parties in the case, but the controversy in *Gibbons v. Ogden* was representative of a widespread problem involving many states, and Chief Justice Marshall had to handle the case in such a manner as to effectively solve the entire problem, and not just the fact situation involved in the case. This may account for the different approach he took in this case.

[For more information on concurrent state and federal power, see Casenote Law Outline on Constitutional Law, Chapter 2, § I, Federal-State Relations in General.]

QUICKNOTES
DORMANT COMMERCE CLAUSE - The regulatory effect of the commerce clause on state activity affecting interstate commerce, where Congress itself has not acted to control the activity; a provision inferred from, but not expressly present in, the language of the Commerce Clause.

INTERSTATE COMMERCE - Commercial dealings between two parties located in different states or located in one state and accomplished through a point in another state or a foreign country; commercial dealings transacted between two states.

COOLEY v. BOARD OF WARDENS

Ship consignee (D) v. State board (P)

53 U.S. (12 How.) 299 (1851).

NATURE OF CASE: Action for violation of a state local pilot law.

FACT SUMMARY: Cooley (D) violated a Pennsylvania law requiring all ships using the port of Philadelphia to engage a local pilot.

CONCISE RULE OF LAW: The states may regulate those areas of interstate commerce which are local in nature and do not demand one national system of regulation by Congress.

FACTS: In 1803, Pennsylvania passed a law which required every ship entering or leaving the port of Philadelphia to use a local pilot. The law imposed a penalty of half the pilotage fee which was paid to the Board of Wardens (P) and put in a fund for retired pilots and their dependents. Cooley (D), who was a consignee of two ships which had left the port without a local pilot, was held liable under the law. Cooley (D) challenged the right of the state to impose regulations on pilots because it interfered with interstate commerce. The Board of Wardens (P) relied on an act of Congress in 1789 which stated that all pilots in the rivers, harbors, and ports of the United States shall continue to be regulated in conformity with the existing laws of the states and such laws as the states shall enact for that purpose, until Congress enacts legislation to the contrary.

ISSUE: Is the grant of power to Congress to regulate interstate and foreign commerce an exclusive grant prohibiting the states from legislating, even in areas of primarily local concern?

HOLDING AND DECISION: (Curtis, J.) No. The states may regulate those areas of interstate commerce which are local in nature and do not demand one national system of regulation by Congress. It is evident from the Congressional Act of 1789 that Congress recognized that the states can, in some areas, enact regulations that have an effect on interstate commerce. Some subjects of commerce demand a single uniform national rule and therefore Congress has exclusive jurisdiction over those areas. However, there are some subjects that are primarily local in nature and therefore require many different rules to meet the local necessities. The problem concerning pilots is local in nature and therefore Congress does not have exclusive power over this area. In the Act that Congress passed allowing the states to regulate pilots, Congress has recognized that the problems involved with pilots do not demand one uniform rule and thus allowed the states to regulate pilots. The Court held that the grant of the power over commerce to Congress did not imply a prohibition on the states to exercise the same power, but it is the exercise of the power by Congress that may make the exercise of the same power by the states unlawful. The Court noted that its decision in this case applied only to its facts and did not attempt to delineate the dividing line between those subjects of commerce that were primarily local and those which were primarily national in scope. The decision of the lower courts upholding Cooley's (D) fine was affirmed.

EDITOR'S ANALYSIS: The local interest versus the national interest test is still used by the court today. In applying this test the Court balances the national interest against the local interest and also determines if the local regulation discriminates against interstate commerce. If the local interest outweighs the national interest and the regulation does not discriminate against interstate commerce, the states are allowed to regulate that subject of commerce. If it appears that the state regulation has placed a burden on interstate commerce, the Court has drawn the line and refused to hold the state regulations valid even though a local subject may be involved.

[For more information on the national-local rule, see Casenote Law Outline on Constitutional Law, Chapter 6, § I, The Dormant or "Negative" Commerce Clause.]

QUICKNOTES

COMMERCE CLAUSE - Article 1, section 8, clause 3 of the United States Constitution, granting Congress the power to regulate commerce with foreign countries and between the states.

INTERSTATE COMMERCE - Commercial dealings between two parties located in different states or located in one state and accomplished through a point in another state or a foreign country; commercial dealings transacted between two states.

PHILADELPHIA v. NEW JERSEY
State (P) v. State (D)
437 U.S. 617 (1978).

NATURE OF CASE: Appeal from decision upholding constitutionality of state commerce statute.

FACT SUMMARY: The New Jersey Supreme Court upheld a New Jersey law prohibiting the importation of waste originating in another state into New Jersey (D) on the basis that it protected a legitimate health interest of the state of New Jersey (D).

CONCISE RULE OF LAW: State laws which are basically protectionist in nature unduly burden interstate commerce and thus are unconstitutional.

FACTS: New Jersey enacted a statute which prohibited the importation of solid or liquid waste which was collected or originated in another state. The law was challenged by private landfill owners in New Jersey (D), and the trial court held that it unduly burdened interstate commerce by discriminating against products from other states. The New Jersey Supreme Court reversed, holding the law advanced legitimate health and safety concerns and thus did not unduly burden interstate commerce. The U.S. Supreme Court granted certiorari.

ISSUE: Do state laws which are basically protectionist in nature unduly burden interstate commerce?

HOLDING AND DECISION: (Stewart, J.) Yes. State laws which are basically protectionist in nature unduly burden interstate commerce and are unconstitutional. Even if New Jersey's (D) ultimate purpose was to protect the health and safety of its citizens, it may not accomplish this by discriminating against articles of commerce coming from outside the state. Discrimination must be based on some property of the goods other than geographic origin. This law treats inherently similar products differently based solely on place of origin. As a result, it improperly discriminates against out-of-state production and unduly burdens interstate commerce. Reversed.

DISSENT: (Rehnquist, J.) New Jersey (D) recognized the health and safety problems associated with the use of landfills in disposing of waste. Under its inherent police power, that state could validly limit the amount of waste its citizens had to deal with by limiting the use of its land as a dump site for any other state.

EDITOR'S ANALYSIS: This case reaffirms the Court's holding in *Dean Milk Co. v. Madison*, 340 U.S. 349 (1951). It recognizes that waste is an element of commerce, and its disposal must be regulated as is all commerce. Because no federal regulation exists on the interstate transport and disposition of waste, states may regulate it only if done in a way which is not unduly burdensome. Since the Dean Milk decision, discrimination based on point of origin has been held unduly burdensome.

[For more information on state discriminatory effects on interstate commerce, see Casenote Law Outline on Constitutional Law, Chapter 6, § I, The Dormant or "Negative" Commerce Clause.]

QUICKNOTES

CERTIORARI - The informing of a higher court by a lower court, through the examination of a certified copy of the case, enabling the higher court to determine whether any irregularities occurred in the lower court's proceedings.

INTERSTATE COMMERCE - Commercial dealings between two parties located in different states or located in one state and accomplished through a point in another state or a foreign country; commercial dealings transacted between two states.

POLICE POWER - The power of a government to impose restrictions on the rights of private persons, as long as those restrictions are reasonably related to the promotion and protection of public health, safety, morals and the general welfare.

NOTES:

DEAN MILK CO. v. CITY OF MADISON
Milk products distributor (P) v. Municipality (D)
340 U.S. 349 (1951).

NATURE OF CASE: Action challenging the validity of a city ordinance regulating the sale of milk and milk products within the municipality's jurisdiction.

FACT SUMMARY: A Madison (D) ordinance made it unlawful to sell any milk as pasteurized unless it had been processed and bottled at an approved pasteurization plant located within five miles of the city.

CONCISE RULE OF LAW: A locality may not discriminate against interstate commerce, even to protect the health and safety of its people if reasonable alternatives exist which do not discriminate and are adequate to conserve legitimate local interests.

FACTS: Dean Milk Co. (P) was an Illinois corporation engaged in distributing milk products in Illinois and Wisconsin. Madison (D) is a city in Wisconsin. A Madison (D) ordinance prohibited the sale of any milk as pasteurized unless it had been processed and bottled at an approved pasteurization plant located within five miles of the city. Dean Milk (P) had pasteurization plants located 65 and 85 miles from Madison (D). Dean Milk (P) was denied a license to sell its milk products within Madison (D) solely because its pasteurization plants were more than five miles away. Dean Milk (P) contended that the ordinance imposed an undue burden on interstate commerce.

ISSUE: Can an ordinance, which in practical effect prevents out-of-state sellers from competing with local producers, be upheld?

HOLDING AND DECISION: (Clark, J.) No. A locality may not discriminate against interstate commerce, even to protect the health and safety of its people, if reasonable alternatives exist which do not discriminate and are adequate to conserve legitimate local interests. The Madison (D) ordinance erects an economic barrier protecting a major local industry against competition from without the state. Hence, it plainly discriminates against interstate commerce. It must be decided whether the ordinance can be justified in view of the local interest and the available methods for protecting those interests. Reasonable and adequate alternatives do exist. Madison (D) could send its inspectors to the distant plants, or it could exclude from its city all milk not produced in conformity with standards as high as those enforced by Madison (D). It could use the local ratings checked by the U.S. Public Health Service to enforce such a provision. The Madison (D) ordinance must yield to the principle that "one State, in its dealings with another, may not place itself in a position of economic isolation."

DISSENT: (Black, J.) Dean Milk's (P) personal preference not to pasteurize within five miles of Madison (D), not the ordinance, keeps its milk out of Madison (D). The lower court found the ordinance to be a good faith attempt to safeguard public health. Never has a bona fide health law been struck down on the ground that equally good or better alternatives exist. At the very least the ordinance should not be invalidated without having the parties present evidence on the relative merits of the Madison (D) ordinance and the alternatives suggested by the court. I do not think that the court can, on the basis of judicial knowledge, guarantee that the substitute methods it proposes would not lower health standards.

EDITOR'S ANALYSIS: In *Nebbia v. New York,* the court sustained the state regulation of minimum milk prices to be paid by dealers to local producers. However in *Baldwin v. Seelig,* the same law was challenged as applied to out-of-state producers. The Supreme Court held that application to be an unconstitutional burden on commerce in that it "set a barrier to traffic between one state and another as effective as if custom duties, equal to the price differential (between the out-of-state price and the minimum price set by New York) had been laid upon the thing transported." Baldwin was heavily relied upon in Dean Milk.

[For more information on state discriminatory effects on interstate commerce, see Casenote Law Outline on Constitutional Law, Chapter 6, § I, The Dormant or "Negative" Commerce Clause.]

QUICKNOTES

INTERSTATE COMMERCE - Commercial dealings between two parties located in different states or located in one state and accomplished through a point in another state or a foreign country; commercial dealings transacted between two states.

UNDUE BURDEN - Unlawfully oppressive or troublesome.

H. P. HOOD & SONS v. DU MOND
Milk distributor (P) v. Milk commissioner (D)
336 U.S. 525 (1949).

NATURE OF CASE: Action challenging the constitutionality of a New York milk dealer licensing law.

FACT SUMMARY: Hood (P), a Boston milk distributor, obtained milk from New York. He was denied a license to establish a receiving depot in New York on the basis of a New York law which makes a condition of the issuance of a license that such issuance will not tend to be destructive of competition in a market already "adequately served."

CONCISE RULE OF LAW: Restrictions, imposed for the avowed purpose and with the practical effect of curtailing the volume of interstate commerce to aid local economic interests, will not be sustained.

FACTS: Hood (P) was a Boston milk distributor who obtained his supply of milk from producers in New York State. He had established three milk receiving and processing depots in New York under licenses from that state. When he applied for a license to open a fourth depot, he was denied. The basis for the denial was that issuance would tend to creative destructive competition in an area already adequately served. In his denial, the milk commissioner (D) stated that the fourth depot would draw milk supplies away from other existing processing plants and would tend to deprive the local market of an adequate supply of milk.

ISSUE: May a state constitutionally enact restrictions with the purpose and effect of curtailing the volume of interstate commerce for the benefit of local economic interests?

HOLDING AND DECISION: (Jackson, J.) No. Restrictions, imposed for the avowed purpose and with the practical effect of curtailing the volume of interstate commerce to aid local economic interests, will not be sustained. There is a distinction between the power of the state to shelter its people from menaces to their health or safety, even when those dangers emanate from interstate commerce, and its lack of power to retard, burden, or constrict the flow of such commerce for their economic advantage. *Baldwin v. Seelig* is a recent explicit condemnation by this court of economic restraints or interstate commerce for local economic advantage. "Our system, fostered by the Commerce Clause, is that every farmer and every craftsperson shall be encouraged to produce by the certainty of free access to every market in the nation, that no home embargoes will withhold exports and no other state will, by customs duties or regulations, exclude them. Such was the vision of the founders; such has been the doctrine of this court which has given it reality." Since the statute, as applied to Hood (P), violates the Commerce Clause and is not authorized by federal legislation pursuant to that Clause, it cannot stand.

DISSENT: (Black, J.) The question here is whether all local phases of interstate business are to be judicially immunized from state laws against destructive competitive business practices. In *Baldwin*, it was because New York attempted to project its law into Vermont that its health purpose was insufficient to outweigh Vermont's interest in controlling its own local affairs. Here, New York does not attempt to regulate the price of milk, rather it seeks to promote health and to protect New York farmers from destructive competition in New York. Such were the purposes of the Pennsylvania Milk Law which was upheld in *Milk Control Board v. Eisenberg Co.* 306 U.S. 346 (1939).

DISSENT: (Frankfurter, J.) In effect the majority holds that no matter how important the prevention of destructive competition may be to the internal economy of a state and no matter how unimportant the interstate commerce affected, a state cannot, as a means of preventing such competition, deny an applicant access to a market within the state if that applicant intends to ship out of state. What is essentially a problem of striking a balance between competing interests should not be treated as an exercise in absolutes.

EDITOR'S ANALYSIS: In *Milk Control Board v. Eisenberg*, a New York milk dealer who bought milk from Pennsylvania producers challenged a Pennsylvania law. The law set the minimum price to be paid by dealers to milk producers. The Supreme Court upheld the law, stating that it did not attempt to regulate shipment to or sale in New York. It also found that the activity affected was essentially local in Pennsylvania, since only a fraction of the milk produced in that state is shipped out of state. The effect on interstate commerce was found to be incidental. *Baldwin* was not controlling. The Court stated that that decision "condemned an enactment aimed solely at interstate commerce, attempting to affect and regulate the price of milk in a sister state" and amounted, in effect, to a tariff.

[For more information on the anti-embargo rule, see Casenote Law Outline on Constitutional Law, Chapter 6, § I, The Dormant or "Negative" Commerce Clause.]

QUICKNOTES

PAROCHIAL - Regional or narrow in scope.

INTERSTATE COMMERCE - Commercial dealings between two parties located in different states or located in one state and accomplished through a point in another state or a foreign country; commercial dealings transacted between two states.

SOUTHERN PACIFIC CO. v. ARIZONA
Railroad company (D) v. State (P)
325 U.S. 761 (1945).

NATURE OF CASE: Action to recover statutory penalties for violation of the Arizona Train Limit Law.

FACT SUMMARY: The Arizona Train Limit Law prohibited the operation within the state of passenger trains more than 14 cars long and freight trains more than 70 cars long.

CONCISE RULE OF LAW: In deciding whether a state law places an unreasonable burden on interstate commerce, and hence cannot be sustained, the Court must balance the nature and extent of the burden which would be imposed by the statute against the merits and purposes to be derived from the state regulation.

FACTS: The Arizona Train Limit Law made it unlawful to operate within the state a train of more than 14 passenger cars or 70 freight cars. It authorized the state to recover a money penalty for each violation. Arizona (P) brought this action against Southern Pacific (D) to recover the statutory penalties for operative trains within the state in violation of the Law. The trial court decided for Southern Pacific (D) on the basis of detailed findings. The state supreme court reversed. It thought that the statute was enacted within the state's police power and that it bore some reasonable relation to the health, safety, and well-being of the state's people. Hence, the Court thought, the statute should not be overturned notwithstanding its admittedly adverse effect on interstate commerce.

ISSUE: In determining whether a state law imposes an unallowable burden on interstate commerce, is it for the courts to balance the burden to be imposed against the merits and purposes to be derived from the law?

HOLDING AND DECISION: (Stone, C.J.) Yes. Wide scope has been left to the states for regulating matters of local concern, but such regulation must not materially restrict the free flow of interstate commerce or interfere with it in matters requiring national uniformity. The courts must determine the nature and extent of the burden which a state regulation would impose on interstate commerce, and then balance that burden against the benefits and merits to be derived from the regulation. In this case, the findings show that the operations of trains of more than 14 passenger cars and more than 70 freight cars is standard practice of the major U.S. railroads. If train length is to be regulated, national uniformity in regulation, such as only Congress can impose, is "practically indispensable to the operation of an efficient and economic national railway system." The findings leave no doubt that the Arizona Train Limit Law imposes a serious burden on interstate commerce. The practical effect of the law is to control train operations beyond the boundaries of the state because of the necessity of breaking up and reassembling long trains before entering and leaving the regulating state. Further, the Arizona law has no reasonable relation to safety. It in fact makes train operation more dangerous, as is demonstrated by the increase in accidents due to the increase in the number of trains. The purpose

of the Act was to cut down on "slack action accidents." Slack action is increased as train length is increased. However, the trial court found that such accidents occurred as frequently in Arizona as in Nevada, where train length is unregulated. Hence, the total effect of the law as a safety measure in reducing accidents is so slight as to not outweigh the national interest in keeping interstate commerce free from substantial interference and from subjection to local regulation which does not have a uniform effect on the interstate train journey which it interrupts. Arizona (P) relies on *South Carolina v. Barnwell*. However, that case concerned the state's power to regulate the use of its highways, a field over which the state has a far more extensive control than over railroads. Here, Arizona's (P) safety interest is clearly outweighed by the national interest in an adequate, economical, and efficient railway system. The state supreme court's decision sustaining the statute is reversed.

DISSENT: (Black, J.) The trial court, in making findings of fact as to the validity of the reasons for the enactment of the Arizona Train Limit Law, acted as a "super legislature." The state supreme court did not discuss the lower court's findings of fact, and it properly designated that the statute bore a reasonable relation to its purpose as a safety measure. Congress deliberately left this area to the states. The majority's decision seems to be the result of their belief that both the Arizona legislature and Congress made wrong policy decisions in permitting a law which limits train length to stand. It seems that maintaining low railroad operation costs outweighs the personal safety of railway employees, many of whom have been killed and injured in slack action accidents.

DISSENT: (Douglas, J.) The courts should intervene only where state laws discriminate against interstate commerce or are out of harmony with laws which Congress has enacted.

EDITOR'S ANALYSIS: In *Southern Pacific*, the Court employs the balancing of interests test, which, as the dissenting opinion points out, is a departure from the *Barnwell* rational basis test. The following are examples of regulations which were held not to unreasonably burden commerce (or where a national interstate commerce interest did not outweigh the state's benefits). A requirement that all persons operating trains within the state (even those in purely interstate movement) be licensed to insure their skill and fitness was upheld. Likewise, the Court upheld "full crew" laws defining the size of train crews. Laws prescribing reasonable safety and comfort devices and others limiting the speed of trains within city limits, as well as those regulating grade crossing, were also upheld.

[For more information on state safety regulations on commerce, see Casenote Law Outline on Constitutional Law, Chapter 6, § I, The Dormant or "Negative" Commerce Clause.]

QUICKNOTES

POLICE POWER - The power of a government to impose restrictions on the rights of private persons, as long as those restrictions are reasonably related to the promotion and protection of public health, safety, morals and the general welfare.

KASSEL v. CONSOLIDATED FREIGHTWAYS CORP.

State (D) v. Common carrier (P)

450 U.S. 662 (1981).

NATURE OF CASE: Appeal from decision holding that an Iowa statute unconstitutionally burdened interstate commerce.

FACT SUMMARY: Consolidated Freightways Corp. (P) challenged the constitutionality of an Iowa statute which prohibited the use of certain large trucks within the state boundaries.

CONCISE RULE OF LAW: A state safety regulation will be unconstitutional if its asserted safety purpose is outweighed by its degree of interference with interstate commerce.

FACTS: The State of Iowa passed a statute restricting the length of vehicles that may use its highways. The state law set a general length limit of 55 feet for most vehicles, and 60 feet for trucks pulling two trailers ("doubles"). Iowa was the only state in the western or midwestern United States to outlaw the use of 65-foot doubles. Consolidated Freightways Corp. (P), one of the largest common carriers in the country, alleged that the Iowa statute unconstitutionally burdened interstate commerce. The district court and the court of appeals found the statute unconstitutional and Kassel (D), on behalf of the state, appealed.

ISSUE: Will a state safety regulation be held to be unconstitutional if its asserted safety purpose is outweighed by the degree of interference with interstate commerce?

HOLDING AND DECISION: (Powell, J.) Yes. While bona fide state safety regulations are entitled to a strong presumption of validity, the asserted safety purpose must be weighed against the degree of interference with interstate commerce. Less deference will be given to the findings of state legislators where the local regulation has a disproportionate effect on out-of-state residents and businesses. Here, the State of Iowa failed to present any persuasive evidence that 65-foot doubles are less safe than 55-foot single trailers. Consolidated Freightways Corp. (P) demonstrated that Iowa's law substantially burdens interstate commerce by compelling trucking companies either to route 65-foot doubles around Iowa or use the smaller trucks allowed by the state statute. Thus the Iowa statute is in violation of the Commerce Clause. Affirmed.

CONCURRENCE: (Brennan, J.) In ruling on the constitutionality of state safety regulations, the burdens imposed on commerce must be balanced against the regulatory purposes identified by the state legislators. Protectionist legislation is unconstitutional under the Commerce Clause, even if its purpose is to promote safety, rather than economic, purposes.

DISSENT: (Rehnquist, J.) A sensitive consideration must be made when weighing the safety purposes of a statute against the burden on interstate commerce. A state safety regulation is invalid if its asserted safety justification is merely a pretext for discrimination against interstate commerce. The Iowa statute is a valid highway safety regulation and is entitled to the strongest presumption of validity.

EDITOR'S ANALYSIS: Traditionally, states have been free to pass public safety regulations restricting the use of highways and railway facilities. However, state safety regulations have been struck down when only a marginal increase in safety causes a substantial burden on interstate commerce. This case simply follows this rationale.

[For more information on state safety regulation burdening interstate commerce, see Casenote Law Outline on Constitutional Law, Chapter 6, § I, The Dormant or "Negative" Commerce Clause.]

QUICKNOTES

COMMERCE CLAUSE - Article 1, section 8, clause 3 of the United States Constitution, granting Congress the power to regulate commerce with foreign countries and between the states.

INTERSTATE COMMERCE - Commercial dealings between two parties located in different states or located in one state and accomplished through a point in another state or a foreign country; commercial dealings transacted between two states.

PER SE - An activity that is so inherently obvious that it is unnecessary to examine its underlying validity.

SALUTARY - Remedial or beneficial.

NOTES:

SOUTH-CENTRAL TIMBER DEVELOPMENT, INC. v. WUNNICKE

Timber company (P) v. State (D)
467 U.S. 82 (1984).

NATURE OF CASE: Appeal from finding of congressional authorization of state regulation.

FACT SUMMARY: Alaska offered to sell large amounts of state-owned timber if the buyers, including South-Central Timber (P), agreed to process it within state boundaries, but South-Central Timber (P) wanted to buy the timber and ship it to Japan for processing.

CONCISE RULE OF LAW: If a state imposes burdens on commerce within a market in which it is a participant, but which have a substantial regulatory effect outside of that particular market, they are per se invalid under the Federal Commerce Clause.

FACTS: Alaska offered for sale a large quantity of state-owned timber. However, it required potential purchasers to agree to process the timber within state boundaries before shipment out of Alaska. This law was enacted to protect existing timber-processing industries within the state and to obtain further revenue from the timber beyond its sale. South-Central Timber (P) wanted to buy Alaska timber and also wanted to ship it beyond Alaskan borders to Japan for processing. South-Central (P) challenged the constitutional validity of the Alaska requirement on Commerce Clause grounds. Alaska responded by asserting that the in-state processing requirement was exempt from invalidation under the Commerce Clause under the "market participant" doctrine. The court of appeals found that Congress had authorized Alaska's processing requirement, and South-Central (P) appealed to the U.S. Supreme Court.

ISSUE: If a state imposes burdens on commerce within a market in which it is a participant, but those burdens have a substantial regulatory effect outside of that particular market, are they per se invalid under the Federal Commerce Clause?

HOLDING AND DECISION: (White, J.) Yes. The market participant doctrine allows a state to impose burdens on interstate commerce within the market in which it is a participant but allows it to go no further. The state may not impose conditions, whether by statute, regulation, or contract, that have a substantial regulatory effect outside of that particular market. "Market" for Commerce Clause purposes is narrowly defined and precludes a state's exercise of leverage in the market in which it is directly participating in order to regulate a "downstream" market. Here, Alaska is a direct participant in the timber market but not in the processing market. Although Alaska may legitimately prefer its own residents in the initial disposition of goods, in other words, when it is a "private trader" in the immediate transaction, it may not

attach restrictions on dispositions subsequent to the goods coming to rest in private hands after Alaska no longer has a proprietary interest in them. Alaska may not govern the private, separate economic relationships of its trading partners downstream; as a typical seller, it has no say over how the product is used after sale. Because Alaska's local-processing requirement burdens interstate commerce, it is per se invalid under the Federal Commerce Clause. Reversed and remanded.

DISSENT: (Rehnquist, C.J.) The distinction drawn in the plurality opinion between market participation and market regulation is unconvincing and artificial. Alaska could have chosen a number of constitutionally valid ways of requiring the buyers of its timber process it within the state, all of which in substance are the same as the contractual provisions the plurality found violative of the Commerce Clause. For instance, Alaska could have chosen to sell its timber only to those companies that themselves own and operate processing plants in Alaska, or the statute itself could have paid to have the logs processed and then sold only processed, rather than unprocessed, logs. The plurality approach is unduly formalistic.

EDITOR'S ANALYSIS: The facts of this case closely resemble the facts of an earlier Supreme Court case, in which the court struck down a Louisiana law prohibiting export from the state of any shrimp from which the heads and hulls had not been removed. See *Foster-Fountain Packing Co. v. Haydel*, 278 U.S. 1 (1928). The Court rejected the claim that the fact that the shrimp were owned by the state authorized the state to impose such limitations. The case, as here, involved a natural resource which the court noted could have been retained for use and consumption within its borders, but because Louisiana permitted its shrimp to be taken and sold in interstate commerce, it released its right to and terminated its control of the shrimp so taken.

[For more information on market participant exception, see Casenote Law Outline on Constitutional Law, Chapter 6, § I, The Dormant or "Negative" Commerce Clause.]

QUICKNOTES

COMMERCE CLAUSE - Article 1, section 8, clause 3 of the United States Constitution, granting Congress the power to regulate commerce with foreign countries and between the states.

MARKET PARTICIPANT DOCTRINE - Allows states acting as market participants (i.e. businesses) to be exempted from the dormant clause.

PER SE - An activity that is so inherently obvious that it is unnecessary to examine its underlying validity.

PACIFIC GAS & ELECTRIC CO. v. STATE ENERGY RESOURCES CONSERVATION & DEVELOPMENT COMM'N

Electric utility company (P) v. State agency (D)
461 U.S. 190 (1983).

NATURE OF CASE: Action seeking a declaratory judgment.

FACT SUMMARY: Pacific Gas (P) maintained that certain provisions of California's Warren-Alquist Act were invalid because it was preempted by Congress' passage of the Atomic Energy Act of 1954.

CONCISE RULE OF LAW: In passing the Atomic Energy Act of 1954, Congress preempted state regulation of the radiological safety aspects involved in the construction and operation of nuclear plants but intended for the states to retain their traditional responsibility in the field of regulating electrical utilities for determining questions of need, reliability, cost, and other related state concerns.

FACTS: In challenging the validity of various provisions of California's Warren-Alquist State Energy Resources Conservation and Development Act, Pacific Gas (P) claimed that such regulation as it attempted was preempted by the Atomic Energy Act which Congress enacted in 1954. Of particular concern was a provision imposing a moratorium on the certification of new nuclear plants until the State Energy Resources and Conservation Commission (Energy Commission) (D) "finds that there has been developed and that the United States through its authorized agency has approved and there exists a demonstrated technology or means for the disposal of high-level nuclear waste." Disposal was defined as a "method for the permanent and terminal disposition of high-level nuclear waste," a goal which was not even close to being reached. The district court held that the aforementioned nuclear moratorium provision was not preempted because it saw in certain sections of the Atomic Energy Act congressional authorization for states to regulate nuclear power plants "for purposes other than protection against radiation hazards."

ISSUE: Has Congress, in passing the Atomic Energy Act of 1954, totally preempted any state regulation of nuclear power or power plants?

HOLDING AND DECISION: (White, J.) No. The intent of Congress in passing the Atomic Energy Act of 1954 was to give the federal government exclusive regulatory power over the radiological safety aspects involved in the construction and operation of a nuclear plant. It did not intend to preempt the states from exercising their traditional responsibility in the field of regulating electrical utilities (nuclear or otherwise) for determining questions of need, reliability, cost, and other related state concerns. California has maintained that its moratorium provisions are aimed at economic problems, arguing that without a permanent nuclear waste disposal system the nuclear waste problem could become critical and lead to unpredictably high costs to either contain the problem or shut down reactors. Accepting this avowed economic purpose as the rationale for enacting the moratorium provision, the statute lies outside the occupied field of nuclear safety regulation. It does not conflict with federal regulation of nuclear waste disposal. In fact, its very words accept that it is the federal responsibility to develop and license such technology and it

nowhere seeks to impose its own state standards on nuclear waste disposal. It does not conflict with the Nuclear Regulatory Commission's decision to continue licensing reactors despite the uncertainty surrounding the waste disposal problem or with Congress' recent passage of legislation directed at that problem. The NRC's imprimatur indicates only that it is safe to proceed with such plants, not that it is economically wise to do so. Since the NRC order does not and could not compel a utility to develop a nuclear plant, compliance with both it and California's challenged statutory provision is possible. Furthermore, because the NRC's regulations are aimed at insuring that plants are safe, not necessarily that they are economical, California's statutory provision does not interfere with the objective of the federal regulation. Finally, there is little doubt that a primary purpose of the Atomic Energy Act was and is the promotion of nuclear power. But, as the court of appeals noted, the promotion of nuclear power was not intended by Congress to be accomplished "at all costs." The elaborate licensing and safety provisions and the continued preservation of state regulation in traditional areas belie that. Thus, it cannot be said that California's statutory provision "frustrates" the Atomic Energy Act's purpose of developing the commercial use of nuclear power. Quite simply, there has been no preemption with regard to the type of provision California enacted. Affirmed.

CONCURRENCE IN PART: (Blackmun, J.) I cannot join in that part of the Court's opinion that suggests that a state may not prohibit the construction of nuclear power plants if the state is motivated by concerns about the safety of such plants. In passing the Atomic Energy Act, Congress intended only to encourage the development of nuclear technology so as to make another source of energy available to the states. It did not intend to force the states to accept this particular source. Thus, a state ban on nuclear plant construction for safety reasons would not conflict with Congress' objectives or purposes.

EDITOR'S ANALYSIS: There are instances in which Congress explicitly preempts state authority by so stating in express terms in the federal statute itself. More often, however, Congress' intent to supersede state law altogether is to be found: 1) from a "scheme of federal regulation so pervasive as to make reasonable the inference that Congress left no room to supplement it;" or 2) because "the Act of Congress touches a field in which the federal interest is so dominant that the federal system will be assumed to preclude enforcement of state laws on the same subject;" or 3) because "the object sought to be obtained by the federal law and the character of obligations imposed by it may reveal the same purpose." *Fidelity Federal Savings & Loan Ass'n v. de la Cuesta*, 458 U.S. ___ (1982).

[For more information on preemption doctrine, see Casenote Law Outline on Constitutional Law, Chapter 2, § I, Federal-State Relations in General.]

QUICKNOTES

DECLARATORY JUDGMENT - A judgment of the rights between opposing parties in a justiciable controversy that does not grant coercive relief (i.e. damages), but is binding.

PRE-EMPTION - Judicial preference recognizing the procedure of federal legislation over state legislation of the same subject matter.

UNITED BUILDING & CONSTRUCTION TRADES COUNCIL v. CAMDEN
Trade council (P) v. City (D)
465 U.S. 208 (1984).

NATURE OF CASE: Appeal from judgment upholding constitutionality of a municipal residency ordinance.

FACT SUMMARY: The New Jersey Supreme Court held that a municipal ordinance, which required that 40% of all workers on city construction projects be residents of the city, was not covered by the Privileges and Immunities Clause.

CONCISE RULE OF LAW: The Privileges and Immunities Clause applies to municipal ordinances which discriminate on the basis of municipal residence.

FACTS: The City of Camden (D), New Jersey, enacted an ordinance requiring that contractors and subcontractors working on city construction projects employ a workforce of 40% Camden (D) residents. The Trades Council (P) sued, contending the ordinance discriminated against non-city residents in violation of the Privileges and Immunities Clause. The Supreme Court of New Jersey upheld the ordinance, holding that the Privileges and Immunities Clause did not apply to municipal ordinances which discriminate on the basis of municipal residence because the discrimination applies to both New Jersey residents outside Camden (D) as well as out-of-state residents. Therefore, no discrimination based on state residence was made by the ordinance, and it did not come under the Privileges and Immunities Clause. The U.S. Supreme Court took jurisdiction.

ISSUE: Does the Privileges and Immunities Clause apply to municipal ordinances which discriminate on the basis of municipal rather than state citizenship?

HOLDING AND DECISION: (Rehnquist, J.) Yes. The Privileges and Immunities Clause applies to municipal ordinances which discriminate on the basis of municipal residence. Ordinances are enacted under the municipality's power derived from the state. Thus, ordinances are not outside the Clause merely because they are enacted by a municipality. Further, although New Jersey residents living outside of Camden (D) were affected by the ordinance along with out-of-state residents, New Jersey residents had the opportunity to expand or contract municipal power by voting in state elections. Out-of-state residents had no such power. Therefore, the clause applies. The ordinance affected the rights of non-residents to pursue a livelihood of their choosing. This is clearly a fundamental privilege protected by the Clause. Because no trial was held, it is necessary that the decision of the supreme court of New Jersey be reversed and the case remanded to determine whether Camden's (D) economic problems were sufficient to justify the discrimination placed on non-residents by the ordinance.

DISSENT: (Blackman, J.) The Court erroneously extends the scope of the Privileges and Immunities Clause without textual or historical support. Because the Clause was not intended to apply to intrastate discrimination, the ordinance was valid.

EDITOR'S ANALYSIS: In this case, the court points out that although the ordinance may have been valid under the Commerce Clause, as the City was acting as a market participant, such an analysis does not apply under the Privileges and Immunities Clause. That Clause imposes a direct restraint on state action in the interest of interstate harmony.

QUICKNOTES

COMMERCE CLAUSE - Article 1, section 8, clause 3 of the United States Constitution, granting Congress the power to regulate commerce with foreign countries and between the states.

MARKET PARTICIPANT DOCTRINE - Allows states acting as market participants (i.e. businesses) to be exempted from the dormant clause.

PRIVILEGED AND IMMUNITIES CLAUSE OF ARTICLE IV, § 2 - Provision in the constitution that accords the advantages of citizenship equally to the citizens of each state; out-of-state citizens must therefore be given the same privileges as a state's own citizens.

NOTES:

NOTES

CHAPTER 6
SEPARATION OF POWERS

QUICK REFERENCE RULES OF LAW

1. **Executive Encroachment on Legislative Powers.** The President, as leader of the executive branch, is bound to enforce the laws within the limits of the authority expressly granted to him by the Constitution, and he cannot usurp the lawmaking power of Congress by an assertion of an unspecified aggregation of his specified powers. (Youngstown Sheet & Tube Co. v. Sawyer [The Steel Seizure Case])

   [For more information on exclusive congressional authority to legislate domestically, see Casenote Law Outline on Constitutional Law, Chapter 5, § II, Major Issues under the Doctrine of Separation of Powers.]

2. **Congressional Encroachments on Executive Power.** The cancellation provisions authorized by the Line Item Veto Act are not constitutional. (Clinton v. New York)

3. **Executive Encroachment on Legislative Powers.** The president lacks the plenary power to settle claims against foreign governments through an Executive Agreement; however, where Congress at least acquiesces in the president's actions, the president can settle such claims. (Dames & Moore v. Regan)

   [For more information on scope of presidential powers, see Casenote Law Outline on Constitutional Law, Chapter 4, § I, Presidential Powers.]

4. **Congressional Encroachments on Executive Power.** Because it constitutes an exercise of legislative power and is thus subject to the bicameralism and presentment requirements of Article I of the Constitution, the federal statute purporting to authorize a one-house veto of the Attorney General's decision to allow a particular deportable alien to remain in the United States is unconstitutional. (INS v. Chadha)

   [For more information on bicamerality and presentment requirements, see Casenote Law Outline on Constitutional Law, Chapter 5, § II, Major Issues under the Doctrine of Separation of Powers.]

5. **Congressional Control Over Executive Officers.** The assignment of executive powers to an agent or officer of the legislative branch violates the doctrine of separation of powers. (Bowsher v. Synar)

   [For more information on Separation of Powers, see Casenote Law Outline on Constitutional Law, Chapter 5, § II, Major Issues under the Doctrine of Separation of Powers.]

6. **Congressional Control Over Executive Officers.** Congress' creation of the independent counsel was not an unconstitutional usurpation of power. (Morrison v. Olson)

   [For more information on the Appointment Power, see Casenote Law Outline on Constitutional Law, Chapter 4, § I, Presidential Powers.]

7. **Executive Privilege and Immunities.** Absent a claim of need to protect military, diplomatic, or sensitive national security secrets, an absolute, unqualified presidential privilege of immunity from judicial process under all circumstances does not exist. (United States v. Nixon)

   [For more information on presidential privileged communications, see Casenote Law Outline on Constitutional Law, Chapter 4, § II, Presidential Immunities and Privileges.]

8. **Executive Privilege and Immunities.** Presidential immunity does not apply to civil damages litigation arising out of unofficial events occurring prior to the assumption of office. (Clinton v. Jones)

   [For more information on presidential and congressional immunity, see Casenote Law Outline on Constitutional Law, Chapter 4, § II, Presidential Immunities and Privileges.]

DAMES & MOORE v. REGAN

Creditor (P) v. Federal government (D)

453 U.S. 654 (1981).

NATURE OF CASE: Review of appeal of decision issuing an order of attachment pursuant to a breach of contract.

FACT SUMMARY: Dames & Moore (P) filed suit to recover funds owed on a contract with the government of Iran, but the order of attachment was voided by an Executive Agreement.

CONCISE RULE OF LAW: The president lacks the plenary power to settle claims against foreign governments through an Executive Agreement; however, where Congress at least acquiesces in the president's actions, the president can settle such claims.

FACTS: In November of 1979 President Carter, acting pursuant to the International Emergency Economic Powers Act (IEEPA), froze Iranian assets in the United States after Americans were taken hostage in Tehran. The Americans held hostage were subsequently released on January 20, 1981, pursuant to an Executive Agreement entered into the day before. The agreement included a promise to settle all claims and litigation between the countries through arbitration. Dames & Moore (P), holders of an attachment order against Iranian assets, took exception with this agreement and filed suit. The litigation eventually reached the Supreme Court.

ISSUE: Does the president possess plenary powers to settle claims against foreign governments through an Executive Agreement?

HOLDING AND DECISION: (Rehnquist, J.) No. The president lacks the plenary power to settle claims against foreign governments through an Executive Agreement; however, where Congress at least acquiesces in the president's actions, the president can settle such claims. When Congress implicitly or explicitly authorizes presidential action, the action is given the greatest presumption of validity. Here, while the president's exact decision was not contemplated in the IEEPA, substantial powers to seize and handle foreign assets was conferred in the president by Congress. Dames & Moore (P) would have to show that the government as a whole lacks the power to settle claims with foreign entities when it is in the interest of the United States to do so; such a heavy burden has not been met. There is a long history of congressional acquiescence to international agreements settling claims between citizens of the United States and nationals of other countries. However, there is no independent source of presidential authority to settle such claims. Had Congress not implicitly approved of the action, the president would have been beyond his bounds. But, in this case, he acted under the implied authority of Congress.

EDITOR'S ANALYSIS: Justice Rehnquist cites the concurring opinion of Justice Jackson in the case of *Youngstown Sheet & Tube Co. v. Sawyer*, 343 U.S. 579 (1952). In that case, Justice Jackson divided presidential authority into three categories: express or implied grants of power from Congress, actions in the face of congressional silence, and actions in direct contravention to congressional legislation. When acting against the wishes of Congress, the president's power was limited to express constitutional grants in Article II. At the other extreme, presidential power was at its greatest when acting with congressional approval, as Justice Rehnquist found to be the case here.

[For more information on scope of presidential powers, see Casenote Law Outline on Constitutional Law, Chapter 4, § I, Presidential Powers.]

QUICKNOTES

EXECUTIVE AGREEMENT - An agreement with a foreign nation that is binding on the country, entered into by the President without Senate approval.

ORDER OF ATTACHMENT - An order mandating the seizing of the property of one party in anticipation of, or in order to satisfy, a favorable judgment obtained by another party.

PLENARY - Unlimited and open; as broad as a given situation may require.

NOTES:

CLINTON v. CITY OF NEW YORK
Parties not identified.
524 U.S. 417, 118 S. Ct. 2091 (1998).

NATURE OF CASE: Challenge to the constitutionality of new presidential powers.

FACT SUMMARY: The Line Item Veto Act of 1996 allowed the president to cancel provisions that have been signed into law. Parties affected by President Clinton's cancellation of a provision of the Balanced Budget Act of 1997 challenged the constitutionality of the Act.

CONCISE RULE OF LAW: The cancellation provisions authorized by the Line Item Veto Act are not constitutional.

FACTS: President Clinton used his authority under the Line Item Veto Act of 1996 to cancel a provision of the Balanced Budget Act of 1997. This forced New York to repay certain funds to the federal government under the Medicaid program and removed a tax benefit to food processors acquired by farmers' cooperatives. New York City and several private organizations challenged the constitutionality of the Medicaid cancellation and the Snake River Potato Growers (a farmer's cooperative) challenged the food processors provision.

ISSUE: Are the cancellation provisions authorized by the Line Item Veto Act constitutional?

HOLDING AND DECISION: (Stevens, J.) No. The cancellation provisions authorized by the Line Item Veto Act are not constitutional. The Line Item Veto Act gives the President the power to "cancel in whole" three types of provisions that have already been signed into law: (1)any dollar amount of discretionary budget authority; (2) any item of new direct spending; or (3) any limited tax benefit. With respect to each cancellation, the President must determine that it will (i) reduce the Federal budget deficit; (ii) not impair any essential government functions; and (iii) not harm the national interest. A cancellation takes effect upon receipt by Congress of the notification of the cancellation. However, a majority vote of both Houses is sufficient to make the cancellation null and void. Although the Constitution expressly authorizes the President to veto a bill under Article I, § 7, it is silent on the subject of unilateral Presidential action that repeals or amends parts of duly enacted statues as authorized under the Line Item Veto Act. Constitutional silence should be construed as express prohibition. If there is to be a new role for the president in the procedure to determine the final text of a law, such a change must come through the amendment procedures and not by legislation.

CONCURRENCE: (Kennedy, J.) Separation of powers was designed to protect liberty, because the concentration of power in any single branch is a threat to liberty.

CONCURRENCE AND DISSENT: (Scalia, J.) If the Line Item Veto Act authorized the President to "decline to spend" any item of spending rather than "canceling" it, it would have been constitutional. Given that there is only a technical difference between the two actions and that it is no different from what Congress has permitted the President to do since the formation of the Union, the Line Item Veto does not offend Article I, § 7.

DISSENT: (Breyer, J.) Given how complex our nation has become, Congress cannot divide bills into thousands or tens of thousands of separate appropriations bills, each of which the President would have to veto or sign separately. Therefore, the Line Item Veto may help representative government work better.

EDITOR'S ANALYSIS: The majority did not comment on the wisdom of the Line Item Veto Act, because they found this step unnecessary given their finding that the Act was unconstitutional. Justice Kennedy did not let that stop him, since he felt that the Line Item Veto Act affected the separation of powers which in turn threatened liberty.

QUICKNOTES
LINE ITEM VETO ACT - Act authorizes a President to veto specified items in appropriation bills.

SEPARATION OF POWERS - The system of checks and balances preventing one branch of government from infringing upon exercising the powers of another branch of government.

NOTES:

YOUNGSTOWN SHEET & TUBE CO. v. SAWYER

Steel companies (P) v. Federal government (D)
343 U.S. 579 (1952).

NATURE OF CASE: Suit for declaratory and injunctive relief from a presidential order.

FACT SUMMARY: Faced with an imminent steel strike during the Korean War, the President ordered governmental seizure of the steel companies to prevent the strike. The companies challenged his power to take such action as being without constitutional authority or prior congressional approval.

CONCISE RULE OF LAW: The President, as leader of the executive branch, is bound to enforce the laws within the limits of the authority expressly granted to him by the Constitution, and he cannot usurp the lawmaking power of Congress by an assertion of an unspecified aggregation of his specified powers.

FACTS: As a result of long, but unsuccessful, negotiations with various steel companies, the United Steelworkers of America served notice of an intent to strike in April, 1952. Through the last months of the negotiations the President had utilized every available administrative remedy to effect a settlement and avert a strike. Congress had engaged in extensive debate on solutions but had passed no legislation on the issue. By order of the President, the Secretary of Commerce seized the steel companies so that steel production would not be interrupted during the Korean War. The steel companies sued in federal district court to have the seizure order declared invalid and to enjoin its enforcement. The government asserted that the President had "inherent power" to make the order and that it was "supported by the Constitution, historical precedent and court decisions." The district court granted a preliminary injunction which was stayed the same day by the court of appeals. The Supreme Court granted certiorari and ordered immediate argument.

ISSUE: May the President, relying on a concept of inherent powers, and in his capacity as Commander-in-Chief, make an order which usurps the lawmaking authority of Congress on the basis of a compelling need to protect the national security?

HOLDING AND DECISION: (Black, J.) No. There is, admittedly, no express congressional authority for these seizures, and so, if any authority for the President's act can be found, it must come from the Constitution. In the absence of express authority for the President's act, it is argued that the power can be implied from the aggregate of his express powers granted by the Constitution. This order cannot be justified by reliance on the President's role as Commander-in-Chief. Even though the term "theater of war" has enjoyed an expanding definition, it cannot embrace the taking of private property to prevent a strike. The President's powers in the area of legislation are limited to proposing new laws to Congress or vetoing laws which he deems inadvisable. This order is not executive implementation of a congressional act but a legislative act performed by the President. Only Congress may do what the President has attempted here. The Constitution is specific in vesting the lawmaking powers in Congress, and we, therefore, affirm the district court's decision to enjoin the enforcement of this order.

CONCURRENCE: (Frankfurter, J.) This decision does not attempt to define the limits of presidential authority. The President cannot act in contravention of an express congressional act, nor may he act where Congress has done nothing. Were this a case of a long history of congressional acquiescence to presidential practice our decision might be different, but no such showing has been made.

CONCURRENCE: (Jackson, J.) The power of the President to act can be viewed as three separate categories of circumstances. First, the President's power is at its maximum when he acts pursuant to express or implied congressional authority. Second, in the absence of a congressional grant of power, the President acts solely on the basis of his powers as specified in the Constitution. Third, when the President acts in contravention of congressional action, he may do so only where it can be shown that Congress has exceeded its constitutional powers and the President is acting in his own sphere of authority. It is in this last area where presidential acts are subject to the closest scrutiny. This order is clearly not in the first category. His act cannot be justified in the second category since Congress has limited seizure powers to specific instances not embracing this order. The constitutional grant of powers to the President is in specific terms that do not permit any loose aggregation to create powers not specified. There is little question that Congress could have authorized those seizures and this very power denies the same authority to the President. Finally, the President's act is justified by arguing it is the result of powers accruing to his office by custom and practice of previous administrations. Present unconstitutional acts cannot be justified by the prior unconstitutional acts of others. Presidential power may, in fact, enlarge due to congressional inaction, but the courts will not assist or approve this process.

DISSENT: (Vinson, Reed, Minton, JJ.) The majority's opinion has left the President powerless to act at the very time the need for his independent and immediate action is greatest. From Washington to Roosevelt, history is replete with examples of needed presidential action in the face of congressional inaction. Jefferson's Louisiana Purchase, Lincoln's Emancipation Proclamation, Wilson's War Labor Board with accompanying industrial seizures, and Roosevelt's seizure of an aircraft plant to avert a strike are but a few examples of presidential action that received subsequent, not prior, congressional or judicial authorization.

The President's seizure in this case is in accord with congressional intent to support the resistance of aggression in the world and is in furtherance of his duty to execute the laws of this nation. The executive is the only branch of government that may, by design, act swiftly to meet national emergencies. This decision emasculates that necessary power.

EDITOR'S ANALYSIS: Justice Black's broad language was criticized by many scholars as being overly expansive for the case presented. However, other authorities pointed out that the broad arguments advanced by the government required a broad response. During oral argument before the court, the government counsel stated that while the Constitution imposed limits on congressional and judicial powers, no such limits were imposed on the presidency. While supplemental briefs were filed modifying this position, the damage may already have been done. The Court was faced with a paucity of judicial precedents. The President and Congress have traditionally preferred political rather than judicial solutions to their conflicts. This practice avoids the limitations imposed on future actions by binding judicial precedents. And, as can be seen by the cases of Marbury v. Madison and United States v. Nixon, the executive branch has not fared well when it has submitted to judicial jurisdiction.

[For more information on exclusive congressional authority to legislate domestically, see Casenote Law Outline on Constitutional Law, Chapter 5, § II, Major Issues under the Doctrine of Separation of Powers.]

QUICKNOTES

EXECUTIVE ORDER - An order issued by the President, or another executive need of government, which has the force of law.

PRELIMINARY INJUNCTION - A judicial mandate issued to require or restrain a party from certain conduct; used to preserve a trial's subject matter or to prevent threatened injury.

IMMIGRATION AND NATURALIZATION SERVICE v. CHADHA

Federal agency (D) v. Illegal immigrant (P)
462 U.S. 919 (1983).

NATURE OF CASE: Consolidated actions challenging the constitutionality of a federal statute.

FACT SUMMARY: Chadha (P) and others challenged the constitutionality of a federal statute which purported to authorize one House of Congress, by resolution, to invalidate the decision of the Attorney General (made under authority delegated by Congress) to allow a particular deportable illegal immigrant to remain in the United States.

CONCISE RULE OF LAW: Because it constitutes an exercise of legislative power and is thus subject to the bicameralism and presentment requirements of Article I of the Constitution, the federal statute purporting to authorize a one-house veto of the Attorney General's decision to allow a particular deportable alien to remain in the United States is unconstitutional.

FACTS: Three cases consolidated on appeal all presented the question of the constitutionality of a federal statute which authorized either House of Congress, by resolution, to invalidate the decision of the Attorney General (made pursuant to authority delegated by Congress) to allow a particular deportable alien to remain in the United States. After such a one-house veto effectively overturned the Attorney General's decision to let Chadha (P) and certain other individuals remain in the United States, each instituted action challenging the constitutionality of the aforesaid statute. Chadha (P) filed a petition for a review of his deportation order, with the INS (D) actually agreeing with his contention that the statute was unconstitutional. The court of appeals held that the statute violated the doctrine of separation of powers.

ISSUE: Is it constitutional for Congress to statutorily authorize a one-house veto of a decision the Attorney General makes, under authority delegated to him by Congress, to allow a particular deportable alien to remain in the United States?

HOLDING AND DECISION: (Burger, C.J.) No. The Constitution does not permit Congress to statutorily authorize a one-house veto of a decision the Attorney General makes, pursuant to authority delegated to him by Congress, to allow a particular deportable alien to remain in the United States. Such an action is clearly an exercise of legislative power, which makes it subject to the bicameralism and presentment requirements of Article I of the Constitution unless one of the express constitutional exceptions authorizing one House to act alone applies. None of them apply. Thus, to accomplish what has been attempted by one House of Congress in this case requires action in conformity with the

express procedures of the Constitution's prescription for legislative action, passage by a majority of both Houses, and presentment to the President (for his signing or his veto). Such requirements were built into the Constitution to act as enduring checks on each branch and to protect the people from the improvident exercise of power by mandating certain prescribed steps. In attempting to bypass those steps, Congress has acted unconstitutionally. Affirmed.

CONCURRENCE: (Powell, J.) This case should be decided on the narrower ground that Congress assumes a judicial function in violation of the principle of separation of powers when it finds that a particular person does not satisfy the statutory criteria for permanent residence in this country. The Court's broader decision will apparently invalidate every use of the legislative veto, which is a procedure that has been much used by Congress and one it clearly views as essential to controlling the delegation of power to administrative agencies. While one may reasonably disagree with Congress' assessment of the veto's utility, the respect due its judgment as a coordinate branch of government cautions that our holding should be no more extensive than necessary to decide this case.

DISSENT: (White, J.) Today's decision sounds the death knell for nearly two hundred statutory provisions in which Congress has reserved a "legislative veto," which has become a central means by which Congress secures the accountability of executive and independent agencies. Without this particular tool, Congress faces a Hobson's choice: either to refrain from delegating the necessary authority, leaving itself with a hopeless task of writing laws with the requisite specificity to cover endless special circumstances across the entire policy landscape, or, in the alternative, to abdicate its lawmaking function to the executive branch and independent agencies. Thus, the apparent sweep of the Court's decision today, which appears to invalidate all legislative vetoes irrespective of form or subject, is regrettable. Furthermore, the Court's decision fails to recognize that the legislative veto is not the type of action subject to the bicameralism and presentment requirements of Article I. Only bills and their equivalent are subject to such requirements. The initial legislation delegating to the Attorney General the power to make a decision on the deportation of a particular alien complied with the Article I requirements. Congress' power to exercise a legislative veto over that decision cannot be viewed, then, as the power to write new law without bicameral approval or presidential consideration. If Congress can delegate lawmaking power to executive agencies, it is most difficult to understand Article I as forbidding Congress from simply reserving a check on legislative power for itself. Without the veto, agencies to whom power has been delegated may issue regulations having the force of law without bicameral approval and without the President's signature. It is thus not apparent why the reservation of a veto over the exercise of that legislative power must be subject to a more exacting test. In both cases, it is enough that the initial statutory authorizations comply with the Article I requirements.

EDITOR'S ANALYSIS: It is only within the last 50 years that the legislative veto has come into widespread use. When the federal government began its massive growth in response to the Depression, the legislative veto was "invented" as one means of keeping a check on the sprawling new structure. While many commentators, upon the Court's announcement of this decision, opined that the result was a major shift of power from the legislative branch to the executive branch, Congress through more restrictive draftsmanship should actually see minimal diminishment of its control of those areas over which it desires to retain control.

[For more information on bicamerality and presentment requirements, see Casenote Law Outline on Constitutional Law, Chapter 5, § II, Major Issues under the Doctrine of Separation of Powers.]

QUICKNOTES

BICAMERALISM - The necessity for approval by a majority of both houses of Congress when ratifying legislation, or approving other legislative action.

LEGISLATIVE VETO - A statutory provision that contemplates the Congressional ability to require the President or another part of the executive branch to act, or to refrain from taking action.

PRESENTMENT - The act of bringing a Congressional decision before the President for his approval or veto.

SEPARATION OF POWERS DOCTRINE - Each branch of government is precluded from interfering with the authority of another.

NOTES:

BOWSHER v. SYNAR

Federal government (D) v. Challenger to legislation (P)
478 U.S. 714 (1986).

NATURE OF CASE: Direct appeal to consider constitutionality of "Gramm-Rudman-Hollings Act" reporting provisions.

FACT SUMMARY: Bowsher (D) took a direct appeal to the Supreme Court from a district court ruling invalidating the reporting provisions of the "Gramm-Rudman-Hollings" deficit control act, finding the assignment of certain functions under the Act to the Comptroller General violated the doctrine of separation of powers.

CONCISE RULE OF LAW: The assignment of executive powers to an agent or officer of the legislative branch violates the doctrine of separation of powers.

FACTS: In 1985, the President signed into law the Gramm-Rudman-Hollings Deficit Control Act. The Act called for automatic reductions through the implementation of the so-called reporting provisions of the Act. Under these provisions, deficits are estimated, and if excessive, the Directors of the Office of Management and Budget and the Congressional Budget Office were to calculate necessary, program-by-program reductions, which are reported to the Comptroller General. After reviewing these figures, the Comptroller General reports his conclusions to the President, who is required to implement the reductions specified in the report. Anticipating constitutional challenge, the Act contained a fall-back reporting provision, whereby the Directors would report to a specially created Committee on Deficit Reduction, which in turn would report a joint resolution to both houses, which would then be voted on and amended. If the resolution were passed and signed by the President, the resolution would become the basis of the mandated reductions. Hours after the Act was signed, Synar (P) filed a complaint seeking declaratory relief that the Act was unconstitutional. The district court invalidated the reporting provisions, and a direct appeal was taken to the Supreme Court.

ISSUE: Does the assignment of executive powers to an agent or officer of the legislative branch violate the doctrine of separation of powers?

HOLDING AND DECISION: (Burger, C.J.) Yes. The assignment of executive powers to an agent or officer of the legislative branch violates the doctrine of separation of powers. [The Court quickly disposed of standing issues.] The Constitution does not contemplate an active role for Congress in the supervision of officers charged with the execution of the laws. Congress would thereby retain a sort of Congressional veto. The Comptroller General is subject to removal by Congress, and these removal powers dictate that he will be subservient to congressional control. Further, Congress has consistently viewed the Comptroller General as an officer of the legislative branch. There is no question that the Comptroller General acts in an executive capacity by executing the Act's reduction reporting provisions. By law, the President is required to implement the reductions of the Comptroller General. By placing the execution of the Act in the hands of an officer controlled by Congress, the doctrine of separation of powers is violated. Affirmed.

CONCURRENCE: (Stevens, J.) While Congress may infrustrate legislative powers to independent agencies or the Executive, when it elects to exercise such power itself, it may not authorize a lesser representative of the legislative branch to act on its behalf.

DISSENT: (White, J.) The majority's conclusion rests on the premise that any direct involvement of Congress in the removal of officers charged with the execution of laws violates the separation of powers. It is unrealistic to think that the Comptroller General is subservient to Congress. The Act itself represents a Congressional choice as to how to execute the Act, and the President has chosen not to upset the choice. Since there is no threat to the balance of authority, the Act need not be struck down.

EDITOR'S ANALYSIS: One of the alternatives posited by the dissent ignores the 60-year evolution of the office of the Comptroller General. To invalidate the Congressional removal provisions would presumably leave removal in the hands of the executive branch and would wreak havoc with the office as to any number of legislative functions the Comptroller General's office performs.

[For more information on Separation of Powers, see Case note Law Outline on Constitutional Law, Chapter 5, § II, Major Issues under the Doctrine of Separation of Powers.]

QUICKNOTES

CONGRESSIONAL VETO - The effort deemed unconstitutional exercised by Congress to engage in decision-making ability over the executive branch of government.

DECLARATORY RELIEF - A judgment of the rights between opposing parties that does not grant coercive relief (i.e. damages) but is binding.

SEPARATION OF POWERS - The system of checks and balances preventing one branch of government from infringing upon exercising the powers of another branch of government.

MORRISON v. OLSON

*Federal government (D) v. Subject of special prosecutor
investigation (P)*
337 U.S. 654 (1988).

NATURE OF CASE: Review of invalidation of the Ethics in Government Act.

FACT SUMMARY: The Ethics in Government Act, which created the independent counsel/special prosecutor, was challenged as unconstitutional.

CONCISE RULE OF LAW: Congress' creation of the independent counsel was not an unconstitutional usurpation of power.

FACTS: In 1978, Congress passed the Ethics in Government Act. One facet of this legislation was the creation of the office of the independent counsel. The pertinent provisions mandated that, upon receipt of certain information, the Attorney General may determine whether evidence of official wrongdoing warrants appointment of a special prosecutor. The results are reported to a special court. The court is empowered to appoint a special prosecutor, who would be given broad investigative powers. The only power to remove the prosecutor lay in impeachment or by the Attorney General, after a showing of good cause. The Act contained certain requirements of reporting to Congress. Olson (P), a subject of an inquiry by a special prosecutor, challenged the Act as violative of the Appointments Clause and separation of powers. The district court upheld the law, but the court of appeals reversed. The Supreme Court granted review.

ISSUE: Was Congress' creation of the independent counsel an unconstitutional usurpation of power?

HOLDING AND DECISION: (Rehnquist, C.J.) No. Congress' creation of the independent counsel was not an unconstitutional usurpation of power. The Appointments Clause mandates that only the president may appoint "principal" United States officers. However, Congress may invest in the Judiciary the power to appoint inferior officers. This Court is of the opinion that independent counsels are inferior officers. He is subordinate to the Attorney General, his role is restricted to the investigation and possible prosecution of a number of federal crimes, and his tenure is limited. Also, this Court rejects the argument that the Appointments Clause does not permit "inter-branch" appointments, exemplified by the Act's provision of a judicial body appointing an executive officer. No restriction is to be found in the Appointments Clause. This Court further rejects the argument that the Act violates the longstanding prohibition on vesting in courts' executive powers. The special court does have certain supervisory powers, but it is the special prosecutor, not the special court, that carries out executive functions. Finally, this Court rejects the argument that the Act violates separation of

powers. Congress, in passing the Act, did not attempt to usurp executive or judicial authority. Rather than take such authority unto itself, it created an executive and judicial office not unduly beholden to itself. This was not a violation of separation of powers. This being so, the Act is valid. Reversed.

DISSENT: (Scalia, J.) The Act is a clear violation of the concept of separation of powers. The only relevant questions are: (1) Is the investigation/prosecution of a federal crime an exercise of purely executive power, and (2) does the statute deprive the President of exclusive control over the exercise of that power? The Constitution and precedent mandate an affirmative answer to the former question, and any reasonable reading of the act requires a similar answer to the latter. This being so, the Act violates separation of powers.

EDITOR'S ANALYSIS: The Court has made some important separation of powers decisions in recent years. Probably the most important other decision was *INS v. Chadha*, 462 U.S. 919 (1983). This decision struck down legislation review of executive actions. In the present case, the Court distinguished Chadha by holding that the Ethics Act did not directly give Congress more power.

[For more information on the Appointment Power, see Case note Law Outline on Constitutional Law, Chapter 4, § I, Presidential Power.]

QUICKNOTES

APPOINTMENTS CLAUSE - Article II, section 2, clause 2 of the United States Constitution conferring power upon the president to appoint ambassadors, public ministers and consuls, judges of the Supreme Court and all other officers of the United States with the advice and consent of the Senate.

ETHICS IN GOVERNMENT ACT - Allows for the appointment of special independent counsel to investigate high ranking government officials.

INDEPENDENT COUNSEL - An officer, whose appointment is authorized by the Ethics in Government Act, who is charged with the investigation of possible criminal activity by high level government officials.

INFERIOR OFFICERS - Members of the executive branch having less power or authority in relation to others.

SEPARATION OF POWERS - The system of checks and balances preventing one branch of government from infringing upon exercising the powers of another branch of government.

UNITED STATES v. NIXON

Federal government (P) v. President (D)
418 U.S. 683 (1974).

NATURE OF CASE: Certiorari granted after denial of a motion to quash a third-party subpoena duces tecum.

FACT SUMMARY: Nixon (D) challenged a subpoena served on him as a third party requiring the production of tapes and documents for use in a criminal prosecution.

CONCISE RULE OF LAW: Absent a claim of need to protect military, diplomatic, or sensitive national security secrets, an absolute, unqualified presidential privilege of immunity from judicial process under all circumstances does not exist.

FACTS: After the grand jury returned an indictment charging seven defendants with various offenses relating to Watergate, Special Prosecutor Jaworski moved for the issuance of a subpoena duces tecum to obtain Watergate-related tapes and documents from Nixon (D). Jaworski claimed that the materials were important to the government's proof at the criminal proceeding against the seven defendants. The subpoena was issued, and Nixon (D) turned over some materials. His lawyer then moved to quash the subpoena. Nixon (D) contended that the separation of powers doctrine precludes judicial review of a presidential claim of privilege and that the need for confidentiality of high-level communication requires an absolute privilege as against a subpoena.

ISSUE: Does the President possess an absolute executive privilege which is immune from judicial review?

HOLDING AND DECISION: (Burger, C.J.) No. Absent a claim of need to protect military, diplomatic, or sensitive national security secrets, an absolute, unqualified presidential privilege of immunity from judicial process under all circumstances does not exist. First of all, Nixon (D) claimed the court lacks jurisdiction to issue the subpoena because the matter was an intrabranch dispute within the executive branch. However, courts must look behind names that symbolize the parties to determine whether a justiciable case or controversy exists. Here, the Special Prosecutor, with his asserted need for the subpoenaed material, was opposed by the President with his assertion of privilege against disclosure. This setting assures that there is the necessary concreteness and adversity to sharpen the presentation of the issues. Against Nixon's (D) claim of absolute privilege immune from judicial review, this court reaffirms the holding of Marbury v. Madison that "it is emphatically the province of the Judicial Department to say what the law is," and this is true with respect to a claim of executive privilege. Absent a claim of need to protect military, diplomatic, or sensitive national security secrets, neither the doctrine of the separation of powers nor the generalized need for the confidentiality of high-level communica-

tions, without more, can sustain an absolute unqualified presidential privilege. Now that the court has decided that legitimate needs of judicial process may outweigh presidential privilege, it is necessary to resolve those competing interests in this case. It is true that the need for confidentiality justifies a presumptive privilege for presidential communications. However, our criminal justice system depends on a complete presentation of all relevant facts. To ensure this presentation, compulsory process must be available. Here, Jaworski has demonstrated a specific need at a criminal trial for the material sought. Nixon (D) has not based his claim of privilege on the military or diplomatic content of the materials but rather on a generalized interest in confidentiality. The allowance of this privilege based on only a generalized interest in confidentiality to withhold relevant evidence in a criminal trial would cut deeply into the guarantee of due process and cannot prevail.

EDITOR'S ANALYSIS: On July 16, 1973, Alexander Butterfield testified before the Senate Select Committee on presidential campaign activities that conversations in President Nixon's offices had been recorded automatically at Nixon's direction. Nixon declined to comply with requests for the tapes from Special Prosecutor Cox and the Senate Select Committee. Nixon maintained that the tapes would remain under his personal control. When a subpoena for the tapes was issued, Nixon replied that he asserted executive privilege and that the President is not subject to compulsory process from the courts. The grand jury then instructed the Special Prosecutor to seek an order for the production of the tapes. It was that enforcement proceeding which produced the first ruling in the case. Judge Sirica ordered the President to produce the items for in-camera inspection. The court of appeals affirmed. *Nixon v. Sirica*, 487 F.2d. 700, 1973

[For more information on presidential privileged communications, see Casenote Law Outline on Constitutional Law, Chapter 4, § II, Presidential Immunities and Privileges.]

QUICKNOTES

ABSOLUTE PRIVILEGE - Unconditional or unqualified immunity enjoyed by a person

EXECUTIVE PRIVILEGE - The right of the executive branch to refuse to disclose confidential communications if such exemption is necessary for the effective discharge of its official duties.

SUBPOENA DUCES TECUM - A court mandate compelling the production of documents under a witness' control.

CLINTON v. JONES

President of the United States (D) v. Female state employee (P)

520 U.S. 681, 117 S. Ct. 1636 (1997).

NATURE OF CASE: Review of judgment denying presidential immunity and request to postpone trial in sexual harassment case.

FACT SUMMARY: Jones (P) claimed Clinton (D) sexually harassed her during events that took place prior to Clinton (D) assuming the presidency.

CONCISE RULE OF LAW: Presidential immunity does not apply to civil damages litigation arising out of unofficial events occurring prior to the assumption of office.

FACTS: In May of 1991, Jones (P) worked as a state employee at a conference for which Clinton (D) gave a speech. Jones (P) claimed that a state police officer persuaded her to go to Clinton's (D) hotel room, where Clinton (D) proceeded to make sexual advances toward her. Jones (P) allegedly experienced on-the-job retaliation because she rejected these advances. When Clinton (D) was elected president in 1992, Jones (P) claimed she was defamed when spokesmen for Clinton (D) denied her allegations, branding Jones (P) a liar. On May 6, 1994, Jones (P) filed suit in district court, and Clinton (D) filed a motion to dismiss based on presidential immunity. The district court denied the motion to dismiss, but delayed the trial until after Clinton (D) leaves office. Both parties appealed and the court of appeals affirmed the denial of the motion to dismiss, but reversed the delay in the trial. Clinton (D) appealed.

ISSUE: Does presidential immunity apply to civil damages litigation arising out of unofficial events occurring prior to the assumption of office?

HOLDING AND DECISION: (Stevens, J.) No. Presidential immunity does not apply to civil damages litigation arising out of unofficial events occurring prior to the assumption of office. Here, Clinton (D) cannot claim presidential immunity because his actions occurred in an unofficial capacity during a time prior to his assuming the presidency. Because the conduct occurred in an unofficial capacity, this ruling will not make any president unduly cautious in the discharge of his official duties. With respect to the separation of powers, the litigation of questions that relate entirely to the unofficial conduct of the individual who happens to be president poses no perceptible risk of misallocation of either judicial power or executive power. Affirmed.

CONCURRENCE: (Breyer, J.) Although the Constitution does not automatically grant Clinton (D) an immunity from civil lawsuits, a federal judge may not interfere with Clinton's (D) discharge of his public duties once Clinton (D) sets forth and explains how they conflict with judicial proceedings.

EDITOR'S ANALYSIS: Intergovernmental immunity generally applies in situations where states attempt to regulate and tax the property and activities of the federal government. The federal government's power is derived from the Supremacy Clause and, generally, the federal government is given greater immunity than state governments. This case brings up an unexplored area where the limits of presidential immunity extend as it relates to the private, unofficial acts of the president.

[For more information on presidential and congressional immunity, see Casenote Law Outline on Constitutional Law, Chapter 4, § II, Presidential Immunities and Privileges.]

QUICKNOTES

EXECUTIVE PRIVILEGE - The right of the executive branch to refuse to disclose confidential communications if such exemption is necessary for the effective discharge of its official duties.

NOTES:

CHAPTER 7
THE BILL OF RIGHTS AND THE POST-CIVIL WAR AMENDMENTS: "FUNDAMENTAL" RIGHTS AND THE "INCORPORATION" DISPUTE

QUICK REFERENCE RULES OF LAW

1. **The Pre-Civil War Situation.** The amendments to the Constitution were intended as limitations solely on the exercise of power by the U.S. Government and are not applicable to the legislation of the states. (Barron v. Mayor and City Council of Baltimore)

   [For more information on application of the Bill of Rights, see Casenote Law Outline on Constitutional Law, Chapter 7, § I, The Bill of Rights and the Fourteenth Amendment.]

2. **The Purpose and Impact of the Post-Civil War Amendments.** The Fourteenth Amendment protects the privileges and immunities of national, not state, citizenship, and neither the Equal Protection, Due Process, or Privileges and Immunities Clauses of that amendment may be used to interfere with state control of the privileges and immunities of state citizenship. (Slaughter-House Cases)

   [For more information on Fourteenth Amendment privileges and immunities of national citizenship, see Casenote Law Outline on Constitutional Law, Chapter 7, § I, The Bill of Rights and the Fourteenth Amendment.]

3. **The Purpose and Impact of the Post-Civil War Amendments.** Durational residency requirements violate the fundamental right to travel by denying a newly arrived citizen the same privileges and immunities enjoyed by other citizens in the same state, and are therefore subject to strict liability. (Saenz v. Roe)

4. **Due Process and the "Incorporation" Controversy.** The right to a jury trial in serious criminal cases punishable by at least two years in prison is a fundamental right which must be recognized by the states as part of their obligation to extend due process of law to all persons within their jurisdiction. (Duncan v. Louisiana)

   [For more information on procedural due process in criminal cases, see Casenote Law Outline on Constitutional Law, Chapter 7, § II, The Meaning of Fourteenth Amendment "Liberty" and "Due Process."]

BARRON v. MAYOR AND CITY COUNCIL OF BALTIMORE

Wharf owner (P) v. Municipality (D)

32 U.S. (7 Pet.) 243 (1833).

NATURE OF CASE: Action to recover damages.

FACT SUMMARY: Barron (P) claimed that the City (D) made his wharf useless by diverting the streams during its construction work.

CONCISE RULE OF LAW: The amendments to the Constitution were intended as limitations solely on the exercise of power by the U.S. Government and are not applicable to the legislation of the states.

FACTS: Barron (P) sued the City (D) for making his wharf in Baltimore Harbor useless. He claimed that the City (D) had diverted the flow of streams during its street construction and that this diversion had deposited earth near the wharf, causing the water to become too shallow for most vessels. Barron (P) claimed that the action violated the Fifth Amendment guarantee that property will not be taken without just compensation.

ISSUE: Is state legislation subject to the limitations imposed by the amendments to the United States Constitution?

HOLDING AND DECISION: (Marshall, J.) No. The amendments to the Constitution were intended as limitations solely on the exercise of power by the U.S. Government and are not applicable to the legislation of the states. The Constitution and its amendments were established by the people of the United States for themselves, for their own government, and not for the governments of the states. The people and each state established their own constitution. The constitutional amendments restrain only the power of the federal government and are not applicable to the actions of the state governments. Article I, § 10 expressly lists the restrictions upon the state governments. We find no reason why if the amendments were to apply to the states, there are not express words so stating. The amendments contain no expression indicating an intent to apply them to the states. Hence, because there is no conflict here between the City (D) and state's action and the federal Constitution, this court has no jurisdiction over this action.

EDITOR'S ANALYSIS: There were relatively few references to individual rights in the original Constitution. Its major concern was with governmental structures and relationships. The most important limitation on state power protective of individual rights was the Contract Clause. Nor was there a significant broader spectrum of individual rights restrictions on the national government. In response to the demand for additional constitutional protection of individual as well as states' rights, the first ten amendments were proposed and ratified. Since federal criminal decisions were not ordinarily reviewable by the Supreme Court, it had little occasion for interpretation of the Bill of Rights prior to the Civil War.

[For more information on application of the Bill of Rights, see Casenote Law Outline on Constitutional Law, Chapter 7, § I, The Bill of Rights and the Fourteenth Amendment.]

QUICKNOTES

CONTRACT CLAUSE - Article 1, section 10 of the Constitution prohibiting states from passing any "law impairing the Obligation of Contracts."

JUST COMPENSATION - The right guaranteed by the Fifth Amendment to the United States Constitution of a person, when his property is taken for public use by the state, to receive adequate compensation in order to restore him to the position he enjoyed prior to the appropriation.

TAKING - Governmental use or dispossession of private property.

NOTES:

SLAUGHTER-HOUSE CASES
Butchers (P) v. State (D)
83 U.S. (16 Wall.) 36 (1873).

NATURE OF CASE: Appeal of state enforcement of a monopoly.

FACT SUMMARY: Louisiana created a 25-year slaughterhouse monopoly to which several butchers who were not included objected.

CONCISE RULE OF LAW: The Fourteenth Amendment protects the privileges and immunities of national, not state, citizenship, and neither the Equal Protection, Due Process, or Privileges and Immunities Clauses of that amendment may be used to interfere with state control of the privileges and immunities of state citizenship.

FACTS: A Louisiana law of 1869 granted a monopoly to one Slaughterhouse Company for the three largest parishes in that state. Butchers (P), who were not included in the monopoly, challenged the law creating it on the grounds that it violated the Thirteenth Amendment ban on involuntary servitude and the Fourteenth Amendment protections of the privileges and immunities of national citizenship and equal protection and due process of law. From a judgment sustaining the law, the butchers (P) appealed.

ISSUE: Does the Fourteenth Amendment Privileges and Immunities Clause make all privileges and immunities of citizenship federal rights subject to federal enforcement?

HOLDING AND DECISION: (Miller, J.) No. The Fourteenth Amendment protects the privileges and immunities of national, not state, citizenship, and neither the Equal Protection, Due Process, or Privileges and Immunities Clauses of that Amendment may be used to interfere with state control of the privileges and immunities of state citizenship. The underlying purpose of all three of the post-Civil War amendments was to eliminate the remnants of African slavery, not to effect any fundamental change in the relations of the government. The Fourteenth Amendment expressly was adopted to assure only that states would not "abridge the privileges and immunities of citizens of the United States" (i.e., Negro citizens in their pursuit of national rights such as the right to protection on the high seas). Similarly, the Equal Protection and Due Process Clauses of that Amendment were drawn to protect former slaves from state denial of federal rights. No interpretation of this Amendment (or the Thirteenth, which is an even clearer case) may be used to prevent the State of Louisiana from exercising its police power here (to promote public health in slaughterhouses) to define particular privileges and immunities of its citizens. Affirmed.

DISSENT: (Field, J.) Justice Field views the Fourteenth Amendment as protection for all citizens of the fundamental rights of free government from abridgment by the states. Among such rights clearly is the right to an equal opportunity to pursue employment.

DISSENT: (Bradley, J.) Justice Bradley views the Fourteenth Amendment as a ban upon state deprivation of life, liberty, or property without due process of law. He views the purpose of its passage as preventing future insubordination to government by law which fostered the Civil War.

EDITOR'S ANALYSIS: The effect of this decision was to essentially render the Fourteenth Amendment Privileges and Immunities Clause ineffectual as a means of protecting individual rights from state abridgment. In addition, it ruled out the possibility that the Bill of Rights could be enforced upon the states as privileges and immunities of national citizenship. Subsequently, of course, the court adopted the position of Justice Bradley and began selectively incorporating parts of those Amendments into the Fourteenth Amendment Due Process Clause. In addition, the Equal Protection Clause has been used extensively to prohibit state action which is discriminatory in any irrational way (i.e., the rational basis test). Note, finally, that even the Thirteenth Amendment, summarily treated above, has been expanded to bar private discriminatory action which can be identified as a badge of slavery.

[For more information on Fourteenth Amendment privileges and immunities of national citizenship, see Casenote Law Outline on Constitutional Law, Chapter 7, § I, The Bill of Rights and the Fourteenth Amendment.]

QUICKNOTES
EQUAL PROTECTION CLAUSE - A constitutional guarantee that no person should be denied the same protection of the laws enjoyed by other persons in like circumstances.

INVOLUNTARY SERVITUDE - Being in a state of forced labor for the benefit of another person.

MONOPOLY - A privilege or right conferred upon an individual or entity granting it the exclusive power to manufacture, sell and distribute a particular service or commodity; a market condition in which one or a few companies control the sale of a product or service thereby restraining competition in respect to that article or service.

PRIVILEGES AND IMMUNITIES CLAUSE OF 14TH AMENDMENT - A provision in the Constitution that accords the advantages of citizenship equally to the citizens of each state; out-of-state citizens must therefore be given the same privileges as a state's own citizens.

SAENZ v. ROE

New state resident (P) v. State government (D)

526 U.S. 489, 119 S. Ct. 1518 (1999).

NATURE OF CASE: Appeal from an order enjoining implementation of a state statute.

FACT SUMMARY: When California (D) discriminated against citizens who had resided in the state for less then one year in distributing welfare benefits, the state statute was challenged and held to be unconstitutional.

CONCISE RULE OF LAW: Durational residency requirements violate the fundamental right to travel by denying a newly arrived citizen the same privileges and immunities enjoyed by other citizens in the same state, and are therefore subject to strict liability.

FACTS: In 1992, California (D) enacted a statute limiting the maximum first year welfare benefits available to newly arrived residents to the amount they would have received in the state of their prior residence. Saenz (P) and other California residents who were eligible for such benefits challenged the constitutionality of the durational residency requirement, alleging their right to travel was violated. The district court preliminarily enjoined implementation of the statute and the court of appeals affirmed. Congress enacted the Personal Responsibility and Work Opportunity Reconciliation Act of 1996, which expressly authorized states to apply the rules (including benefit amounts) of another state if the family has resided in the state for less than twelve months. California (D) appealed, alleging that the statute should be upheld if it has a rational basis, and that the state's (D) legitimate interest in saving over $10 million a year satisfied that test.

ISSUE: Do durational residency requirements violate the fundamental right to travel by denying a newly arrived citizen the same privileges and immunities enjoyed by other citizens in the same state, and are they thus subject to strict liability?

HOLDING AND DECISION: (Stevens, J.) Yes. Durational residency requirements violate the fundamental right to travel by denying a newly arrived citizen the same privileges and immunities enjoyed by other citizens in the same state, and are therefore subject to strict liability. The first sentence of Article IV, § 2, provides that the citizens of each state shall be entitled to all privileges and immunities of citizens in the several states. The right of a newly arrived citizen to the same privileges and immunities enjoyed by other citizens of the same state is protected not only by the new arrival's status as a state citizen, but also by her status as a citizen of the United States. The Citizenship Clause of the Fourteenth Amendment protects all citizens' right to choose to be citizens of the state wherein they reside. Neither mere rationality nor some intermediate standard

of review should be used to judge the constitutionality of a state rule that discriminates against some of its citizens because they have been domiciled in the state for less than a year. The state's legitimate interest in saving money provides no justification for its decision to discriminate among equally eligible citizens. Affirmed.

DISSENT: (Rehnquist, C.J.) The right to travel and the right to become a citizen are distinct, and one is not a "component" of the other. If states can require an individual to reside in-state for a year before exercising the right to educational benefits, the right to terminate a marriage, or the right to vote in primary elections that all other state citizens enjoy, then it may surely do the same for welfare benefits. California has reasonably exercised its power to protect state resources through an objective, narrowly tailored residence requirement. There is nothing in the Constitution that should prevent the enforcement of that requirement.

DISSENT: (Thomas, J.) The majority attributes a meaning to the Privileges or Immunities Clause that likely was unintended when the Fourteenth Amendment was enacted and ratified. At that time, people understood "privileges or immunities of citizens" to be their fundamental right, rather than every public benefit established by positive law.

EDITOR'S ANALYSIS: The court in this case found that a state violated the Privileges and Immunities Clause when it discriminated against citizens who had been residents for less than one year. The Thomas dissent alleged that this was contrary to the original understanding at the time the Fourteenth Amendment was enacted. The Rehnquist dissent went on to point out that a welfare subsidy is as much an investment in human capital as is a tuition subsidy and their attendant benefits are just as portable.

QUICKNOTES

FOURTEENTH AMENDMENT - Declares that no state shall make or enforce any law which shall abridge the privileges and immunities of citizens of the United States.

RATIONAL BASIS REVIEW - A test employed by the court to determine the validity of a statute in equal protection actions, whereby the court determines whether the challenged statute is rationally related to the achievement of a legitimate state interest.

STRICT SCRUTINY - Method by which courts determine the constitutionality of a law, when a law affects a fundamental right. Under the test, the legislature must have a compelling interest to enact law and measures prescribed by the law must be the least restrictive means possible to accomplish goal.

FUNDAMENTAL RIGHT - A liberty that is either expressly or implicitly provided for in the United States Constitution, the deprivation or burdening of which is subject to a heightened standard of review.

DUNCAN v. LOUISIANA
Defendant (D) v. State (P)
391 U.S. 145 (1968).

NATURE OF CASE: Appeal from conviction of battery and sentence of 60 days with a $150 fine.

FACT SUMMARY: Louisiana's Constitution granted jury trials only in cases in which capital punishment or imprisonment at hard labor may be granted.

CONCISE RULE OF LAW: The right to a jury trial in serious criminal cases punishable by at least two years in prison is a fundamental right which must be recognized by the states as part of their obligation to extend due process of law to all persons within their jurisdiction.

FACTS: Duncan (D) was charged with simple battery, which in Louisiana was punishable by a maximum of two years' imprisonment and a $300 fine. His request for a jury trial was denied by the trial court because the Louisiana (P) constitution granted jury trials only in cases in which capital punishment or imprisonment at hard labor may be imposed.

ISSUE: Does the Fourteenth Amendment guarantee a right of jury trial in all criminal cases which, were they to be tried in a federal court, would come within the Sixth Amendment's guarantee?

HOLDING AND DECISION: (White, J.) Yes. The right to a jury trial in serious criminal cases punishable by at least two years in prison is a fundamental right which must be recognized by the states as part of their obligation to extend due process of law to all persons within their jurisdiction. A right to jury trial is granted to a criminal defendant in order to guard against an overzealous or corrupt prosecutor and the compliant, biased, or eccentric judge. A holding that due process assures a right to jury trial will not cast doubt on the integrity of every trial conducted without a jury. Thus, there is no constitutional problem with accepting waivers, and prosecuting petty crimes without extending the right where defendants are satisfied with bench trials, judicial, or prosecutorial unfairness is less likely. What controls will be the maximum possible sentence and not the punishment actually meted out. The exact line between petty and serious crimes need not be settled here.

CONCURRENCE: (Black, J.) Both total and selective incorporation of the Bill of Rights are to be preferred to assigning no settled meaning to the term "due process" as this will shift from time to time in accordance with changing theories.

CONCURRENCE: (Fortas, J.) Neither logic nor history nor the intent of the Framers of the Fourteenth Amendment require that all of the Sixth Amendment be applied to the states.

DISSENT: (Harlan, J.) The Due Process Clause requires only that state procedures be fundamentally fair in all respects. There is no historical support for the total incorporation theory. The Framers of the Fourteenth Amendment intended that the meaning of "due process" will change as does the experience and conscience of the American people. Selective incorporation lacks guiding standards. The definition of "fundamental" used by the majority is circular since it means "old," "much praised," and "found in the Bill of Rights." Here, there was no indication that Duncan's (D) trial was not a fair one.

EDITOR'S ANALYSIS: One commentator has suggested that, after Duncan, the court, although describing its test as a "fundamental rights" approach, has actually embraced "selective incorporation" in which all of the Bill of Rights, one provision at a time, has been incorporated in fact. Nevertheless, it is still unclear whether by "specific" provisions the court means only the text of the actual amendments or judicial interpretations in decisions involving those rights.

[For more information on procedural due process in criminal cases, see Casenote Law Outline on Constitutional Law, Chapter 7, § II, The Meaning of Fourteenth Amendment "Liberty" and "Due Process."]

QUICKNOTES

DUE PROCESS - Fundamental fairness; the laws fairly administered through the court of justice.

FUNDAMENTAL RIGHT - A basic and essential right; freedoms expressed in the Bill of Rights and implied freedoms not expressly stated in the Constitution.

RIGHT TO JURY TRIAL - The right guaranteed by the Sixth Amendment to the federal constitution that in all criminal prosecutions the accused has a right to a trial by an impartial jury of the state and district in which the crime was allegedly committed.

SELECTIVE INCORPORATION - Doctrine providing that the Bill of Rights is incorporated by the Due Process Clause only to the extent that the Supreme Court decides that the privileges and immunities therein are so essential to fundamental principals of due process to be preserved against both state and federal action.

SIXTH AMENDMENT - Provides the right to a speedy trial by impartial jury, the right to be informed of the accusation, to confront witnesses, and to have the assistance of counsel in all criminal prosecutions.

CHAPTER 8
SUBSTANTIVE DUE PROCESS: RISE, DECLINE, REVIVAL

QUICK REFERENCE RULES OF LAW

1. **The Lochner Era: Judicial Intervention and Economic Regulation.** To be a fair, reasonable, and appropriate use of a state's police power, an act must have a direct relation, as a means to an end, to an appropriate and legitimate state objective. (Lochner v. New York)

   [For more information on liberty of contract, see Casenote Law Outline on Constitutional Law, Chapter 7, § II, The Meaning of Fourteenth Amendment "Liberty" and "Due Process."]

2. **The Modern Era: The Decline of Judicial Scrutiny of Economic Regulation.** Upon proper occasion and by appropriate measures, a state may regulate a business in any of its aspects, including fixing prices. (Nebbia v. New York)

   [For more information on the overthrow of substantive due process and the rational basis test, see Casenote Law Outline on Constitutional Law, Chapter 7, § II, The Meaning of Fourteenth Amendment "Liberty" and "Due Process."]

3. **The Modern Era: The Decline of Judicial Scrutiny of Economic Regulation.** The Due Process Clause will no longer be used to strike down state laws regulating business and industrial conditions because they may be unwise, improvident, or out of harmony with a particular school of thought. (Williamson v. Lee Optical Co.)

   [For more information on overinclusive and underinclusive classifications, see Casenote Law Outline on Constitutional Law, Chapter 8, § II, Rational Basis Review.]

4. **The Takings Clause.** While private property may be regulated to a certain degree, a taking under the Fifth Amendment will be found if the regulation results in a severe diminution of value. At a certain magnitude, there must be an exercise of eminent domain and compensation to sustain the regulatory act. While considerable deference is to be given the legislature's judgment, each case will turn upon its particular facts. (Pennsylvania Coal Co. v. Mahon)

   [For more information on the public use requirement of a taking, see Casenote Law Outline on Constitutional Law, Chapter 6, § IV, The Contract Clause.]

5. **The Contracts Clause.** The reservation of the reasonable exercise of the state's protective power is read into all contracts. A state may affect the obligations between two contracting parties so long as: 1) an emergency exists; 2) the legislation is addressed to a legitimate end; 3) the relief afforded and justified by the emergency could only be of a character appropriate to that emergency; 4) the conditions upon which relief is granted do not appear to be unreasonable; and 5) the legislation is temporary in operation. (Home Building & Loan Ass'n v. Blaisdell)

   [For more information on the Contract Clause, see Casenote Law Outline on Constitutional Law, Chapter 6, § IV, The Contract Clause.]

6. **Contraception.** The right to mental privacy, although not explicitly stated in the Bill of Rights, is a penumbra, formed by certain other explicit guarantees. As such, it is protected against state regulation which sweeps unnecessarily broad. (Griswold v. Connecticut)

[For more information on rights of personal liberty, see Casenote Law Outline on Constitutional Law, Chapter 7, § II, The Meaning of Fourteenth Amendment "Liberty" and "Due Process."]

7. **Abortion.** The right of privacy found in the Fourteenth Amendment's concept of personal liberty and restrictions upon state action is broad enough to encompass a woman's decision whether or not to terminate her pregnancy. (Roe v. Wade)

    [For more information on the right of privacy regarding abortion, see Casenote Law Outline on Constitutional Law, Chapter 7, § II, The Meaning of Fourteenth Amendment "Liberty" and "Due Process."]

8. **Abortion.** A law is unconstitutional as an undue burden on a woman's right to an abortion before fetal viability, if the law places a substantial obstacle in the path of a woman seeking to exercise her right. (Planned Parenthood of Southeastern Pa v. Casey)

    [For more information on the right to privacy, see Casenote Law Outline on Constitutional Law, Chapter 7, § II, The Meaning of Fourteenth Amendment "Liberty" and "Due Process."]

9. **Sexuality.** The Constitution does not grant a fundamental right to engage in consensual homosexual sodomy. (Bowers v. Hardwick)

    [For more information on the right of privacy regarding abortion, see Casenote Law Outline on Constitutional Law, Chapter 7, § II, The Meaning of Fourteenth Amendment "Liberty" and "Due Process."]

10. **Death.** The right to assistance in committing suicide is not a fundamental liberty interest protected by the Due Process Clause. (Washington v. Glucksberg)

    [For more information on substantive due process, see Casenote Law Outline on Constitutional Law, Chapter 7, § II, The Meaning of Fourteenth Amendment "Liberty" and "Due Process."]

LOCHNER v. NEW YORK
Employer bakery (D) v. State (P)
198 U.S. 45 (1905).

NATURE OF CASE: Appeal from conviction for violation of a labor law.

FACT SUMMARY: A state labor law prohibited employment in bakeries for more than 60 hours a week or more than 10 hours a day. Lochner (D) permitted an employee in his bakery to work over 60 hours in one week.

CONCISE RULE OF LAW: To be a fair, reasonable, and appropriate use of a state's police power, an act must have a direct relation, as a means to an end, to an appropriate and legitimate state objective.

FACTS: Lochner (D) was fined for violating a state labor law. The law prohibited employment in bakeries for more than 60 hours a week or more than 10 hours a day. Lochner (D) permitted an employee to work in his bakery for more than 60 hours in one week.

ISSUE: Is a state law regulating the hours bakery employees may work a valid exercise of state police power?

HOLDING AND DECISION: (Peckham, J.) No. The general right to make a contract in relation to one's business is part of the liberty of the individual protected by the Fourteenth Amendment. The right to purchase or sell labor is part of the liberty protected by this amendment. However, the states do possess certain police powers relating to the safety, health, morals, and general welfare of the public. If the contract is one which the state in the exercise of its police power has the right to prohibit, the Fourteenth Amendment will not prevent the state's prohibition. When, as here, the state acts to limit the right to labor or the right to contract, it is necessary to determine whether the rights of the state or the individual shall prevail. The Fourteenth Amendment limits the state's exercise of its police power, otherwise the state would have unbounded power once it stated that legislation was to conserve the health, morals, or safety of its people. It is not sufficient to assert that the act relates to public health. Rather, it must have a more direct relation, as a means to an end, to an appropriate state goal, before an act can interfere with an individual's right to contract in relation to his labor. In this case, there is no reasonable foundation for holding the act to be necessary to the health of the public or of bakery officials. Statutes such as this one are merely meddlesome interferences with the rights of the individual. They are invalid unless there is some fair ground to say that there is material danger to the public health or to the employees' health if the labor hours are not curtailed. It cannot be said that the production of healthy bread depends upon the hours that the employees work. Nor is the trade of a baker an unhealthy one to the degree which would authorize the legislature to interfere with the rights to labor and of free contract. Lochner's (D) conviction is reversed.

DISSENT: (Harlan, J.) Whether or not this be wise legislation is not a question for this Court. It is impossible to say that there is not substantial or real regulation between the statute and the state's legitimate goals. This decision brings under the Court's supervision matters which supposedly belonged exclusively to state legislatures.

DISSENT: (Holmes, J.) The word liberty in the Fourteenth Amendment should not invalidate a statute unless it can be said that a reasonable person would say that the statute infringes fundamental principles of our people and our law. A reasonable person might think this statute valid. Citizens' liberty is regulated by many state laws which have been held to be valid, i.e., the Sunday laws, the lottery laws, laws requiring vaccination.

EDITOR'S ANALYSIS: From the Lochner decision in 1905 to the 1930s the Court invalidated a considerable number of laws on substantive due process grounds, such as laws fixing minimum wages, maximum hours, prices and law regulating business activities. The modern Court claims to have rejected the Lochner doctrine. It has withdrawn careful scrutiny in most economic areas but has maintained and increased intervention with respect to a variety of non-economic liberties. However, not only economic regulations were struck down under Lochner. That doctrine formed the basis for absorbing rights such as those in the First Amendment into the Fourteenth Amendment concept of liberty. Lochner also helped justify on behalf of other non-economic rights such as the right to teach in a foreign language (Meyers v. Nebraska, 262 U.S. 390). Meyers was to be relied upon in the birth control decision, Griswold v. Connecticut.

[For more information on liberty of contract, see Casenote Law Outline on Constitutional Law, Chapter 7, § II, The Meaning of Fourteenth Amendment "Liberty" and "Due Process."]

QUICKNOTES

POLICE POWERS - The power of a state or local government to regulate private conduct for the health, safety and welfare of the general public.

SUBSTANTIVE DUE PROCESS - A constitutional safeguard limiting the power of the state, irrespective of how fair its procedures may be; substantive limits placed on the power of the state.

NEBBIA v. NEW YORK
Grocery store proprietor (D) v. State (P)
291 U.S. 502 (1934).

NATURE OF CASE: Appeal from conviction for violation of an order of the Milk Board.

FACT SUMMARY: The State Milk Board fixed nine cents as the price to be charged for a quart of milk. Nebbia (D) sold two quarts of milk and a loaf of bread for eighteen cents.

CONCISE RULE OF LAW: Upon proper occasion and by appropriate measures, a state may regulate a business in any of its aspects, including fixing prices.

FACTS: In 1933, the New York (P) legislature established a Milk Control Board. The Board was given the power to fix minimum and maximum retail prices to be charged by stores to consumers. The Board fixed the price of a quart of milk at nine cents. Nebbia (D), a grocery store proprietor, charged eighteen cents for two quarts of milk and a five-cent loaf of bread. The law establishing the Board was based on a legislative finding that, "Milk is an essential item of diet. Failure of producers to receive a reasonable return threatens a relaxation of vigilance against contamination. The production of milk is a paramount industry of the state, and largely affects the health and prosperity of its people."

ISSUE: Does the federal Constitution prohibit a state from fixing selling prices?

HOLDING AND DECISION: (Roberts, J.) No. Upon proper occasion and by appropriate measures, a state may regulate a business in any of its aspects, including fixing prices. The general rule is that both the use of property and the making of contracts shall be free from government interference. However, neither property rights nor contract rights are absolute. Equally fundamental with the private interest is the public's to regulate it in the common interest. The Fifth and Fourteenth Amendments do not prohibit governmental regulation for the public welfare. They merely guarantee that regulation shall be consistent with due process. The guarantee of due process demands only that the law shall not be unreasonable, arbitrary, or capricious and that the means selected shall have a real and substantial relation to the object sought to be attained. If an industry is subject to regulation in the public interest, its prices may be regulated. An industry which is "affected with a public industry" is one which is subject to police powers. A state is free to adopt whatever economic policy may be reasonably deemed to promote the public welfare. The courts are without authority to override such policies. If the laws passed have a rational relation to a legitimate purpose and are neither arbitrary nor discriminatory, the requirements of due process are satisfied. Price control may fulfill these requirements as well as any other type of regulation. The New York (P) law

creating the Milk Board and giving it power to fix prices does not conflict with the due process guarantees and is constitutionally valid. Nebbia's (D) conviction is affirmed.

DISSENT: (McReynolds, J.) The Legislative Committee pointed out as the cause of decreased consumption of milk the consumer's reduced buying power. Higher store prices will not enlarge this power, nor will they increase production. This statute arbitrarily interferes with citizens' liberty since the means adopted do not reasonably relate to the end sought, the promotion of the public welfare.

EDITOR'S ANALYSIS: The early attitude of the court had been that the states could regulate selling prices only for industries affecting the public interest. Regulation of prices and rates charged by public utilities, dairies, grain elevators, etc., were upheld, but regulation of the prices of theater tickets or ice were not. Nebbia held that price control regulation was to be treated the same as other police powers and a rational relation to a legitimate goal was all that was necessary. The dissent, representing the court's earlier position, does not want to treat the legislation with the deference exercised by the majority. In its judgment, the method adopted by New York does not rationally relate to its goal. Nebbia represents the modern position of the court, which is to presume the propriety of the legislation.

[For more information on the overthrow of substantive due process and the rational basis test, see Casenote Law Outline on Constitutional Law, Chapter 7, § II, The Meaning of Fourteenth Amendment "Liberty" and "Due Process."]

QUICKNOTES

DUE PROCESS - The constitutional mandate requiring the courts to protect and enforce individuals' rights and liberties consistent with prevailing principals of fairness and justice and prohibiting the federal and state governments from such activities that deprive its citizens of a life, liberty or property interest.

PRICE FIXING - A collaboration by competing companies to uniformly set price levels.

WILLIAMSON v. LEE OPTICAL CO.

State (P) v. Optical company (D)
348 U.S. 483 (1955).

NATURE OF CASE: Appeal from a district court's judgment holding unconstitutional three sections of a state ophthalmology law.

FACT SUMMARY: A state law prohibited any person from fitting or duplicating lenses without a prescription from an ophthalmologist or optometrist. It also prohibited soliciting the sale of frames and the renting of space in a retail store to any person purporting to do eye examination.

CONCISE RULE OF LAW: The Due Process Clause will no longer be used to strike down state laws regulating business and industrial conditions because they may be unwise, improvident, or out of harmony with a particular school of thought.

FACTS: A state law prohibited any person who was not a licensed ophthalmologist or optometrist from fitting or duplicating lenses without a prescription from a licensed optometrist or ophthalmologist. Opticians are artisans qualified to grind lenses, fill prescriptions, and fit frames. The effect of the provision was to prevent opticians from fitting old glasses into new frames or duplicating a lost or broken lens without a prescription. Two other sections of the Act prohibited soliciting the sale of frames, mountings, or other optical appliances and the renting of space in a retail store to one purporting to do eye examinations.

ISSUE: Does a state law regulating the fitting and selling of eye lenses and frames conflict with the Due Process Clause?

HOLDING AND DECISION: (Douglas, J.) No. The Due Process Clause will no longer be used to strike down state laws, regulating business or industrial conditions, because they may be unwise, improvident, or out of harmony with a particular school of thought. For protection against abuses by the legislature, the people must resort to the polls, not the courts. The state law in question here may exact needless wasteful requirements in many cases. But it is for the legislatures, not the courts, to balance the advantages and disadvantages of the new requirement. The legislature may have concluded that the cases in which prescriptions are essential are frequent enough to justify requiring one in every case. Since frames and mountings are used only in conjunction with lenses, and lenses enter the field of health, the legislature might have concluded that to regulate one it had to regulate the other. Finally, the last provision appeared to be an attempt to rid the profession of commercialism. Hence, it cannot be said that the regulation had no rational relation to legitimate objectives.

EDITOR'S ANALYSIS: An example of the Court's deference to legislative judgments is *Ferguson v. Skrupa*, 372 U.S. 726 (,1963), where the court reversed the invalidation of a state statute regulating the business of debt-adjusting. The law prohibited that business except as an incident to the practice of law. The Supreme Court spoke of its abandonment of the use of the vague contours of the Due Process Clause to nullify laws which a majority of the Court believed to be economically unwise. "We refuse to sit as a super legislature to weigh the wisdom of legislation," the Court stated.

[For more information on overinclusive and underinclusive classifications, see Casenote Law Outline on Constitutional Law, Chapter 8, § II, Rational Basis Review.]

QUICKNOTES

COMMERCIALISM – Relating to advertisement or profit.

DUE PROCESS CLAUSE - Clauses found in the Fifth and Fourteenth Amendments to the United States Constitution providing that no person shall be deprived of "life, liberty, or property, without due process of law."

LEGISLATIVE OBJECTIVES – The goal or purpose motivating the legislture in enacting a particular law.

NOTES:

PENNSYLVANIA COAL CO. v. MAHON
Coal mining company (D) v. Landowner (P)
260 U.S. 393 (1922).

NATURE OF CASE: Action by property owner to enjoin certain operations on adjacent property.

FACT SUMMARY: A Pennsylvania statute forbade the mining of coal in such fashion as to cause the subsidence of any structure used as a human habitation.

CONCISE RULE OF LAW: While private property may be regulated to a certain degree, a taking under the Fifth Amendment will be found if the regulation results in a severe diminution of value. At a certain magnitude, there must be an exercise of eminent domain and compensation to sustain the regulatory act. While considerable deference is to be given the legislature's judgment, each case will turn upon its particular facts.

FACTS: In 1878, the Pennsylvania Coal Co. (D) conveyed some land but reserved in the deed the right to remove all coal under the land. The grantee agreed to assume any resulting damage. Mahon (P), who later acquired the land, was bound by the deed. Mahon (P), wanting to prevent further mining under the land, claimed that a 1922 state law changed the coal company's (D) rights. The act forbade the mining of coal in such manner as to cause the subsistence of any structure used as a human habitation with certain exceptions. Mahon's (P) injunction was denied, the trial court maintaining that the Act would be unconstitutional if applied to the present case. On appeal, the state supreme court reversed, holding that the statute was a legitimate exercise of the police power.

ISSUE: Must a state which, through legislation, destroys previously existing contractual and property rights between private parties to the extent of severe diminution of property value give compensation to the affected party?

HOLDING AND DECISION: (Holmes, J.) Yes. While private property may be regulated to a certain degree, a taking under the Fifth Amendment will be found if the regulation results in a severe diminution of value. At a certain magnitude, there must be an exercise of eminent domain and compensation to sustain the regulatory act. While considerable deference is to be given the legislature's judgment, each case will turn upon its particular facts. Where damage is inflicted on a single private house, even if similar damage is inflicted on others in different places, there is no public interest. On the other hand, the damage to the coal company's (D) contractual and property rights is considerable. The act cannot be sustained where, as an exercise of the police power, it affects reserved rights. To make coal mining commercially unprofitable is, in effect, to destroy it. The rights of the public in a street purchased by eminent domain are those it has paid for. A strong public desire to improve the public condition

is not enough to justify achieving it by a shorter cut than the constitutional way of paying for the charge. This is a question of degree and cannot be disposed of by general propositions. So long as private individuals or communities take the risk of contracting for or purchasing only surface rights, they must bear the loss.

DISSENT: (Brandeis, J.) Every restriction on the use of property is an abridgment by the state of rights in property without making compensation. Here, the restriction was only against a noxious use of property which remains in the Coal Company's (D) possession. The Company (D), once it discontinues its noxious use, is free to enjoy its property as before. A restriction does not cease to be public simply because some individuals may be benefitted. The means chosen here may be the only way to prevent the subsistence of land. Because values are relative, the value of the coal kept in place by the restriction should be compared with the value of other parts of the land. The state should not have to follow a theory of reciprocal advantage to justify exercising its police power for the public good. The reciprocal advantage given by the Act to the Coal Company (D) is that of doing business in a civilized community.

EDITOR'S ANALYSIS: Eventually, the same analysis of the "taking" issue was used in *United States v. Causby*, 328 U.S. 256 (1946). There, a group of chicken farmers who owned land adjacent to a military airport claimed that, as a result of the noise of planes flying over their property, their chickens were frightened literally to death and egg production fell off. Rejecting the government's argument that any damage was merely consequential of the public's right of freedom of transit, Justice Douglas, writing for the majority, stated, "It is the owner's loss, not the taker's gain, which is the measure of the value of the property taken. . . . The owner's right to possess and exploit the land — that is to say, his beneficial ownership of it — would be destroyed. . . . It would not be a case of incidental damages arising from a legalized nuisance." In dissent, Justice Black warned "the effect of the court's decision is to limit, by the imposition of relatively absolute constitutional barriers, possible future adjustments through legislation and regulation which might become necessary with the growth of air transportation, and [because] the Constitution does not contain such barriers."

[For more information on the public use requirement of a taking, see Casenote Law Outline on Constitutional Law, Chapter 6, § IV, The Contract Clause.]

QUICKNOTES

EMINENT DOMAIN - The governmental power to take private property for public use so long as just compensation is paid therefor.

TAKING - A governmental action that substantially deprives an owner of the use and enjoyment of his property, requiring compensation.

HOME BUILDING & LOAN ASSN. v. BLAISDELL
Mortgagor (D) v. Mortgagee (P)
290 U.S. 398 (1934).

NATURE OF CASE: Action to secure an order extending the period of redemption from a foreclosure and sale of real property.

FACT SUMMARY: During the "Great Depression," Minnesota authorized county courts to extend the redemption period from foreclosure sales.

CONCISE RULE OF LAW: The reservation of the reasonable exercise of the state's protective power is read into all contracts. A state may affect the obligations between two contracting parties so long as: 1) an emergency exists; 2) the legislation is addressed to a legitimate end; 3) the relief afforded and justified by the emergency could only be of a character appropriate to that emergency; 4) the conditions upon which relief is granted do not appear to be unreasonable; and 5) the legislation is temporary in operation.

FACTS: In 1933, Minnesota enacted a statute authorizing county courts to extend the period of redemption from foreclosure sales "for such additional time as the court may deem just and equitable (but not extending beyond May 1, 1975)." The Blaisdells (P) applied for a judicial extension, and the court granted the extension but also ordered the Blaisdells (P) to pay Home Building & Loan Association (D), the mortgagor of their home, $40 a month through the extended period. Home (D) appealed on the ground that the Minnesota Act violated article I, § 10 of the U.S. Constitution ("No State shall . . . pass any . . . law impairing the obligation of Contracts"). The state supreme court upheld the Act's constitutionality.

ISSUE: May a state change the existing contractual obligations between two private parties?

HOLDING AND DECISION: (Hughes, C.J.) Yes. The reservation of the reasonable exercise of the state's protective power is read into all contracts. A state may affect the obligations between two contracting parties so long as: 1) an emergency exists; 2) the legislation is addressed to a legitimate end; 3) the relief afforded and justified by the emergency could only be of a character appropriate to that emergency; 4) the conditions upon which relief is granted do not appear to be unreasonable; and 5) the legislation is temporary in operation. The prohibition embodied in the Contract Clause is not an absolute one. The state continues to possess authority to safeguard the vital interests of its people. The protection of contracts presupposes a government which views contractual obligations as worthwhile. A rational compromise must be found between public need and private rights, especially when an emergency is found to exist upon judicial review. Provisions of the Constitution must yield to interpretations which respond to current problems not envisioned by the original Framers. The Contract Clause should not be used to frustrate the states in advancing their fundamental interests. Here, the Act was an appropriate response because: 1) a true emergency in Minnesota existed; 2) the legislation was for the protection of a basic interest of society rather than the advantage of a few individuals; 3) the relief afforded was geared to the emergency (mass foreclosures); 4) the mortgagor's interests (no impairment of the indebtedness, the running of interest, validity of the sale, etc.) are not impaired; and 5) the legislation does not outlast the emergency, being temporary in duration.

DISSENT: (Sutherland, J.) "The phrase 'obligation of a contract' in the constitutional sense imports a legal duty to perform the specified obligation of that contract, not to substitute and perform, against the will of one of the parties, a different, albeit equally valuable, obligation."

EDITOR'S ANALYSIS: Despite the sweeping language of the instant opinion, the court struck down state acts impairing contractual obligations in the following instances: exemption of payments on life insurance policies from garnishment (no time limitation, no limitation of amount to necessities); repeal of law protecting purchasers at state-conducted tax sales from attempts by the state to invalidate the transaction because of irregularities (purchaser had right to rely on earlier law so as to make land marketable); change of procedures for enforcement of payment of benefit assessments pledged as security for Municipal Improvement District bonds. Nonetheless, the Blaisdell decision marked the death knell of the Contract Clause's viability as a means to assail the validity of state laws.

[For more information on the Contract Clause, see ***Casenote Law Outline on Constitutional Law, Chapter 6, § IV, The Contract Clause.]***

QUICKNOTES

CONTRACT CLAUSE - Article I, Section 10 of the Consitution which prohibits states from passing laws impairing contractual obligations.

FORECLOSURE - The termination of a property interest due to non-paymet of a debt and the sale of that property to satisfy the debt.

REDEMPTION - The regaining of possession of property by payment of a debt or fulfillment of other conditions.

GRISWOLD v. CONNECTICUT
Doctor/director (D) v. State (P)
381 U.S. 479 (1965).

NATURE OF CASE: Appeal from conviction for violating state laws prohibiting the counseling of married persons to take contraceptives.

FACT SUMMARY: Doctor (D) and layman (D) were prosecuted for advising married persons on the means of preventing conception.

CONCISE RULE OF LAW: The right to mental privacy, although not explicitly stated in the Bill of Rights, is a penumbra, formed by certain other explicit guarantees. As such, it is protected against state regulation which sweeps unnecessarily broad.

FACTS: Griswold (D), the Executive Director of the Planned Parenthood League of Connecticut, and Dr. Buxton (D) were convicted under a Connecticut law which made counseling of married persons to take contraceptives a criminal offense.

ISSUE: Is the right to privacy in the marital relationship protected by the Constitution despite the absence of specific language recognizing it?

HOLDING AND DECISION: (Douglas, J.) Yes. The various guarantees which create penumbras, or zones, of privacy include the First Amendment's right of association, the Third Amendment's prohibition against the peacetime quartering of soldiers, the Fourth Amendment's prohibition against unreasonable searches and seizures, the Fifth Amendment's Self-Incrimination Clause, and the Ninth Amendment's reservation to the people of unenumerated rights. The Connecticut law, by forbidding the use of contraceptives rather than regulating their manner or sale, seeks to achieve its goals by means having a maximum destructive impact upon that relationship.

CONCURRENCE: (Harlan, J.) The court, instead of focusing on "specific provisions" of the Bill of Rights, should have instead relied on the Due Process Clause in finding this law violative of basic values "implicit in the concept of ordered liberty."

CONCURRENCE: (Goldberg, J.) The Ninth Amendment, while not constituting an independent source of rights, suggests that the list of rights in the first eight amendments is not exhaustive. This right is a "fundamental" one which cannot be infringed on the state's slender justification in protecting marital fidelity.

CONCURRENCE: (White, J.) The Due Process Clause should be the test in determining whether such laws are reasonably necessary for the effectuation of a legitimate and substantial state interest and are not arbitrary or capricious in application. Here, the causal connection between married persons engaging in extramarital sex and contraceptives is too tenuous.

DISSENT: (Black, J.) While the law is offensive, neither the Ninth Amendment nor the Due Process Clause invalidates it. Both lead the court into imposing its own notions as to what are wise or unwise laws. What constitutes "fundamental" values this court is incapable of determining. Keeping the Constitution "in tune with the times" is accomplished only through the amendment process. Similarly, the Due Process Clause is too imprecise and lends itself to subjective interpretation.

DISSENT: (Stewart, J.) The Due Process Clause is not the "guide" because there was no claim here that the statute is unconstitutionally vague or that the defendants were denied any of the elements of procedural due process at their trial. The Ninth Amendment simply restricts the federal government to a government of express and limited powers. Finally, the Constitution is silent on the "right to privacy."

EDITOR'S ANALYSIS: Although the theory of "substantive due process" has declined as a means to review state economic regulation — at least since 1937 — the court, as here, has freely applied strict scrutiny of state laws affecting social areas.

[For more information on rights of personal liberty, see Casenote Law Outline on Constitutional Law, Chapter 7, § II, The Meaning of Fourteenth Amendment "Liberty" and "Due Process."]

QUICKNOTES

PENUMBRA - A doctrine whereby authority of the federal government is implied pursuant to the Necessary and Proper Clause; one implied power may be inferred from the conferring of another implied power.

RIGHT TO PRIVACY - The violation of an individual's right to be protected against unwarranted interference in his personal affairs, falling into one of four categories: (1) appropriating the individual's likeness or name for commercial benefit; (2) intrusion into the individual's seclusion; (3) public disclosure of private facts regarding the individual; and (4) disclosure of facts placing the individual in a false light.

SUBSTANTIVE DUE PROCESS - A constitutional safeguard limiting the power of the state, irrespective of how fair its procedures may be; substantive limits placed on the power of the state.

ROE v. WADE

Single pregnant woman (P) v. State (D)
410 U.S. 113 (1973).

NATURE OF CASE: Challenge to state laws making it a crime to procure an abortion except by medical advice to save the life of the mother.

FACT SUMMARY: Roe (P), a single woman, wished to have her pregnancy terminated by an abortion.

CONCISE RULE OF LAW: The right of privacy found in the Fourteenth Amendment's concept of personal liberty and restrictions upon state action is broad enough to encompass a woman's decision whether or not to terminate her pregnancy.

FACTS: The Texas abortion laws challenged here were typical of those adopted by most states. The challengers were Roe (P), a single pregnant woman, a childless couple with the wife not pregnant (J and M Doe), and a licensed physician with two criminal charges pending (Halford). Only Roe (P) was found to be entitled to maintain the action. Although her 1970 pregnancy had been terminated, her case was not found moot since pregnancy "truly could be capable of repetition, yet evading review."

ISSUE: Does the constitutional right of privacy include a woman's right to choose to terminate her pregnancy?

HOLDING AND DECISION: (Blackmun, J.) Yes. While the Constitution does not explicitly mention any right of privacy, such a right has been recognized. This right of privacy, whether founded in the Fourteenth Amendment's concept of personal liberty and restrictions upon state action, as this court feels it is, or in the Ninth Amendment's reservation of rights to the people, is broad enough to encompass a woman's decision to terminate her pregnancy. A statute regulating a fundamental right, such as the right to privacy, may be justified only by a compelling state interest and such statutes must be narrowly drawn. Here, Texas (D) argued that the fetus is a person within the meaning of the Fourteenth Amendment whose right to life is guaranteed by that Amendment. However, there are no decisions indicating such a definition for "fetus." The unborn have never been recognized in the law as persons in the whole sense. Texas (D) may not, by adopting one theory of life, override the rights of the pregnant woman that are at stake. However, neither are the woman's rights to privacy absolute. The state does have a legitimate interest in preserving the health of the pregnant woman and in protecting the potentiality of life. Each of these interests grows in substantiality as the woman approaches term, and, at a point, each becomes compelling. During the first trimester, mortality in abortion is less than mortality in childbirth. After that point, in promoting its interest in the mother's health, the state may regulate the abortion procedure in ways related to maternal health (i.e., licensing of physicians, facilities, etc.). Prior to viability, the physician, in consultation with the pregnant woman, is free to decide that a pregnancy should be terminated without interference by the state. Subsequent to viability, the state, in promoting its interest in the potentiality of life, may regulate, and even prescribe abortion, except where necessary to save the mother's life. Because the Texas (D) statute makes no distinction between abortions performed in early pregnancy and those performed later, it sweeps too broadly and is, therefore, invalid.

CONCURRENCE: (Stewart, J.) The Texas statute invaded "liberty" protected by the Fourteenth Amendment Due Process Clause. Justice Stewart suggests that substantive due process has been resurrected.

CONCURRENCE: (Douglas, J.) A woman's right to an abortion arises from the periphery of the Bill of Rights. This decision has nothing to do with substantive due process.

DISSENT: (White, J.) This issue, for the most part, should be left with the people. There is nothing in the language or history of the Constitution to support the court's opinion. The Texas statute is not constitutionally infirm because it denies abortions to those who seek to serve only their own convenience rather than to protect their life or health.

DISSENT: (Rehnquist, J.) The test to be applied is whether the abortion law has a rational relation to a valid state objective. Here, the court applies the compelling state interest test. The application of this test requires the court to examine the legislative policies and pass on the wisdom of those policies, tasks better left to the legislature.

EDITOR'S ANALYSIS: *Doe v. Bolton* was the companion case to *Roe v. Wade*. The Georgia laws attacked in *Doe* were more modern than the Texas laws. They allowed a physician to perform an abortion when the mother's life was in danger or the fetus would likely be born with birth defects or the pregnancy had resulted from rape. The court held that a physician could consider all attendant circumstances in deciding whether an abortion should be performed. No longer could only the three situations specified be considered. The court also struck down the requirements of prior approval for an abortion by the hospital staff committee and of inconfirmation by two physicians. They concluded that the attending physician's judgment was sufficient. Lastly, the court struck down the requirement that the woman be a Georgia resident.

[For more information on the right of privacy regarding abortion, see Casenote Law Outline on Constitutional Law, Chapter 7, § II, The Meaning of Fourteenth Amendment "Liberty" and "Due Process."]

QUICKNOTES

MOOTNESS - Judgment on the particular issue would not resolve the controversy.

BOWERS v. HARDWICK
State officials (D) v. Homosexual man (P)
478 U.S. 186 (1986).

NATURE OF CASE: Appeal from decision finding state sodomy statute unconstitutional.

FACT SUMMARY: Bowers (D) and other state officials appealed from a court of appeals decision finding the Georgia sodomy statute unconstitutional in that it violated Hardwick's (P) fundamental rights, since it applied to consensual, homosexual sodomy.

CONCISE RULE OF LAW: The Constitution does not grant a fundamental right to engage in consensual homosexual sodomy.

FACTS: Hardwick (P), a gay man, was charged with violating a state law criminalizing sodomy. After a preliminary hearing, the district attorney decided not to present the matter to the grand jury unless further evidence developed. Hardwick (P) brought suit, challenging the constitutionality of the statute in that it criminalized consensual sodomy. He claimed the law as administered by the state placed him in imminent danger of arrest and was unconstitutional on a number of grounds. The district court dismissed the action for failing to state a claim, relying heavily on the Supreme Court decision in *Doe v. Commonwealth's Attorney for the City of Richmond*, 425 v. 901 (1976), which summarily affirmed a case involving a similar Virginia sodomy statute. The court of appeals reversed, finding that the statute violated Hardwick's (P) fundamental rights because the homosexual activity was a private and intimate association beyond the reach of state regulation. From this decision, Bowers (D) and other state officials appealed.

ISSUE: Does the Constitution grant a fundamental right to engage in consensual homosexual sodomy?

HOLDING AND DECISION: (White, J.) No. The Constitution does not grant a fundamental right to engage in consensual homosexual sodomy. None of the fundamental rights announced in previous cases bears any resemblance to the claimed constitutional right to engage in sodomy asserted in the present case. Fundamental liberties identified by this Court and deserving of heightened judicial scrutiny have either been liberties implicit in the concept of ordered liberty or liberties deeply rooted in this nation's history and traditions. Neither of these formulations would extend the liberty sought in the present case. Great restraint should be used when expanding the contours of constitutional due process. The fact that the conduct in question occurred in the privacy of the home does not necessarily shield it from regulation, as can be seen in statutes punishing a number of other victimless and/or sex crimes. The conduct at issue is not a fundamental right, and the state has provided a rational basis for the statute. Reversed.

CONCURRENCE: (Burger, C.J.) This is a question not of personal preference but of the legislative authority of the state, and nothing in the Constitution forbids the state statute at issue.

CONCURRENCE: (Powell, J.) Hardwick (P) may be protected under the Eighth Amendment, but he has not been tried, sentenced, or convicted, and has not raised any Eighth Amendment issues.

DISSENT: (Blackmun, J.) The state in the present case is legislating particular forms of private, consensual sexual conduct. The Court's obsession with homosexual activity is difficult to justify, since the statute's language encompasses non-homosexual conduct. The Court fails to comprehend the magnitude of the liberty interest at stake in this case.

DISSENT: (Stevens, J.) The essential liberty to choose how to conduct private sexual conduct surely encompasses the right to engage in nonreproductive, sexual conduct that others may find offensive or immoral. The state cannot justify the selective application of the statute in question, given the conceded unconstitutionality of the statute as applied to nonhomosexual conduct. Hardwick (P) at this state of the litigation has stated a constitutional claim sufficient to withstand a motion to dismiss.

EDITOR'S ANALYSIS: Also plaintiffs in the original action were a "Doe" couple, who had alleged that they wished to engage in the proscribed activity and were chilled and deterred by the existence of the statute and Hardwick's (P) arrest. The district court dismissed their claim for lack of standing, as the selective enforcement of the law left them in no immediate danger, and this judgment was upheld by the court of appeals. The "Does" did not challenge this holding in the present case.

[For more information on Rights of Personal Liberty, see Casenote Law Outline on Constitutional Law, Chapter 7, § II, The Meaning of Fourteenth Amendment "Liberty" and "Due Process."]

QUICKNOTES
FUNDAMENTAL RIGHT - A liberty that is either expressly or impliedly provided for in the United States Constitution, the deprivation or burdening of which is subject to a heightened standard of review.

GRAND JURY - A group summoned to investigate, inform, and accuse persons of crimes when sufficient evidence exists to do so.

PLANNED PARENTHOOD OF SOUTHEASTERN PENNSYL-VANIA v. CASEY

Clinics/doctors (P) v. State (D)
505 U.S.833 (1992).

NATURE OF CASE: Appeal of order upholding abortion statutes, except a husband-notification provision.

FACT SUMMARY: Planned Parenthood (P) facially challenged the constitutionality of Pennsylvania's (D) abortion law.

CONCISE RULE OF LAW: A law is unconstitutional as an undue burden on a woman's right to an abortion before fetal viability, if the law places a substantial obstacle in the path of a woman seeking to exercise her right.

FACTS: The Pennsylvania Abortion Control Act required (a) a doctor to provide a woman seeking an abortion with information designed to persuade her against abortion and imposed a waiting period of at least 24 hours between provision of the information and the abortion; (b) a minor to obtain consent of one parent or a judge's order before having an abortion; (c) a married woman to sign a statement averring that her husband had been notified, her husband was not the father, her husband forcibly had impregnated her, or that she would be physically harmed if she notified her husband; and (d) a public report on every abortion, detailing information on the facility, physician, patient, and steps taken to comply with the Act. The name of the patient was confidential. It provided the first three provisions would not apply in a "medical emergency," i.e., a condition a doctor determines to require immediate abortion to avert death or serious risk of substantial, irreversible impairment of a major bodily function. Five clinics (P), including Planned Parenthood (P), and five doctors (P) sued Pennsylvania (D), including Governor Casey (D), claiming the Act was unconstitutional on its face. The district court held the entire Act invalid under *Roe v. Wade*, 410 U.S. 113 (1973). The court of appeals reversed, upholding the entire Act except the husband-notification requirement. Planned Parenthood et al. (P) appealed.

ISSUE: Is a law unconstitutional as an undue burden on a woman's right to an abortion before fetal viability, if the law places a substantial obstacle in the path of a woman's exercise of her right?

HOLDING AND DECISION: (O'Connor, Kennedy, and Souter, JJ.) Yes. A law is unconstitutional as an undue burden on a woman's right to an abortion before fetal viability, if the law places a substantial obstacle in the path of a woman seeking to exercise her right. For two decades people have organized lives relying on the availability of abortion. The Court rarely resolves a controversy as intensely divisive as in *Roe*. Such a decision only should be overturned if it proves unworkable or if new information arises which renders the decision unjustified in the present. *Roe* is neither unworkable nor based on outdated assumptions.

Medical technology has altered the age of viability, but that does not affect the validity of viability as a dividing line. Viability is the point at which a fetus can be said to be an independent life, so that the state's interest in protecting it then outweighs the mother's decision-making interest. The Court and the nation would be seriously damaged if the Court were to overturn *Roe* simply on the basis of a philosophical disagreement with the 1973 Court, or as a surrender to political pressure. The liberty rights of women and the personal, intimate nature of child bearing sharply limit state power to insist a woman carry a child to term or accept the state's vision of her role in society. Thus, the integrity of the Court, stare decisis, and substantive due process require the central principle of *Roe* to be reaffirmed: a state may not prevent a woman from making the ultimate decision to terminate her pregnancy before viability. *Roe* also recognized the state interest in maternal health and in protecting potential life. Application of the rigid trimester framework often ignored state interests, leading to striking down abortion regulations which in no real sense deprived women of the ultimate decision. Therefore, the trimester framework must be rejected and undue burden analysis put in its place. Here, the information requirement is not an undue burden. Truthful, nonmisleading information on the nature of abortion procedure, health risks, and consequences to the fetus is reasonable to ensure informed choice, one which might cause a woman to choose childbirth. The 24-hour waiting period does not create a health risk and reasonably furthers the state interest in protecting the unborn. Requiring a period of reflection to make an informed decision is reasonable. A waiting period may increase cost and risk of delay, but on a facial challenge it cannot be called a substantial obstacle. Prior cases establish that a state may require parental consent before abortions by minors, provided there is a judicial bypass procedure. On its face, the statute's definition of "medical emergency" is not too narrow. The reporting requirement is reasonably directed to the preservation of maternal health, providing a vital element of medical research, and the statute protects patient confidentiality. The husband-notification requirement imposes an undue burden on abortion rights of the abused women who fear for their safety and the safety of their children and are likely to be deterred from procuring an abortion as surely as if the state outlawed abortion. A husband has a strong interest in his wife's pregnancy, but before birth it is a biological fact that regulation of the fetus has a far greater impact on the woman. The husband-notification requirement is unconstitutional, and the rest of the statute is valid. Affirmed.

CONCURRENCE AND DISSENT: (Stevens, J.) A burden is "undue" if it is too severe or lacks legitimate justification. The information, waiting period, and parental consent requirements, as well as the husband-notification requirement, are invalid. The Court's opinion implicitly reaffirms its holding that a fetus is not a "person" within the meaning of the Fourteenth Amendment. The state interest in protecting potential life is legitimate but not grounded in the Constitution. A woman has constitutional liberty rights to bodily integrity and to decide personal and private matters. So, the state may promote a preference for childbirth, but decisional autonomy must limit the state's power to interject into a woman's most personal deliberations its own views of what is best. Pennsylvania's law goes too far by requiring a doctor to provide information designed to persuade a woman to opt against abortion, just as she is weighing her personal choice. In contrast, the requirement of informing a woman of the nature and risks of abortion and childbirth enhances decision-making. The 24-hour waiting period illegitimately rests on assumptions that a decision to terminate pregnancy is wrong, and that a woman is unable to make decisions. There is no legitimate reason to require a woman who has agonized over her decision to leave the hospital and return another day.

CONCURRENCE AND DISSENT: (Blackmun, J.) The Court correctly reaffirms a woman's right to abortion. However, that right should remain fundamental, and any state-imposed burden upon it should be subjected to the strictest judicial scrutiny. Categorizing a woman's right to abortion as merely a "liberty interest" is not sufficient. In striking down the husband-notification requirement, the Court sets up a framework for evaluating abortion regulations in the social context of women facing issues of reproductive choice. The Court failed to strike down the information, waiting period, parental consent, and reporting requirements on their face, but the Court's standard at least allows future courts to hold that in practice such regulations are undue burdens. The reporting requirement does not further maternal health. Fearing harassment, many doctors will stop performing abortions if their names appear on public reports. However, none of these requirements would survive under the strict-scrutiny standard of review. The trimester framework should be maintained. No other approach better protects a woman's fundamental right while accommodating legitimate state interests. The Court's cases do not create a list of personal liberties: they are a principled account of how these rights are grounded in a general right of privacy.

DISSENT: (Rehnquist, C.J.) *Roe* was wrongly decided, has led to a confusing body of law, and should be overturned. The Court's decision, replacing *Roe's* strict scrutiny standard and trimester framework with a new, unworkable undue burden test, cannot be justified by stare decisis. Authentic principles of stare decisis do not require erroneous decisions to be maintained. The Court's integrity is enhanced when it repudiates wrong decisions. Americans have grown accustomed to *Roe*, but that should not prevent the Court from correcting a wrong decision. The Fourteenth Amendment concept of liberty does not incorporate any all-encompassing right of privacy. Unlike marriage, procreation, and contraception, abortion terminates potential life and must be analyzed differently. Historic traditions of the American people, critical to an understanding of fundamental rights, do not support a right to abortion. A woman's interest in having an abortion is liberty protected by due process, but states may regulate abortion in ways rationally related to a legitimate state interest. All provisions of the Pennsylvania law do so and are constitutional. The husband-notification requirement is reasonably related to promoting state interests in protecting the husband's interests, potential life, and the integrity of marriage.

DISSENT: (Scalia, J.) The limits on abortion should be decided democratically. The Constitution is silent on abortion, and American traditions have allowed it to be proscribed. Applying the rational basis test, the Pennsylvania law should be upheld in its entirety. *Roe* was wrongly decided. It begged the question by assuming a fetus is merely potential human life. The whole argument of abortion opponents is that the state seeks to protect human life. *Roe* also failed to produce a settled body of law. *Roe* did not resolve the deeply divisive issue of abortion. It made compromise impossible and elevated the issue to a national level where it has proven infinitely more difficult to resolve. Here, the Court claims to rely on stare decisis but throws out *Roe's* trimester framework. The new undue burden standard is meaningless in application, giving a district judge freedom to strike down almost any abortion restriction he does not like. The Court's suggestion that public opposition to an erroneous decision mitigates against overturning it is appalling.

EDITOR'S ANALYSIS: The Court also affirmed *Roe's* holding that after viability the state may regulate, or even proscribe, abortion, except where it is necessary to preserve the life or health of the mother. This is only the second time in modern Supreme Court jurisprudence that an opinion has been jointly authored. Justice Kennedy's portion of the opinion addresses the importance of public faith in and acceptance of the Court's work by opening with the statement: "Liberty finds no refuge in a jurisprudence of doubt." Justice O'Connor expounds on the essential nature of a woman's right to an abortion, while Justice Souter performs the stare decisis analysis, concluding that there is no reason to reverse the essential holding of *Roe*. It appears that the instant case marks the first time the Court has downgraded a fundamental right to a protected liberty and by so doing removed from the usual strict scrutiny standard of review.

[For more information on the right to privacy, see Casenote Law Outline on Constitutional Law, Chapter 7, § II, The Meaning of Fourteenth Amendment "Liberty" and "Due Process."]

QUICKNOTES

FUNDAMENTAL RIGHT - A basic and essential right; freedoms expressed in the Bill of Rights and implied freedoms not expressly stated in the Constitution.

STARE DECISIS - Doctrine whereby courts follow legal precedent unless there is good cause for departure.

STRICT SCRUTINY - Method by which courts determine the constitutionality of a law, when a law affects a fundamental right. Under the test, the legislature must have a compelling interest to enact law and measures prescribed by the law must be the least restrictive means possible to accomplish goal.

SUBSTANTIVE DUE PROCESS - A constitutional safeguard limiting the power of the state, irrespective of how fair its procedures may be; substantive limits placed on the power of the state.

UNDUE BURDEN - Unlawfully oppressive or troublesome.

VIABILITY - The point at which a newborn child is capable of existing outside the womb.

WASHINGTON v. GLUCKSBERG
State (D) v. Doctors (P)
521 U.S. 702, 117 S. Ct. 2258 (1997).

NATURE OF CASE: Review of judgment declaring that a state law prohibiting assisted suicide was unconstitutional.

FACT SUMMARY: A group of Washington physicians (P) and a nonprofit organization (P) that counseled people considering physician-assisted suicide filed suit seeking a declaration that the state's assisted-suicide ban was facially unconstitutional.

CONCISE RULE OF LAW: The right to assistance in committing suicide is not a fundamental liberty interest protected by the Due Process Clause.

FACTS: A Washington law stated that "a person is guilty of promoting a suicide attempt when he knowingly causes or aids another person to attempt suicide." Breaking the law was a felony punishable by up to five years' imprisonment and up to a $10,000 fine. Washington also had a Natural Death Act which stated that withholding or withdrawal of life-sustaining treatment at a patient's discretion did not constitute a suicide. Physicians (P) practicing in Washington and Compassion in Dying (P), a nonprofit organization that counseled people considering physician-assisted suicide, filed suit seeking a declaration that the ban on assisted suicide was unconstitutional. The physicians (P), who treated many terminally ill, suffering patients, declared that they would have assisted some of these patients in ending their lives were it not for Washington's law. The district court found the statute invalid, and the court of appeals ultimately affirmed. The appellate court held that the Constitution encompasses a due process liberty interest in controlling the time and manner of one's death, and that the state's assisted-suicide ban was unconstitutional as applied to terminally ill competent adults who wish to hasten their deaths with medication prescribed by their physicians. The Supreme Court granted certiorari.

ISSUE: Is the right to assistance in committing suicide a fundamental liberty interest protected by the Due Process Clause?

HOLDING AND DECISION: (Rehnquist, C.J.) No. The right to assistance in committing suicide is not a fundamental liberty interest protected by the Due Process Clause. In almost every state and every western democracy, it is a crime to assist a suicide. These laws reflect a longstanding commitment to the protection and preservation of human life. In 1991, Washington voters rejected a ballot measure that would have permitted a form of physician-assisted suicide. The Court must exercise extreme prudence in expanding the Due Process Clause to include new fundamental rights and liberties. In Cruzan v. Director, Missouri Dept. of Health, 497 U.S. 261 (1990), the Court suggested that

the Due Process Clause protects the right to refuse unwanted lifesaving medical treatment. The physicians' (P) reliance on Cruzan is misplaced. At common law, forced medication was a battery; however, the decision to commit suicide has never been afforded similar legal protection. Washington (D) also has a fundamental interest in protecting the integrity of the medical profession, and the American Medical Association has concluded that physician-assisted suicide is fundamentally incompatible with the physician's role as a healer. Finally, the state has an interest in protecting vulnerable groups from abuse, neglect, and mistakes. There is a very real risk of subtle coercion and undue influence in end-of-life situations that legalized physician-assisted suicide would likely exacerbate. Therefore, the statute does not violate the Fourteenth Amendment either on its face or as applied. Reversed.

CONCURRENCE: (O'Connor, J.) While the majority correctly holds that there is no generalized "right" to commit suicide, the question of whether a mentally competent person experiencing great suffering has a constitutional right to control the circumstances of his or her imminent death should not be precluded by this decision.

CONCURRENCE: (Stevens, J.) The Court's holding that Washington's statute is not invalid on its face does not foreclose the possibility that some applications of the statute might well be invalid. While the Court correctly held that Cruzan does not decide the issue here, Cruzan did give recognition to an individual's interest in making decisions about how to confront an imminent death. Furthermore, the state's interest in supporting a general rule banning the practice of physician-assisted suicide does not have the same force in all cases.

CONCURRENCE: (Souter, J.) While Washington (D) has persuasively demonstrated that its ban on physician-assisted suicide should not be found facially unconstitutional, this does not preclude the possibility that the individual interests at stake here will at some point or in some cases be held "fundamental." While that day is yet to come, the Court has presently correctly deferred to Washington's institutional legislative competence.

CONCURRENCE: (Breyer, J.) The Court has misstated the claimed liberty interest. A more accurate formulation would use words like a "right to die with dignity" and would be closely linked with a right to avoid severe physical pain connected with death. Nevertheless, given the facts at hand, the Court need not decide now whether or not such a right is "fundamental."

EDITOR'S ANALYSIS: The four concurring justices all left the door wide open for the Court to revisit this decision given a more fact-specific case. While they all strongly suggested that an individual under certain, limited circumstances may have a constitutionally protected right to assisted suicide, they were cautious in taking that leap given the specific question at issue here. While several states, including Washington and California, have voted down statutes permitting physician-assisted suicide, it is likely that one will eventually pass, and the Court will again be presented with these issues.

[For more information on substantive due process, see Casenote Law Outline on Constitutional Law, Chapter 7, § II, The Meaning of Fourteenth Amendment "Liberty" and "Due Process."]

QUICKNOTES

DUE PROCESS CLAUSE - Clauses found in the Fifth and Fourteenth Amendments to the United States Constitution providing that no person shall be deprived of "life, liberty, or property, without due process of law."

LIBERTY INTEREST - A right conferred by the Due Process Clauses of the state and federal constitutions.

BATTERY - Unlawful contact with the body of another person.

NOTES:

9

CHAPTER 9
EQUAL PROTECTION

QUICK REFERENCE RULES OF LAW

1. **Scrutiny of Means in Economic Regulations.** The Equal Protection Clause does not require that a statute eradicate all evils of the same type or none at all. (Railway Express Agency v. New York)

   [For more information on hypothetical purposes under the rational basis test, see Casenote Law Outline on Constitutional Law, Chapter 8, § II, Rational Basis Review.]

2. **Scrutiny of Means in Economic Regulations.** Social and economic legislation enacted by Congress will be upheld under the Equal Protection Clause if it is rationally related to a permissible government objective. (U.S. Railroad Retirement Bd v. Fritz)

   [For more information on the debate over enhanced rationality review, see Casenote Law Outline on Constitutional Law, Chapter 8, § II, Rational Basis Review.]

3. **Strict Scrutiny of Disadvantaging Racial and Ethnic Classifications.** A state law restricting the freedom to marry solely because of racial classification violates the Equal Protection Clause. (Loving v. Virginia)

   [For more information on strict scrutiny review, see Casenote Law Outline on Constitutional Law, Chapter 8, § III, Strict Scrutiny Review: Suspect Classifications.]

4. **The Unconstitutionality of Racial Segregation.** The "separate but equal" doctrine has no application in the field of education, and the segregation of children in public schools based solely on their race violates the Equal Protection Clause. (Brown v. Board of Education [Brown I])

   [For more information on strict scrutiny review of racial segregation in public schools, see Casenote Law Outline on Constitutional Law, Chapter 8, § III, Strict Scrutiny Review: Suspect Classifications.]

5. **The Unconstitutionality of Racial Segregation.** The cases are remanded to the lower courts to enter orders consistent with equitable principles of flexibility and requiring the defendant to make a prompt and reasonable start toward full racial integration in public schools. (Brown v. Board of Education [Brown II])

   [For more information on school desegregation "with all deliberate speed," see Casenote Law Outline on Constitutional Law, Chapter 8, § III, Strict Scrutiny Review: Suspect Classifications.]

6. **Suspect Classification and Forbidden Discrimination.** Laws which establish classifications by gender must serve important governmental objectives and must be substantially related to achievement of those objectives to be constitutionally in line with the Equal Protection Clause. (Craig v. Boren)

   [For more information on heightened scrutiny based on gender classification, see Casenote Law Outline on Constitutional Law, Chapter 8, § IV, Heightened Scrutiny for Certain Other Classifications.]

7. **Suspect Classification and Forbidden Discrimination.** Public schools may not exclude women. (United States v. Virginia)

   [For more information on gender classification, see Casenote Law Outline on Constitutional Law, Chapter 8, § IV, Heightened Scrutiny for Certain Other Classifications.]

8. **Disability, Age, Poverty.** Laws impacting the mentally retarded are not to be given heightened constitutional scrutiny. (Cleburne v. Cleburne Living Center, Inc.)

    [For more information on equal protection and strict scrutiny review, see Casenote Law Outline on Constitutional Law, Chapter 8, § III, Strict Scrutiny Review: Suspect Classifications.]

9. **Sexual Orientation.** Colorado's Amendment 2 violates the Equal Protection Clause because it singles out a class of citizens — homosexuals — for disfavored legal status. (Romer v. Evans)

    [For more information on inclusive classification, see Casenote Law Outline on Constitutional Law, Chapter 8, § II, Rational Basic Review.]

10. **Proving Purposeful Discrimination.** A law or official governmental practice must have a "discriminatory purpose," not merely a disproportionate effect on one race, in order to constitute "invidious discrimination" under the Fifth Amendment Due Process Clause or the Fourteenth Amendment Equal Protection Clause. (Washington v. Davis)

    [For more information on requirement of discriminatory intent, see Casenote Law Outline on Constitutional Law, Chapter 8, § III, Strict Scrutiny Review: Suspect Classifications.]

11. **Proving Purposeful Discrimination.** At-large voting systems which dilute the voting power of members of a racial group must be shown to be maintained for a discriminatory purpose, and not merely discriminatory in impact, in order to establish that they violate the Equal Protection Clause. (Rogers v. Lodge)

    [For more information on neutral criteria maintained for a discriminatory purpose, see Casenote Law Outline on Constitutional Law, Chapter 8, § III, Strict Scrutiny Review: Suspect Classifications.]

12. **The "Benign" Use of Racial Criteria.** Race may not be made the sole criterion for an admissions decision. (Regents of Univ. of California v. Bakke)

    [For more information on "benign" racial classifications, see Casenote Law Outline on Constitutional Law, Chapter 9, § I, "Benign" Suspect or Quasi-Suspect Classifications.]

13. **The "Benign" Use of Racial Criteria.** Local governments may enact affirmative action programs only where evidence of past discrimination exists and where the programs are aimed at rectifying such past discrimination. (Richmond v. J.A. Croson Co.)

    [For more information on race-conscious remedies, see Casenote Law Outline on Constitutional Law, Chapter 9, § I, "Benign" Suspect or Quasi-Suspect Classifications.]

14. **The "Benign" Use of Racial Criteria.** Federal programs that set racial classifications for awarding contracts or jobs will be subject to strict judicial scrutiny. (Adarand Constructors, Inc. v. Pena)

    [For more information on affirmative action, see Casenote Law Outline on Constitutional Law, Chapter 9, § I, "Benign" Suspect or Quasi-Suspect Classifications.]

15. **Denials and "Dilution" of Voting Rights.** The right to vote is a fundamental and basic right, and where such rights are asserted under the Equal Protection Clause, classifications which might restrain those rights must be closely scrutinized and carefully confined. Lines drawn on the basis of wealth or property, like those of race, are traditionally disfavored. (Harper v. Virginia State Board of Elections)

[For more information on restrictions on right to vote are subject to strict scrutiny review, see Casenote Law Outline on Constitutional Law, Chapter 9, § II, Fundamental Rights and Equal Protection.]

16. **Denials and "Dilution" of Voting Rights.** Legal classifications must be tailored so that exclusion of a certain class of persons is necessary to achieve an articulated state goal. (Kramer v. Union Free School District No. 15)

[For more information on voting qualifications, see Casenote Law Outline on Constitutional Law, Chapter 9, § II, Fundamental Rights and Equal Protection.]

17. **Vote "Dilution": The Reapportionment Cases, Gerrymandering, and Race-Conscious Districting.** The Equal Protection Clause guarantees the opportunity for equal protection by all voters in the election of state legislators and requires that the seats in both houses of a bicameral state legislature must be apportioned on a population basis. (Reynolds v. Sims)

[For more information on equal protection and voter dilution, see Casenote Law Outline on Constitutional Law, Chapter 9, § II, Fundamental Rights and Equal Protection.]

18. **Vote "Dilution": The Reapportionment Cases, Gerrymandering, and Race-Conscious Districting.** When determining unconstitutional vote dilution, the challenging party must show a discriminatory vote dilution to make out a prima facie case. (Davis v. Bandemer)

[For more information on voting rights and equal protection, see Casenote Law Outline on Constitutional Law, Chapter 9, § II, Fundamental Rights and Equal Protection.]

19. **Vote "Dilution": The Reapportionment Cases, Gerrymandering, and Race-Conscious Districting.** An allegation that a reapportionment scheme is so irrational on its face that it can be understood only as an effort to segregate voters based on race without sufficient justification states a cognizable claim under the Fourteenth Amendment. (Shaw v. Reno [Shaw I])

[For more information on gerrymander, see Casenote Law Outline on Constitutional Law, Chapter 9, § II, Fundamental Rights and Equal Protection.]

20. **Access to Courts.** A state may not condition appeals from trial court decrees terminating parental rights on the affected parent's ability to pay record preparation fees. (M.L.B. v. S.L.J.)

[For more information on fundamental rights and equal protection, see Casenote Law Outline on Constitutional Law, Chapter 9, § II, Fundamental Rights and Equal Protection.]

21. **Refusals to Expand Fundamental Interests Analysis to Redress of Economic Inequalities.** Education is not a fundamental right, and students who live in school districts with a lower property tax base do not constitute a suspect classification, so a school financing system is not subject to strict standard of judicial review on an equal protection challenge to the financing system. (San Antonio Independent School District v. Rodriquez)

[For more information on education not constituting a fundamental right, see Casenote Law Outline on Constitutional Law, Chapter 9, Equal Protection (II), § II, Fundamental Rights and Equal Protection.]

RAILWAY EXPRESS AGENCY v. NEW YORK
Trucking company (D) v. City (P)
336 U.S. 106 (1949).

NATURE OF CASE: Appeal from conviction for violation of a state advertising statute.

FACT SUMMARY: New York (P) had a regulation which prohibited advertising on vehicles but allowed advertising on business vehicles so long as the vehicles are engaged in their owner's usual work and are not used mainly for advertising.

CONCISE RULE OF LAW: The Equal Protection Clause does not require that a statute eradicate all evils of the same type or none at all.

FACTS: A New York City (P) regulation prohibited advertising on vehicles. The statute did not prohibit, however, advertising on business vehicles so long as the vehicles are engaged in their owner's usual work and are not used merely or mainly for advertising. Railway (D) is engaged in a nationwide express business. It operated 1900 trucks in New York City (P). It sold space on the exterior of its trucks for advertising. Such advertising was generally unconnected with its business.

ISSUE: Does a regulation which prohibits general advertisements on vehicles while allowing advertisement of products sold by vehicle owners violate equal protection?

HOLDING AND DECISION: (Douglas, J.) No. The Equal Protection Clause does not require that a statute eradicate all evils of the same type or none at all. The court of special sessions concluded that advertising on vehicles using the streets of New York City (P) constituted a distraction to vehicle drivers and pedestrians, therefore affecting the public's safety in the use of the streets. The local authorities may well have concluded that those who advertise their own products on their trucks do not present the same traffic problem in view of the nature and extent of their advertising. The court cannot say that such a judgment is now an allowable one. The classification has relation to the purpose for which it is made and does not contain the kind of discrimination against which the Equal Protection Clause protects. The fact that New York City (P) does not eliminate all distractions from its streets is immaterial. It is no requirement of equal protection that all evils of the same genus be eradicated or none at all. Conviction affirmed.

CONCURRENCE: (Jackson, J.) Laws must not discriminate between people except upon some reasonable differentiation fairly related to the object of regulation. There is a real difference between doing in self-interest and doing for hire so that it is one thing to tolerate an action done in self-interest and another thing to permit the same action to be done for hire.

EDITOR'S ANALYSIS: Traditionally, the Equal Protection Clause supported only minimal judicial intervention. During the late sixties, however, it became the favorite and most far-reaching tool for judicial protection of fundamental rights not specified in the Constitution. For many years, the impact of the Equal Protection Clause was a very limited one. During the decades of extensive court intervention with state economic legislation, substantive due process, not equal protection, provided the cutting edge to determine a statute's constitutionality. Also, as the concurring opinion points out, equal protection demanded only a "reasonable differentiation fairly related to the object of regulation." As demonstrated by this case, the rational classification requirement could be satisfied fairly easily, as the courts were extremely deferential to legislative judgment and easily convinced that the means used might relate rationally to a plausible end.

[For more information on hypothetical purposes under the rational basis test, see Casenote Law Outline on Constitutional Law, Chapter 8, § II, Rational Basis Review.]

QUICKNOTES

EQUAL PROTECTION - A constitutional guarantee that no person shall be denied the same protection of the laws enjoyed by other persons in life circumstances.

RATIONAL BASIS REVIEW - A test employed by the court to determine the validity of a statute in equal protection actions, whereby the court determines whether the challenged statute is rationally related to the achievement of a legitimate state interest.

NOTES:

UNITED STATES RAILROAD RETIREMENT BOARD v. FRITZ

Federal agency (D) v. Restored railroad employees (P)
449 U.S. 166 (1980).

NATURE OF CASE: Appeal from finding of unconstitutionality of Railroad Retirement Act of 1974.

FACT SUMMARY: Fritz (P) and other active and retired railroad workers alleged that the portions of the Railroad Retirement Act of 1974 which denied them retirement benefits violated equal protection standards.

CONCISE RULE OF LAW: Social and economic legislation enacted by Congress will be upheld under the Equal Protection Clause if it is rationally related to a permissible government objective.

FACTS: Congress enacted the Railroad Retirement Act of 1974 to place that industry's retirement system on a sound financial basis. Under the former system, a person who worked for both railroad and nonrailroad employers received both railroad retirement benefits and Social Security retirement benefits. Under the 1974 act, railroad employees who had qualified for both sets of benefits as of the effective date of the legislation, but who had not yet actually retired, were entitled to receive benefits under both retirement schemes if they had either performed some railroad service during 1974 or as of December 31, 1974, had been employed by the railroad industry for 12 of the preceding 30 calendar months or had completed 25 years of railroad service as of December 31, 1974. Fritz (P) claimed that the distinctions used to determine eligibility for both sets of benefits violated equal protection standards. The lower court agreed, and the Board (D) appealed.

ISSUE: Will social and economic legislation enacted by Congress be upheld under equal protection provisions if it is rationally related to a permissible government objective?

HOLDING AND DECISION: (Rehnquist, J.) Yes. In the field of economic and social welfare, a legislative classification complies with equal protection standards if it has a reasonable basis. A classification is not unconstitutional merely because it results in some inequality. Here, because Congress could have eliminated dual benefits for all classes of employees, it was permissible for Congress to draw lines between groups of employees for the purpose of phasing out those benefits. The test used to determine benefits is not a patently arbitrary method of accomplishing the congressional objective. Reversed.

CONCURRENCE: (Stevens, J.) To be valid, there must be a correlation between the statutory classification and either the actual purpose of the statute or a legitimate legislation objective. The congressional purpose of eliminating dual benefits is

legitimate, and the timing of the employee's railroad service is a reasonable basis for the statutory classification.

DISSENT: (Brennan, J.) A legislative classification may be upheld only if it bears a rational relationship to a legitimate state purpose. Congress has stated that a principal purpose of the act was to preserve the vested earned benefits of retirees who had already qualified for them. Because the statutory classification here deprives some retirees of vested dual benefits, it is not rationally related to Congress' stated purpose and therefore violates equal protection standards.

EDITOR'S ANALYSIS: The Supreme Court has used a reasonableness standard when reviewing legislative and administrative classifications contained in socioeconomic legislation. To be reasonable, a law or regulation must have a legitimate public purpose based upon some conception of the public good. However, the Court has traditionally given great deference to congressional determinations of the nature of public good.

[For more information on the debate over enhanced rationality review, see Casenote Law Outline on Constitutional Law, Chapter 8, § II, Rational Basis Review.]

QUICKNOTES

EQUAL PROTECTION - A constitutional guarantee that no person shall be denied the same protection of the laws enjoyed by other persons in life circumstances.

RATIONAL BASIS REVIEW - A test employed by the court to determine the validity of a statute in equal protection actions, whereby the court determines whether the challenged statute is rationally related to the achievement of a legitimate state interest.

NOTES:

LOVING v. VIRGINIA
Interracial couple (D) v. State (P)
388 U.S. 1 (1967).

NATURE OF CASE: Appeal after conviction for violation of state law barring interracial marriage.

FACT SUMMARY: Loving (D), a white man, and Jeter (D), a black woman, both Virginia residents, were married in the District of Columbia. When they returned to Virginia, they were indicted for violating the state's ban on interracial marriage.

CONCISE RULE OF LAW: A state law restricting the freedom to marry solely because of racial classification violates the Equal Protection Clause.

FACTS: In June 1958, Loving (D) a white man, and Jeter (D), a black woman, both Virginia residents, were married in the District of Columbia, pursuant to its laws. Shortly after their marriage, the Lovings (D) returned to Virginia and were indicted for violating the state's law barring interracial marriage. They pleaded guilty and were sentenced to one year in jail. The trial judge suspended the sentence for 25 years on the condition that the Lovings (D) leave the state and not return for 25 years. In 1963, they filed a motion to have the judgment vacated and set aside.

ISSUE: Does a state law restricting the freedom to marry solely because of racial classifications violate the Equal Protection Clause?

HOLDING AND DECISION: (Warren, C. J.) Yes. A state law restricting the freedom to marry solely because of racial classification violates the Equal Protection Clause. At the very least, the Equal Protection Clause demands that racial classifications, especially suspect in criminal statutes, be subjected to the most rigid scrutiny. If they are ever to be upheld, they must be shown to be necessary to the accomplishment of some legitimate state objective. Here, there is no question that Virginia's miscegenation statutes rest solely upon distinctions drawn according to race. The statutes proscribe generally accepted conduct if engaged in by members of different races. The fact that the statute prohibits only interracial marriages involving white persons indicates that its aim is to maintain white supremacy. There is patently no legitimate overriding purpose independent of invidious discrimination which justifies the classification. A statute restricting marriage solely because of race violates the Equal Protection Clause. These statutes also deprive the Lovings (D) of liberty without due process. Since marriage is a basic human civil right, to deny this freedom on so insupportable a basis as racial classifications deprives all the state's citizens of liberty without due process of the law.

CONCURRENCE: (Stewart, J.) It is simply not possible for a state law to be valid under the Constitution, which makes the criminality of an act depend upon the race of the actor.

EDITOR'S ANALYSIS: In *McLaughlin v. Florida*, 379 U.S. 184 (1964), a state law banning habitual nighttime cohabitation between whites and blacks not married to each other was held to violate the Equal Protection Clause, since other nonmarried couples were not subject to prosecution for the same acts. Ordinances establishing ghettos in which blacks must reside were found to violate the clause (*Buchanan v. Warley*, 245 U.S. 60 [1917]), as was judicial enforcement of covenants restricting ownership land to whites (*Shelley v. Kramer*, 334 U.S. 1 [1948]); racial discrimination in the selection of jurors (*Patton v. Mississippi*, 332 U.S. 463 [1947]); hiring blacks for certain occupations; and establishing racial qualifications for public offices (*Anderson v. Martin*, 375 U.S. 399 [1964]).

[For more information on strict scrutiny review, see Casenote Law Outline on Constitutional Law, Chapter 8, § III, Strict Scrutiny Review: Suspect Classifications.]

QUICKNOTES
EQUAL PROTECTION CLAUSE - A constitutional guarantee that no person should be denied the same protection of the laws enjoyed by other persons is circumstances.

INVIDIOUS DISCRIMINATION - Unequal treatment of a class of persons that with particularly malicious or hostile.

MISCEGENATION - Marriage between two persons of different races.

STRICT SCRUTINY - Method by which courts determine the constitutionality of a law, when a law affects a fundamental right.

SUSPECT CLASSIFICATION - A class of persons that have historically been subject to discriminatory treatment; statutes drawing a distinction between persons based on a suspect classification, i.e. race, nationality or alienage, are subject to a strict scrutiny standard of review.

NOTES:

BROWN v. BOARD OF EDUCATION (I)
Students (P) v. School board (D)
347 U.S. 483 (1954).

NATURE OF CASE: Black minors sought the court's aid in obtaining admission to the public schools of their community on a nonsegregated basis.

FACT SUMMARY: Black children were denied admission to public schools attended by white children.

CONCISE RULE OF LAW: The "separate but equal" doctrine has no application in the field of education, and the segregation of children in public schools based solely on their race violates the Equal Protection Clause.

FACTS: Black children had been denied admission to public schools attended by white children under laws requiring or permitting segregation according to race. It was found that the black children's schools and the white children's schools had been or were being equalized with respect to buildings, curricula, qualifications, and salaries of teachers.

ISSUE: Does segregation of children in public schools solely on the basis of race, even though the physical facilities are equal, deprive the children of the minority group of equal protection of the law?

HOLDING AND DECISION: (Warren, C.J.) Yes. The "separate but equal" doctrine has no application in the field of education, and the segregation of children in public schools based solely on their race violates the Equal Protection Clause. First, intangible as well as tangible factors may be considered. Hence, the fact that the facilities and other tangible factors in the schools have been equalized is not controlling. Segregation of white and black children in public schools has a detrimental effect on the black children because the policy of separating the races is usually interpreted as denoting the inferiority of the black children. A sense of inferiority affects children's motivation to learn. Segregation tends to deprive black children of some of the benefits they would receive in an integrated school. Any language in *Plessy v. Ferguson*, 163 U.S. 537 (1896), contrary to this is rejected. The "separate but equal" doctrine has no place in the field of education. Separate facilities are inherently unequal. Such facilities deprive black children of their right to equal protection of the laws.

EDITOR'S ANALYSIS: In *Plessy v. Ferguson*, the court sustained a Louisiana statute requiring "equal, but separate accommodations" for black and white railway passengers. The separate but equal doctrine was born and under it a long line of statutes providing separate but equal facilities were upheld. Justice Harlan was the only dissenter in *Plessy*. He stated, "The arbitrary separation of citizens, on the basis of race, while they are on a public highway . . . cannot be justified upon any legal grounds. The thin disguise of equal accommodations for passengers in railway cars will not mislead anyone, nor atone for the wrong done this day." After the 1954 decision in *Brown v. Board of Education*, the court found segregation unconstitutional in other public facilities as well. Despite the emphasis on the school context in *Brown*, the later cases resulted in per curiam orders simply citing *Brown*. Facilities which were desegregated included beaches, buses, golf courses, and parks.

[For more information on strict scrutiny review of racial segregation in public schools, see Casenote Law Outline on Constitutional Law, Chapter 8, § III, Strict Scrutiny Review: Suspect Classifications.]

QUICKNOTES

EQUAL PROTECTION - A constitutional guarantee that no person shall be denied the same protection of the laws enjoyed by other persons in life circumstances.

SEGREGATION - The use of separate institutions and facilities for persons of different races.

SEPARATE BUT EQUAL DOCTRINE - Doctrine pursuant to the holding in Plessy v. Ferguson that "separate but equal" facilities for persons of different races does not violate equal protection.

NOTES:

BROWN v. BOARD OF EDUCATION (II)
(IMPLEMENTATION DECISION)
Students (P) v. School board (D)
349 U.S. 294 (1955).

NATURE OF CASE: Decision to determine the manner in which relief from segregation in public schools is to be accorded.

FACT SUMMARY: In May 1954, the court decided that racial discrimination in public education is unconstitutional. It requested further arguments on the question of relief.

CONCISE RULE OF LAW: The cases are remanded to the lower courts to enter orders consistent with equitable principles of flexibility and requiring the defendant to make a prompt and reasonable start toward full racial integration in public schools.

FACTS: These cases were decided in May 1954. The opinions declared that racial discrimination in public education is unconstitutional. They are incorporated here. Because the cases arose under various local conditions and their disposition would involve a variety of local problems, the court requested additional arguments on the question of relief. All provisions of federal, state, and local laws which permit segregation in public schools must be modified.

ISSUE: Shall relief in the public school racial desegregation cases be accorded by remanding the cases to the lower courts to enter orders requiring integration?

HOLDING AND DECISION: (Warren, C.J.) Yes. School authorities have the primary responsibility for assessing and solving the problem of achieving racial integration in the public schools. It will be for courts to consider whether the school authorities' actions are good faith implementation of the governing constitutional principles. Because of their proximity to local conditions and the possible need for further hearings, the courts which originally heard these cases can best perform this judicial appraisal. In doing so, the courts will be guided by the equitable principles of practical flexibility in shaping remedies and the facility for adjusting and reconciling public and private needs. The courts will require that the defendants make a prompt and reasonable start toward full racial integration in the public schools. Once such a start is made, the courts may determine that additional time is required to carry out the May 1954 ruling. However, the burden rests upon the defendant to determine that such time is necessary and consistent with good faith compliance with the Constitution. The courts may consider problems related to administration, the facilities, school transportation systems, and revision of school districts and local laws. They will also consider the adequacy of any plans proposed by the defendants and will retain jurisdiction during the transition period. The cases are remanded to the lower courts to enter orders consistent with this opinion as necessary to insure that the parties to these cases are admitted to public schools on a racially nondiscriminatory basis with all deliberate speed.

EDITOR'S ANALYSIS: After its promulgation of general guidelines in Brown II in 1955, the court maintained silence about implementation for several years. Enforcement of the desegregation requirement was left largely to lower court litigation. In 1958, the court broke its silence in *Cooper v. Aaron*, 358 U.S. 1, where it reaffirmed the Brown principles in the face of official resistance in Little Rock, Arkansas. It was not until the early sixties, however, that the court began to consider the details of desegregation plans. During the late sixties, court rulings on implementation came with greater frequency, specificity, and urgency. Finally, in *Alexander* v. *Holmes County Board of Education*, 369 U.S. 19 (1969), the court called for an immediate end to dual school systems.

[For more information on school desegregation "with all deliberate speed," see Casenote Law Outline on Constitutional Law, Chapter 8, § III, Strict Scrutiny Review: Suspect Classifications.]

QUICKNOTES

GOOD FAITH COMPLIANCE - A sincere or unequivocal intention to fulfil an obligation or to comply with specifically requested conduct.

REMAND - To send back for additional scrutiny or deliberation.

NOTES:

CRAIG v. BOREN
Males 18-20 years of age (P) v. State (D)
429 U.S. 190 (1976).

NATURE OF CASE: Appeal from an action to have an Oklahoma statute declared unconstitutional.

FACT SUMMARY: Craig (P) appealed after a federal district court upheld two sections of an Oklahoma statute prohibiting the sale of "nonintoxicating" 3.2% beer to males under the age of 21 and to females under the age of 18 on the ground that such a gender-based differential did not constitute a denial to males 18-20 years of age equal protection of the laws.

CONCISE RULE OF LAW: Laws which establish classifications by gender must serve important governmental objectives and must be substantially related to achievement of those objectives to be constitutionally in line with the Equal Protection Clause.

FACTS: Craig (P) brought suit to have two sections of an Oklahoma statute, which prohibits the sale of "nonintoxicating" 3.2% beer to males under the age of 21 and to females under the age of 18, declared unconstitutional. Craig (P) contended that such a gender-based differential constituted a denial to males 18-20 years of age of the equal protection of the laws in violation of the Fourteenth Amendment. Boren (D), representing the state of Oklahoma, argued that this law was enacted as a traffic safety measure and that the protection of public health and safety was an important function of state and local governments. Boren (D) introduced statistical data demonstrating that 18-20-year-old male arrests for "driving under the influence" and "drunkenness" substantially exceeded female arrests for the same age period. The district court upheld the ordinance on the ground that it served the important governmental objective of traffic safety. Craig (P) appealed.

ISSUE: Are laws which establish classifications by gender constitutional if they do not serve important governmental objectives and are not substantially related to achievement of those objectives?

HOLDING AND DECISION: (Brennan, J.) No. Laws which establish classifications by gender must serve important governmental objectives and must be substantially related to achievement of those objectives to be constitutionally in line with the Equal Protection Clause. It appears that the objective underlying the statute in controversy is the enhancement of traffic safety. Clearly, the protection of public health and safety represents an important function of state and local governments. However, the statistics presented by Boren (D) in this court's view cannot support the conclusion that the gender-based distinction closely serves to achieve the objective. The most relevant of the statistical surveys presented as evidence by Boren (D) in support of the statute, arrests of 18-20-year-olds for alcohol related driving offenses, establish 2% more males than females are arrested for that offense. Such a disparity can hardly form the basis for employment of a gender line as a classifying device. Certainly, if maleness is to serve as a proxy for drinking and driving, a correlation of 2% must be considered unduly tenuous. Indeed, prior cases have consistently rejected the use of sex as a decision-making factor. Therefore, since the gender-based differential does not serve an important governmental objective, the Oklahoma statute constitutes a denial of the equal protection of the laws to males aged 18-20 and is unconstitutional. The judgment of the district court is reversed.

CONCURRENCE: (Powell, J.) The state legislature, by the classification it has chosen, has not adopted through the enactment of the statute a means that bears a fair and substantial relation to the objective of traffic safety.

CONCURRENCE: (Stevens, J.) It is difficult to believe that the statute in question was actually intended to cope with the problem of traffic safety, since it has only a minimal effect on access to a not-very-intoxicating beverage and does not prohibit its consumption.

DISSENT: (Rehnquist, J.) The court's disposition of this case is objectionable on two grounds. First is its conclusion that men challenging a gender-based statute which treats them less favorably than women may invoke a more stringent standard of judicial review than pertains to most other types of classifications. Second is the court's enunciation of this standard, without citation to any source, as being that "classifications by gender must serve important governmental objectives and must be substantially related to achievement of those objectives." The Equal Protection Clause contains no such language, and none of our previous cases adopt that standard.

EDITOR'S ANALYSIS: Cases concerning whether males and females should be considered as reaching a majority age equally has met with some stiff opposition. In *Stanton v. Stanton*, a Utah justice observed: "Regardless of what a judge may think about equality, his thinking cannot change the facts of life. To judicially hold that males and females attain their maturity at the same age is to be blind to the biological facts of life."

[For more information on heightened scrutiny based on gender classification, see Casenote Law Outline on Constitutional Law, Chapter 8, § IV, Heightened Scrutiny for Certain Other Classifications.]

QUICKNOTES
PROXY - A person authorized to act for another.

UNITED STATES v. VIRGINIA
Federal Government (P) v. State (D)
518 U.S. 515, 116 S. Ct. 2264 (1996).

NATURE OF CASE: Appeal from final judgment upholding a college's male-only admission policy.

FACT SUMMARY: Virginia Military Institute (VMI) (D), a state-sponsored university, had a policy of excluding women from attending.

CONCISE RULE OF LAW: Public schools may not exclude women.

FACTS: Since 1839, VMI (D), a Virginia (D) public institution, had been a male-only college that sought to train "citizen-soldiers." In 1990, the Attorney General (P) sued VMI (D) and Virginia (D), claiming that the admission policy violated the Equal Protection Clause. Virginia (D) eventually proposed a remedial plan under which a parallel program would be developed for women. The Virginia Women's Institute for Leadership (VWIL) would be created at Mary Baldwin College. The trial court and an appellate court upheld this remedial plan, but the Attorney General (P) appealed and the Supreme Court granted a writ of certiorari.

ISSUE: May public schools exclude women?

HOLDING AND DECISION: (Ginsburg, J.) No. Public schools may not exclude women. States must show that a sex-based government action serves important governmental objectives and that the discriminatory means employed are substantially related to the achievement of those objectives. There must an exceedingly persuasive justification for the action. This heightened review standard prevents classifications that perpetuate the legal, social, and economic inferiority of women. While single-sex education may provide benefits to some students, Virginia (D) has not shown that it pursued this option as a means to providing a diversity of educational opportunities. On the other hand, the historical record shows that Virginia (D) has systematically prevented women from obtaining higher education until relatively recently. The fact that women have been successfully integrated into the armed forces and service academies demonstrates that VMI's (D) stature will not be downgraded by admitting women. The proposed VWIL does not qualify as VMI's (D) equal in terms of faculty, facilities, course offerings, and its reputation. Accordingly, since Virginia (D) is unable to provide substantial equal opportunities for women who desire to attend VMI (D), the male-only admission policy is unconstitutional. Reversed.

CONCURRENCE: (Rehnquist, J.) The majority decision is correct but there is no basis for stating that states must demonstrate an exceedingly persuasive justification to support sex-based classifications.

DISSENT: (Scalia, J.) The majority sweeps away an institution that has thrived for 150 years and the precedents of this Court to embark on a course of proscribing its own elite opinions on society. Virginia (D) has an important interest in providing education, and single-sex instruction is an approach substantially related to this goal. The proposed VWIL was designed for women and not designed to be exactly equal to VMI (D).

EDITOR'S ANALYSIS: Justice Scalia's dissent carries a tone of disgust for the majority opinion. As he did in *Romer v. Evans*, 517 U.S. 620 (1996), Scalia states that the majority seeks to satisfy some unidentified group of antimajoritarian elites. This attitude is unusual for a member of the Supreme Court since dissents are usually restricted to attacks on the majority's legal reasoning.

[For more information on gender classification, see Casenote Law Outline on Constitutional Law, Chapter 8, § IV, Heightened Scrutiny for Certain Other Classifications.]

QUICKNOTES
CERTIORARI - A discretionary writ issued by a superior court to an inferior court in order to review the lower court's decisions; the Supreme Court's writ ordering such review.

NOTES:

CLEBURNE v. CLEBURNE LIVING CENTER, INC.

Municipality (D) v. Zoning permit applicant (P)

473 U.S. 432 (1985).

NATURE OF CASE: Appeal of order voiding municipal special use permit ordinance.

FACT SUMMARY: Cleburne Living Center, Inc. (P) contended that laws impacting the mentally retarded should be given heightened constitutional scrutiny.

CONCISE RULE OF LAW: Laws impacting the mentally retarded are not to be given heightened constitutional scrutiny.

FACTS: The city of Cleburne, Texas, (D) had zoned multiple-residence dwellings as R-3. Most R-3 structures required no permit; however, any proposed home for the mentally retarded did. The Cleburne Living Center, Inc. (P) applied for such a permit. Responding to objections from nearby residents, the city council refused the application. The Center (P) challenged the ordinance as a denial of equal protection. The Fifth Circuit, applying a heightened level of scrutiny towards the mentally retarded, voided the ordinance. The Supreme Court granted review.

ISSUE: Are laws impacting the mentally retarded to be given heightened constitutional scrutiny?

HOLDING AND DECISION: (White, J.) No. Laws impacting the mentally retarded are not to be given heightened scrutiny. This Court has defined certain characteristics to be so irrelevant to a person's potential contribution to society that, when combined with their political minority status, the conclusion follows that they are entitled to special protection under the Equal Protection Clause. Examples include race, alienage, and religious belief. Mental retardation does not fit this profile. The retarded person's status does relate to his ability to contribute to society. Second, there is ample evidence that lawmakers are responsive to retarded people's plights, showing that they are not politically powerless. Finally, if a large and amorphous class such as the mentally retarded were to be given special Fourteenth Amendment protection, it is hard to see where the process would stop. For these reasons, the Court concludes that the mentally retarded are not entitled to heightened scrutiny. [The Court went on to hold that, even under low-level scrutiny, the ordinance failed to pass constitutional scrutiny.] Affirmed.

CONCURRENCE: (Stevens, J.) The Court's equal protection analysis is better seen as a continuum than specific levels of scrutiny.

CONCURRENCE AND DISSENT: (Marshall, J.) The ordinance in question would no doubt survive the Court's classic "rational basis" test. What the Court has done is fashion a heightened level of scrutiny without so stating.

EDITOR'S ANALYSIS: The Court's Equal Protection Clause analysis continues to evolve. As of the time of this case, three levels of scrutiny existed: rational basis, heightened, and strict. In years past, strict scrutiny automatically led to invalidation, rational basis to approval. As this case shows, this is no longer true.

[For more information on equal protection and strict scrutiny review, see Casenote Law Outline on Constitutional Law, Chapter 8, § III, Strict Scrutiny Review: Suspect Classifications.]

QUICKNOTES

EQUAL PROTECTION - A constitutional guarantee that no person shall be denied the same protection of the laws enjoyed by other persons in life circumstances.

HEIGHTENED SCRUTINY - A purposefully vague judicial description of all levels of scrutiny more exacting than minimal scrutiny.

QUASI-SUSPECT CLASS - A specific class of persons subjected to unequal treatment but deserving less than strict scrutiny.

NOTES:

ROMER v. EVANS
Parties not identified.
517 U.S. 620, 116 S. Ct. 1620 (1996).

NATURE OF CASE: Appeal of order enjoining enactment of an amendment to a state constitution.

FACT SUMMARY: A Colorado (D) constitutional amendment, Amendment 2, which struck down local antidiscrimination laws based on sexual orientation, was challenged for being violative of the Equal Protection Clause.

CONCISE RULE OF LAW: Colorado's Amendment 2 violates the Equal Protection Clause because it singles out a class of citizens — homosexuals — for disfavored legal status.

FACTS: In 1992, Colorado (D) amended its state constitution by a statewide referendum. Amendment 2, as it was designated, provided that the state and local branches of government were forbidden from enacting any laws or regulations that would protect homosexuals from discrimination. Amendment 2 was challenged in court as unconstitutional for violating the Equal Protection Clause. Colorado (D) responded that Amendment 2 simply denied homosexuals any special rights given to protected classes, such as minorities. The trial court enjoined enactment of Amendment 2, the Colorado Supreme Court affirmed, and the Supreme Court granted certiorari to decide the issue.

ISSUE: Does Colorado's Amendment 2 violate the Equal Protection Clause because it singles out a class of citizens — homosexuals — for disfavored legal status?

HOLDING AND DECISION: (Kennedy, J.) Yes. Colorado's Amendment 2 violates the Equal Protection Clause because it singles out a class of citizens — homosexuals — for disfavored legal status. The Colorado Supreme Court construction of Amendment 2 found that its objective was to repeal existing antidiscrimination ordinances. Thus, Amendment 2 is far-reaching in that it places homosexuals in a solitary class, withdrawing legal protection against discrimination and forbidding reinstatement of these policies except by constitutional amendment. Thus, it imposes a special disability on homosexuals who can now only change the law by amending the state constitution, no matter how local the harm. Generally, legislative classifications are constitutional if they bear a rational relation to a legitimate end. However, Amendment 2 identifies persons by a single trait and denies them protection across the board. Therefore, it violates the principle that the government remain open on impartial terms to all who seek its assistance. Finally, equal protection means that the desire to harm a politically unpopular group is not a legitimate government interest. Amendment 2 is extraordinary and explainable only by animus toward homosexuals. Accordingly, Amendment 2 violates the Equal Protection Clause and is unconstitutional. Affirmed.

DISSENT: (Scalia, J.) Amendment 2 only prohibits the special treatment of homosexuals in that they may not obtain preferential treatment without amending the state constitution. Surely, Colorado has the right to be hostile toward homosexuals just as they may have animosity toward murderers or polygamists. In fact, laws against polygamy are the best analogy and have been ignored by the majority. Also, since homosexuals are segregated in certain communities they possess political power much greater than their numbers. Amendment 2 seeks to counter this disproportionate political power. The majority has taken the side of the elites in this culture law.

EDITOR'S ANALYSIS: Justice Scalia's dissenting opinion is astonishing for its not-at-all disguised animosity toward homosexuals, who will no doubt be surprised to find that they are politically powerful. The dissent is also remarkable for its tone of disgust toward the majority. At the heart of the majority decision is the recognition that homosexuality is more of a status (like sex, race, or ethnicity) than a conduct or lifestyle.

QUICKNOTES

EQUAL PROTECTION - A constitutional guarantee that no person shall be denied the same protection of the laws enjoyed by other persons in life circumstances.

NOTES:

WASHINGTON v. DAVIS
Federal agency (D) v. Civil service applicants (P)
426 U.S. 229 (1976).

NATURE OF CASE: Action for a declaratory judgment.

FACT SUMMARY: A qualifying test for positions as police officers in the District of Columbia was failed by a disproportionately high number of Negro applicants (P).

CONCISE RULE OF LAW: A law or official governmental practice must have a "discriminatory purpose," not merely a disproportionate effect on one race, in order to constitute "invidious discrimination" under the Fifth Amendment Due Process Clause or the Fourteenth Amendment Equal Protection Clause.

FACTS: In order to be accepted in the District of Columbia Metropolitan Police Department, all applicants must receive a grade of at least 40 on "Test 21." This test was developed by the Civil Service Commission for use throughout the federal service to test "verbal ability, vocabulary, reading and comprehension." After failing this test, several Negro applicants (P) brought an action against the Commissioners of the United States Civil Service Commission (D) for a declaratory judgment that "Test 21" was unconstitutional. In this action, the Negro applicants (P) claimed that "Test 21" was unlawfully discriminatory against Negroes and, therefore, was in violation of the Fifth Amendment Due Process Clause. After the test was invalidated by the court of appeals, the Commissioners (D) appealed to this court.

ISSUE: Does a law or official governmental practice constitute "invidious discrimination" merely because it affects a greater proportion of one race than another?

HOLDING AND DECISION: (White, J.) No. A law or official governmental practice must have a "discriminatory purpose," not merely a disproportionate effect on one race, in order to constitute "invidious discrimination" under the Fifth Amendment Due Process Clause or the Fourteenth Amendment Equal Protection Clause. Of course, a disproportionate impact may be relevant as "evidence" of a "discriminatory purpose." However, such impact "is not the sole touchstone of invidious racial discrimination forbidden by the constitution," and, standing alone, "it does not trigger the rule that racial classifications are to be subjected to the strictest scrutiny." Here, "Test 21" is racially "neutral" on its face (i.e., it is designed to disqualify anyone who cannot meet the requirements of the police training program). As such, it is valid even though it has a disproportionate effect on Negroes. Reversed.

CONCURRENCE: (Stevens, J.) There is no "purposeful discrimination" here, since "Test 21" serves "the neutral and legitimate purpose of requiring all applicants to meet a uniform minimum standard of literacy."

EDITOR'S ANALYSIS: Generally classifications based upon race are considered "suspect" and, therefore, subjected to "strict scrutiny" under the Equal Protection Clause or the Due Process Clause (i.e., such classifications must be justified by a "compelling state interest"). However, as this case illustrates, such "strict scrutiny" is only applied when there is "purposeful discrimination." As such, the court (as here) can avoid applying "strict scrutiny" by finding that any discriminatory impact is merely incidental. Note that here the court also avoided applying the strict standard in Title VII of the Civil Rights Act of 1964 (by saying that only the constitutional issue was raised). Under Title VII, whenever hiring and promotion practices disqualify disproportionate numbers of blacks, they must be justified by more than a rational basis (i.e., must be validated in terms of job performance) even if no discriminatory purpose is shown.

[For more information on requirement of discriminatory intent, see Casenote Law Outline on Constitutional Law, Chapter 8, § III, Strict Scrutiny Review: Suspect Classifications.]

QUICKNOTES

DECLARATORY JUDGMENT - A judgment of the court establishing the rights of the parties.

DISCRIMINATORY PURPOSE - Intent to discriminate; established an Equal Protection violation.

INVIDIOUS DISCRIMINATION - Unequal treatment of a class of persons that is particularly malicious or hostile.

NOTES:

ROGERS v. LODGE
Citizens (P) v. County (D)
458 U.S. 613 (1982).

NATURE OF CASE: Appeal of an order declaring a county election system unconstitutional.

FACT SUMMARY: Burke County, Georgia's at-large election system was challenged on the ground it denied equal protection by diluting the voting power of black citizens.

CONCISE RULE OF LAW: At-large voting systems which dilute the voting power of members of a racial group must be shown to be maintained for a discriminatory purpose, and not merely discriminatory in impact, in order to establish that they violate the Equal Protection Clause.

FACTS: Burke County, Georgia maintained an at-large voting system which required a candidate for office receive a majority of all votes cast to win. Even though the population of the county was over 50% black, and blacks represented 38% of the registered voters, no black had ever been elected to the County Board of Governors. The black citizens (P) challenged this system on the basis that it unconstitutionally diluted their voting power. The district court found that the county's history of past discriminatory voting requirements and the unresponsiveness of county officials to black concerns effectively precluded blacks from participating in county government and showed the system was maintained for a discriminatory purpose thereby violating the Equal Protection Clause.

ISSUE: Must at-large voting systems which dilute the voting power of members of a racial group be shown to be maintained for a discriminatory purpose, and not merely discriminatory in impact, in order to establish that they violate the Equal Protection Clause?

HOLDING AND DECISION: (White, J.) Yes. At-large voting systems which dilute the voting power of a racial group must be shown to be maintained for a discriminatory purpose, and not merely discriminatory in impact, in order to establish that they violate the Equal Protection Clause. Discriminatory purpose shows an intent to discriminate, which is the essence of an equal protection violation. The existence of a discriminatory purpose is, therefore, a factual question to be resolved in light of all the circumstances of the case, including but not limited to discriminatory impact. The district court considered not only the impact but also the history of discrimination and the system's effective preclusion of blacks from representation due to white block voting allowing officials to disregard black needs. As a result, it found, as a matter of fact, that the system was maintained for a discriminatory purpose and thereby violated the Equal Protection Clause. The findings not being clearly erroneous must be upheld. Affirmed.

DISSENT: (Powell, J.) The factors considered by the district court in this case to show discriminatory purpose are insufficient to establish such a showing. Further, the district courts should be required to focus on objective factors which are "direct, reliable, and unambiguous indices of discriminatory intent," thereby forgoing inquiry into the subjective motivations of state officials.

EDITOR'S ANALYSIS: This case applies the rule of *Washington v. Davis*, 426 U.S. 229 (1976), that merely because a law is racially discriminatory in impact does not render it unconstitutional and that a showing of discriminatory purpose must be made. In *Mobile v. Bolden*, 446 U.S. 55 (1980), the court on almost identical facts, held a statute not discriminatory in purpose. The distinction, if any, was seen by the court in this case to rest on the fact the district court applied the correct legal principle here and these findings of fact not being clearly erroneous, must be upheld, while in the Mobile case, the lower court applied an incorrect legal standard to determine a statute unconstitutional.

[For more information on neutral criteria maintained for a discriminatory purpose, see Casenote Law Outline on Constitutional Law, Chapter 8, § III, Strict Scrutiny Review: Suspect Classifications.]

QUICKNOTES

AT-LARGE VOTING SYSTEM - Voting that takes place over a broad area instead of a designated district of that area.

EQUAL PROTECTION CLAUSE - A constitutional guarantee that no person should be denied the same protection of the laws enjoyed by other persons in like circumstances.

DISCRIMINATORY IMPACT - The effect of an action that affects one group of persons more significantly than another; insufficient to prove discriminatory intent on its own.

DISCRIMINATORY PURPOSE - Intent to discriminate; must be shown to establish an Equal Protection violation.

NOTES:

CITY OF RICHMOND v. J.A. CROSON CO.
Municipality (D) v. Contractor (P)
488 U.S. 469 (1989).

NATURE OF CASE: Appeal from invalidation of affirmative action program.

FACT SUMMARY: Richmond (D) enacted an ordinance requiring participation of minority contractors on city projects, which Croson (P) challenged as unconstitutional.

CONCISE RULE OF LAW: Local governments may enact affirmative action programs only where evidence of past discrimination exists and where the programs are aimed at rectifying such past discrimination.

FACTS: Croson (P) bid on a Richmond (D) project and was granted preliminary acceptance. Under a city ordinance, Croson (P) was required to subcontract out 30% of the work to minority-owned contractors. Croson (P) was unable to find a qualified minority subcontractor whose participation would not significantly increase the project cost. Croson (P) unsuccessfully sought a waiver, and then sued, contending the ordinance was facially unconstitutional. The district court upheld the plan, even though no evidence of actual past discrimination was presented. The court of appeals affirmed, yet on remand struck down the program as violating equal protection and due process. The Supreme Court granted review.

ISSUE: Are city affirmative action programs valid only where aimed at remedial action for past discrimination?

HOLDING AND DECISION: (O'Connor, J.) Yes. Local governments may enact affirmative action programs aimed at rectifying past discrimination. In this case, only generalized evidence of past discrimination was presented in support of the plan. Without specific evidence of such discrimination, it is impossible to determine the scope of such discrimination either in size or application to particular minority groups. Further, such cannot be relied upon to conclude that remedial action is necessary. Thus, in the absence of such evidence, the plan is unconstitutional. Affirmed.

CONCURRENCE: (Stevens, J.) While affirmative action is a legitimate goal, it is constitutional only to remedy actual past discrimination.

CONCURRENCE: (Kennedy, J.) This statute falls short of constitutional standards by exceeding the scope of discrimination shown.

CONCURRENCE: (Scalia, J.) While strict scrutiny must be applied to all legislation which advocates discrimination based on race, affirmative action programs which are aimed at ameliorating past discrimination cannot be valid.

DISSENT: (Marshall, J.) This statute is precisely the type of remedial aid needed to even the books on past discrimination. The fact of discrimination is unquestioned, and the lack of specificity does not render it invalid.

DISSENT: (Blackmun, J.) This decision is a regression back to the days when discrimination was tolerated and fostered.

EDITOR'S ANALYSIS: This decision was based upon the Court's holding in the cases of *Fullilove v. Klutznick* (1980), and *Wygant v. Jackson Board of Education* (1986). These cases adopted the standards of review for "set aside" provisions, wherein governments require minority participation in government work up to a certain percentage. The Court split upon the usual ideological lines with Justices O'Connor, Scalia, Kennedy, and Rehnquist on the side of striking down the measure, and the more liberal branch of Justices Blackmun, Brennan, and Marshall opining that the program was valid.

[For more information on race-conscious remedies, see Casenote Law Outline on Constitutional Law, Chapter 9, § I, "Benign" Suspect or Quasi-Suspect Classifications.]

QUICKNOTES

AFFIRMATIVE ACTION - A form of benign discrimination designed to remedy existing discrimination by favoring one group over another.

PAST DISCRIMINATION - A history of unequal treatment experienced by a specific class of persons.

REMEDIAL ACTION – Actions taken pursuant to the Fourteenth and Fifteenth Amendment to provide remedies for violations of those amednemnts.

ADARAND CONSTRUCTORS, INC. v. PENA
Contractor (P) v. Federal Government (D)
515 U.S. 200, 115 S. Ct. 2097 (1995).

NATURE OF CASE: Review of dismissal of action seeking damages and injunctive relief for constitutional violation.

FACT SUMMARY: A federal program favoring minority-owned businesses was challenged by Adarand Constructors (P), a white contractor who lost a job to an Hispanic-owned company, as violative of equal protection.

CONCISE RULE OF LAW: Federal programs that set racial classifications for awarding contracts or jobs will be subject to strict judicial scrutiny.

FACTS: A general contractor to a project involving the federal government solicited bids for the subcontracts. For the guardrail portion of this highway project, Adarand Constructors (P), a white contractor, submitted the low bid. The general contractor, however, signed a competing Hispanic-owned company because of a congressionally created program that awarded contractors bonus monies for hiring minority-owned businesses. Adarand (P) sued in district court, contending that the program violated equal protection. The district court evaluated the program under a relaxed standard resembling intermediate scrutiny, held the program valid, and dismissed. The Tenth Circuit affirmed, and the Supreme Court granted review.

ISSUE: Will federal programs that set racial classifications for awarding contracts or jobs be subject to strict judicial scrutiny?

HOLDING AND DECISION: (O'Connor, J.) Yes. Federal programs that set racial classifications for awarding contracts or jobs will be subject to strict judicial scrutiny. Three general propositions exist with respect to governmental racial classifications. The first is skepticism: all such classifications are inherently suspect. The second is consistency: the standard of review does not vary depending on race. The third proposition is congruence: that which applies to the states must apply to the national government as well. From this, the proposition naturally follows that any person of any race has the right to demand that any governmental actor explain, through the standard of strict scrutiny, why he is being treated differently than a person of another race. Consequently, any racial classification scheme enacted by Congress must pass strict scrutiny, which is to say, must be narrowly tailored to serve a compelling governmental interest. This was not the standard used by the courts below. The matter must be remanded for a determination under the strict scrutiny standard.

CONCURRENCE: (Scalia, J.) Government can never have a compelling interest in discriminating on the basis of race to "make up" for past discrimination. We are just one race in the eyes of government.

CONCURRENCE: (Thomas, J.) There is a moral and constitutional equivalence between all racial distinctions, "benign" or otherwise, that justifies subjecting them to strict scrutiny analysis.

DISSENT: (Stevens, J.) There is no moral or constitutional equivalence between a policy designed to perpetuate racial subjugation and one designed to eradicate it.

EDITOR'S ANALYSIS: Subjecting affirmative action policies to a rigorous examination will inevitably jeopardize a whole host of programs designed to convey special federal benefits to members of minority groups. However, Justice O'Connor stopped short of the Scalia-Thomas approach that would simply bar all racial preferences as unconstitutional. Instead, she invites the executive and legislative branches to take unspecified steps to address "the unhappy persistence of both the practice and the lingering effects of racial discrimination."

[For more information on affirmative action, see Casenote Law Outline on Constitutional Law, Chapter 9, § I, "Benign" Suspect or Quasi-Suspect Classifications.]

QUICKNOTES

AFFIRMATIVE ACTION - A form of benign discrimination designed to remedy existing discrimination by favoring one group over another.

INJUNCTIVE RELIEF - A count order issued as a remedy, requiring a person to do, or prohibiting that person formn doing, a specific act.

STARE DECISIS - Doctrine whereby courts follow legal precedent unless there is good cause for departure.

STRICT SCRUTINY - Method by which courts determine the constitutionality of a law, when a law affects a fundamental right. Under the test, the legislature must have a compelling interest to enact law and measures prescribed by the law must be the least restrictive means possible to accomplish goal.

REGENTS OF UNIV. OF CALIFORNIA v. BAKKE

University (D) v. Applicant (P)

438 U.S. 265 (1978).

NATURE OF CASE: Action alleging violation of Title VI of Civil Rights Act and Fourteenth Amendment.

FACT SUMMARY: Bakke (P) was denied admission to U.C., Davis Medical School (D) because it employed a racial quota to aid minorities.

CONCISE RULE OF LAW: Race may not be made the sole criterion for an admissions decision.

FACTS: Bakke (P) applied for admission to the University of California, Davis (D) Medical School. The school (D) admitted 100 students per year. However, the Regents (D) had adopted a policy of setting aside a minimum number of seats for minority applicants to increase the number of minority members in the medical profession. Members of minorities were screened by a separate admissions panel and were subject to lesser standards in the admissions. While disadvantaged whites were to be considered by the board, no recommendation for admission under the special program was ever granted. Bakke (P) was denied admission to the medical school in 1973 and again in 1974. In both years, Bakke's (P) overall test scores and grade point were significantly higher than many of those admitted under the minorities program. Bakke (P) filed suit seeking mandatory, injunctive, and declaratory relief to compel his admission to the school (D). Bakke (P) alleged that the special admissions program violated the Equal Protection Clause and § 601 of Title VI of the C.R.A. of 1964. The trial court found that the Regents (D) were using a racial quota, reserving 16 places out of the 100 available each year for minority students. The court held that the school (D) could not take race into account in making admissions decisions. Bakke (P) was denied a seat, however, since he had failed to establish that he would have been admitted but for the special admissions program. On appeal, the state supreme court applied strict scrutiny standards to the program, since it involved a racial classification. The court found that the goals of integrating the medical profession and increasing services available to minority group patients did not justify the admissions program. The court found that the program violated the Fourteenth Amendment and that there were less intrusive means available to accomplish the state's (D) purpose. The court found that Bakke (P) had been discriminated against and ordered his admission, finding that the school (D) had not carried its burden of proof to establish that he would not have been admitted even without the program. The school (D) appealed, alleging that benign discrimination was not violative of the Fourteenth Amendment.

ISSUE: May race be made the sole criterion for an admissions decision?

HOLDING AND DECISION: (Powell, J.) No. Race may not be made the sole criterion for an admissions decision. Before reaching the constitutional issue, we must first determine whether the program is invalid under Title VI since this would obviate the necessity of determining constitutional issues. We do not need to pass upon the issue of standing under Title VI, since this was neither briefed nor argued by the parties. Section 601 states that no person shall, on the ground of race, color or national origin, be excluded from participation in any program or benefit receiving federal financial assistance. Based on its legislative history, we find that Title VI proscribes only those racial classifications which would violate the Equal Protection Clause of the Fifth Amendment. When racial classifications are involved, strict judicial scrutiny is required even where the class being subjected to the discrimination is white males. The Fourteenth Amendment, regardless of its original roots, is now applied to eliminate discrimination against any group. We decline to restrict its reach to encompass only minorities. Discrimination is never benign. White males may be the minority in certain areas and allegedly benign discrimination may actually have more invidious purposes. While racial classifications have been approved as remedial devices where a court has found prior racial discrimination, U.C., Davis (D) has no history of discrimination. To justify the use of a suspect classification such as race, a state must establish that it has a constitutionally permissible purpose or interest which is substantial and the classification is necessary to accomplish it. The Regents (D) allege that the classification is necessary to increase the number of minority doctors, counter the effect of societal discrimination, increase the number of physicians willing to practice in minority areas, and obtain the benefit of a racially diverse student body. Davis (D) has no history of racial discrimination and it may not employ racial quotas merely to assume that its student body will have a set percentage of students from each of the races. Racial classifications to eliminate societal discrimination have never been sanctioned. The school (D) is in the business of educating, not formulating social and legislative policy. Since there is no showing that minority applicants will practice in disadvantaged areas or are in anyway required to do so, the school (D) cannot justify its admission policy on this basis. While an ethnically diverse student body is a legitimate and important purpose, it is only one of the elements in the range of factors which must be considered by a school in attaining a goal of a heterogeneous student body. A school may not base its admissions policies solely on the criterion of race. Racial quotas are violative of the Equal Protection Clause. Race may be considered, but only as one of the factors involved in the admissions decision. Race may be deemed a "plus" so long as all other relevant factors are considered. Affirmed.

CONCURRENCE AND DISSENT: (Brennan, J.) The central import of the opinion herein is that race may be taken into account when it does not demean or insult any racial group, but is used to remedy past disadvantages suffered by the minority or group. Based on our nation's past history of discrimination, affirmative action programs are necessary to make up for past acts of societal discrimination. Title VI could not have been intended to reach such programs. This is borne out by the fact that many affirmative action programs are required as a condition to federal funding. Therefore, we find that classifications need not be color blind where race is used to eliminate the effects of past discrimination so long as it is not the sole criterion used, i.e., racial quotas. The government must establish that no less intrusive method for accomplishing its purpose is available. Davis (D) had a sound basis for determining that minorities were seriously underrepresented and had been subjected to prior acts of societal and government discrimination. This condition would be perpetuated absent some affirmative action program. Moreover, judicial decrees in California had established discriminatory official acts which had the effect of exacerbating the situation. We feel that the Davis (D) program was remedial. The admissions program did not stigmatize any race, minority or majority. The number of minority applicants admitted was less than their proportion of the population in California. No quota within these minorities was established and the best qualified of minority applicants were admitted. In light of the circumstances and objectives herein, race was a reasonable criterion. We would, therefore, reverse the finding that the program was unconstitutional.

SEPARATE OPINION: (White, J.) I find that there is no private cause of action available under § 601.

SEPARATE OPINION: (Marshall, J.) The Thirteenth and Fourteenth Amendments were designed to eliminate discrimination against minorities. They should not be applied to benign discrimination programs.

SEPARATE OPINION: (Blackmun, J.) The Equal Protection Clause cannot be used as a shield to perpetuate the supremacy of the majority.

CONCURRENCE AND DISSENT: (Stevens, J.) This is not a class action and the scope of the opinion is far beyond that which is necessary to conclude the controversy between Bakke (P) and Davis (D). I would affirm on the basis of the plain language of § 601. Race cannot be used under it and Davis' (D) admissions policy clearly violates this prohibition.

EDITOR'S ANALYSIS: Bakke, based on the failure of the Court to achieve any consensus, stands merely for the proposition that

racial quotas cannot be used where there is no court finding of discrimination. The loose standards enunciated herein should allow a school to establish what amounts to a racial quota merely by giving inordinate weight to race in its admissions decision. That is, of course, if any schools will want to bother now that they are under no legal obligation to do so.

[For more information on "benign" racial classifications, see Casenote Law Outline on Constitutional Law, Chapter 9, § I, "Benign" Suspect or Quasi-Suspect Classifications.]

QUICKNOTES

AFFIRMATIVE ACTION PROGRAM - A program designed to create benign discrimination for the purpose of remedying existing discrimination by favoring one group over another.

EQUAL PROTECTION - A constitutional guarantee that no person shall be denied the same protection of the laws enjoyed by other persons in life circumstances.

FOURTEENTH AMENDMENT - Declares that no state shall make or enforce any law which shall abridge the privileges and immunities of citizens of the United States.

THIRTEENTH AMENDMENT - The constitutional provision which abolished slavery in the United States.

NOTES:

HARPER v. VIRGINIA STATE BOARD OF ELECTIONS

Residents (P) v. State (D)

383 U.S. 663 (1966).

NATURE OF CASE: Suits challenging the constitutionality of Virginia's poll tax.

FACT SUMMARY: Harper (P) and other Virginia residents brought this suit to have Virginia's (D) poll tax declared unconstitutional.

CONCISE RULE OF LAW: The right to vote is a fundamental and basic right, and where such rights are asserted under the Equal Protection Clause, classifications which might restrain those rights must be closely scrutinized and carefully confined. Lines drawn on the basis of wealth or property, like those of race, are traditionally disfavored.

FACTS: Harper (P) and other Virginia residents brought these suits to have Virginia's (D) poll tax declared unconstitutional. The three-judge district court, feeling bound by the court's decision in Breedlove v. Suttles, dismissed the complaint. Harper (P) appealed. The law at issue conditions the right to vote in state elections upon the payment of a poll tax.

ISSUE: Is a poll tax, the payment of which is a required prerequisite for voting, constitutional?

HOLDING AND DECISION: (Douglas, J.) No. A state violates the Equal Protection Clause whenever it makes the affluence of the voter or the payment of a fee an electoral standard. The right to vote is a basic and fundamental one, especially since it preserves other rights. Any alleged infringement on the right to vote must be carefully scrutinized. A state's interest, when it comes to voting, is limited to the power to fix qualifications. Wealth, like race or creed or color, is irrelevant to one's ability to participate intelligently in the electoral process. Further lines drawn on the basis of wealth or property, like those of race, are traditionally disfavored. The requirement of the payment of a fee as a condition of obtaining a ballot causes invidious discrimination. Breedlove sanctioned this use of the poll tax, and to that extent it is overruled.

DISSENT: (Black, J.) So long as a distinction drawn is not irrational, unreasonable, or invidious, it must be upheld. There are certainly rational reasons for Virginia's poll tax, such as the state's desire to collect revenue and its belief that voters who pay poll tax will be interested in furthering the state's welfare. Hence, the tax must be upheld. If it is to be struck down, it should be done by the legislature rather than the courts.

DISSENT: (Harlan, J.) The Equal Protection Clause does not impose upon this country an ideology of unrestrained equalitarianism.

EDITOR'S ANALYSIS: If, as the dissenters in Harper argue, the poll tax classification is not wholly "irrational," the case represents a greater intervention than the courts undertook under old equal protection. There is some question as to whether this greater scrutiny was because the "fundamental rights" of voting are affected or because "lines drawn on the basis of wealth" are traditionally disfavored. In *McDonald v. Board of Election Commissioners*, 394 U.S. 802 (1969), the Court sees wealth as an independent ground (apart from impact on fundamental rights) for strict scrutiny. There is a series of cases preceding and following Harper (among them Reynolds v. Sims) which support the invoking of strict scrutiny when voting rights are affected.

[For more information on restrictions on right to vote are subject to strict scrutiny review, see Casenote Law Outline on Constitutional Law, Chapter 9, § II, Fundamental Rights and Equal Protection.]

QUICKNOTES

EQUAL PROTECTION CLAUSE - A constitutional guarantee that no person should be denied the same protection of the laws enjoyed by other persons in like circumstances.

FUNDAMENTAL RIGHT - A liberty that is either expressly or impliedly provided for in the United States Constitution, the deprivation or burdening of which is subject to a heightened standard of review.

POLL TAX - A specific amount taxed to persons of a certain class living in a designated area.

KRAMER v. UNION FREE SCHOOL DISTRICT

Ineligible voter (P) v. School district (D)

395 U.S. 621 (1969).

NATURE OF CASE: Appeal from dismissal of a complaint to overturn voter eligibility requirements.

FACT SUMMARY: Kramer (P) claimed that Union's (D) School District voter eligibility requirements denied him equal protection of the laws.

CONCISE RULE OF LAW: Legal classifications must be tailored so that exclusion of a certain class of persons is necessary to achieve an articulated state goal.

FACTS: The New York Education Code provided that in certain school districts residents may vote in a school district election only if they or their spouse own or lease taxable real property within the district, or are parents or have custody of children enrolled in local public schools. Kramer (P), an unmarried man who neither owned nor leased taxable real property, argued that the voter eligibility requirements denied him equal protection. Union (D) argued that the state has a legitimate interest in limiting the right to vote in school district elections and may reasonably conclude that parents are those primarily interested in school affairs. A three-judge federal district court dismissed Kramer's (P) complaint, and he appealed.

ISSUE: Must legal classifications be tailored so that exclusion of a certain class of persons is necessary to achieve an articulated state goal?

HOLDING AND DECISION: (Warren, C.J.) Yes. Legal classifications must be tailored so that exclusion of a certain class of person is necessary to achieve an articulated state goal. As statutes distributing voting rights are at the foundation of representative society, any unjustified discrimination in who may vote undermines the legitimacy of representative government. Thus a statute which allows some to vote while prohibiting others must promote a compelling state interest to be valid. Assuming for purposes of argument that New York can limit the right to vote in school district elections to persons primarily interested in school affairs, that statute does not accomplish that goal. The statute excludes persons who have a distinct and direct interest in school affairs while it includes those whose interest is remote and indirect. Here, Kramer (P), who lives with his parents and pays state and federal taxes, cannot vote, while an unemployed man who pays no taxes, but who rents an apartment in the district, can vote. Reversed.

DISSENT: (Stewart, J.) The statute does not impinge on constitutionally protected rights "for the constitution of the United States does not confer the right of suffrage upon any one." Accordingly, the "compelling state interest" test should not have

been applied. The classification appeared to have been rationally related to a permissible legislative end and should have been upheld.

EDITOR'S ANALYSIS: It appears that the court will not be quick to sustain "interest" voting tests but will tend to uphold competency voting tests such as requirements based on age and sanity. It is not a denial of equal protection for the state to deny ex-convicts the right to vote. An interest classification that has been upheld involved only allowing landowners in a water storage district to vote. The district had a very limited purpose, *Salyer Land Co. v. Tulare Lake Basin Water Storage District,* 410 U.S. 719 (1973).

[For more information on voting qualifications, see Casenote Law Outline on Constitutional Law, Chapter 9, § II, Fundamental Rights and Equal Protection.]

QUICKNOTES

EQUAL PROTECTION CLAUSE - A constitutional guarantee that no person should be denied the same protection of the laws enjoyed by other persons in like circumstances.

NOTES:

REYNOLDS v. SIMS

Parties not identified.
377 U.S. 533 (1964.)

NATURE OF CASE: Appeal from a decision of a federal district court holding invalid the existing and two proposed plans for apportionment.

FACT SUMMARY: The federal district court held that the existing and two proposed plans for apportionment of seats in the Alabama legislature violated the Equal Protection Clause.

CONCISE RULE OF LAW: The Equal Protection Clause guarantees the opportunity for equal protection by all voters in the election of state legislators and requires that the seats in both houses of a bicameral state legislature must be apportioned on a population basis.

FACTS: The federal district court for the Middle District of Alabama held that the existing and two legislatively proposed plans for the apportionment of seats in the two Houses of the Alabama legislature violated the Equal Protection Clause. The court ordered into effect a temporary reapportionment plan comprised of part of the proposed plans.

ISSUE: Does the Equal Protection Clause require that seats in both houses of a bicameral state legislature be apportioned on a population basis?

HOLDING AND DECISION: (Warren, C.J.) Yes. Concededly, the basic aim of legislative apportionment is the achieving of fair and effective representation for all citizens. The Equal Protection Clause guarantees the opportunity for equal participation by all voters in the election of state legislators. Overweighting and overvaluation of the votes of persons living in one area has the effect of dilution and undervaluation of those living in another area. Diluting the weight of votes because of place of residence impairs basic constitutional rights under the Fourteenth Amendment, just as much as invidious discrimination based upon race. It is argued that the apportionment issue is a political one which the court should leave alone. However, a denial of constitutionally protected rights demands judicial protection. The weight of a citizen's vote cannot be made to depend on where he lives. The Equal Protection Clause requires that the seats in both houses of a bicameral state legislature must be apportioned on a population basis. Analogy to the federal system will not sustain a system not based on population. The federal system grew out of compromise and concession needed to band together states which formerly were independent. Political subdivisions of states (cities, counties) never were independent entities. The decision does not mean that the two bodies in a state legislature cannot consist of different constituencies, have different length terms, represent geographical districts of different sizes or be of different sizes. It does mean that in apportionment's overriding objective — whatever the method used — must be substantial equality of population among the various districts. Neither history, nor economics, nor other group interests, will justify disparity from population-based representation. One factor which could justify some deviation from such representation is political subdivisions. Decennial reapportionment would meet the requirement for reasonable currency. It will be for the federal courts to devise the particular remedies to be utilized in such cases. Here the action taken by the federal district court is affirmed.

DISSENT: (Harlan, J.) State legislative apportionments are wholly free of constitutional limitations save those imposed by the Republican Form of Government Clause (Article IV, § 4). This decision places basic aspects of state political systems under the overlordship of the federal judiciary, a move that is ill-advised and constitutionally impermissible.

DISSENT: (Stewart, J.) The Equal Protection Clause demands but two basic attributes of any state legislative apportionment plan. The plan must be a rational one, and it must not permit the systematic frustration of the will of a majority of the voters. Beyond this, there is nothing in the federal Constitution to prevent a state from choosing any electoral legislative plan it thinks best-suited to the interests, temper, and customs of its people.

EDITOR'S ANALYSIS: For many years, the Court refused jurisdiction of cases challenging the fairness of the representation in state legislatures, on the ground that the issue involved was a "political question." The Court abandoned this position in *Baker v. Carr* and ever since has held that the federal courts have the jurisdiction to determine the fairness and validity of state legislative apportionment plans. The result has been that a traditionally political question has become justiciable, and the courts have exerted what was traditionally deemed a legislative power in determining what is, and what is not, a fair plan of legislative apportionment.

[For more information on equal protection and voter dilution, see Casenote Law Outline on Constitutional Law, Chapter 9, § II, Fundamental Rights and Equal Protection.]

QUICKNOTES

APPORTIONMENT - The division of property costs in proportion to the parties' respective interests therein.

BICAMERALISM - The necessity of approval by a majority of both houses of Congress in ratifying legislation or approving other legislative action.

EQUAL PROTECTION CLAUSE - A constitutional guarantee that no person should be denied the same protection of the laws enjoyed by other persons in like circumstances.

INVIDIOUS DISCRIMINATION - Unequal treatment of a class of persons that is particularly malicious or hostile.

POLITICAL QUESTION - An issue that is more appropriately left to the determination of another governmental branch and which the court declines to hear.

REAPPORTIONMENT PLAN - The alteration of a voting districts' boundaries or composition to reflect the population of that district.

DAVIS v. BANDEMER
State (D) v. Democrats (P)
478 U.S. 109 (1986).

NATURE OF CASE: Review of a judgment sustaining an equal protection challenge to Indiana's 1981 state apportionment.

FACT SUMMARY: Democrats (P) challenged a state reapportionment plan that did not include exactly proportional representation.

CONCISE RULE OF LAW: When determining unconstitutional vote dilution, the challenging party must show a discriminatory vote dilution to make out a prima facie case.

FACTS: In 1981, the Republican-controlled state legislature of Indiana reapportioned the state. The districts were of roughly equal population. The plan was apparently drafted without much debate due to the limited amount of information available to voting politicians. In the next election, Democrats (P) won majority popular votes but received less than half of the seats in the house and senate. The Democrats (P) then filed suit. The district court found that both discriminatory intent and actual discrimination had been proven. The decision was appealed.

ISSUE: When determining unconstitutional vote dilution, must the challenging party show a discriminatory vote dilution to make out a prima facie case?

HOLDING AND DECISION: (White, J.) Yes. When determining unconstitutional vote dilution, the challenging party must show a discriminatory vote dilution to make out a prima facie case. The Constitution mandates one-person, one-vote. However, there is no requirement that all districts in a voting region have mathematically equivalent proportional representations of the various voting populations. Here, a single election was used as evidence of an equal protection voting violation. But it would be next to impossible to conclude that actual discrimination had occurred after a single election. Since there is no requirement that districts contain populations exactly proportional to the total population, the election result will most likely vary from the total popular vote. Furthermore it would be a difficult task to ascertain how to apportion districts to even achieve exactly proportional representation of all population groups. Reversed.

DISSENT: (Powell, J.) An analysis should be used that focuses upon whether voting districts have been deliberately distorted and are arbitrary. The shape of districts is very telling when searching for an improper purpose in reapportionment. Other relevant considerations include legislative goals and procedures, evidence concerning population disparities, and statistics showing vote dilution.

EDITOR'S ANALYSIS: Commentators have suggested that the Court opened a can of worms when it agreed that there was even a justiciable issue on the question of whether political parties deserved protection from discriminatory reapportionment. Traditionally, the focus was on protecting racial minorities. This case added yet another factor to complicate the reapportionment picture.

[For more information on voting rights and equal protection, see Casenote Law Outline on Constitutional Law, Chapter 9, § II, Fundamental Rights and Equal Protection.]

QUICKNOTES

PRIMA FACIE CASE - An action where the plaintiff introduces sufficient evidence to submit the issue to the judge or jury for determination.

PROPORTIONAL REPRESENTATION - An election method designed to permit the proportional representation of minority gorup interests.

REAPPORTIONMENT PLAN - The alteration of a voting districts' boundaries or composition to reflect the population of that district.

NOTES:

SAN ANTONIO IND. SCHOOL DIST. v. RODRIGUEZ
School district (D) v. Students (P)
411 U.S. 1 (1973).

NATURE OF CASE: Class action to declare state educational funding plan unconstitutional.

FACT SUMMARY: The Texas state educational system was partially funded through the use of local property taxes resulting in a lower per-pupil expenditure in the poorer school districts. This system was challenged as a denial of equal protection to those students who resided in the poorer districts.

CONCISE RULE OF LAW: Education is not a fundamental right, and students who live in school districts with a lower property tax base do not constitute a suspect classification, so a school financing system is not subject to strict standard of judicial review on an equal protection challenge to the financing system.

FACTS: Public elementary schools in Texas were funded by a combination of state and district contributions. Each district supplemented the state contribution to education by a property tax on property within the district. This system resulted in significant disparities in per-pupil expenditures among the various districts which resulted from the difference in taxable property values in the district: the richer districts spent up to $594 per pupil, and the poorer districts spent $356. Rodriguez (P) was the parent of a child in a district with a low per-pupil expenditure and brought a class action suit on behalf of all children similarly situated. Rodriguez (P) alleged that the state's reliance on property tax to finance education favored the more affluent districts and therefore violated the Equal Protection Clause because of the disparities in expenditures. Rodriguez (P) further alleged that this discrimination on the basis of wealth is a suspect classification and that education is a fundamental right, requiring a strict standard of judicial review.

ISSUE: Is this a proper case to examine the state's action under a strict standard of judicial review either because the action discriminated against a suspect class or interfered with a fundamental right?

HOLDING AND DECISION: (Powell, J.) No. The strict scrutiny standard is not appropriate in this case because it involves neither a suspect classification nor a fundamental right, and the state system does not violate the Equal Protection Clause because it bears a rational relationship to a legitimate state interest. The system does not disadvantage a suspect class because there is no definable class of "poor" people that are discriminated against. The poorest families are not necessarily residents of the poorest property tax districts. The system does not result in an absolute deprivation of a desired benefit because

all students in Texas get an adequate education despite the differences in per-pupil expenditures. Education is not a fundamental right. The fundamental nature of a right is established only if that right is explicitly or implicitly guaranteed by the Constitution. Rodriguez (P) argues that education is guaranteed because it is a necessary prerequisite to the exercise of other constitutionally protected rights, such as the right to free speech. This "nexus" theory is unacceptable because it is unlimited in scope. Even if it were assumed that education is constitutionally protected because it is a prerequisite to other rights, there is no evidence that the level of education given to the students in the poorer district falls short of the minimum education that would be required. Additionally, this is an inappropriate case for the use of a strict judicial scrutiny test because it is an attack on state expenditure of taxes, a field in which the court, because of its lack of expertise, has traditionally deferred to state legislative judgments. It also involves considerations of educational policy, another area in which the court should not interfere because of its lack of experience. The Texas system is, then, not a violation of the Equal Protection Clause because it does bear a rational relationship to a legitimate state purpose. Although the system may be imperfect and result in some inequalities, the financing system is not so irrational as to constitute invidious discrimination. Such a financing system is common practice among the states, and suggested alternatives to this system are untested.

CONCURRENCE: (Stewart, J.) All laws have some measure of discriminatory treatment. The Equal Protection Clause is used only to test the validity of classifications created by state laws, and, unless a fundamental right or suspect classification is involved, the Clause is violated only by classifications that are wholly arbitrary or capricious.

DISSENT: (White, Douglas, Brennan, JJ.) In this case, the means chosen to further a permissible state goal, local control of education, are not rationally related to that goal. The state must establish a financing system which provides a rational basis for encouraging local control and not the current system which gives unequal treatment to groups which are determined on the basis of criteria wholly unrelated to that goal.

DISSENT: (Marshall, Douglas, JJ.) Rather than dividing all cases into either strict scrutiny or rational basis test, the court should adopt a sliding scale approach to testing violations of the Equal Protection Clause based on the constitutional and societal importance of the affected interest and the invidiousness of the basis on which the state has drawn the classification. The fundamental nature of a right is not entirely derived from the face of the Constitution, but the proper question is the extent to which constitutionally protected rights are dependent on interests not verbalized in the Constitution. As the connection between the two increases, the unarticulated interests become more fundamental and the level of judicial scrutiny increases. On this basis education is a fundamental right because of the close relationship between education and other constitutionally protected rights such as freedom of speech and the right to vote. Past cases have shown that the court will carefully scrutinize discriminations based on wealth. Here, a careful scrutiny of the asserted state interest in local control of education shows that this interest is offered merely as an excuse for interdistrict inequality. Therefore, the financing system is a violation of the Equal Protection Clause.

EDITOR'S ANALYSIS: Under the holding of this case, no right or interest is considered fundamental, requiring strict judicial review under the Equal Protection Clause, unless that right is explicitly or implicitly guaranteed by the Constitution. Education is not a fundamental interest because it is not so protected, and the court also holds that wealth is not a suspect classification. Since the strict standard is not required, the classification will be upheld if it has a rational relationship to a legitimate state interest and is not invidiously discriminatory, a test that is very easy for the state to meet. This case clearly indicates that the current court will not extend the fundamental right and suspect classification analysis beyond the traditionally well-established categories, such as classification based on race.

[For more information on education not constituting a fundamental right, see Casenote Law Outline on Constitutional Law, Chapter 9, § II, Fundamental Rights and Equal Protection.]

QUICKNOTES

EQUAL PROTECTION CLAUSE - A constitutional guarantee that no person should be denied the same protection of the laws enjoyed by other persons in like circumstances.

FUNDAMENTAL RIGHT - A liberty that is either expressly or impliedly provided for in the United States Constitution, the deprivation or burdening of which is subject to a heightened standard of review.

INVIDIOUS DISCRIMINATION - Unequal treatment of a class of persons that is particularly malicious or hostile.

RATIONAL BASIS TEST - A test employed by the court to determine the validity of a statute in equal protection actions, whereby the court determines whether the challenged statute is rationally related to the achievement of a legitimate state interest

STRICT SCRUTINY - Method by which courts determine the constitutionality of a law, when a law affects a fundamental right. Under the test, the legislature must have a compelling interest to enact law and measures prescribed by the law must be the least restrictive means possible to accomplish goal.

SUSPECT CLASSIFICATION - A class of persons that have historically been subject to discriminatory treatment; statutes drawing a distinction between persons based on a suspect classification, i.e. race, nationality or alienage, are subject to a strict scrutiny standard of review.

NOTES:

SHAW v. RENO
Voters (P) v. State (D)
509 U.S. 630, 113 S. Ct. 630 (1993).

NATURE OF CASE: Appeal of dismissal of action challenging a congressional redistricting plan.

FACT SUMMARY: Shaw (P) alleged that a North Carolina reapportionment plan that included one majority-black district with boundary lines of dramatically irregular shape constituted unconstitutional racial gerrymandering.

CONCISE RULE OF LAW: An allegation that a reapportionment scheme is so irrational on its face that it can be understood only as an effort to segregate voters based on race without sufficient justification states a cognizable claim under the Fourteenth Amendment.

FACTS: North Carolina, after becoming entitled to a twelfth seat in the U.S. House of Representatives as a result of the 1990 census, enacted a reapportionment plan that included one majority-black district with boundary lines of dramatically irregular shape. Shaw (P), on behalf of a number of voters, sued, alleging the creation of the irregular district was unconstitutional racial gerrymandering under the Fourteenth Amendment. The district court dismissed the action for failure to state a cognizable claim. Shaw (P) appealed to the Supreme Court.

ISSUE: Does an allegation that a reapportionment scheme is so irrational on its face that it can be understood only as an effort to segregate voters based on race without sufficient justification state a cognizable claim under the Fourteenth Amendment?

HOLDING AND DECISION: (O'Connor, J.) Yes. An allegation that a reapportionment scheme is so irrational on its face that it can be understood only as an effort to segregate voters based on race without sufficient justification states a cognizable claim under the Fourteenth Amendment. The Fourteenth Amendment requires that legislation which is unexplainable on grounds other than race be narrowly tailored to further a compelling governmental interest, even if facially race-neutral. An example of such unexplainable legislation would be a reapportionment plan so highly irregular on its face that it rationally cannot be understood as anything other than an effort to segregate voters on the basis of race. Such a plan perpetuates impermissible racial stereotypes by reinforcing the perception that members of the same racial group, regardless of age or economic status, share the same political ideology. Shaw's (P) complaint alleged that the North Carolina plan was such a plan and thus stated a cognizable claim. The case of *United Jewish Organizations of Williamsburgh, Inc. v. Carey*, 430 U.S. 144 (1977) is distinguishable: there a claim by a Hasidic community split between two districts under a reapportionment plan was not upheld because the plaintiffs did not make the kind of claim made here and was therefore not controlling. Reversed.

DISSENT: (White, J.) Shaw (P) failed to state a claim because no cognizable injury was alleged. There is neither an outright deprivation of the right to vote nor a demonstration that the challenged action had the intent and effect of unduly diminishing a group's influence on the political process.

DISSENT: (Stevens, J.) The Equal Protection Clause prohibits states from creating bizarre district boundaries such as the one at issue for the sole purpose of making it more difficult for members of a minority group to win an election. However, it does not prohibit gerrymandering when the majority acts to facilitate the election of a member of a group that lacks power because it remains underrepresented in the state legislature.

DISSENT: (Souter, J.) There is no justification for treating the narrow category of bizarrely shaped district claims differently from other districting claims.

EDITOR'S ANALYSIS: Though the holding of Shaw is limited, the Court spoke extensively in dicta about what constituted sufficient justification for race-based districting. If on remand a plan were found to be in fact racial gerrymandering, the plan must then be found narrowly tailored to further a compelling governmental interest. This high level of scrutiny is imposed because the Court believes racial classifications with respect to voting rights "carry particular dangers" such as "Balkanizing" citizens into competing racial factions, thus moving the country away from the goal of a political system in which race is irrelevant. In the Shaw case, the challenged district was unusually long and narrow and ran along an interstate. One pundit suggested that if a driver on the interstate opened his car doors, he would risk running over every voter in the district.

[For more information on gerrymander, see Casenote Law Outline on Constitutional Law, Chapter 9, § II, Fundamental Rights and Equal Protection.]

QUICKNOTES

FOURTEENTH AMENDMENT - Declares that no state shall make or enforce any law which shall abridge the privileges and immunities of citizens of the United States.

GERRYMANDER - The designation of voting districts in a geographic area to provide unfair advantage to one political party over another.

REAPPORTIONMENT PLAN - The alteration of a voting districts' boundaries or composition to reflect the population of that district.

M.L.B v. S.L.J.

Mother (P) v. State (D)

519 U.S. 102, 117 S. Ct. 555 (1996).

NATURE OF CASE: Appeal from decree terminating parental rights.

FACT SUMMARY: A Mississippi court dismissed M.L.B.'s (P) appeal of the termination of her parental rights to her two minor children when she was unable to pay the required record preparation fees.

CONCISE RULE OF LAW: A state may not condition appeals from trial court decrees terminating parental rights on the affected parent's ability to pay record preparation fees.

FACTS: A Mississippi court ordered M.L.B.'s (P) parental rights to her two minor children terminated. M.L.B. (P) sought to appeal the termination decree, but the state required that she pay in advance over $2,000 in record preparation fees. Because M.L.B. (P) did not have the money to pay the fees, her appeal was dismissed. The Supreme Court granted certiorari to determine whether the Due Process and Equal Protection Clauses of the Fourteenth Amendment permitted such appeals to be conditioned on the ability to pay certain fees.

ISSUE: May a state condition appeals from trial court decrees terminating parental rights on the affected parent's ability to pay record preparation fees?

HOLDING AND DECISION: (Ginsburg, J.) No. A state may not condition appeals from trial court decrees terminating parental rights on the affected parent's ability to pay record preparation fees. Fee requirements are generally examined only for their rationality. While the Court has not prohibited state controls on every type of civil action, it has consistently distinguished those involving intrusions on family relationships. However, the stakes for M.L.B. (P), i.e., the forced dissolution of her parental rights, are far greater than any monetary loss. Mississippi's interest, on the other hand, in offsetting the costs on its court system, is purely financial. Decrees forever terminating parental rights fit in the category of cases in which a state may not "bolt the door to equal justice." Reversed.

DISSENT: (Thomas, J.) The majority's new-found constitutional right to free transcripts in civil appeals cannot be effectively restricted to this case. M.L.B. (P) requested relief under both the Due Process and Equal Protection Clauses, yet the majority does not specify the source of relief it has granted. Mississippi's transcript rule reasonably obliges all potential appellants to bear the cost of availing themselves of a service that the state is not constitutionally required to provide. The Equal Protection Clause is not a panacea for all perceived social and economic inequity.

EDITOR'S ANALYSIS: While the majority's rationale in granting M.L.B. (P) relief may have been vaguely articulated, as the dissent has alleged, it would seem that the issues at stake here go beyond simple textual analysis. It is not merely M.L.B.'s (P) rights that must be considered, but the impact that the termination of those rights will have on her two minor children. It will likely not be as great of a problem as the dissent suggests to limit the application of this holding to similarly situated parents.

[For more information on fundamental rights and equal protection, see Casenote Law Outline on Constitutional Law, Chapter 9, § II, Fundamental Rights and Equal Protection.]

QUICKNOTES

CERTIORARI - A discretionary writ issued by a superior court to an inferior court in order to review the lower court's decisions; the Supreme Court's writ ordering such review.

DUE PROCESS CLAUSE - Clauses found in the Fifth and Fourteenth Amendments to the United States Constitution providing that no person shall be deprived of "life, liberty, or property, without due process of law."

EQUAL PROTECTION CLAUSE - A constitutional guarantee that no person should be denied the same protection of the laws enjoyed by other persons in like circumstances.

FUNDAMENTAL RIGHT - A liberty that is either expressly or impliedly provided for in the United States Constitution, the deprivation or burdening of which is subject to a heightened standard of review.

NOTES:

10

CHAPTER 10
THE POST-CIVIL WAR AMENDMENTS AND CIVIL RIGHTS LEGISLATION: CONSTITUTIONAL RESTRAINTS ON PRIVATE CONDUCT; CONGRESSIONAL POWER TO IMPLEMENT THE AMENDMENTS

QUICK REFERENCE RULES OF LAW

1. **The Problem of State Action.** The Fourteenth Amendment does not reach private acts of discrimination but encompasses only state action which is discriminatory. (Civil Rights Cases)

   [For more information on state action requirement, see Casenote Law Outline on Constitutional Law, Chapter 10, § I, State Action.]

2. **Significant State "Involvement."** Judicial enforcement of a private racially restrictive covenant is considered state action for Fourteenth Amendment purposes. (Shelly v. Kraemer)

   [For more information on state action through judicial enforcement, see Casenote Law Outline on Constitutional Law, Chapter 10, § I, State Action.]

3. **Significant State "Involvement."** Racial discrimination by a business, which is located in and constitutes part of a state-owned public facility, is considered to be state action and is forbidden by the Fourteenth Amendment. (Burton v. Wilmington Parking Authority)

   [For more information on state action through partnership, sponsorship, or association, see Casenote Law Outline on Constitutional Law, Chapter 10, State Action and Congressional Authority to Reach Private Action to Protect Civil Rights, § I, State Action.]

4. **Significant State "Involvement."** Evidence showing a heavily regulated private utility, enjoying at least a partial monopoly in the providing of electrical service, which elected to terminate service to a customer in a manner found by the state public utilities commission to be permissible under state law, does not demonstrate a sufficiently close nexus between the state and the utility's action to make that action state action. (Jackson v. Metropolitan Edison Co.)

   [For more information on state action through the undertaking of public functions, see Casenote Law Outline on Constitutional Law, Chapter 10, § I, State Action.]

5. **Congressional Power to Reach Private Interferences With Constitutional Rights.** The Enabling Clause of the Fourteenth Amendment permits Congress to reach private action (e.g., conspiracy) which abridges Fourteenth Amendment rights if and only if some active state involvement in such action is also present, but the right of travel is a right so fundamental to the concept of federal union that Congress has an inherent power to reach private action which abridges it independently. (United States v. Guest)

   [For more information on conspiracies against the rights of citizens, see Casenote Law Outline on Constitutional Law, Chapter 10, § II, Congressional Authority to Reach Private Action Infringing Civil Rights.]

6. **Congressional Power to Reach Private Conduct Under the 13th Amendment.** Congress, pursuant to the authority vested in it by the Thirteenth Amendment which clothes "Congress with power to pass all laws necessary and proper for abolishing all badges and incidents of slavery, may validly bar all racial discrimination, private as well as public, in the sale or rental of property." (Jones v. Alfred H. Mayer Co.)

[For more information on the Thirteenth Amendment congressional power to prohibit private discrimination in housing, see Casenote Law Outline on Constitutional Law, Chapter 10, § II, Congressional Authority to Reach Private Action Infringing Civil Rights.]

7. **Congressional Protection of Voting Rights.** A federal statute enacted pursuant to the Enabling Clause of the Fourteenth Amendment supersedes any state constitutional or statutory provision which is in conflict with the federal law. (Katzenbach v. Morgan)

    [For more information on the Morgan theory, see Casenote Law Outline on Constitutional Law, Chapter 10, § II, Congressional Authority to Reach Private Action Infringing Civil Rights.]

8. **Confinement of Congress's Civil Rights Enforcement Power to "Proportional" and "Congruent" Remedies.** The RFRA unconstitutionally exceeds Congress's enforcement power under the Due Process Clause of the Fourteenth Amendment. (City of Boerne v. Flores)

    [For more information on scope of congressional power to redefine amendments, see Casenote Law Outline on Constitutional Law, Chapter 10, § II, Congressional Authority to Reach Private Action Infringing Civil Rights.]

9. **Confinement of Congress's Civil Rights Enforcement Power to "Proportional" and "Congruent" Remedies.** Section 13891 of the Violence Against Women Act may not be upheld as an exercise of Congress' remedial power under § 5 of the Fourteenth Amendment. (United States v. Morrison)

    [For more information on the exercise of congress's remedial power, see Casenote Law Outline on Constitutional Law, Chapter 10, § II, Congressional Authority to Reach Private Action Infringing Civil Rights.]

CIVIL RIGHTS CASES
Citizens (P) v. Federal government (D)
109 U.S. 3 (1883).

NATURE OF CASE: Actions challenging the constitutionality of § 1 of the Civil Rights Act of 1875.

FACT SUMMARY: Private citizens of five states who had suffered either criminal indictments or civil penalty actions for violating § 1 of the Civil Rights Act of 1875 challenged its constitutionality.

CONCISE RULE OF LAW: The Fourteenth Amendment does not reach private acts of discrimination but encompasses only state action which is discriminatory.

FACTS: In § 1 of the Civil Rights Act of 1875, Congress provided that all persons were entitled to full and equal enjoyment of accommodations provided by public inns, public conveyances on land or water, theaters, and other places of public amusement, regardless of race. The statute went on to provide that violation of its provisions was a misdemeanor and also declared that aggrieved persons could recover $500 "for every such offense." Five individuals, private citizens, who had excluded blacks from such facilities, challenged the constitutionality of the law and their indictments or fines.

ISSUE: Can the Fourteenth Amendment reach private acts of discrimination?

HOLDING AND DECISION: (Bradley, J.) No. The Fourteenth Amendment does not reach private acts of discrimination but encompasses only state action which is discriminatory. Since the Fourteenth Amendment is concerned with prohibiting certain types of state laws and actions, it cannot reach private acts of discrimination such as occurred in these cases. Thus, it gives Congress no power to enact laws reaching private acts of discrimination, as this law attempts to do. While the Thirteenth Amendment does reach private as well as state actions, it gives Congress power to deal only with problems of involuntary servitude and not mere racial discrimination. Thus, the challenged law is unconstitutional.

DISSENT: (Harlan, J.) The Thirteenth Amendment was designed to destroy any and all burdens and disabilities constituting badges of slavery and servitude, such as racial discrimination, and not just the institution of slavery. Furthermore, the Fourteenth Amendment affirmatively establishes the citizenship of all persons born or naturalized in the United States and is thus not limited to prohibiting certain state actions. Even if it were, railroads, inns, and public places of amusement can be seen as agents of the state whose actions are reachable anyway.

EDITOR'S ANALYSIS: Although the Court would probably reach the opposite result were this case decided today, it continues to hold to the position that the Fourteenth Amendment can reach only state action and not private discrimination. The difference is that the Court has changed its concept of state action to include private actions attributable to the state through agency theories, etc.

[For more information on state action requirement, see Casenote Law Outline on Constitutional Law, Chapter 10, § I, State Action.]

QUICKNOTES
DISCRIMINATION - Unequal treatment of a class of persons.

STATE ACTION - Actions brought pursuant to the Fourteenth Amendment claiming that the government violated the plaintiff's civil rights.

NOTES:

SHELLEY v. KRAEMER
Purchaser (D) v. Property owner (P)
334 U.S. 1 (1948).

NATURE OF CASE: Action to enforce a restrictive covenant in the sale of real property.

FACT SUMMARY: Kraemer (P) sought to void a sale of real property to Shelley (D) from a Mr. Fitzgerald, relying on a racially restrictive covenant.

CONCISE RULE OF LAW: Judicial enforcement of a private racially restrictive covenant is considered state action for Fourteenth Amendment purposes.

FACTS: On February 16, 1911, 30 out of a total of 39 owners of property fronting both sides of Labadie Avenue between Taylor Avenue and Cora Avenue in St. Louis signed an agreement, which was subsequently recorded, providing in part that the property could not be used or occupied by anyone of the Negro or Mongolian race for a period of 50 years. This covenant was to be valid whether it was included in future conveyances or not and was to attach to the land as a condition precedent to the sale of the property. On August 11, 1945, Shelley (D), a Negro, purchased a parcel of land subject to the restrictive covenant from a Mr. Fitzgerald. Shelley (D) did not have any actual knowledge of the restrictive agreement at the time of the purchase. On October 9, 1945, Kraemer (P), an owner of other property subject to the terms of the restrictive covenant, brought suit in the circuit court of St. Louis to enjoin Shelley (D) from taking possession of the property and to divest title from Shelley (D) and revest title in Fitzgerald or in such person as the court should direct. The trial court held for Shelley (D), but on appeal the supreme court of Missouri reversed their decision. Shelley (D) contended that the restrictive covenant violated the Equal Protection Clause of the Fourteenth Amendment. Kraemer (P) contended that no state action was involved in the private restrictive covenant, and even if there were state action, the courts would enforce a restrictive covenant barring whites from purchasing certain land and so there was equal protection of the law. He further contended that if he was not allowed to enforce the covenant he would be denied equal protection of the law.

ISSUE: Does the Equal Protection Clause of the Fourteenth Amendment prevent judicial enforcement by state courts of restrictive covenants based on race or color?

HOLDING AND DECISION: (Vinson, C.J.) Yes. Judicial enforcement of a private racially restrictive covenant is considered state action for Fourteenth Amendment purposes. Because the restrictive covenants did not involve any action by the state legislature or City Council, the restrictive covenant itself did not violate any rights protected by the Fourteenth Amendment, since it was strictly a private covenant. But the judicial enforcement of the covenant did qualify as state action.

From the time of the adoption of the Fourteenth Amendment until the present, the court has consistently ruled that the action of the states to which the amendment has reference includes action of state courts and state judicial officers. In this case because there was a willing buyer and seller, Shelley (D) would have been able to enforce the restrictive covenants only with the active intervention of the state courts. The court rejected Kraemer's (P) argument that since the state courts would enforce restrictive covenants excluding white persons from ownership of property there was no denial of equal protection. The court stated that equal protection of the law is not achieved through indiscriminate imposition of inequalities. As to Kraemer's (P) contention that he was being denied equal protection of the laws because his restrictive covenant was not being enforced, the court stated that the Constitution does not confer the right to demand action by the state that would result in the denial of equal protection of the laws to other individuals. Therefore, in granting judicial enforcement of the restrictive agreement, the state has denied Shelley (D) equal protection of the laws and the action of the state courts cannot stand. The court noted that the enjoyment of property rights, free from discrimination by the states, was among the objectives sought to be effectuated by the framers of the Fourteenth Amendment.

EDITOR'S ANALYSIS: The Court in its post-*Shelley v. Kraemer* decisions has given this decision a fairly narrow reading. A broad reading of this case requires that whenever a state court enforces a private racial restrictive covenant that such action constitutes state action which is forbidden by the Fourteenth Amendment. In cases where the ruling in this case could have been found to be applicable, the Court has used a different rationale. Some of the Court's statements suggest that more state involvement than evenhanded enforcement of private biases was necessary to find unconstitutional state action. Justice Black, in a dissenting opinion, stated that the decision in this case is applicable only in cases involving property rights.

[For more information on state action through judicial enforcement, see Casenote Law Outline on Constitutional Law, Chapter 10, § I, State Action.]

QUICKNOTES

EQUAL PROTECTION - A constitutional guarantee that no person shall be denied the same protection of the laws enjoyed by other persons in like circumstances.

RESTRICTIVE COVENANT - A promise contained in a deed to limit the uses to which the property will be made.

STATE ACTION - Actions brought pursuant to the Fourteenth Amendment claiming that the government violated the plaintiff's civil rights.

BURTON v. WILMINGTON PARKING AUTHORITY

Negro customer (P) v. Municipal authority (D)

365 U.S. 715 (1961).

NATURE OF CASE: Action seeking declaratory and injunctive relief for racial discrimination.

FACT SUMMARY: Wilmington Parking Authority (D) leased space in a parking facility to Eagle Coffee Shoppe for use as a restaurant, and they refused to serve Burton (P), a Negro.

CONCISE RULE OF LAW: Racial discrimination by a business, which is located in and constitutes part of a state-owned public facility, is considered to be state action and is forbidden by the Fourteenth Amendment.

FACTS: Wilmington Parking Authority (D) was going to erect a public parking facility, but before it started construction it was advised that the anticipated revenue from the parking of cars and proceeds from the sale of its bonds would not be sufficient to finance the construction costs of the facility. To secure additional capital, the Authority (D) decided to enter into long-term leases with responsible tenants for commercial use of some of the space available in the projected garage building. A 20-year lease was entered into with Eagle Coffee Shoppe, Inc. for a space to be used as a restaurant. Even though the Authority (D) had the power to adopt rules and regulations requiring that the restaurant services be made available to the general public, the lease contained no such requirement of Eagle Coffee Shoppe. Under a Delaware statute, Eagle Coffee Shoppe was classified as a restaurant and not an inn and, therefore, was not required to serve all persons entering their shop. Burton (P) attempted to enter the restaurant but was refused service because he was a Negro. As a result, Burton (P) filed an action seeking declaratory and injunctive relief against Wilmington Parking Authority (D) claiming that as the restaurant was the Authority's (D) lessee, and the Authority (D) was an agency of the state, that the discrimination was therefore state action. However, the Supreme Court of Delaware held that Eagle was acting in a purely private capacity under its lease and that the action was not that of the Authority (D) and was not, therefore, state action. The court based its conclusion on the fact that only 15% of the total cost of the facility was advanced from public funds and that the revenue from parking was only 30.5% of the total income. Eagle had expended considerable amounts of its own funds on furnishings and there was no public entrance direct from the parking area. The only connection Eagle had with the public facility was the payment of $28,700 in rent annually. The decision was appealed to the Supreme Court.

ISSUE: Is racial discrimination by a business which leases facilities from the state considered to be state action?

HOLDING AND DECISION: (Clark, J.) Yes. The Court held that the restaurant was so closely tied in with the Parking Authority (D) that the discriminatory action by the restaurant was considered to be state action. The Court pointed out that the land and building were publicly owned and that the costs of land acquisition, construction, and maintenance were defrayed entirely from donations by the City of Wilmington from loans and revenue bonds, and from the proceeds of rentals and parking services out of which the loans and bonds were payable. The Court didn't feel that the figures used by the Delaware Supreme Court were very accurate. The Court also noted that the restaurant operated as an integral part of a public building devoted to a public parking service and that part of the facility was open to the public while in another part Negroes were refused service. The fact that the Parking Authority (D) didn't require in the lease that the restaurant be open to the public doesn't allow the restaurant to discriminate against Negroes with impunity. By its inaction, the Authority (D), and through it the state, made itself a party to the refusal of service. Because of the financial interdependence between the Authority (D) and the restaurant, and because of the physical relation of the facility, the discriminatory action by the restaurant cannot be considered purely private action. The Court also pointed out that it is impossible for the Court to create a formula by which it can be determined what is state action. It is necessary to look at the facts in each case in order to determine if state action is involved. Reversed and remanded.

CONCURRENCE: (Stewart, J.) The Court's decision could have been reached by a more direct route. The statute which permits a restaurant to refuse service to individuals with impunity has been construed by the Delaware Supreme Court to authorize racial discrimination. As such, the statute itself should have been declared unconstitutional.

DISSENT: (Harlan, J.) The majority did not define what the requirements were for a finding of state action other than to piece together various factual tidbits. But, beyond that, it is not clear on what basis the Delaware Supreme Court's decision rested. If their decision interpreted the statute as authorizing racial discrimination, it was clearly unconstitutional. If, on the other hand, their decision merely reaffirmed the common-law right of a business to serve only when it pleases, then, and only then, would the "state action" issue be squarely before this Court.

EDITOR'S ANALYSIS: As Justice Stewart pointed out in his dissent, the Court, in this case did not clearly define the requirements for a finding of state action. In subsequent cases, however, it became clearer that the critical factor in the *Burton* case was the leasing of public property to a private enterprise for its exclusive use. The City of Montgomery, Alabama, rented or granted the exclusive use of certain public recreation areas to private groups that practiced racial discrimination. The Court found no difficulty in invalidating this practice. But a more troublesome problem was presented by the grant of nonexclusive permits to such groups. A case involving such nonexclusive use was remanded for further findings on how much restriction was placed on free public access by these nonexclusive permits. Finally, in *Moose Lodge v. Irvis*, 407 U.S. 163 (1972), the court found that the granting of a liquor license to a private fraternal organization which discriminated was not sufficient state action to involve the Equal Protection Clause.

[For more information on state action through partnership, sponsorship, or association, see Casenote Law Outline on Constitutional Law, Chapter 10, § I, State Action.]

QUICKNOTES

DECLARATORY RELIEF - A judgment of the rights between opposing parties that does not grant coercive relief (i.e. damages,) but is binding.

EQUAL PROTECTION CLAUSE - A constitutional guarantee that no person should be denied the same protection of the laws enjoyed by other persons in like circumstances.

INJUNCTIVE RELIEF - A court order requiring a person to do, or prohibiting that person from doing, a specific act.

RACIAL DISCRIMINATION - Unequal treatment of a class of persons based on their racial identity.

STATE ACTION - Activity where the state is involved sufficiently enough to permit protection under due process.

NOTES:

JACKSON v. METROPOLITAN EDISON CO.

Customer (P) v. Utility company (D)

419 U.S. 345 (1974).

NATURE OF CASE: Federal civil rights action under 42 U.S.C. § 1983.

FACT SUMMARY: Jackson (P) claimed that Metropolitan's (D) (a privately owned utility company) action in terminating service to her for nonpayment without notice, a hearing, or an opportunity to pay, constituted state action and violated due process.

CONCISE RULE OF LAW: Evidence showing a heavily regulated private utility, enjoying at least a partial monopoly in the providing of electrical service, which elected to terminate service to a customer in a manner found by the state public utilities commission to be permissible under state law, does not demonstrate a sufficiently close nexus between the state and the utility's action to make that action state action.

FACTS: Metropolitan (D) is a privately owned utility which holds a certificate of public convenience issued by the state public utilities commission, empowering it to deliver electricity. It has filed a general tariff with the commission, a provision of which states Metropolitan's (D) right to terminate electricity to a user for nonpayment. Metropolitan (D) terminated Jackson's (P) electric service for nonpayment. She claims that this constituted state action and because it was done without notice, a hearing, or opportunity to pay, such action deprived her of her property (her alleged right to reasonably continuous electrical service) without due process.

ISSUE: Where a heavily regulated public utility, which enjoys at least a partial monopoly, elects to terminate service to a customer in a manner found by the state public utilities commission to be permissible under state law, does such termination constitute state action?

HOLDING AND DECISION: (Rehnquist, J.) No. Evidence showing a heavily regulated private utility, enjoying at least a partial monopoly in the providing of electrical service, which elected to terminate service to a customer in a manner found by the state public utilities commission to be permissible under state law, does not demonstrate a sufficiently close nexus between the state and the utility's action to make that action state action. The mere fact that a business is subject to detailed and extensive state regulation does not convert its action into state action. Nor does the fact that it enjoys a monopoly make its action state action. It's true that Metropolitan's (D) services affect the public interest. However, the actions of all businesses which affect the public interest cannot be called state action. Metropolitan (D) is not performing a public function since state law imposes no obligation on the state to furnish utility service. Finally, the state public utilities commission's approval of Metropolitan's (D) tariff merely constituted a finding by the commission that Metropolitan's (D) termination procedure was permissible under state law. It did not convert Metropolitan's (D) actions into state actions. Hence, the evidence did not demonstrate a sufficiently close nexus between the state and Metropolitan's (D) action so that Metropolitan's (D) termination of services may be treated as state action.

DISSENT: (Douglas, J.) The proper question in a state action case is whether the aggregate of all relevant factors compels a finding of state involvement, not whether any single factor supports such a finding. Where the evidence shows a monopoly providing essential public services subject to state power to regulate, the monopoly's actions are sufficiently intertwined with the state to make its action state action.

DISSENT: (Marshall, J.) State authorization and approval of "private" conduct supports a finding of state action. The majority's analysis would seem to apply as well to a company which refused service to blacks, welfare recipients, or any other group. I cannot believe this court would hold that the state's involvement with Metropolitan (D) was not sufficient to require that it not discriminate. However, nothing in the majority's analysis suggests otherwise.

EDITOR'S ANALYSIS: In *Moose Lodge v. Irvis*, 407 U.S. 163 (1972), the lodge refused service to a black guest of a lodge member. The guest claimed that although the lodge was a private club, its action was unconstitutional because it held a state liquor license. The Court held that the state was not sufficiently implicated in the lodge's discriminatory policies to make its action state action. The dissent argued that the "state was putting the weight of its liquor license, concededly a valued and important adjunct to a private club, behind racial discrimination."

[For more information on state action through the undertaking of public functions, see Casenote Law Outline on Constitutional Law, Chapter 10, § I, State Action.]

QUICKNOTES

MONOPOLY - A privilege or right conferred upon an individual or entity granting it the exclusive power to manufacture, sell and distribute a particular service or commodity; a market condition in which one or a few companies control the sale of a product or service thereby restraining competition in respect to that article or service.

PRIVATE FIGURES/CITIZENS - An individual that does not hold a public office or that is not a member of the armed forces.

PUBLIC UTILITY - A private business that provides a service to the public which is of need.

STATE ACTION - Activity where the state is involved sufficiently enough to permit protection under due process.

TARIFF - A duty or fee paid when articles are imported into the United States.

UNITED STATES v. GUEST

Federal government (P) v. Conspirators (D)
383 U.S. 745 (1966).

NATURE OF CASE: Appeal of dismissal of civil rights law indictment.

FACT SUMMARY: Guest (D) and others were charged with violating various civil rights of Georgia Negroes.

CONCISE RULE OF LAW: The Enabling Clause of the Fourteenth Amendment permits Congress to reach private action (e.g., conspiracy) which abridges Fourteenth Amendment rights if and only if some active state involvement in such action is also present, but the right of travel is a right so fundamental to the concept of federal union that Congress has an inherent power to reach private action which abridges it independently.

FACTS: Guest (D) and others were indicted under 18 U.S.C. § 241 with conspiring to deprive Negro citizens of Georgia of the free exercise and enjoyment of "several specified rights secured by the Constitution and laws of the United States." Two counts of the indictment specifically charged them with: 1) preventing Negroes from using public facilities maintained by the State of Georgia (protected by the Fourteenth Amendment); and 2) preventing Negroes from using public highways and roads in interstate commerce (protected by the "right to travel"). From a dismissal of the indictments, the United States (P) appealed.

ISSUE: May Congress constitutionally legislate to protect federal civil rights from private abridgment?

HOLDING AND DECISION: (Stewart, J.) Yes. The Enabling Clause of the Fourteenth Amendment permits Congress to reach private action (e.g., conspiracy) which abridges Fourteenth Amendment rights as long as some active state involvement in such action is also present but the right to travel is a right so fundamental to the concept of federal union that Congress has an inherent power to reach private action which abridges it independently. It is true that Fourteenth Amendment rights are broad and not fully delineated, but this does not justify preventing Congress from protecting those rights which are established on some kind of vagueness theory as the federal court below has done. The indictment below adequately set out violations of federal civil rights which Congress is empowered to protect. The dismissal of the indictments below must be reversed.

CONCURRENCE: (Clark, J.) The Enabling Clause of the Fourteenth Amendment permits Congress to ban wholly private action which abridges Fourteenth Amendment rights, regardless of the existence or nonexistence of state involvement.

DISSENT: (Harlan, J.) There is no basis for congressional power to reach either private violations of the Fourteenth Amendment

(which expressly require state action) or private violations of the right to travel (which traditionally require governmental action).

CONCURRENCE AND DISSENT: (Brennan, J.) State action is not necessary for Congress to proscribe private conduct which abridges any "right secured by the Constitution." The Court above found that the possibility of state involvement with the alleged conspiracy to deny Negroes access to Georgia public facilities was enough to sustain the indictment. Proof of such state action, difficult as it will be to provide, will undermine the ultimate prosecution of the case improperly. The Enabling Clause of the Fourteenth Amendment allows Congress to make any laws which it reasonably believes necessary to the enforcement of that Amendment. Clearly, preventing private conspiracies which deny equal use of public facilities to Negroes is within the scope of that clause.

EDITOR'S ANALYSIS: This case points up the continuous expansion of the Enabling Clause of the Fourteenth Amendment so as to permit Congress to reach wholly private acts of discrimination with its laws. In 1945, in *Screws v. United States*, 325 U.S. 91 (1945), the Court upheld federal legislation which punished state officials who acted "under color of state law." In 1966, in *United States v. Price*, 383 U.S. 787 (1966), the Court upheld federal legislation which punished private individuals who acted jointly with state officials to abridge the civil rights of others. In *Guest* a majority of the Court (six Justicies: Brennan, Warren, Douglas, Clark, Black, and Fortas) approved the power of Congress to punish wholly private action which serves to abridge civil rights of others. Note that the conduct which the Fourteenth Amendment's Enabling Clause thus allows Congress to proscribe is not necessarily itself unconstitutional (no state action), but merely is such as might result in deprivation of some constitutional right.

[For more information on conspiracies against the rights of citizens, see Casenote Law Outline on Constitutional Law, Chapter 10, § II, Congressional Authority to Reach Private Action Infringing Civil Rights.]

QUICKNOTES

ABRIDGMENT - A diminishing or curtailing of rights.

ENABLING CLAUSE OF 14th AMENDMENT - A constitutional provision giving the power to implement and enforce the law.

FEDERAL CIVIL RIGHTS – rights protected by the federal cponstitution.

FOURTH AMENDMENT - Provides that persons be secure as to their person and private belongings against unreasonable searches and seizures.

FRANCHISOR - A supplier of goods or services, who agrees to permit a re-seller to sell the good or service or to otherwise conduct business on behalf of the franchise.

JONES v. ALFRED H. MAYER CO.
Buyer (P) v. Real estate company (D)
392 U.S. 409 (1968).

NATURE OF CASE: Action for injunctive and other relief to deal with refusal of property owners to sell to Negroes.

FACT SUMMARY: Jones (P) brought suit in federal district court against the Alfred H. Mayer Co. (D) alleging that Mayer (D) refused to sell a home to him for the sole reason that Jones (P) was a Negro.

CONCISE RULE OF LAW: Congress, pursuant to the authority vested in it by the Thirteenth Amendment which clothes "Congress with power to pass all laws necessary and proper for abolishing all badges and incidents of slavery, may validly bar all racial discrimination, private as well as public, in the sale or rental of property."

FACTS: Relying upon 42 U.S.C. § 1982 (all citizens have the same right to inherit, purchase, lease, hold, and convey real and personal property as is enjoyed by white citizens), Jones (P) brought suit in federal district court against the Alfred H. Mayer Co. (D) alleging that Mayer (D) refused to sell a home to him for the sole reason that Jones (P) was a Negro.

ISSUE: 1) Does purely private discrimination, unaided by any action on the part of the state, violate § 1982 if its effect were to deny a citizen the right to rent or buy property solely because of his race or color?; 2) Does Congress have the power under the Constitution to do what § 1982 purports to do?

HOLDING AND DECISION: (Stewart, J.) 1) Yes. Section 1982 is only a limited attempt to deal with discrimination in a select area of real estate transactions, even though, on its face, § 1982 appears to prohibit all discrimination against Negroes in the sale or rental of property. If § 1982, originally enacted as § 1 of the Civil Rights Act of 1866, had been intended to grant nothing more than an immunity from governmental interference, then much of § 2 of the 1866 Act, which provides for criminal penalties where a person has acted "under color" of any law, would have been meaningless. The broad language of § 1982 was intentional. Congress, in 1866, had before it considerable evidence showing private mistreatment of Negroes. The focus of Congress, then, was on private groups (e.g., the KKK) operating outside the law. 2) Yes. At the very least, the Thirteenth Amendment includes the freedom to buy whatever a white man can buy, and the right to live wherever a white man can live.

DISSENT: (Harlan, J.) The term "right" in § 1982 operates only against state-sanctioned discrimination. There is a difference between depriving a man of a right and interfering with the enjoyment of that right in a particular case. The enforcement provisions of the 1866 Act talk about "law, statute, ordinance, regulation, or custom." As for legislative history, residential racial segregation was the norm in 1866. The Court has always held that the Fourteenth Amendment reaches only "state action."

EDITOR'S ANALYSIS: In *Sullivan v. Little Hunting Park, Inc.*, 396 U.S. 229 (1969), the Court invalidated a refusal by a homeowner's association to permit a member to assign his recreation share to a Negro. Once again, Harlan in dissent questioned whether the Court should expand a century-old statute to encompass today's real estate transactions. After these two cases, it is questionable whether the Court will place any limits or its reading of the Thirteenth Amendment when reviewing legislation aimed at private discrimination.

[For more information on the Thirteenth Amendment congressional power to prohibit private discrimination in housing, see Casenote Law Outline on Constitutional Law, Chapter 10, § II, Congressional Authority to Reach Private Action Infringing Civil Rights.]

QUICKNOTES

13th AMENDMENT - The constitutional provision which abolished slavery in the United States.

42 U.S.C. § 1982 - "All citizens of the United States shall have the same right in every state at territory, as is enjoyed by white citizens thereof to inherit, purchase, lease, sell, hold, and convey real and personal property."

CITY OF BOERNE v. FLORES
City (D) v. Archbishop (P)
521 U.S. 507 (1997).

NATURE OF CASE: Review of judgment sustaining the constitutionality of the Religious Freedom Restoration Act of 1993.

FACT SUMMARY: After the city of Boerne (D) denied Archbishop Flores (P) a building permit to expand a church, he contended that the permit denial violated the Religious Freedom Restoration Act (RFRA).

CONCISE RULE OF LAW: The RFRA unconstitutionally exceeds Congress's enforcement power under the Due Process Clause of the Fourteenth Amendment.

FACTS: The Religious Freedom Restoration Act (RFRA) prohibited the government from substantially burdening a person's exercise of religion, even if the burden is the result of a generally applicable law, unless the government has a compelling interest and is using the least restrictive means. Boerne (D) enacted a city ordinance requiring city preapproval for any construction on any of the city's historic landmarks. Archbishop Flores (P) sought a building permit to expand his church, a historic landmark. Boerne (D) denied the permit and Flores (P) sued, invoking the RFRA. The district court determined that the RFRA exceeded congressional power, but the Fifth Circuit reversed, holding the Act constitutional. Boerne (D) appealed.

ISSUE: Does the RFRA unconstitutionally exceed Congress's enforcement power under the Due Process Clause of the Fourteenth Amendment?

HOLDING AND DECISION: (Kennedy, J.) Yes. The RFRA unconstitutionally exceeds Congress's enforcement power under the Due Process Clause of the Fourteenth Amendment. Here, Congress, with the RFRA, attempts to replace, with the compelling interest test, this Court's decision asserting that the compelling interest test is inappropriate in cases involving general prohibitions with free exercise challenges. See *Employment Div., Oregon Dept. of Human Resources v. Smith*, 494 U.S. 872 (1990). Such an action violates the long tradition of separation of powers established by the Constitution. The judiciary is to determine the constitutionality of laws and the powers of the legislature are defined and limited. While Congress can enact remedial, preventive legislation that deters violations, the RFRA is not a preventive law. Instead, the RFRA redefines the scope of the Free Exercise Clause and nothing in our history extends to Congress the ability to take such action. The RFRA is so out of proportion to a supposed remedial or preventive object that it cannot be regarded as a response to unconstitutional behavior. Reversed.

EDITOR'S ANALYSIS: The Religious Freedom Restoration Act was one of the four federal laws overturned by the Supreme Court during its 1997 term. Although the Court has endorsed judicial restraint in recent years, it has not hesitated to quash improper intrusions on its authority to set unconstitutional standards. The Court, however, chose not to revisit the religious freedom issue in its Boerne decision, leaving intact the ruling in Smith that inspired Congress to pass the RFRA. In *Smith*, the Court approved Oregon's use of its ban on peyote to prohibit the drug's use in Native American religious rituals. The RFRA was intended to guarantee religious observance a higher degree of statutory protection than the *Smith* Court thought necessary.

[For more information on scope of congressional power to redefine amendments, see Casenote Law Outline on Constitutional Law, Chapter 10, § II, Congressional Authority to Reach Private Action Infringing Civil Rights.]

QUICKNOTES

DUE PROCESS CLAUSE - Clauses found in the Fifth and Fourteenth Amendments to the United States Constitution providing that no person shall be deprived of "life, liberty, or property, without due process of law."

FOURTEENTH AMENDMENT - Declares that no state shall make or enforce any law which shall abridge the privileges and immunities of citizens of the United States.

FREE EXERCISE CLAUSE - The guarantee of the First Amendment to the United States Constitution prohibiting Congress from enacting laws regarding the establishment of religion or prohibiting the free exercise thereof.

NOTES:

KATZENBACH v. MORGAN
Voters (P) v. State (D)
384 U.S. 641 (1966).

NATURE OF CASE: Challenge to constitutionality of federal statute.

FACT SUMMARY: As part of the Voting Rights Act, Congress inserted a provision that prohibited restrictions on the right to register to vote and the applicant's inability to read and write English where the applicant had at least a sixth-grade education in a Puerto Rican school where instruction was primarily in Spanish. New York had a statutory requirement of an ability to read and write English as a prerequisite to voter registration.

CONCISE RULE OF LAW: A federal statute enacted pursuant to the Enabling Clause of the Fourteenth Amendment supersedes any state constitutional or statutory provision which is in conflict with the federal law.

FACTS: New York had a statute which required all persons seeking to register to vote be able to read and write the English language. In the Voting Rights Act of 1965, Congress inserted a provision which prohibited a requirement of ability to read and write English where the person seeking to vote had completed at least a sixth-grade education in Puerto Rico where the language of instruction is primarily Spanish. This suit was instituted by a group of registered voters in New York who challenged that the provision of the federal statute insofar as it would prohibit enforcement of the New York requirement. At issue were the several hundred thousand Puerto Rican immigrants in New York who were prevented from voting by the New York statute, but who would be qualified under the federal law. The Attorney General of New York filed a brief in which he argued that the federal legislation would supersede the state law only if the state law were found to violate the provisions of the Fourteenth Amendment without reference to the federal statute. Also advanced was the argument that the federal statute violated the Equal Protection Clause of the Fourteenth Amendment, since it discriminated between non-English-speaking persons from Puerto Rico and non-English-speaking persons from other countries.

ISSUE: Does a federal statute enacted pursuant to the Enabling Clause of the Fourteenth Amendment supersede conflicting state law by reason of the Supremacy Clause of the U.S. Constitution?

HOLDING AND DECISION: (Brennan, J.) Yes. There is no need to determine if the New York English literacy law is violative of the Fourteenth Amendment Equal Protection Clause in order to validate the federal law respecting voter qualifications. If Congress were limited to restricting only those state laws that violated the Amendment, there would be no need for the federal

law, since the state law could be invalidated in the courts. Rather, the test must be whether the federal legislation is appropriate to enforcement of the Equal Protection Clause. Section 5 of the Fourteenth Amendment is to be read to grant the same powers as the Necessary and Proper Clause of Article I, § 8. Therefore, the federal statute must be examined to see if it is "plainly adapted to that end" and whether it is not prohibited by but is consistent with "the letter and spirit of the Constitution." It was well within congressional authority to say that the need to vote by the Puerto Rican community warranted intrusion upon any state interests served by the English literacy test. The federal law was "plainly adapted" to furthering the aims of the Fourteenth Amendment. There is a perceivable basis for Congress to determine that this legislation was a proper way to resolve an inequity resulting from Congress's evaluation that an invidious discrimination existed. As to the contention that the federal law itself violates the Equal Protection Clause, the law does not restrict anyone's voting rights, but rather extends the franchise to a previously ineligible group. This was a reform measure and Congress need not correct an entire evil with one law but may "take one step at a time, addressing itself" to that problem which seems most pressing. We hold, therefore, that the federal law was a proper exercise of the powers granted Congress by the Fourteenth Amendment and that the Supremacy Clause prevents enforcement of the New York statute insofar as it is inconsistent with the federal law.

DISSENT: (Harlan, J.) The majority has confused the question of legislative enforcement power with the area of proper judicial review. The question here is whether the state law is so arbitrary or irrational as to violate the Equal Protection Clause. And that is a judicial, not legislative, determination. The majority has validated a legislative determination by Congress that a state law is violative of the Constitution. There is no record of any evidence secured by Congress to support this determination. The judiciary is the ultimate arbiter of constitutionality, not Congress.

EDITOR'S ANALYSIS: As has occurred before, there was a footnote to the decision which caused as much controversy as the decision itself. In this footnote, the Court stated that Congress could enact legislation giving force to the Fourteenth Amendment that expanded the rights provided in the Amendment, but could not dilute or restrict the Amendment by legislation. In other words, Congress can make determinations of constitutionality so long as they expand rights but cannot make those determinations if they restrict rights. However, there is serious debate as to whether allowing Congress to take an independent role in interpreting the Constitution can be justified under any circumstances in view of *Marbury v. Madison*, 5 U.S. (1 Cranch) 137 (1803). Once loosed in this area, can any restraint be thereafter imposed? Congress has traditionally tried to stay within judicially circumscribed bounds of constitutionality. But, if it has an "independent role" in this area, the restraints are removed. An example is shown in the Omnibus Crime Control Act, where congress made legislative inroads to judicially granted rights as expressed in the Miranda decision. The Court can always rule on these inroads, but is it not better that Congress not be encouraged to embark on them in the first instance?

[For more information on the Morgan theory, see Casenote Law Outline on Constitutional Law, Chapter 10, § II, Congressional Authority to Reach Private Action Infringing Civil Rights.]

QUICKNOTES

SUPREMACY CLAUSE - Art. VI, Sec. 2, of the Constitution, which provides that federal action must prevail over inconsistent state action.

UNITED STATES v. MORRISON

Federal government (P) v. Students (D)

529 U.S. 598, (2000).

NATURE OF CASE: Suit alleging sexual assault in violation of the Violence Against Women Act.

FACT SUMMARY: Brzonkala (P) brought suit against two football-playing male students (D) and Virginia Polytechnic University under the Violence Against Women Act.

CONCISE RULE OF LAW: Section 13891 of the Violence Against Women Act may not be upheld as an exercise of Congress' remedial power under § 5 of the Fourteenth Amendment.

FACTS: Brzonkala (P), a student at Virginia Polytechnic Institute, complained that football-playing students Morrison (D) and Crawford (D) assaulted and repeatedly raped her. Virginia Tech's Judicial Committee found insufficient evidence to punish Crawford (D), but found Morrison (D) guilty of sexual assault and sentenced him to immediate suspension for two semesters. The school's vice president set this aside as excessive punishment. Brzonkala (P) then dropped out of the university and brought suit against the school and the male students (D) under the Violence Against Women Act, 42 U.S.C. § 13981, providing a federal cause of action of a crime of violence motivated by gender.

ISSUE: May § 13891 of the Violence Against Women Act be upheld as an exercise of Congress' remedial power under § 5 of the Fourteenth Amendment?

HOLDING AND DECISION: (Rehnquist, C.J.) No. Section 13891 of the Violence Against Women Act may not be upheld as an exercise of Congress' remedial power under § 5 of the Fourteenth Amendment. This case required the Court to address the Constitutionality of 42 U.S.C. § 13981, which provides a federal civil remedy for victims of gender-motivated violence. Since every law enacted by Congress must be based upon a power enumerated in the Constitution, and the Court concludes that the Commerce Clause does not provide Congress with the authority to enact § 13981, the Court addresses Brzonkala's (P) alternative argument that § 5 of the Fourteenth Amendment authorized the statutory cause of action under Congress' remedial power. This argument is based on the assertion that there is pervasive bias in various state justice systems against victims of gender-motivated violence and is supported by a voluminous congressional record. Case law had established that state-sponsored gender discrimination violates equal protection unless it serves important governmental objectives and the discriminatory means employed are substantially related to the achievement of such objectives. While sex discrimination is one of the objects of the Fourteenth Amendment, the amendment only prohibits state action. In two cases, United States v. Harris and the Civil Rights Cases, the Court interpreted the Fourteenth Amendment's provisions and concluded that laws enacted to punish private persons were beyond the scope of Congress' § 5 power. Brzonkala (P) also argued that here there has been gender-disparate treatment by state officials, whereas in those cases there was no indication of state action. Section 13891 is unlike any of the § 5 remedies that this Court has previously upheld since it has no consequence on any public official involved in investigating or prosecuting Brzonkala's (P) assault. Congress' power under § 5 does not extend to the enactment of § 13891. Affirmed.

DISSENT: (Breyer, J.) I doubt the Court's reasoning rejecting Congress' source of authority under § 5 of the Fourteenth Amendment. This Court has held that Congress may enact remedial legislation that prohibits conduct that is not itself unconstitutional.

EDITOR'S ANALYSIS: The primary issue here is that the federal government is seeking to regulate areas traditionally regulated exclusively by the states. The majority concludes that the regulation and punishment of intrastate violence that is not directed to the instrumentalities of interstate commerce is the exclusive jurisdiction of local government. What the dissent argues here is that Congress in this case has amassed substantial findings to demonstrate that such intrastate violence does have an effect on the instrumentalities of commerce.

[For more information on the exercise of Congress's remedial power, see Casenote Law Outline on Constitutional Law, Chapter 10, § II, Congressional Authority to reach private action infringing civil rights.]

QUICKNOTES

REMEDIAL ACTION – Actions taken pursuant to the Fourteenth and Fifteenth Amendment to provide remedies for violations of those amednemnts.

FOURTEENTH AMENDMENT - No state shall deny to any person within its jurisdiction the equal protection of the laws.

COMMERCE CLAUSE - Article 1, section 8, clause 3 of the United States Constitution, granting Congress the power to regulate commerce with foreign countries and between the states.

EQUAL PROTECTION - A constitutional guarantee that no person shall be denied the same protection of the laws enjoyed by other persons in like circumstances.

NOTES

CHAPTER 11
FREEDOM OF SPEECH WHY GOVERNMENT RESTRICTS SPEECH UNPROTECTED AND LESS PROTECTED EXPRESSION

QUICK REFERENCE RULES OF LAW

1. **Incitement.** The test to determine the constitutionality of a statute restricting free speech is whether, under the circumstances, the speech is of such a nature as to create a clear and present danger that it will bring about the substantive evils which Congress has a right to prevent. (Schenck v. United States)

   [For more information on clear and present danger test, see Casenote Law Outline on Constitutional Law, Chapter 11, § II, The First Amendment and "Dangerous" Speech Having Social or Political Aims.]

2. **Incitement.** The United States may constitutionally restrict speech that has the intended effect of hindering the United States in a war effort by means of riots and sedition. (Abrams v. United States)

   [For more information on restricted speech, see Casenote Law Outline on Constitutional Law, Chapter 11, § II, The first Amendment and "Dangerous" speech having social or political aims.]

3. **Incitement.** An opinion critical of a draft statute, no matter how seditious in nature, cannot be deemed to be advocacy of the violation of that statute unless there is a direct urging of such violation. (Masses Publishing Co. v. Patten)

   [For more information on unlawful or subversive advocacy directed at the state or major state goals, see Casenote Law Outline on Constitutional Law, Chapter 11, § II, The First Amendment and "Dangerous" Speech Having Social or Political Aims.]

4. **The "Red Scare" Cases.** Under its police powers, a state may validly forbid any speech or publication which has a tendency to produce action dangerous to public security, even where such speech or publication presents no clear and present danger to the security of the public. (Gitlow v. New York)

   [For more information on the clear and present danger test inapplicability to advocating overthrow of the government by force or violence, see Casenote Law Outline on Constitutional Law, Chapter 11, § II, The First Amendment and "Dangerous" Speech Having Social or Political Aims.]

5. **The "Red Scare" Cases.** A state may, in the exercise of its police power, punish abuses of freedom of speech where such utterances are inimical to the public welfare as tending to incite crime, disturb the peace, or endanger organized government through threats of violent overthrow. (Whitney v. California)

   [For more information on the clear and present imminent danger test, see Casenote Law Outline on Constitutional Law, Chapter 11, § II, The First Amendment and "Dangerous" Speech Having Social or Political Aims.]

6. **The Smith Act Prosecutions.** Where an offense is specified by a statute in nonspeech or nonpress terms, a conviction relying upon speech or press as evidence of violation may be sustained only when the speech or publication created a clear and present danger of attempting or accomplishing the prohibited crime. (Dennis v. United States)

   [For more information on the advocation of the overthrow of the government by force or violence as unprotected speech, see Casenote Law Outline on Constitutional Law, Chapter 11, § II, The First Amendment and "Dangerous" Speech Having Social or Political Aims.]

7. **The Modern Incitement Test.** The constitutional guarantees of freedom of speech and freedom of press do not permit a state to forbid or proscribe advocacy of the use of force or of law violation except where such advocacy is directed to inciting or producing imminent lawless action and is likely to produce or incite such action. (Brandenburg v. Ohio)

   [For more information on incitement, see Casenote Law Outline on Constitutional Law, Chapter 11, § II, The First Amendment and "Dangerous" Speech Having Social or Political Aims.]

8. **Fighting Words.** A state cannot bar the use of offensive words either because such words are inherently likely to cause a violent reaction or because the state wishes to eliminate such words to protect the public morality. (Cohen v. California)

   [For more information on offensive speech, see Casenote Law Outline on Constitutional Law, Chapter 11, § IV, Indecent and Offensive Speech.]

9. **Hostile Audiences.** When clear and present danger of riot, disorder, interference with traffic on the streets, or other immediate threat to public safety, peace, or order, appear, the state has the power to punish or prevent such disorder. (Feiner v. New York)

   [For more information on the hostile audience and the abusive speaker doctrine, see Casenote Law Outline on Constitutional Law, Chapter 12, § I, First Amendment Variables.]

10. **Libel.** The First Amendment requires that a public official may not recover damages for defamatory falsehoods relating to his official conduct unless he proves that the statement involved was made with "actual malice — that is, with knowledge that it was false or with reckless disregard of whether it was false or not." (New York Times Co. v. Sullivan)

    [For more information on defamation and freedom of speech's actual malice test, see Casenote Law Outline on Constitutional Law, Chapter 11, § II, The First Amendment and "Dangerous" Speech Having Social or Political Aims.]

11. **Hate Speech.** Where content discrimination in an ordinance is not reasonably necessary to achieve a city's compelling interests, the ordinance cannot survive First Amendment scrutiny. (R.A.V. v. City of St. Paul)

    [For more information on fighting words and hostile audiences, see Casenote Law Outline on Constitutional Law, Chapter 11, § II, The First Amendment and "Dangerous" Speech Having Social or Political Aims.]

12. **Obscenity.** Obscenity is not a constitutionally protected expression and if the material, taken as a whole, has a dominant theme which appeals to prurient interest as judged by contemporary community standards, then it may be proscribed. (Roth v. United States / Alberts v. California)

    [For more information on obscenity, see Casenote Law Outline on Constitutional Law, Chapter 11, Freedom of Speech (I), § III, Erotic, Obscene, and Pornographic Expression.]

13. **Obscenity.** Material is obscene and not protected by the First Amendment if: 1) the average person, applying contemporary community standards, would find that the work, taken as a whole, appeals to the prurient interest; 2) the work depicts in a patently offensive way sexual conduct specifically defined by the applicable state law; and 3) the work, taken as a whole, lacks serious literary, artistic, political, or scientific value. (Miller v. California)

    [For more information on the First Amendment protection of serious literary artistic, political, or scientific value, see Casenote Law Outline on Constitutional Law, Chapter 11, § III, Erotic, Obscene, and Pornographic Expression.]

14. Obscenity. A state can forbid the dissemination of obscene material to consenting adults in order to preserve the quality of the community and to prevent the possibility of resulting antisocial behavior. (Paris Adult Thratre I v. Slaton)

[For more information on the legitimate state interest in prohibiting obscenity, see Casenote Law Outline on Constitutional Law, Chapter 11, § III, Erotic, Obscene, and Pornographic Expression.]

15. Pornography as Subordination of Women. Ordinances that discriminate on the basis of the content of speech are unconstitutional in violation of the First Amendment. (American Booksellers Ass'n v. Hudnut)

[For more information on Offensive speech, see Casenote Law Outline on Constitutional Law, Chapter 11, § IV, Indecent and offensive speech.]

16. Sexually Explicit but Non-Obscene Expression. Government may validly regulate speech which is indecent but not obscene. (FCC v. Pacifica Foundation)

[For more information on regulation of indecent speech, see Casenote Law Outline on Constitutional Law, Chapter 11, § IV, Indecent and Offensive Speech.]

17. Sexually Explicit but Non-Obscene Expression. Content-based government regulations on speech are unconstitutional unless the government can demonstrate that it has a compelling interest for the regulation and that the regulation is the least restrictive means of achieving that interest. (Reno v. American Civil Liberties Union)

[For more information on content-based restrictions on speech, see Casenote Law Outline on Constitutional Law, Chapter 12, § I, First Amendment Variables.]

18. Commercial Speech. The First Amendment guarantee of freedom of speech extends to the recipients as well as the sources of the speech; and, as such, the consumer's interest in the free flow of advertising information brings such "commercial speech" within the protection of the First Amendment. (Virginia Pharmacy Board v. Virginia Citizens Consumer Council)

[For more information on the First Amendment protection of truthful commercial speech, see Casenote Law Outline on Constitutional Law, Chapter 11, § V, Commercial Speech.]

19. Commercial Speech. Where there is a substantial governmental interest, a restriction on commercial speech protected by the First Amendment is constitutional if it directly advances that interest and is not more extensive than is necessary to serve that interest. (Central Hudson Gas v. Public Service Comm'n)

[For more information on truthful, commercial speech regulation, see Casenote Law Outline on Constitutional Law, Chapter 11, Freedom of Speech (I), § V, Commercial Speech.]

20. Commercial Speech. Complete bans on truthful commercial advertising are unconstitutional. (44 Liquormart, Inc. v. Rhode Island)

[For more information on Government regulation of commercial speech, see Casenote Law Outline on Constitutional Law, Chapter 11, § IV, Commercial speech.]

P 997

SCHENCK v. UNITED STATES
Publisher (D) v. Federal government (P)
249 U.S. 47 (1919).

NATURE OF CASE: Appeal from conviction for conspiracy to violate the Espionage Act, conspiracy to use the mails for transmissions of non-mailable material, and unlawful use of the mails.

FACT SUMMARY: During a time of war, Schenck (D) mailed circulars to draftees which were calculated to cause insubordination in the armed services and to obstruct the U.S. recruiting and enlistment program in violation of military laws.

CONCISE RULE OF LAW: The test to determine the constitutionality of a statute restricting free speech is whether, under the circumstances, the speech is of such a nature as to create a clear and present danger that it will bring about the substantive evils which Congress has a right to prevent.

FACTS: During a time of war, Schenck (D) mailed circulars to draftees. The circulars stated that the Conscription Act was unconstitutional and likened conscription to conviction. They intimated that conscription was a monstrous wrong against humanity in the interest of Wall Street's chosen few and described nonconscription arguments as coming from cunning politicians and a mercenary capitalist press. They urged: "Do not submit to intimidation," but advised only peaceful actions such as a petition to repeal the Conscription Act. Schenck (D) did not deny that the jury could find that the circulars could have no purpose except to influence draftees to obstruct the carrying out of the draft.

ISSUE: Does the right to freedom of speech depend upon the circumstances in which the speech is spoken?

HOLDING AND DECISION: (Holmes, J.) Yes. The character of every act depends on the circumstance in which it is done. The most stringent protection of free speech would not protect a person's falsely shouting fire in a theatre and causing a panic. "The question in every case is whether the words are used in such circumstances and are of such a nature as to create a clear and present danger that they will bring about the substantive evils that Congress has a right to prevent. It is a question of proximity and degrees. During a war, things that could be said during peaceful times may be such a hindrance to the war effort that they will not be permitted." Schenck's (D) convictions are affirmed.

EDITOR'S ANALYSIS: The Court's first significant encounter with the problem of articulating the scope of constitutionally protected speech came in a series of cases involving agitation against the draft and war during World War I (Schenck, Frohwerk, Debs). Schenck announces the "clear and present danger" test,

the test for determining the validity of legislation regulating speech. In Schenck, Holmes rejected perfect immunity for speech. But he also rejected a far more restrictive, far more widely supported, alternative test: that "any tendency in speech to produce bad acts, no matter how remote, would suffice to validate a repressive statute."

[For more information on clear and present danger test, see Casenote Law Outline on Constitutional Law, Chapter 11, § II, The First Amendment and "Dangerous" Speech Having Social or Political Aims.]

QUICKNOTES

CLEAR AND PRESENT DANGER TEST - Doctrine that restraints on freedom of speech are permissible if the speech incites persons to engage in unlawful conduct.

CONSPIRACY - Concerted action by two or more persons to accomplish some unlawful purpose.

FREEDOM OF SPEECH - The right to express oneself without governmental restrictions on the content of that expression.

NOTES:

20 years

ABRAMS v. UNITED STATES
Russian immigrants (D) v. Federal government (P)
250 U.S. 616 (1919).

NATURE OF CASE: Appeal of convictions under the Espionage Act.

FACT SUMMARY: Russian immigrants (D) issued fliers that advocated a general strike in ammunition factories to prevent ammunition from being used against Russian revolutionaries.

CONCISE RULE OF LAW: The United States may constitutionally restrict speech that has the intended effect of hindering the United States in a war effort by means of riots and sedition.

FACTS: During World War I, in 1918, the United States sent forces to Russia following the overthrow of the Czarist government as part of a strategic operation against Germany on the eastern front. Russian immigrants (D) to the U.S. circulated literature advocating a general strike in ammunition plants to hinder the U.S. effort, as they perceived it, to crush the revolutionary struggle in Russia. The Russians (D) were charged under the Espionage Act for inciting actions that hindered the U.S. war effort. Abrams (D) and others appealed.

ISSUE: Can the U.S. government properly restrict speech that has the intended effect of hindering the United States in a war effort by means of riots and sedition?

hindering prod. of war material

HOLDING AND DECISION: (Clark, J.) Yes. The United States may constitutionally restrict speech that has the intended effect of hindering the United States in a war effort by means of riots and sedition. Individuals may be held accountable for the intended consequences of their actions. While speech is protected by the Constitution, it is not without limits. When speech is intended to incite riots and rebellion in such a critical time as that of war, it cannot be given the protection normally accorded to speech in the United States. Here, the Russian immigrants (D) hoped to generate a sympathetic revolution in the United States for the purpose of defeating military plans in Europe. Such a goal was so contrary to the concerns of the United States during time of war that it could not be permitted to proceed. Affirmed.

follows Debs (could Q "probable effect") [efficacy]

DISSENT: (Holmes, J.) This decision deeply undermines the liberties that the First Amendment was drafted to protect. Expression of dissenting opinions is the very foundation of freedom. It is only the present danger of immediate evil or an intent to bring it about that warrants Congress's setting a limit to expression of opinion. These convictions on the basis of two leaflets should not be sustained.

EDITOR'S ANALYSIS: Holmes' famous dissent sounds as though it requires greater immediacy of threat than his opinion, a few months earlier in *Schenck v. United States*, 249 U.S. 47 (1919), which articulated the clear and present danger test. Commentators have found support for this interpretation in other writings of Holmes. It appears that he realized the need to leave some element in place to protect speech, even while permitting some level of protection against dangerous speech.

[For more information on the restricted speech, see Casenote Law Outline on Constitutional Law, Chapter 11, § II, The first Amendment and "Dangerous" speech having social or political aims.]

QUICKNOTES

FIRST AMENDMENT - Prohibits Congress from enacting any law respecting an establishment of religion, prohibiting the free exercise of religion, abridging freedom of speech or the press, the right of peaceful assembly and the right to petition for a redress of grievances.

ESPIONAGE ACT – Federal law prohibiting espionage.

FREEDOM OF SPEECH - The right to express oneself without governmental restrictions on the content of that expression.

SEDITION - Unlawful action advocating the overthrow of the government.

NOTES:

③ *p1005 - doctrine gen. language on persecution for opinions*

right not lessened, but govt interest strengthened

⟵ ① → *clear/present danger test always same War makes dangers in general "more present" but principle of FS is always the same.*

② *Q of punish't - Holmes - even't intent, only nominal punish't - what legal principle?*

[handwritten: 1008]

[handwritten: RCSvesh— Marc Antony for final]

MASSES PUBLISHING CO. v. PATTEN

Publishing company (P) v. Postmaster (D)

244 Fed. 535 (S.D.N.Y. 1917).

NATURE OF CASE: Action for preliminary injunction.

FACT SUMMARY: Patten (D) refused Masses Publishing Company's (P) magazine access through mails for violating the 1917 Espionage Act.

CONCISE RULE OF LAW: An opinion critical of a draft statute, no matter how seditious in nature, cannot be deemed to be advocacy of the violation of that statute unless there is a direct urging of such violation.

FACTS: Masses Publishing Co. (P) published a monthly magazine called "The Masses," which contained cartoons and text of a politically revolutionary nature. During the First World War, Masses (P) ran political material in the magazine violently attacking the draft and the war and expressing sympathy for conscientious objectors. In July of 1917, under directions from the Postmaster General, Patten (D), Postmaster of New York, told Masses (P) that their August issue would be denied use of the mails. Patten (D) stated that the magazine violated the Espionage Act of 1917 by: 1) making false statements with the intent to interfere with the operation of the military forces of the U.S.; 2) arousing discontent among potential draftees and thereby promoting insubordination among troops already in the war; and 3) counseling resistance and disobedience to the law. Masses (P) brought this suit for a preliminary injunction against Patten's (D) refusal to accept the magazine in the mails.

ISSUE: Where a person's publications or utterances stop short of directly advocating resistance to a law, is that person nonetheless to be held responsible for attempting to cause its violation?

HOLDING AND DECISION: (Hand, J.) No. Unless there is some direct advocacy by a person for others to resist a particular law, then that person may not be held responsible for attempting to cause a violation of the law. Here, the publications of Masses (P) may have created national dissension and thereby assisted, indirectly, the cause of the enemy. But the statute in question provides that such publications be willfully false and made with the intent to interfere with military operations. The publications were mere opinions and not publications of facts. Thus, they fall within the scope of the right to criticize, normally the privilege of individuals in countries dependent on free expression of opinions as an ultimate source of authority. The statute was intended to prevent the spreading of false rumors embarrassing to the military, not the dissemination of inflammatory public opinion. It is also contended by Patten (D) that to allow Masses (P) to arouse discontent among the public as to the conduct of the war and draft causes insubordination among wartime troops. But to interpret the word "causes" too broadly would be to suppress all hostile

[handwritten left margin: urging a "duty or obligation" to resist]

criticism of the war except those officially sanctioned opinions. There are recognized limits to criticisms of existing laws or policies of war. One may not counsel or advise others to violate the law as it stands. The present statute is limited to punishing direct advocacy of resistance to recruiting and enlistment. Neither the cartoons or text of Masses' (P) publications fall within this test.

EDITOR'S ANALYSIS: The present test, later supplanted with the "clear and present danger" test, as to what type of conduct constitutes advocacy of resistance to law, focuses on the speaker and the value of the speech. This decision weighs the value of content of freely spoken opinions against its impact on the orderly conduct of governmental policy. The burden is on the government as accuser to show that such speech or publication is so detrimental to the orderly process of government that freedom of speech should bow to governmental will. The Masses case takes a liberal view of First Amendment rights and allows the free expression of opinion that falls short of direct advocacy of resistance to governmental authority. Judge Hand's decision in this case was overturned by the court of appeals on the ground that a person would be held accountable for the natural consequences of his words. If his words strongly imply that a particular law should be violated, that person will not be immune from prosecution merely because he omitted a direct appeal for violations. Judge Hand later wrote to a friend that his opinion in this case had apparently received little or no professional approval.

[For more information on unlawful or subversive advocacy directed at the state or major state goals, see Casenote Law Outline on Constitutional Law, Chapter 11, § II, The First Amendment and "Dangerous" Speech Having Social or Political Aims.]

QUICKNOTES

FIRST AMENDMENT - Prohibits Congress from enacting any law respecting an establishment of religion, prohibiting the free exercise of religion, abridging freedom of speech or the press, the right of peaceful assembly and the right to petition for a redress of grievances.

INJUNCTION - A remedy imposed by the court ordering a party to cease the conduct of a specific activity.

inst. competency

Congress (N.Y. leg.)
decide clear/
presentness

GITLOW v. NEW YORK
Publisher (D) v. State (P)
268 U.S. 652 (1925).

NATURE OF CASE: Appeal from a conviction for criminal anarchy.

FACT SUMMARY: Gitlow (D) printed and circulated literature advocating a Communist revolt against the U.S. government.

CONCISE RULE OF LAW: Under its police powers, a state may validly forbid any speech or publication which has a tendency to produce action dangerous to public security, even where such speech or publication presents no clear and present danger to the security of the public.

FACTS: Gitlow (D) was a member of the Left Wing Section of the Socialist Party in New York (P), and he was responsible for printing the official organ of the Left Wing called the "Revolutionary Age." In this paper, Gitlow (D) printed articles advocating the accomplishment of the Communist revolution through militant revolutionary socialism. Gitlow (D) further advocated a class struggle mobilization of the proletariat through mass industrial revolts and political strikes to conquer and destroy the U.S. Government and replace it with a "dictatorship of the proletariat." Although there was no evidence that these writings resulted in any such action, Gitlow (D) was arrested, tried, and convicted for advocating the overthrow of the government by force under a New York (P) criminal anarchy act. At trial, Gitlow's (D) counsel urged that since there was no resulting action flowing from the publication of the Gitlow (D) "Manifesto," the statute penalized the mere utterance of doctrine having no propensity toward incitement of concrete action.

ISSUE: Is a state statute, punishing the mere advocacy of overthrowing the government by force, an unconstitutional denial of the freedom of speech and press as protected under the First Amendment and applied to the states by the Fourteenth Amendment?

HOLDING AND DECISION: (Sanford, J.) No. Under its police powers, a state may validly forbid both speech and publication if they have a tendency to result in action that is dangerous to public security, even though such utterances present no "clear and present danger." The New York (P) criminal anarchy act did not punish the utterance of abstract doctrine, having no quality of incitement to action. It prohibits advocacy to overthrow organized government by unlawful means. These words imply advocacy of action. Clearly, Gitlow's (D) "Manifesto," which spoke in terms of "mass action" of the proletariat for the "Communist reconstruction of society — the struggle for these," is language of direct incitement. The means suggested imply force and violence and are inherently unlawful in a constitutional form of government based on law and order. Although freedom of speech and press are protected by the First and Fourteenth Amendments, it is fundamental that this freedom is not absolute. The police power extends to a state the right to punish those who abuse this freedom by advocating action inimical to the public welfare, tending to corrupt public morals, incite to crime, or to threaten the public security. The state need not wait for such dangers to arise. It may punish utterances likely to bring about such substantive evils. The "clear and present danger" test announced in the *Schenck* case does not apply here since the legislature has previously determined the danger of the substantive evils which may arise from specified utterances. As long as the statute is constitutional and the use of the language sought to be penalized comes within the prohibition, the statute will be upheld. And it is not necessary that the defendant advocates some definite or immediate act of force or violence. It is sufficient if they were expressed in general terms.

DISSENT: (Holmes, J.) The "clear and present danger" test applies, and there was no clear and present danger here. The followers of Gitlow (D) were too few to present one. Every idea is an incitement. The only meaning of free speech is to allow everyone to have their say.

EDITOR'S ANALYSIS: The Gitlow case is an example of what has been termed the "bad tendency" test. This test punishes utterances whose meaning lies somewhere between "clear and present danger" and mere advocacy of abstract ideas. The key question here is whether the language "tends" to produce action resulting in a danger to public security. The holding of the Court in this case, while recognizing Gitlow's (D) constitutional rights of free speech and press, bypassed these rights by saying that the New York (P) statute did not unduly restrict such freedom. However, in light of the modern test of "clear and present danger," it seems that the "bad tendency" test is all but dead. The "clear and present danger" test requires language that results in imminent lawless action. Tendency is not enough. It is important to note that the "bad tendency" test has not been used by the Court since *Gitlow*.

[For more information on the clear and present danger test inapplicability to advocating overthrow of the government by force or violence, see Casenote Law Outline on Constitutional Law, Chapter 11, § II, The First Amendment and "Dangerous" Speech Having Social or Political Aims.]

QUICKNOTES

CLEAR AND PRESENT DANGER TEST - Doctrine that restraints on freedom of speech are permissible if the speech incites persons to engage in unlawful conduct.

FIRST AMENDMENT - Prohibits Congress from enacting any law respecting an establishment of religion, prohibiting the free exercise of religion, abridging freedom of speech or the press, the right of peaceful assembly and the right to petition for a redress of grievances.

FREEDOM OF SPEECH - The right to express oneself without governmental restrictions on the content of that expression.

POLICE POWER - The power of a government to impose restrictions on private persons, as long as those restrictions are reasonably related to the promotion of the public welfare, health, safety, and morals.

PROLETARIAT - The laboring class; those unskilled persons wihtout property or capital.

WHITNEY v. CALIFORNIA
Communist party member (D) v. State (P)
274 U.S. 357 (1927).

NATURE OF CASE: Appeal from conviction for violation of Criminal Syndicalism Act.

FACT SUMMARY: Whitney (D), organizer and member of the Communist Labor Party of California, was convicted of aiding in that organization's violation of the Criminal Syndicalism Act.

CONCISE RULE OF LAW: A state may, in the exercise of its police power, punish abuses of freedom of speech where such utterances are inimical to the public welfare as tending to incite crime, disturb the peace, or endanger organized government through threats of violent overthrow.

FACTS: In 1919, Whitney (D) attended a convention of the Socialist Party. When the convention split into factions, Whitney (D) went with the radicals and helped form the Communist Labor Party. Later that year, Whitney (D) attended another convention to organize a new California unit of CLP. There, Whitney (D) supported a resolution that endorsed political action and urged workers to vote for CLP member-candidates at all elections. This resolution was defeated and a more extreme program of action was adopted, over Whitney's (D) protests. At trial, upon indictment for violation of the California Criminal Syndicalism Act, which held it unlawful to organize a group that advocated unlawful acts of violence as a means of effecting change in industrial ownership and in political change, Whitney (D) contended that she never intended the CLP to become a terrorist organization. Whitney (D) further contended that since she had no intent to aid the CLP in a policy of violent political reform, her mere presence at the convention was not a crime. Whitney (D) contends that the Act thus deprived her of her liberty without due process and freedom of speech, assembly, and association.

ISSUE: Is a state statute that punishes a person for becoming a knowing member of an organization that advocates use of unlawful means to effect its aims, a violation of due process and a restraint of freedom of speech, assembly, and association secured by the Constitution?

HOLDING AND DECISION: (Sanford, J.) No. Freedom of speech, secured by the Constitution, does not confer an absolute right to speak, without responsibility. A state may in the exercise of its police power, punish abuses of freedom of speech where such utterances are inimical to the public welfare as tending to incite crime, disturb the peace, or endanger organized government through violent overthrow. Here, the Syndicalism Act of California declared that to become a knowing member of or to assist in an organization that advocates crimes involving danger to the public peace and security of the state was punishable in the exercise of the state's police powers. The essence of the offense was the combining with others to accomplish desired ends through advocacy and use of criminal means. This is in the nature of

criminal conspiracy and involves an even greater danger to public security than individual acts. Miss Whitney's (D) contentions that the California Criminal Syndicalism Act as applied to her in this case is unconstitutional is foreclosed to the court, since it is an effort to review a trial verdict.

CONCURRENCE: (Brandeis, J.) Whitney (D) is here punished for a step in the preparation of incitement which only threatens the public remotely. The Syndicalism Act of California aims at punishing those who propose to preach, not put into action, criminal syndicalism. The right of freedom of speech, assembly, and association, protected by the Due Process Clause of the Fourteenth Amendment and binding on the states, are restricted if they threaten political, moral, or economic injury to the state. However, such restriction does not exist unless speech would produce a clear and imminent danger of some substantive evil to the state. The Court has not yet fixed standards in determining when a danger shall be clear. But no danger flowing from speech can be deemed clear and present unless the threatened evil is so imminent that it may strike before opportunity for discussion on it. There must be, however, probability of serious injury to the state. As to review by this Court of an allegation of unconstitutionality of a criminal syndicalism act, whenever fundamental rights of free speech and assembly are alleged to have been invaded, the defendant must be allowed to present the issue of whether a clear and present danger was imminent by his actions. Here, mere advocacy of revolution by mass action at some future date was within the Fourteenth Amendment protection. But our power of review was lacking since there was evidence of a criminal conspiracy and such precludes review by this court of errors at a criminal trial absent a showing that constitutional rights were deprived. *what does th me*

EDITOR'S ANALYSIS: The Whitney case is important for having added to the Schenck test of "clear and present danger" the further requirement that the danger must be "imminent." The Brandeis opinion in the Whitney case should be viewed as a dissenting opinion. His addition of "imminent" flies directly in the face of the majority opinion that punished "mere advocacy" of threatened action against the state. The "mere advocacy" test has not survived. Today, through the Smith Act that continues to punish criminal syndicalism, "mere advocacy" is not punishable. The urging of action for forcible overthrow is necessary before punishment will be imposed. Thus, the "urging of action" is the modern test of "clear and present imminent danger" espoused by Brandeis in Whitney.

[For more information on the clear and present imminent danger test, see Casenote Law Outline on Constitutional Law, Chapter 11, § II, The First Amendment and "Dangerous" Speech Having Social or Political Aims.]

QUICKNOTES
FREEDOM OF ASSOCIATION - The right to peaceably assemble.

Cf Fiske
facts-only preamble to IWW const. It did not prove advocation of crimel violnel unlawful (Kor more?)

HERNDON - 1937 Jlobvts blackcommsk orgner in GA, Merely advocated 'ideal', not enough
DEJONGE (1937) - 7 OR syndicalism law. Attended Comm Party meetng - not enough (J Hughes) [w/o content of

DENNIS v. UNITED STATES
Communist party leaders (D) v. Federal government (P)
341 U.S. 494 (1951).

NATURE OF CASE: On rit of certiorari to review convictions of conspiracy to overthrow the government by force or violence.

FACT SUMMARY: Dennis (D) and other Communist Party leaders were convicted for violation of the Smith Act, which is directed at conspiracy to teach or advocate the overthrow of the government by force or violence.

CONCISE RULE OF LAW: Where an offense is specified by a statute in nonspeech or nonpress terms, a conviction relying upon speech or press as evidence of violation may be sustained only when the speech or publication created a clear and present danger of attempting or accomplishing the prohibited crime.

FACTS: The Smith Act made it unlawful to advocate or teach the overthrow of the government by force or violence, or to organize people to teaching and advocating. It also prohibited a conspiracy to do any of the above. Dennis (D) and other Communist Party leaders were convicted of conspiracy to overthrow the government by force or violence. The evidence showed that the Communist Party was a highly disciplined organization, adept at infiltration into strategic positions, use of aliases, and double-meaning language. The Party was rigidly controlled and tolerated no dissension. The Party literature and statements advocated a successful overthrow of the government by force and violence.

ISSUE: Does the Smith Act, which punishes advocacy of the overthrow of the government by force or violence and conspiracy to so advocate, violate the First Amendment, inherently or as applied to Communist Party leaders?

HOLDING AND DECISION: (Vinson, J.) No. In determining the constitutionality of a statute which restricts First Amendment rights, the test is: where the offense is specified in nonspeech on nonpress terms, a conviction relying upon speech or press as evidence of violation may be sustained only when the speech or publication created a clear and present danger of attempting or accomplishing the prohibited crime. Here, the Smith Act seeks to protect the government from overthrow by force or violence. This is certainly a substantial enough interest for the government to limit speech. Now it must be determined whether a clear and present danger existed. Success or probability of success of an attempt to overthrow the government is not a criterion of whether that attempt constitutes a clear and present danger. The question is whether the gravity of the evil, discounted by its improbability, justifies such an invasion of free speech as is necessary to avoid the danger. Here, the formation by Dennis (D) and the others of such a highly organized conspiracy with rigidly disciplined

members subject to call when the leaders felt the time had come, coupled with the inflammable nature of world conditions, similar uprisings in other countries, and our relations with Communist countries convince us that a clear and present danger existed here. Convictions affirmed.

CONCURRENCE: (Frankfurter, J.) The validity of the statute depends on a balancing of competing interests, such as the nature of the speech and the nature of the advocacy. This balancing should be done by the legislatures not by the courts. The courts can overturn a statute, including statutes dealing with First Amendment rights, only if there is no reasonable basis for it.

CONCURRENCE: (Jackson, J.) A statute making it a criminal offense to conspire for the purpose of teaching and advocating the overthrow of the government by force or violence may be applied without infringing free speech rights even where there is no clear and present danger.

DISSENT: (Black, J.) First Amendment rights should have a preferred position in a free society. Laws restricting those rights should not be sustained by the courts on the grounds of mere reasonableness.

DISSENT: (Douglas, J.) A restriction of First Amendment rights can only be sustained where there is plain and objective proof of danger that the evil advocated is imminent. This was not shown here, where it is inconceivable that Dennis (D) and other Communists advocating the violent overthrow of the government have any chance of success.

EDITOR'S ANALYSIS: After Dennis, the government brought Smith Act cases against a number of Communists who were lower echelon rather than leaders. In *Yates v. U.S.*, 354 U.S. 298 (1957), the Court reversed the convictions of 14 defendants. It distinguished and explained Dennis on the ground that it had involved group indoctrination toward future violent action, under circumstances which reasonably justified the apprehension that violence would result. In *Scales v. U.S.*, 367 U.S. 203 (1961), the Court sustained the membership clause of the Smith Act, making it clear that to be convicted under that clause one must have had knowledge of an organization's illegal advocacy and must have joined the group with the specific intent of furthering its illegal aims.

[For more information on the advocation of the overthrow of the government by force or violence as unprotected speech, see Casenote Law Outline on Constitutional Law, Chapter 11, § II, The First Amendment and "Dangerous" Speech Having Social or Political Aims.]

QUICKNOTES

CONSPIRACY - Concerted action by two or more persons to accomplish some unlawful purpose.

BRANDENBURG v. OHIO
Ku Klux Klan leader (D) v. State (P)
395 U.S. 444 (1969).

NATURE OF CASE: Appeal from conviction for violation of the Ohio criminal syndicalism statute.

FACT SUMMARY: Brandenburg (D) was convicted under a state statute which proscribes advocacy of the duty, necessity, or propriety of crime, sabotage, violence, or unlawful methods of terrorism as a means of accomplishing reform.

CONCISE RULE OF LAW: The constitutional guarantees of freedom of speech and freedom of press do not permit a state to forbid or proscribe advocacy of the use of force or of law violation except where such advocacy is directed to inciting or producing imminent lawless action and is likely to produce or incite such action.

FACTS: Brandenburg (D), a Ku Klux Klan leader, was convicted under Ohio's (P) criminal syndicalism statute. The statute prohibited advocacy of the duty, necessity, or propriety of crime, sabotage, violence, or unlawful methods of terrorism as a means of accomplishing reform, and the assembling with any group formed to teach or advocate the doctrine of criminal syndicalism. The case against Brandenburg (D) rested on some films. One film showed 12 hooded figures, some carrying firearms, gathered around a wooden cross which they burned. Scattered words could be heard that were derogatory to Jews and blacks. Brandenburg (D) made a speech and stated, "We are not a revengent group, but if our President, our Congress, and our Supreme Court, continues to suppress the White, Caucasian race, it's possible that there might have to be some revengence taken."

ISSUE: Does a statute which proscribes advocacy of the use of force, where such advocacy is directed to inciting or producing imminent lawless action, and is likely to produce or incite such action violate the rights guaranteed by the First and Fourteenth Amendments?

HOLDING AND DECISION: [Per curiam.] Yes. The constitutional guarantees of free speech and free press do not permit a state to forbid or proscribe advocacy of the use of force or of law violation except where such advocacy is directed to inciting or producing imminent lawless action and is likely to incite or produce such action. The mere abstract teaching of the moral propriety or even moral necessity for a resort to force and violence is not the same as preparing a group for violent action and steering it to such action. A statute which fails to draw this distinction impermissibly intrudes upon the freedoms guaranteed by the First and Fourteenth Amendments. It sweeps within its condemnation speech which the Constitution has immunized from governmental control. The Ohio statute purports to punish mere advocacy and to forbid assembly with others merely to advocate the described type of action. Hence, it cannot be sustained. Brandenburg's (D) conviction is reversed.

CONCURRENCE: (Black and Douglas, J.) The line between what is permissible and not subject to control and what may be made impermissible and subject to regulation is the line between ideas and overt acts. Apart from rare exceptions, speech is immune from prosecution.

EDITOR'S ANALYSIS: This case demonstrates that imminence of danger is an essential requirement to the validity of any statute curbing freedom of speech. This requirement was reiterated in *Bond v. Floyd*, 385 U.S. 116 (1966), in which the Court reversed a state legislature's resolution excluding Bond from membership. The exclusion was based on the ground that Bond could not take the oath to support the state and U.S. Constitutions after his endorsement of a SNCC statement and his remarks criticizing the draft and the Vietnam war. The Court found no incitement to violation of law in Bond's remarks.

[For more information on incitement, see Casenote Law Outline on Constitutional Law, Chapter 11, § II, The First Amendment and "Dangerous" Speech Having Social or Political Aims.]

QUICKNOTES

FREEDOM OF SPEECH - The right to express oneself without governmental restrictions on the content of that expression.

FREEDOM OF THE PRESS - The right to publish and publicly disseminate one's views.

COHEN v. CALIFORNIA
Defendant (D) v. State (P)
403 U.S. 15 (1971).

NATURE OF CASE: Criminal prosecution for violation of disturbing the peace statute.

FACT SUMMARY: Cohen (D) wore a jacket with the words "Fuck the Draft" on it in a courthouse corridor and was arrested and convicted under a disturbing the peace statute.

CONCISE RULE OF LAW: A state cannot bar the use of offensive words either because such words are inherently likely to cause a violent reaction or because the state wishes to eliminate such words to protect the public morality.

FACTS: Cohen (D) was arrested in a courthouse because he was wearing a jacket bearing the words, "Fuck the Draft." Cohen (D) did not engage in any act of violence or any other unlawful act. There was also no evidence that anyone who saw the jacket became violently aroused or even protested the jacket. Cohen (D) testified that he wore the jacket to inform people of his feelings against the Vietnam war and the draft. He was convicted under a statute prohibiting "maliciously and willfully disturbing the peace or quiet ... by offensive conduct." The state court held that "offensive conduct" meant conduct which had a tendency to provoke others to disturb the peace.

ISSUE: Can a state constitutionally prevent the use of certain words on the ground that the use of such words is offensive conduct?

HOLDING AND DECISION: (Harlan, J.) No. A state cannot constitutionally prohibit the use of offensive words either because such words are inherently likely to cause a violent reaction or because the state wishes to eliminate such words to protect the public morality. Here, Cohen (D) could not be punished for criticizing the draft, so the statute could be upheld, if at all, only as a regulation of the manner, not the substantive content, of his speech. Cohen's (D) speech does not come within any of the exceptions to the general rule that the form and content of speech cannot be regulated: (1) this is not a prohibition designed to protect courthouse decorum because the statute is not so limited; (2) this is not an obscenity case because Cohen's (D) words were not erotic; (3) this is not a case of fighting words which are punishable as inherently likely to provoke a violent reaction because here the words were not directed as a personal insult to any person; and (4) this is not a captive audience problem since a viewer could merely avert his eyes, there is no evidence of objection by those who saw the jacket, and the statute is not so limited. The state tries to justify the conviction because the words are inherently likely to cause a violent reaction, but this argument cannot be upheld because these are not fighting words and there is no evidence that words that are merely offensive would cause such a response. Next, the state justifies the conviction on the ground that the state is guardian of the public morality. This argument is unacceptable because "offensive" is an unlimited concept and forbidding the use of such words would also cause the risk of suppressing the accompanying ideas. Therefore, there is no valid state interest which supports the regulation of offensive words in public.

DISSENT: (Blackmun, J.) Cohen's (D) conviction can be upheld both because his speech was fighting words and also because his act was conduct and not speech. Additionally, the state court subsequently restricted the statute in question to the fighting words context, so the case should be remanded and reconsidered under this construction.

EDITOR'S ANALYSIS: This case reasserts the Chaplinsky holding that fighting words are not protected by the First Amendment. Fighting words, then, are only those words which are likely to cause an immediate breach of the peace by another person, and are not just offensive words. More importantly, this case holds that a state has no valid interest in preventing the use of offensive words when there is no competing privacy interest. Here, the public in general has no right to protection from hearing either offensive words or offensive ideas.

[For more information on offensive speech, see Casenote Law Outline on Constitutional Law, Chapter 11, § IV, Indecent and Offensive Speech.]

QUICKNOTES

DECORUM - Observance of commonly-accepted standards of propriety.

FIGHTING WORDS - Unprotected speech that inflicts injury by their very utterance and provokes violence from the audience.

FEINER v. NEW YORK
Public speaker (D) v. State (P)
340 U.S. 315 (1951).

NATURE OF CASE: Appeal from conviction for disorderly conduct.

FACT SUMMARY: Feiner (D) gave an open-air speech before a racially mixed audience. The crowd that gathered forced pedestrians into the street. Feiner (D) urged black people to rise up in arms against whites and fight for equal rights. He refused to stop when asked to do so by a police officer and was arrested.

CONCISE RULE OF LAW: When clear and present danger of riot, disorder, interference with traffic on the streets, or other immediate threat to public safety, peace, or order, appear, the state has the power to punish or prevent such disorder.

FACTS: Feiner (D) addressed an open-air meeting. A racially mixed crowd of about eighty people gathered. The crowd forced pedestrians walking by into the street. In response to a complaint about the meeting, two police officers arrived. They heard Feiner (D) urge black people to take up arms and fight against whites for equal rights. The remarks stirred up the crowd a little, and one person commented on the police's inability to control the crowd. Another threatened violence if the police did not act. The officers finally "stepped in to prevent it all resulting in a fight." They asked Feiner (D) to stop speaking twice. He ignored them, and they arrested him.

ISSUE: May a speaker be arrested because of the reaction engendered by his speech?

HOLDING AND DECISION: (Vinson, C.J.) Yes. When clear and present danger of riot, disorder, interference with traffic on the streets, or other immediate threat to public safety, peace, or order, appears, the state has the power to punish or prevent such disorder. Here, the crowd's behavior and Feiner's (D) refusal to obey the police requests presented a sufficient danger to warrant his arrest and to persuade the Court that Feiner's (D) conviction for violation of public peace, order and authority does not exceed the bounds of proper state police action. Feiner (D) was neither arrested nor convicted for the making or the content of his speech. Rather, it was the reaction it engendered. The community's interest in maintaining peace and order on its streets must be protected. Hence, Feiner's (D) conviction is affirmed.

DISSENT: (Black, J.) "I will have no part or parcel in this holding which I view as a long step toward totalitarian authority. Disagreement, mutterings, objections from a crowd do not indicate imminent threat of a riot. Nor does one threat to assault the speaker. Even assuming that a critical situation existed, it was the police's duty to protect Feiner's (D) right to speak, which they made no effort to do. Finally, a person making a lawful address is not required to be silent merely because an officer so directs. Here, Feiner (D) received no explanation as to why he was being directed to stop speaking. This decision means that the police have the discretion to silence minority views in any city as soon as the customary hostility to such views develops."

EDITOR'S ANALYSIS: As Feiner demonstrates, free speech is not an absolute right. The conflicting interest of community order must also be considered. Feiner points out the question of whether the boundaries of protected speech depend on the content of the speech and the speaker's words or on the environment, the crowd reaction or potential crowd reaction. This question arose again in *Gregory v. Chicago*, 394 U.S. 111 (1969), which reversed convictions of disorderly conduct. There, participants in a "peaceful and orderly procession" to press their claims for desegregation were arrested when, after the number of bystanders increased, and some became unruly, they were asked to disperse and did not. The majority asserted that this was a simple case as the marchers' peaceful conduct was a protected activity within the First Amendment. The concurring opinion saw Gregory as involving some complexities, since, as the judge noted, both the demonstrators and the officers had tried to restrain the hecklers but were unable to do so. He concluded that "this record is a crying example of a need for some narrowly drawn law," rather than the sweeping disorderly conduct law.

[For more information on the hostile audience and the abusive speaker doctrine, see Casenote Law Outline on Constitutional Law, Chapter 12, § I, First Amendment Variables.]

QUICKNOTES

CLEAR AND PRESENT DANGER - A threat that is proximate and impending.

FIRST AMENDMENT - Prohibits Congress from enacting any law respecting an establishment of religion, prohibiting the free exercise of religion, abridging freedom of speech or the press, the right of peaceful assembly and the right to petition for a redress of grievances.

FREEDOM OF SPEECH - The right to express oneself without governmental restrictions on the content of that expression.

NEW YORK TIMES CO. v. SULLIVAN
Newspaper publisher (D) v. Public official (P)
376 U.S. 254 (1964).

NATURE OF CASE: Appeal of defamation judgment.

FACT SUMMARY: New York Times (D) published an editorial advertisement in which false statements were made which concerned Sullivan (P).

CONCISE RULE OF LAW: The First Amendment requires that a public official may not recover damages for defamatory falsehoods relating to his official conduct unless he proves that the statement involved was made with "actual malice — that is, with knowledge that it was false or with reckless disregard of whether it was false or not."

FACTS: Sullivan (P) was a commissioner in the city of Montgomery, Alabama, charged with supervision of the Police Department. During a series of civil rights demonstrations in that city in 1960, the New York Times (D) published an editorial advertisement entitled, "Heed Their Rising Voices," in which several charges of terrorism were leveled at the Police Department. The falsity of some of these statements was uncontroverted. The advertisement charged that nine students at a local college had been expelled for leading a march on the state capitol when, in fact, the reason had been an illegal lunch counter sit-in. The advertisement charged that the police had padlocked the dining hall of the college to starve the demonstrators into submission when, in fact, no padlocking had occurred. Other false statements also were made. Sullivan (P) brought a defamation action against New York Times (D) for these statements and recovered $500,000. Under Alabama law, a publication is libel per se (no special damages need be proved — general damages are presumed), whenever a defamatory falsehood is shown to have injured its subject in his public office or impute misconduct to him in his office. New York Times (D) appealed the Alabama judgment, challenging this rule.

ISSUE: Are defamatory falsehoods regarding public officials protected by constitutional guarantees of freedom of speech and press?

HOLDING AND DECISION: (Brennan, J.) Yes. The First Amendment requires that a public official may not recover damages for defamatory falsehoods relating to his official conduct unless he proves that the statement involved was made with "actual malice — that is, with knowledge that it was false or with reckless disregard of whether it was false or not." First Amendment protections do not turn upon the truth, popularity, or social utility of ideas and beliefs which are involved. Rather, they are based upon the theory that erroneous statements are inevitable in free debate and must be protected if such freedom is to survive. Only where malice is involved do such protections cease. Here, the Alabama rule falls short of this standard and the

evidence at trial was insufficient to determine its existence. Reversed and remanded.

CONCURRENCE: (Black, J.) All statements about public officials should be constitutionally protected — even malicious ones.

EDITOR'S ANALYSIS: N.Y. Times is the landmark case in constitutional defamation law. The subsequent cases have expanded this concept even further. In *Rosenblatt v. Baer*, the Court defined "public official" as anyone having substantial responsibility for conduct of government affairs. In *Curtis Publishing v. Butts*, 388 U.S. 130 (1967), New York Times was extended to "public figures" as well as officials. In Gertz, however, the Court retreated a bit by stating that, "As long as they do not impose liability without fault, the states may define for themselves the appropriate standard of liability for publisher . . . of defamatory falsehood injurious to a private individual." Note that the Court has also taken steps to toughen the New York Times' recklessness standard. In *St. Amont v. Thompson*, the Court ruled that recklessness was not to be measured by the reasonable man standard, but rather by the subjective standard of whether or not the defendant in the case subjectively entertained serious doubts about the truth of his statements.

[For more information on defamation and freedom of speech's actual malice test, see Casenote Law Outline on Constitutional Law, Chapter 11, § II, The First Amendment and "Dangerous" Speech Having Social or Political Aims.]

QUICKNOTES
ACTUAL MALICE - Knowledge of falsity or reckless disregard of the truth of falsehood.

DEFAMATION - An intentional false publication, communicated publicly in either oral or written form, subjecting a person to scorn, hatred or ridicule, or injuring him or her in relation to his or her occupation or business.

FIRST AMENDMENT - Prohibits Congress from enacting any law respecting an establishment of religion, prohibiting the free exercise of religion, abridging freedom of speech or the press, the right of peaceful assembly and the right to petition for a redress of grievances.

PUBLIC FIGURE - Persons who have achieved or assumed a special prominence in society, either willingly or by virtue of their social status.

REASONABLE PERSON STANDARD - The standard of care exercised by a hypothetical person who possesses the intelligence, education, knowledge, attention, and judgment required by society of its members when governing behavior; the standard applies to a person's judgment when determining breach of a duty under the theory of negligence.

RECKLESSNESS - The conscious disregard of substantial and justifiable risk.

ROTH v. UNITED STATES /ALBERTS v. CALIFORNIA
Publisher (D) v. Federal government (P)
354 U.S. 476 (1957).

NATURE OF CASE: Appeal from criminal conviction under an obscenity statute.

FACT SUMMARY: Two defendants were convicted under obscenity statutes for selling obscene material. Roth (D) was convicted under a federal statute, Alberts (D) under a state statute.

CONCISE RULE OF LAW: Obscenity is not a constitutionally protected expression and if the material, taken as a whole, has a dominant theme which appeals to prurient interest as judged by contemporary community standards, then it may be proscribed.

FACTS: Roth (D) was a publisher and seller of books, magazines, and photographs. He was convicted under a federal statute for mailing obscene circulars and advertising and an obscene book. Alberts (D) was convicted under a California (P) statute which prohibited the keeping for sale of obscene and indecent books or the writing, composing, and publishing of an obscene advertisement therefor.

ISSUE: Is obscenity outside the protection of the First Amendment freedom of expression guarantees and is there a proper standard for defining prohibitable conduct?

HOLDING AND DECISION: (Brennan, J.) Yes. Obscenity is not a constitutionally protected expression and if the material, taken as a whole, has a dominant theme which appeals to prurient interest as judged by contemporary community standards, then it may be proscribed. The apparently unconditional phrasing of the First Amendment has been held by this Court not to protect every utterance. However, all ideas having even the slightest degree of socially redeeming value are fully protected unless they encroach upon the limited areas of more important interests. Obscenity has been held to carry no socially redeeming value and is, therefore, outside the protection of the First Amendment. A properly drawn and enforced statute outlawing obscenity will withstand the test of constitutionality. The portrayal of sex is not obscenity per se, as is evidenced by the large range of classic presentations in art, literature, and scientific works. Any attempt to proscribe obscenity must clearly define that which is prohibited. A work must be judged in its entirety, not by selected portions since many valuable and socially important materials could thereby be suppressed. The test should be whether, to the average person, applying contemporary community standards, the dominant theme of the material, taken as a whole, appeals to prurient interest. The words of this standard are sufficiently clear to give notice as to what is, or is not, permissible conduct. Both defendants were convicted under statutes applying the stated standard and both convictions are affirmed.

CONCURRENCE: (Warren, C.J.) It is constitutionally permissible to punish individuals for the commercial exploitation of the morbid and shameful craving for materials with prurient effect.

CONCURRENCE AND DISSENT: (Harlan, J.) The majority opinion seems to assume that obscenity is a distinct classification of material which is readily recognizable. This recognition is left, ostensibly, to the trier of fact in the trial court. But where appellate review is undertaken, the appellate court itself must reexamine the material to determine if it is, in fact, obscene. This means that no generalized standard has been promulgated. This Court may be required to review each conviction on a case-by-case basis. The majority adopts the standard used in the Model Penal Code. Yet, the two statutes, one state, the other federal, set down different standards from the Code and from each other. The majority ignored this disparity in upholding the validity of the statutes and the convictions. Since the matter of sexual conduct is predominantly an area of state, not federal, concern, this Court should not strike down the determination by California (P) in this area. I would confirm Albert's (D) conviction. The Roth (D) conviction is another matter. When the federal government attempts to impose a national standard restricting expression, a serious threat to freedom is presented. This decision sets too dangerous a precedent and I would reverse Roth's (D) conviction.

DISSENT: (Douglas and Black, JJ.) The First Amendment is expressed in absolute terms and any law which purports to regulate material which can only produce thoughts is a clearly impermissible encroachment on these absolute guarantees. While the state and federal governments can regulate conduct, they should not be allowed to regulate the thought which precedes the conduct.

EDITOR'S ANALYSIS: The purported standard of the Roth case soon became a thorn in the side of the Court. As Justice Harlan had predicted, the Court was reduced to a case-by-case review of obscenity convictions. In each case, the Court was forced to make a factual analysis of the material to determine if it was obscene. This despite the fact the same determination had already been made in every lower court. The one clarification of the Roth standard came in *Jacobellis v. Ohio* (378 U.S. 184) in 1964. In that case, a split Court stated the "community standard" was a national standard since a national constitution was being applied. The other noteworthy concept to come from that case was from Justice Stewart. He stated that the Court was attempting to deal with "hard core" pornography. While he admitted he could not define that term, he stated he knew it when he saw it, and the motion picture involved in that case was not it.

[For more information on obscenity, see Casenote Law Outline on Constitutional Law, Chapter 11, § III, Erotic, Obscene, and Pornographic Expression.]

QUICKNOTES

OBSCENITY - Actions that corrupt the public morals through their indecency.

PRURIENT - Refers to the shameful and morbid interest in nudity or sex.

R.A.V. v. CITY OF ST. PAUL

Teenager (D) v. Municipality (P)

505 U.S. 377, 112 S. Ct. 2709 (1992).

NATURE OF CASE: Appeal from reversal of dismissal of "hate crime" prosecution.

FACT SUMMARY: When R.A.V. (D) was charged with allegedly burning a cross inside the fenced yard of a black family, the City of St. Paul (P) charged R.A.V. (D) under the Bias-Motivated Crime Ordinance.

CONCISE RULE OF LAW: Where content discrimination in an ordinance is not reasonably necessary to achieve a city's compelling interests, the ordinance cannot survive First Amendment scrutiny.

FACTS: R.A.V. (D) and several other teenagers allegedly assembled a crudely made cross and burned it inside the fenced yard of a black family. This conduct could have been punished under any of a number of laws, but the City of St. Paul (P) chose to charge R.A.V. (D) under the Bias-Motivated Crime Ordinance, which made criminally punishable conduct known as "hate crimes." R.A.V. (D) moved to dismiss on the ground that the ordinance was substantially overbroad and impermissibly content-based and therefore facially invalid under the First Amendment. The trial court granted this motion, but the Minnesota Supreme Court reversed because the modifying phrase "arouses anger, alarm or resentment in others" limited the reach of the ordinance to conduct that amounted to "fighting words," and therefore the ordinance reached only expression "that the First Amendment does not protect." The court also concluded that the ordinance was not impermissibly content-based because it was a narrowly tailored means toward accomplishing the compelling governmental interest of protecting the community against bias-motivated threats to public safety and order.

ISSUE: Where content discrimination in an ordinance is not reasonably necessary to achieve a city's compelling interests, can the ordinance survive First Amendment scrutiny?

HOLDING AND DECISION: (Scalia, J.) No. Where content discrimination in an ordinance is not reasonably necessary to achieve a city's compelling interests, the ordinance cannot survive First Amendment scrutiny. Assuming that all of the expression reached by the ordinance is proscribable under the fighting words doctrine, the ordinance is nonetheless facially unconstitutional in that it prohibits otherwise permitted speech solely on the basis of the subjects the speech addresses. Some areas of speech can, consistent with the First Amendment, be regulated because of their constitutionally proscribable content, namely, obscenity, defamation, and fighting words. Although the Minnesota Supreme Court construed the modifying phrase in the ordinance to reach only those symbols or displays that amount to

fighting words, the remaining, unmodified terms make clear that the ordinance applies only to fighting words that insult, or provoke violence, on the basis of race, color, creed, religion, or gender. The First Amendment does not permit St. Paul (P) to impose special prohibitions on those speakers who express views on disfavored subjects. Burning a cross in someone's front yard is reprehensible, but St. Paul (P) has sufficient means at its disposal to prevent such behavior without adding the First Amendment to the fire. Reversed and remanded.

CONCURRENCE: (White, J.) The judgment of the Minnesota Supreme Court should be reversed. However, this case could easily be decided under First Amendment law by holding that the ordinance is fatally overbroad because it criminalizes not only unprotected expression but expression protected by the First Amendment. The Court's new "underbreadth" creation serves no desirable function.

CONCURRENCE: (Blackmun, J.) The result of the majority opinion is correct because this particular ordinance reaches beyond fighting words to speech protected by the First Amendment. However, by its decision today, the majority appears to relax the level of scrutiny applicable to content-based laws, thus weakening the traditional protections of speech.

CONCURRENCE: (Stevens, J.) The majority establishes a near-absolute ban on content-based regulation. Content-based distinctions are an inevitable and indispensable aspect of First Amendment law. On the basis of content, the First Amendment does not protect the right to fix prices, breach contracts, make false warranties, place bets, threaten, or coerce. "Unprotected" or "proscribable" categories are based on content. Courts must consider the content and context of regulated speech and the scope of restrictions. This ordinance regulates low-value speech, fighting words, and only expressive conduct, not written or spoken words. The context is confrontational and potentially violent situations. Cross-burning is not a political statement, it is the first step in an act of assault which can be no more protected than holding a gun to someone's head. The scope of the restriction is quite narrow. R.A.V. (D) is free to burn a cross or express racial supremacy, so long as the burning is not so threatening and so directed at an individual as to by its very execution inflict injury. That the ordinance singles out threats based on race, color, creed, religion, or gender is justifiable because these threats cause more harm to society and individuals than others. While not invalid as a content-based speech regulation, the ordinance is, however, overbroad.

EDITOR'S ANALYSIS: The text of the St. Paul Bias-Motivated Crime Ordinance provides that: "Whoever places on public or private property a symbol, object, appellation, characterization or graffiti, including, but not limited to, a burning cross or Nazi swastika, which one knows or has reasonable grounds to know arouses anger, alarm or resentment in others on the basis of race, color, creed, religion or gender commits disorderly conduct and shall be guilty of a misdemeanor." The flaw in the wording of the ordinance was that it required the person who committed the hateful act to discern the reaction of the victim to the perpetrator's conduct. It is likely that hate crime ordinances which are worded to punish conduct intended by the perpetrator to frighten, anger, etc., on the basis of race, religion, etc., would be upheld. Even if no hate crime ordinance could be upheld, the hateful conduct could still be punished under criminal trespass, arson, battery, homicide statutes, etc.

→ VA v Black!

[For more information on fighting words and hostile audiences, see Casenote Law Outline on Constitutional Law, Chapter 11, § II, The First Amendment and "Dangerous" Speech Having Social or Political Aims.]

QUICKNOTES

CONTENT-BASED - Refers to statutes that regulate speech based on its content.

CONTENT-NEUTRAL - Refers to statutes that regulate speech regardless of their content.

FIGHTING WORDS - Any words that have the tendency to incite an immediate, violent reaction in the listener or hearer.

OVERBREADTH - Refers to a statute that proscribes lawful as well as unlawful conduct.

NOTES:

MILLER v. CALIFORNIA
Bookseller (D) v. State (P)
413 U.S. 15 (1973).

NATURE OF CASE: Criminal prosecution for knowingly distributing obscene matter.

FACT SUMMARY: Miller (D) sent out advertising brochures for adult books to unwilling recipients.

CONCISE RULE OF LAW: Material is obscene and not protected by the First Amendment if: 1) the average person, applying contemporary community standards, would find that the work, taken as a whole, appeals to the prurient interest; 2) the work depicts in a patently offensive way sexual conduct specifically defined by the applicable state law; and 3) the work, taken as a whole, lacks serious literary, artistic, political, or scientific value.

FACTS: Miller (D) conducted a mass mailing campaign to advertise the sale of adult books. The advertising brochures were themselves found obscene. These brochures were sent to unwilling recipients who had not requested the material. Miller (D) was convicted of violating a statute which forbade knowingly distributing obscene matter.

ISSUE: Is the *Memoirs* requirement that material must be "utterly without redeeming social value" to be considered obscene, a proper constitutional standard?

HOLDING AND DECISION: (Burger, C. J.) No. Material is obscene and not protected by the First Amendment if: 1) the average person, applying contemporary community standards, would find that the work, taken as a whole, appeals to the prurient interest; (2) the work depicts in a patently offensive way sexual conduct specifically defined by the applicable state law; and (3) the work, taken as a whole, lacks serious literary, artistic, political or scientific value. If material meets this definition of obscenity, then the state can prohibit its distribution if the mode of distribution entails the risk of offending unwilling recipients or exposing the material to juveniles. The burden of proof of the *Memoirs* test, that the material be utterly without redeeming value, is virtually impossible for the prosecution to meet and must be abandoned. There is no fixed national standard of "prurient interest" or "patently offensive" and these first two parts of the test are questions of fact to be resolved by the jury by applying contemporary community standards.

DISSENT: (Douglas, J.) The test put forth by the majority offers no guidelines for defining obscenity. "Offensive" is so vague as to completely destroy the protection of the First Amendment.

DISSENT: (Brennan, J.) The statute in question is unconstitutionally overbroad and therefore invalid on its face.

EDITOR'S ANALYSIS: The Miller test of obscenity is the most current test. If the three requirements are met, then the material in question is considered obscene and outside the protection of the First Amendment. Miller is a turnaround from Memoirs for many reasons: the Memoirs standard was too difficult to prove: the lower courts had no clearcut guidelines because Memoirs was a plurality opinion; the Court decided to use local community standards to allow greater jury power; and the Court was beginning to feel institutional pressures, since every obscenity question was a constitutional question. Therefore, Miller was an attempt by the Court to decentralize decision making.

[For more information on the First Amendment protection of serious literary artistic, political, or scientific value, see Casenote Law Outline on Constitutional Law, Chapter 11, § III, Erotic, Obscene, and Pornographic Expression.]

QUICKNOTES

BURDEN OF PROOF - The duty of a party to introduce evidence to support a fact that is in dispute in an action.

OBSCENITY - Conduct tending to corrupt the public morals by its indecency or lewdness.

OVERBROAD - Refers to a statute that proscribes lawful as well as unlawful conduct.

PRURIENT - Refers to the shameful and morbid interest in nudity or sex.

NOTES:

PARIS ADULT THEATRE I v. SLATON

Movie theatres (D) v. State (P)

413 U.S. 49 (1973).

NATURE OF CASE: Civil proceeding to enjoin continued showing of two adult films.

FACT SUMMARY: Two adult films were shown at theaters (D) which advertised the nature of the films and required proof that all patrons were over 21.

CONCISE RULE OF LAW: A state can forbid the dissemination of obscene material to consenting adults in order to preserve the quality of the community and to prevent the possibility of resulting antisocial behavior.

FACTS: Two movie theatres (D) in Atlanta showed "adult" films exclusively. The State of Georgia (P) sought to enjoin the showing of sexually explicit movies in these theatres under an obscenity statute. It was determined that the exterior advertising was not obscene or offensive, but that there were signs at the entrance stating that patrons must be 21 years of age and able to prove it. There was a further warning that those who would be offended by nudity should not enter. However, the films in question included, in addition to nudity, various simulated sex acts.

ISSUE: Can a state prohibit the dissemination of obscene material if the material is distributed only to consenting adults?

HOLDING AND DECISION: (Burger, C.J.) Yes. A state has a valid interest in preventing exposure of obscene material to consenting adults. Even if exposure to juveniles and unwilling observers is prevented, the state has a further interest in preserving the quality of life, the community environment, and possible threats to public safety, which will allow the regulation of obscenity. Even if there is no conclusive scientific proof that exposure to obscenity adversely affects either an individual or society, it is for the legislature, not the courts, to resolve these empirical uncertainties. A legislature can determine that a connection between obscenity and antisocial behavior exists, even in the absence of conclusive proof. Here, even though only consenting adults are involved, the state can make a judgment that public exhibition of obscenity has a tendency to injure the community and can, therefore, enjoin the distribution of obscenity.

DISSENT: (Brennan, J.) Prior obscenity standards have proved unworkable because they fail to give adequate notice of the definition of obscenity, producing a chilling effect on constitutionally protected speech. Because of the vague nature of these standards, every case is marginal, producing a vast number of constitutional questions which creates institutional stress in the judicial system. States do have a valid interest in protecting children and unconsenting adults from exposure to allegedly obscene material, but other possible state interests, as discussed in the majority opinion, are vague, speculative, and cannot be proven. Therefore, in the absence of threat of exposure to juveniles or unconsenting adults, material cannot be suppressed, but the state can regulate the manner of distribution.

EDITOR'S ANALYSIS: The Court, in three companion cases to the principal case, also upheld obscenity convictions on seizures involving the importation of films from a foreign country, the interstate transportation of obscene materials for private use, and the sale of an obscene book that contained no pictures. In 1974, however, the Court overturned an obscenity conviction for the showing of "Carnal Knowledge," a film with an MPAA rating of "R." While asserting that the finding of obscenity was essentially a question of fact for the jury, the Court warned that the jury did not have an unbridled discretion in this area. In another case, the Court also stated that the community standard to be applied was local, not national. Justice Brennan dissented, arguing that requiring a national distributor to comply with numerous local standards was totally unreasonable.

[For more information on the legitimate state interest in prohibiting obscenity, see Casenote Law Outline on Constitutional Law, Chapter 11, § III, Erotic, Obscene, and Pornographic Expression.]

QUICKNOTES

CHILLING EFFECT - Resulting in the inhibition or restriction of an activity.

OBSCENITY - Actions that corrupt the public morals through their indecency.

NOTES:

juveniles + public safety

AMERICAN BOOKSELLERS ASSOCIATION, INC. v. HUDNUT

Book publishers association (P) v. Municipality (D)
771 F.2d. 323 (7th Cir. 1985).

see KAV, Rotush

NATURE OF CASE: Appeal from decision invalidating municipal ordinance.

nice

FACT SUMMARY: Hudnut (D) appealed from a decision finding an Indianapolis municipal statute defining pornography in violation of the First Amendment since it discriminated on the basis of the content of speech.

CONCISE RULE OF LAW: Ordinances that discriminate on the basis of the content of speech are unconstitutional in violation of the First Amendment.

FACTS: Indianapolis enacted a municipal statute defining pornography as a practice that discriminates against women and which could be redressed through the administrative and judicial methods used for other discrimination. More specifically, the statute defines pornography as the graphic sexually explicit subordination of women, whether in pictures or in words, and listed a number of examples that would qualify as pornography. The American Booksellers Association, Inc. (P) brought suit, contending that the ordinance was unconstitutional in that it discriminated on the basis of the content of speech. The district court agreed, and from this decision, Hudnut (D) appealed.

ISSUE: Are ordinances that discriminate on the basis of the content of speech unconstitutional in violation of the First Amendment?

HOLDING AND DECISION: (Easterbrook, J.) Yes. Ordinances that discriminate on the basis of the content of speech are unconstitutional in violation of the First Amendment. There is no question that the ordinance in question in the present case operates in this manner. The city (D) has determined what it considers the appropriate way in which to portray women. Speech that portrays women in positions of equality is allowed, and that which portrays women in positions of subservience is not, regardless of literary or artistic value. This is simply thought control, which cannot be tolerated. Even accepting the premises of the legislation, that pornographic materials, as defined, tend to perpetuate the subordination of women, this ordinance cannot stand. The fact that such speech would tend to perpetuate subordination illustrates its power as speech, and the cornerstone of our society is that our citizens have the absolute right to propagate opinions that our government finds wrongful, or even hateful. Speech is protected regardless of how insidious. This definition of pornography is unconstitutional. Affirmed.

EDITOR'S ANALYSIS: This decision was affirmed upon appeal to the U.S. Supreme Court. Three justices of the Court would have set the case of oral argument. The Court makes it quite clear that regulations on the content of speech, unless proper time, place, and manner restrictions are delineated, will not withstand constitutional challenge.

[For more information on offensive speech, see Casenote Law Outline on Constitutional Law, Chapter 11, § IV, Indecent and offensive speech.]

QUICKNOTES

CONTENT-BASED - Refers to statutes that regulate speech based on its content.

FIRST AMENDMENT - Prohibits Congress from enacting any law respecting an establishment of religion, prohibiting the free exercise of religion, abridging freedom of speech or the press, the right of peaceful assembly and the right to petition for a redress of grievances.

NOTES:

F.C.C. v. PACIFICA FOUNDATION
Federal agency (P) v. Broadcasting company (D)
438 U.S. 726 (1978).

[handwritten:] George Carlin

NATURE OF CASE: Appeal from an F.C.C. disciplinary order.

FACT SUMMARY: The F.C.C. (P) disciplined Pacifica (D) for broadcasting "indecent language" over the radio airwaves.

CONCISE RULE OF LAW: Government may validly regulate speech which is indecent but not obscene.

FACTS: Pacifica (D) broadcasted a monologue performed by comedian George Carlin over its radio station. The monologue sought to express Carlin's view of the public perception of "obscene" language, and included the use of certain words which were considered "indecent" by a listener of the station. This listener filed a complaint with the F.C.C. (P), contending he was harmed by being exposed to Carlin's monologue. The F.C.C. (P) found the words "indecent" and issued an order which would be considered when the station's license came up for renewal. The court of appeals overturned the order as in violation of the First Amendment freedom of speech. It held that because the F.C.C. (P) specifically found the speech not to be obscene, it had no power to regulate it. The Supreme Court granted certiorari.

ISSUE: May government regulate speech which is indecent but not obscene?

HOLDING AND DECISION: (Stevens,) Yes. Government may regulate speech which is indecent yet not obscene. Government may regulate the content of speech where such speech, in context, is vulgar, offensive, and shocking. Patently offensive speech is not entitled to complete constitutional protection. It may be limited under time and place restrictions. As a result, the order was properly issued. Reversed.

CONCURRENCE: (Powell, J.) Limiting speech to appropriate times and places reduces its indecency while still affording access to willing listeners.

DISSENT: (Brennan, J.) The statutory term "indecent" under which the F.C.C. (P) order was issued must be construed only to apply to obscene language. Because this language was held not to be obscene, the order was improper.

EDITOR'S ANALYSIS: Justice Stevens, in this plurality decision, was careful to point out that if there had been any basis for concluding that the F.C.C. (P) characterization of Carlin's monologue rested upon its political content, First Amendment protection might be required. If it is the speaker's opinion being expressed which gives offense, constitutional protection is mandated. In this case the objection was not to Carlin's expressing his opinion, but to the manner in which it was expressed.

[handwritten left margin: Lenny Bruce said niggerlike words of power]
[handwritten: Cohen emotion/ideas intertwined...]

[For more information on regulation of indecent speech, see Casenote Law Outline on Constitutional Law, Chapter 11, § IV, Indecent and Offensive Speech.]

QUICKNOTES
OBSCENITY - Conduct tending to corrupt the public morals by its indecency or lewdness.

NOTES:

[handwritten:]
shit
cocksucker
piss
cunt
motherfucker
ass
damn?

[handwritten:]
"low value"...
↑
no majority
for that
explicit label

[handwritten:]
".. can't separate
political
content from form

Cohen !

only poss. reason is captive audience

[handwritten: CA - internet ① compelling ② least restrictive + kids]

RENO v. AMERICAN CIVIL LIBERTIES UNION

Attorney general (D) v. Union (P)

521 U.S. 844, 117 S. Ct. 2329 (1997).

NATURE OF CASE: Review of judgment striking down provisions of the Communications Decency Act of 1996 (CDA).

FACT SUMMARY: The ACLU (P) challenged the constitutionality of provisions of the CDA that purported to protect minors from harmful transmissions over the Internet.

CONCISE RULE OF LAW: Content-based government regulations on speech are unconstitutional unless the government can demonstrate that it has a compelling interest for the regulation and that the regulation is the least restrictive means of achieving that interest.

FACTS: The CDA contained provisions designed to protect minors from "indecent" and "patently offensive" communication on the Internet. The "indecent transmission" provision prohibited the knowing transmission of obscene or indecent messages to any recipient under eighteen years of age. The "patently offensive display" provision prohibited the knowing sending or displaying of patently offensive messages to a person under eighteen years of age. The ACLU (P) filed an action alleging that the CDA abridged freedom of speech protected by the First Amendment. The district court found in its favor and enjoined the enforcement of the "indecent" communications provisions, but expressly preserved the government's right to investigate and prosecute the obscenity or child pornography activities prohibited by the provision. The court also issued an unqualified injunction against the enforcement of the "patently offensive displays" provision because it contained no separate reference to obscenity or child pornography.

ISSUE: Are content-based government regulations on speech unconstitutional unless the government can demonstrate that it has a compelling interest for the regulation and that the regulation is the least restrictive means of achieving that interest?

HOLDING AND DECISION: (Stevens, J.) Yes. Content-based government regulations on speech are unconstitutional unless the government can demonstrate that it has a compelling interest for the regulation and that the regulation is the least restrictive means of achieving that interest. Although the congressional goal of protecting children from harmful materials is a legitimate and important one, the CDA provisions at issue here are so broad and imprecise that they cannot be upheld. The Internet is a unique medium in that it provides a relatively unlimited, low-cost capacity for communication of all kinds including traditional print and news services, audio, video, still images, and interactive real-time dialogue. It unquestionably deserves the highest level of

First Amendment protection. The breadth of the CDA's coverage is wholly unprecedented and would undoubtedly impact adult as well as minor access to such materials. It does not limit its restrictions to commercial speech or entities, but encompasses anyone posting messages on a computer, regardless of time of day, website, or any other factor. The district court heard evidence that in the near future a reasonably effective and less restrictive method by which parents can prevent their children from accessing sexually explicit material will become widely available. The current provisions cannot stand as they are more likely to interfere with the free exchange of ideas than to encourage it. Affirmed.

[handwritten: ?]

CONCURRENCE AND DISSENT: (O'Connor, J.) The CDA is little more than an attempt by Congress to create "adult zones" on the Internet. Such zoning laws are valid if: (1) they do not unduly restrict adult access to materials, and (2) the materials are such that minors have no right to read or view. The CDA "display" provision and some applications of the "indecency transmission" provision fail to adhere to the first of these requirements, and should therefore be invalidated only to those extents.

EDITOR'S ANALYSIS: Issues surrounding speech, pornography, and access to the Internet will undoubtedly be revisited often in the next several years. The issues are extremely complex because the technology is so novel, and are further complicated by the fact that the Internet extends worldwide. The Court was appropriately cautious in striking down the provisions and leaving the issue in the hands of parents until further developments evolve.

[For more information on content-based restrictions on speech, see Casenote Law Outline on Constitutional Law, Chapter 12, § I, First Amendment Variables.]

QUICKNOTES

CONTENT-BASED - Refers to statutes that regulate speech based on its content.

FIRST AMENDMENT - Prohibits Congress from enacting any law respecting an establishment of religion, prohibiting the free exercise of religion, abridging freedom of speech or the press, the right of peaceful assembly and the right to petition for a redress of grievances.

OBSCENITY - Conduct tending to corrupt the public morals by its indecency or lewdness.

[handwritten: broad communication (not limited like TV/radio)]

VIRGINIA STATE BOARD OF PHARMACY v. VIRGINIA CITIZENS CONSUMER COUNCIL
State board (D) v. Residents (P)
425 U.S. 748 (1976).

NATURE OF CASE: Action for declaratory judgment.

FACT SUMMARY: The State Board (D) was charged with enforcing a state law which made it illegal for a pharmacist to advertise the prices of his prescription drugs.

CONCISE RULE OF LAW: The First Amendment guarantee of freedom of speech extends to the recipients as well as the sources of the speech; and, as such, the consumer's interest in the free flow of advertising information brings such "commercial speech" within the protection of the First Amendment.

FACTS: Virginia law provides that licensed pharmacists are guilty of "unprofessional conduct" if they advertise "in any manner whatsoever, any amount, price, fee, premium, discount, rebate or credit terms . . . for any drugs which may be dispensed only by prescription." Consumer Council (P) is comprised of Virginia residents who require prescription drugs. Citing statistics which show that drugs vary in price strikingly from outlet to outlet (e.g. from $2.59 to $6.00 for one drug), they filed this action to have the advertising ban declared an unconstitutional infringement on their First Amendment right to free speech. From a judgment for the Council (P), the State Board (D) appealed contending that "commercial speech" such as this is not protected by the First Amendment.

ISSUE: Does the First Amendment protect "commercial speech" as manifested in price advertising by professional groups?

HOLDING AND DECISION: (Blackmun, J.) Yes. The First Amendment guarantee of freedom of speech extends to the recipients as well as the sources of the speech; and, as such, the consumer's interest in the free flow of advertising information brings such "commercial speech" within the protection of the First Amendment. The traditional rule that "commercial speech" is not protected has been gradually eroded by the court and today, it is set to rest. Advertising, however tasteless, is information nevertheless and entitled to constitutional deference thereby. To be sure, the holding today does not prevent reasonable regulation as to "time, place, and manner" or prevent illegal or misleading speech. It only recognizes the legitimacy of commercial speech for First Amendment purposes.

CONCURRENCE: (Burger, J.) Ninety-five percent of all drugs sold by pharmacists are prepackaged, requiring little professional expertise for sale. Such is not the case it should be noted, when services by doctors and lawyers are involved.

CONCURRENCE: (Stewart, J.) Today's ruling in no way narrows the government power to promulgate broad regulations for the protection of the public from false or deceptive advertising.

DISSENT: (Rehnquist, J.) The Court's decision today is troublesome for two reasons. First, it extends standing to sue to a group not asserting their right to receive information but rather the right of third parties to publish it. Second, by raising commercial speech to the level of First Amendment protection, the Court has usurped the constitutionally mandated power of state legislatures to regulate public health, etc.

EDITOR'S ANALYSIS: Justice Burger's concurrence to the contrary notwithstanding, this case has brought many observers to the conclusion that advertising bans on professionals are no longer constitutional. Indeed, the American Bar Association and several state bar associations have begun to promulgate standards for advertising by attorneys which will protect the public from the perceived evils of a competitive bar. Consumer Council claims to overrule the 1951 case of Breard v. Alexandria. Note, however, that the ban on door-to-door sales upheld therein, would appear to be precisely the kind of "time, place, and manner restriction" which the Court in Consumer Council expressly sanctioned.

[For more information on the First Amendment protection of truthful commercial speech, see Casenote Law Outline on Constitutional Law, Chapter 11, § V, Commercial Speech.]

QUICKNOTES
COMMERCIAL SPEECH - Any speech that proposes a commercial transaction, or promotes products or services.

TIME, PLACE, MANNER RESTRICTION - Refers to certain types of regulations on speech that are permissible since they only restrict the time, place, and manner in which the speech is to occur.

NOTES:

CENTRAL HUDSON GAS v. PUBLIC SERVICE COMM'N

Gas company (P) v. Federal agency (D)

447 U.S. 557 (1980).

NATURE OF CASE: Action challenging the constitutionality of a federal regulation.

FACT SUMMARY: Central Hudson Gas (P) claimed the First Amendment prohibited the PSC's (D) regulation completely banning promotional advertising by an electrical utility.

CONCISE RULE OF LAW: Where there is a substantial governmental interest, a restriction on commercial speech protected by the First Amendment is constitutional if it directly advances that interest and is not more extensive than is necessary to serve that interest.

FACTS: The PSC (D) banned all promotional advertising by an electrical utility as contrary to the national policy of conserving energy. Central Hudson Gas (P) challenged the regulation on First Amendment grounds.

ISSUE: Can the government place a restriction on commercial speech protected by the First Amendment if it directly advances a substantial governmental interest and is not broader than is necessary to serve that interest?

HOLDING AND DECISION: (Powell, J.) Yes. Commercial speech which concerns lawful activity and is not misleading is protected under the First Amendment, although at a lesser level than other speech. However, this protection prevents governmental restrictions on covered commercial speech unless they advance a substantial governmental interest and are not more extensive than is necessary to serve that interest. These principles produce a four-step analysis which, when applied to this case, indicates the regulation at issue is unconstitutional. It satisfies all the requirements except the last. It is so broad that it suppresses speech about electrical devices or services which would cause no increase in total energy usage and thus be unrelated to the energy conservation interest of the state. Reversed.

CONCURRENCE: (Blackmun, J.) The intermediate level of scrutiny advanced by the four-part analysis the Court sets up in this decision is appropriate for a restraint on commercial speech designed to protect consumers from misleading or coercive speech, or a regulation related to time, place, or manner of commercial speech. It is not, however, properly applied when a state seeks to suppress information about a product in order to manipulate a private economic decision that the state cannot or has not regulated or outlawed directly. No differences between commercial and other protected speech justify suppression of commercial speech in order to influence public conduct through manipulation of the availability of information.

CONCURRENCE: (Stevens, J.) I do not consider this a "commercial speech" case, for the ban at issue would prohibit speech outside the limited boundaries of commercial speech. For example, it would seem to prohibit an electric company's advocacy of the use of electric heat for environmental reasons, as opposed to wood-burning stoves. Thus, I see no need to decide if the four-part analysis the Court adopts adequately protects commercial speech. This is a "regular" speech case. If the perceived harm associated with greater electrical usage is not sufficiently serious to justify direct regulation, surely it does not constitute the kind of clear and present danger that can justify the suppression of speech.

DISSENT: (Rehnquist, J.) In the first place, I cannot agree that the speech of a state-created monopoly, which is the subject of a comprehensive regulatory scheme, is entitled to protection under the First Amendment. Furthermore, I think the Court errs in failing to recognize that the state law at issue in this case is most accurately viewed as an economic regulation and that the speech involved (if it falls within the First Amendment at all) occupies a significantly more subordinate position in the hierarchy of First Amendment values than the Court gives it today. Finally, in reaching its judgment, the Court improperly substitutes its own judgment for that of the state in deciding how a proper ban on promotional advertising should be drafted. On that point, in adopting a "no more extensive than necessary" analysis as the last part of its four-part test, the Court has embraced a test that will unduly impair a state legislature's ability to adopt legislation reasonably designed to promote interests that have always been rightly thought to be of great importance to the state.

EDITOR'S ANALYSIS: Historically, the Court had always held that commercial speech was not within the protections of the First Amendment. In the mid-1970's, however, a new trend began in which the Court recognized that the First Amendment did encompass certain commercial speech and offered it protection, although of a more limited sort than other speech. In recent years, though, there is evidence that the enthusiasm among the Justices for including commercial speech within the First Amendment is waning.

[For more information on truthful, commercial speech regulation, see Casenote Law Outline on Constitutional Law, Chapter 11, § V, Commercial Speech.]

QUICKNOTES

COMMERCIAL SPEECH - Any speech that proposes a commercial transaction, or promotes products or services.

Pol speech   *Thomas - ignore*

(441 iy Mt)

44 LIQUORMART, INC. v. RHODE ISLAND
Liquor distributor (P) v. State (D)
517 U.S.484, 116 S. Ct. 1495 (1996).

NATURE OF CASE: Appeal of decision upholding a state law prohibiting alcohol advertising.

FACT SUMMARY: Rhode Island (D) banned the advertising of retail prices of alcoholic beverages.

CONCISE RULE OF LAW: Complete bans on truthful commercial advertising are unconstitutional.

FACTS: In 1956, Rhode Island (D) enacted a prohibition against advertising the retail price of any alcoholic beverage offered for sale in the state. The law also proscribed the news media from publishing this information. Rhode Island (D) claimed that the law was enacted to reduce market-wide consumption of alcohol. The law was challenged as an unconstitutional abridgement of free speech. The district court concluded that the ban was unconstitutional because liquor price advertising had no impact on levels of alcohol consumption in Rhode Island (D), and thus the ban did not directly advance the State's (D) interest. The court of appeals reversed. The Supreme Court granted certiorari to decide the issue.

ISSUE: Are complete bans on truthful commercial advertising unconstitutional?

HOLDING AND DECISION: (Stevens, J.) Yes. Complete bans on truthful commercial advertising are unconstitutional. Traditionally, commercial messages have provided consumers with information about the availability of goods and services. The common law prohibited fraudulent and misleading advertising. However, prior cases have recognized that regulation of commercial advertising is not protected to the same degree as core First Amendment speech. In *Central Hudson v. Public Service Commission of N.Y.*, 447 U.S. 557 (1980), this Court held that regulation of commercial speech had to be related to a significant state interest and that more limited alternatives are not available. When a state entirely prohibits the dissemination of truthful advertising for reasons unrelated to protecting consumers, strict scrutiny of the law is applicable. In the present case, Rhode Island (D) could reduce alcohol consumption by other methods, such as taxes, rather than through speech regulation. Thus, there is no reasonable relationship between the regulation and state objective. Accordingly, Rhode Island's (D) law is unconstitutional. Reversed.

CONCURRENCE: (Scalia, J.) Although the test enunciated in Central Hudson may not be correct, both parties argued accepting its validity, so it should stand until there is a suitable replacement.

CONCURRENCE: (Thomas, J.) The government's manipulation of consumers' choices by keeping them ignorant is per se illegitimate. Thus, the balancing test of Central Hudson is not appropriate. Accurate commercial speech is entitled to full protection. *(SS)*

CONCURRENCE: (O'Connor, J.) Because Rhode Island's (D) regulation fails even the less stringent standard set out in Central Hudson, nothing here requires adoption of a new analysis for the evaluation of commercial speech regulation.

EDITOR'S ANALYSIS: The Court also overruled the case of *Posados de Puerto Rico Associates v. Tourism Co. of Puerto Rico,* 478 U.S. 328 (1986), in which the Court held that a ban on casino advertising was valid since the state could choose to entirely ban casinos themselves. The decision correctly points out that banning speech may be more intrusive than banning conduct and that the speech ban is not necessarily a lesser included state power. The court also rejected any "vice" exception that Posados may have implied.

[For more information on government regulation of commercial speech, see Casenote Law Outline on Constitutional Law, Chapter 11, § V, Commercial Speech.]

QUICKNOTES
BALANCING TEST – Court's balancing of an individual's constitutional rights against the state's right to protect its citizens.

COMMERCIAL SPEECH - Any speech that proposes a commercial transaction, or promotes products or services.

STRICT SCRUTINY - Method by which courts determine the constitutionality of a law, when a law affects a fundamental right. Under the test, the legislature must have a compelling interest to enact law and measures prescribed by the law must be the least restrictive means possible to accomplish goal.

NOTES:

Rehnquist → dis.
same ridiculous
'greater implies lesser
arg as Posados
+
Grendel dis
opinions

CHAPTER 12
FREEDOM OF SPEECH HOW GOVERNMENT RESTRICTS SPEECH MODES OF ABRIDGMENT AND STANDARDS OF REVIEW
QUICK REFERENCE RULES OF LAW

1. **Content-Neutral Laws and Symbolic Conduct.** When both speech and nonspeech elements are combined in the same conduct, sufficiently important governmental interest in regulating the nonspeech element can justify incidental limitations of First Amendment freedoms. (United States v. O'Brien)

    [For more information on regulation of expressive conduct, see Casenote Law Outline on Constitutional Law, Chapter 12, § I, First Amendment Variables.]

2. **Content-Neutral Laws and Symbolic Conduct.** Burning a U.S flag as a means of political protest may not be criminalized. (Texas v. Johnson)

    [For more information on symbolic speech, see Casenote Law Outline on Constitutional Law, Chapter 12, § 1, First Amendment variables.]

3. **Government's Power to Limit Speech in its Capacity as Proprietor, Educator, Employer, and Patron.** So long as the state's interest is sufficiently substantial to justify the effect of an ordinance, and the effect is no greater than necessary, the state may restrict the posting of messages on public property. (Member, of City Council v. Taxpayers for Vincent)

    [For more information on First Amendment speech regulation, see Casenote Law Outline on Constitutional Law, Chapter 12, § I, First Amendment Variables.]

4. **Government's Power to Limit Speech in its Capacity as Proprietor, Educator, Employer, and Patron.** Expression may be constitutionally restricted to reasonable times, places, and manners. (Clark v. Community for Creative Non-Violence)

    [For more information on regulation of expressive conduct, see Casenote Law Outline on Constitutional Law, Chapter 12, § I, First Amendment Variables.]

5. **Speech and Association by Public Employees and Contractors.** When an employee's speech contributes to his discharge, the court's task is to seek a balance between the interest of the employee, as a citizen, in commenting upon matters of public concern, and the interest of the state, as an employer, in promoting the efficiency of public services it performs through its employees. (Connick v. Myers)

    [For more information on the First Amendment protection of public employee speech and other activities, see Casenote Law Outline on Constitutional Law, Chapter 13, § II, Freedom of Association.]

6. **Prior Restraint.** Freedom of the press is a fundamental right which forms a cornerstone of our Constitution and prior restraint of that freedom will be tolerated only in the most exceptional circumstances involving direct threats to national security or a violent upset of an orderly government. (Near v. Minnesota)

    [For more information on prior restraints on speech, see Casenote Law Outline on Constitutional Law, Chapter 12, § I, First Amendment Variables.]

7. **Prior Restraint.** Any system of prior restraints of expression comes to the Court bearing a heavy presumption against its constitutional validity. (New York Times Co. v. United States [The Pentagon Papers Case])

    [For more information on prior restraint and national security interests, see Casenote Law Outline on Constitutional Law, Chapter 12, § I, First Amendment Variables.]

UNITED STATES v. O'BRIEN

Federal government (P) v. Demonstrator (D)

391 U.S. 367 (1968).

NATURE OF CASE: Appeal from conviction for draft card burning.

FACT SUMMARY: O'Brien (D) was convicted of a violation of a federal statute after he publicly burned his draft card during a demonstration against the compulsory draft and the war in Vietnam.

CONCISE RULE OF LAW: When both speech and nonspeech elements are combined in the same conduct, sufficiently important governmental interest in regulating the nonspeech element can justify incidental limitations of First Amendment freedoms.

FACTS: During a public demonstration directed against the compulsory draft and the war in Vietnam, O'Brien (D) and several others burned their Selective Service Registration Certificates. His act was witnessed by several FBI agents who arrested him. The arrest was for violating a federal statute prohibiting the knowing destruction or knowing mutilation of a Selective Service Certificate. The act also prohibited any changes, alterations, or forgeries of the Certificates. O'Brien (D) was convicted and appealed, contending a violation of his First Amendment right to free speech.

ISSUE: May the government incidentally limit First Amendment rights where it seeks to regulate the nonspeech aspect of conduct composed of both speech and nonspeech elements, where that regulation is supported by a vital governmental interest?

HOLDING AND DECISION: (Warren, C.J.) Yes. The Court considered two aspects of O'Brien's (D) appeal. First, that the statute was unconstitutional in its application to him, and secondly, that the statute was unconstitutional as enacted. Where conduct is composed of speech and nonspeech elements, the speaker can invoke his freedom of speech rights to defend against unwarranted governmental interference. What must be determined is whether the attempted regulation of the nonspeech element also impermissibly inhibits the speech aspect. An incidental restriction on speech can be justified where the government can show a substantial interest in furthering a constitutional power which is not directed at the suppression of speech. In order to facilitate the implementation of the power to raise and support armies, Congress has enacted a system for classifying individuals as to eligibility for military service. The Selective Service cards provide an efficient and reasonable method for identifying those persons previously deemed fit for military service should a national emergency arise. The court found the requirement that the card be in the possession of the holder to be a valid requirement. The Court also found an independent justification for both the possession requirement and the prohibition against mutilation or destruction. While admitting some overlap, the possession requirement was intended for a smooth functioning of the draft system while the prohibition against mutilation was a sabotage prevention measure. A person could destroy another's card while retaining his own intact. The statute was intended as a necessary and proper method to carry out a vital governmental interest. No reasonable alternative is apparent and the narrow construction of the statute indicates it was not intended to suppress communication. As to the contention the statute was unconstitutional on its face, the court found congressional intent to be the smooth functioning of the draft system, not the suppression of anti-war sentiment.

CONCURRENCE: (Harlan, J.) This statute did not prohibit all means of expressing the ideas O'Brien (D) sought to advance. He was free to communicate his concepts in a variety of ways that did not conflict with other governmental interests.

DISSENT: (Douglas, J.) Both the litigants and this Court have failed to address the basic issue of whether the government can enforce conscription for an undeclared war and the case should be remanded for a trial on that point.

EDITOR'S ANALYSIS: Many articles written about this decision have been critical of the court's superficial analysis of the interests involved on both sides of this case. The commentators felt that O'Brien's (D) contention that the draft card was not a vital document was dismissed out of hand. They also felt there should have been a more probing analysis of the operation of the Selective Service System and an examination of the actual, not supposed, importance of the draft card in that system. The strongest criticism of this case has been that the court justified the suppression of expression, not on the basis of a compelling interest but on a bureaucratic system designed for convenience. There was no analysis of alternative systems. Finally, some observers saw in this decision a desire to counterbalance the long string of cases decided by the Warren Court upholding individual rights in the face of much stronger governmental interests.

[For more information on regulation of expressive conduct, see Casenote Law Outline on Constitutional Law, Chapter 12, (II), § I, First Amendment Variables.]

QUICKNOTES

CONSCRIPTION - Compulsory service in the military; the state of being drafted.

FIRST AMENDMENT - Prohibits Congress from enacting any law respecting an establishment of religion, prohibiting the free exercise of religion, abridging freedom of speech or the press, the right of peaceful assembly and the right to petition for a redress of grievances.

SYMBOLIC SPEECH - An activity that expresses an idea without the use of words.

TEXAS v. JOHNSON
State (P) v. Flag owner (D)
491 U.S. 397 (1989).

[handwritten: not fighting words / no invitation / intent]

NATURE OF CASE: Appeal of reversal of conviction for desecration of venerated object.

FACT SUMMARY: Johnson (D), who burned a U.S. flag as a means of political protest, was convicted under Texas (P) law of desecrating a venerated object.

CONCISE RULE OF LAW: Burning a U.S flag as a means of political protest may not be criminalized.

FACTS: Johnson (D) joined a protest at the site of the 1984 Republican National Convention. Except for some minor vandalism in which Johnson (D) took no part, the protest was peaceful. At one point Johnson burned a U.S. flag. He was convicted under a state law criminalizing the desecration of a venerated object. The state court of criminal appeals reversed, holding Johnson's (D) actions protected under the First Amendment. The Supreme Court granted review.

ISSUE: May burning the U.S. flag as a means of political protest be criminalized?

HOLDING AND DECISION: (Brennan, J.) No. Burning a U.S. flag as a means of political protest may not be criminalized. While the First Amendment literally only protects "speech," it has long been the rule that conduct that is meant to express an idea also raises First Amendment concerns. Johnson's (D) behavior undoubtedly was so meant, and Texas (P) conceded this. This being so, the prosecution of Johnson (D) could only be upheld if Texas (P) could show an interest therein unrelated to the suppression of ideas. Two have been offered, keeping the peace and preserving the flag as a symbol of national unity. Here, no breach of the peace occurred, and this court is unwilling to presume that symbolic conduct not directed at any person or group in particular constitutes such a danger to public tranquility that a state may proscribe such conduct. As to the latter justification, it is a core principle of the First Amendment that government may not prohibit expression of an idea because it finds the idea disagreeable. While the Court does not doubt that government is free to promote respect for the flag as a symbol of national unity, it may not compel how a flag, or any symbol, is used. All this being so, the conclusion must be that the law under which Johnson (D) was prosecuted constitutes an abridgement of expressive conduct for which no justification separate from such abridgement can be found, and the statute violates the First Amendment. Affirmed.

DISSENT: (Rehnquist, C.J.) The flag does not represent any idea or point of view. It is a unique symbol of our national heritage and deserves special protection. Beyond that, the acts of

[handwritten: ?? ← There's the idea/pov]

Johnson (D) did have a tendency to incite a breach of the peace. It is more likely to antagonize others than to communicate an idea.

DISSENT: (Stevens, J.) Due to the unique value of the flag as a symbol, government's interest in preserving that value is significant and legitimate. *[handwritten: JP - what are you doing?]*

EDITOR'S ANALYSIS: This was one of the most controversial decisions of the Supreme Court in decades. Almost immediately, calls for a constitutional amendment to overturn the decision were made. Within the year of its decision, Congress had passed a statute, rather than an amendment, in a response that was hoped would pass First Amendment scrutiny. The amendment movement faltered because never in history has the Bill of Rights been amended.

[For more information on symbolic speech, see Casenote Law Outline on Constitutional Law, Chapter 12, § I, First Amendment Variables.]

QUICKNOTES

FIRST AMENDMENT - Prohibits Congress from enacting any law respecting an establishment of religion, prohibiting the free exercise of religion, abridging freedom of speech or the press, the right of peaceful assembly and the right to petition for a redress of grievances.

SYMBOLIC SPEECH - An activity that expresses an idea without the use of words.

SYMBOLIC CONDUCT - Conduct that is expressive of a person's thoughts or opinions.

NOTES:

MEMBERS OF CITY COUNCIL v. TAXPAYERS FOR VINCENT

City council (D) v. Campaign supporters (P)

466 U.S. 789 (1984).

NATURE OF CASE: Appeal of suit challenging a law prohibiting the posting of signs on public property.

FACT SUMMARY: A Los Angeles Municipal Code prohibited the posting of signs on public property, and supporters of Vincent (P), a political candidate, challenged the removal of their signs from utility poles.

CONCISE RULE OF LAW: So long as the state's interest is sufficiently substantial to justify the effect of an ordinance, and the effect is no greater than necessary, the state may restrict the posting of messages on public property.

FACTS: The Los Angeles City Council (D) passed an ordinance prohibiting the posting of signs on public property. Pursuant to the ordinance, city workers removed signs attached to power poles. Some of the signs removed were political message signs for Vincent. Taxpayers for Vincent (P) filed suit, alleging an infringement of speech. The suit was dismissed. The appellate court reversed, and the City (D) appealed to the Supreme Court.

ISSUE: Is it an unconstitutional infringement of speech to prevent political messages from being posted on public property?

HOLDING AND DECISION: (Stevens, J.) No. So long as the state's interest is sufficiently substantial to justify the effect of an ordinance, and the effect is no greater than necessary, the state may restrict the posting of messages on public property. A city has a justified interest in reducing visual blight. To this end, the posting of signs can be regulated withing certain bounds. In this case, the City (D) removed signs from power poles to limit the visual discordance caused by haphazard posting. Since numerous other avenues existed for political speech, the ordinance was not overly restrictive. The ordinance was content neutral and impartially administered. Reversed.

DISSENT: (Brennan, J.) The Court has undermined the First Amendment with its lenient approach toward an argument of aesthetics. The presence of so many signs in Los Angeles indicates that it may be the only avenue of communication feasibly available to many. Such a complete restriction should not be upheld.

EDITOR'S ANALYSIS: Evidently aesthetic concerns are an important matter for government. Given the much grander matters treated in many free-speech cases, it seems unusual that aesthetics would receive such supportive treatment. However, such treatment has been used in several Supreme Court decisions, including *Metromedia, Inc. v. San Diego*, 453 U.S. 490 (1981), so evidently there is harmony on this matter.

[For more information on First Amendment speech regulation, see Casenote Law Outline on Constitutional Law, Chapter 12, § I, First Amendment Variables.]

QUICKNOTES

CONTENT - NEUTRAL - Refers to statutes that regulate speech regardless of its content.

NOTES:

CLARK v. COMMUNITY FOR CREATIVE NON-VIOLENCE

Federal agency (D) v. Organization (P)

468 U.S. 288 (1984).

NATURE OF CASE: Appeal from judgment upholding constitutionality of a state regulation limiting political demonstrations.

FACT SUMMARY: The Community for Creative Non-Violence (CCN) (P) contended that the application of a National Park Service regulation prohibiting camping in certain parks to its demonstration in protest of the plight of the homeless was a violation of their freedom of speech.

CONCISE RULE OF LAW: Expression may be constitutionally restricted to reasonable times, places, and manners.

FACTS: CCN (P) received a permit from the National Park Service allowing them to set up tents in Lafayette Park (across the street from the White House) to protest the plight of the nation's homeless. The permit denied CCN (P) the right to have its members sleep in the tents. This denial was made pursuant to a National Park Service regulation prohibiting camping in Lafayette Park. CCN (P) sued, contending the application of the regulation to its demonstration violated its right to free speech. The district court upheld the regulation, and the court of appeals reversed. The Supreme Court took jurisdiction.

ISSUE: May speech be subjected to reasonable time, place, and manner restrictions?

HOLDING AND DECISION: (White, J.) Yes. Speech may be subject to reasonable time, place, and manner restrictions. Assuming that sleeping, within the context of this case, constitutes expression, it is subject to reasonable time, place, and manner restrictions. The application of the Park Service regulation had nothing to do with the content of the expression. The ban on sleeping was a restriction on the manner of expression. As a result, the application of the regulation did not violate freedom of speech. Reversed.

CONCURRENCE: (Burger, C.J.) Sleeping is conduct, not speech. Therefore, it is not protected by the First Amendment guarantees of free speech.

DISSENT: (Marshall, J.) Sleep in this context went beyond mere conduct. It was symbolic speech, and its ban served no substantial government interest. Therefore, it should not have been suppressed.

EDITOR'S ANALYSIS: The threshold question in cases of this sort is whether the action at issue can be considered speech in a constitutional context. The majority assumed that sleeping in this context was expression, but it failed to hold such. Chief Justice Burger would deny CCN's (P) claim by finding that sleep was conduct and not entitled to First Amendment protection. Justice Marshall on the other hand would characterize sleep as symbolic speech and worthy of protection.

[For more information on regulation of expressive conduct, see Casenote Law Outline on Constitutional Law, Chapter 12, § I, First Amendment Variables.]

QUICKNOTES

SYMBOLIC SPEECH - An activity that expresses an idea without the use of words.

NOTES:

no prior rest, even on ~~tw~~ actual libel

Libel laws can control true 'nuisance'

NEAR v. MINNESOTA

News publisher (D) v. State (P)
283 U.S. 697 (1931).

NATURE OF CASE: Suit for injunction to prevent further publication of a news periodical.

FACT SUMMARY: Near (D) published a news periodical which was found to have violated a statute prohibiting malicious, scandalous, and defamatory newspapers. His periodical was determined to be a public nuisance and an injunction was issued to prevent further publication.

CONCISE RULE OF LAW: Freedom of the press is a fundamental right which forms a cornerstone of our Constitution and prior restraint of that freedom will be tolerated only in the most exceptional circumstances involving direct threats to national security or a violent upset of an orderly government.

FACTS: Near (D) was the publisher of a news periodical which had made charges of extensive corruption and dereliction of duty against several city and county officials, including one member of the grand jury. According to a statute, any person who published or circulated a malicious, scandalous, and defamatory news periodical was guilty of a nuisance. The person found to be committing the nuisance could be enjoined perpetually from committing or maintaining the nuisance. The only defense that could be asserted was that the material was true and was published with good motives and justifiable ends. Near (D) and his periodical were charged under the statute and were adjudged a nuisance, and an injunction was issued restraining him from further violations of the statute.

ISSUE: Since some forms of expression have been found not to enjoy the absolute protection of the First Amendment (e.g., libel), may a state be allowed to impose an injunction, in the nature of a prior restraint on such expression?

HOLDING AND DECISION: (Hughes, C.J.) No. Blackstone noted that prior restraints on the right to publish would destroy freedom of the press. In his view, a person should be allowed to publish anything so long as he was prepared to respond in damages for that which was improper, mischievous, or illegal. Only under the most exceptional circumstances will prior restraint of expression be tolerated. Those circumstances are limited to direct threats to national security or in the incitement to acts of violence or overthrow by force of an orderly government. The criticism of public officials for which Near (D) was convicted was exactly the type of press activity which the First Amendment sought to protect. The statutory defense provided for those charged cannot salvage the unconstitutional invasion of basic rights. Truth was not a requirement to qualify for the freedom of press guarantee. Further, truth alone would not even be a good

defense, for the defendant must also show his proper motives and justifiable ends. The subjects of Near's (D) accusations have not been deprived of their private rights of action against him. The Minnesota statute operates as a prior restraint on the freedom of the press and cannot stand in the face of the strong fundamental guarantees of the First Amendment.

DISSENT: (Butler, J.) The majority misinterprets the application of Blackstone's statement. His reference was to administrative licensors previously restraining even the first publication. Near (D), on the other hand, had already issued his publication when charges were brought against him. He was subject to a court trial, not an administrative sanction. What was proscribed was not his future acts but his past ones. He was enjoined from repeating what had been determined to be an impermissible past act. The majority then states that private actions in libel are an effective and permissible alternative to this statute. It is well known that existing libel laws are an inadequate remedy against the evils sought to be suppressed by this statute.

EDITOR'S ANALYSIS: The Court's distaste for prior restraints on expression has remained unchanged as was evidenced by the Daniel Ellsberg — Pentagon Papers case. Even more recently, the Berger court struck down a Tennessee statute that had prevented a presentation of the stage play "Hair." In the principal case, the majority chose not to discuss another problem area presented by the Minnesota statute. The statute speaks in terms of malicious, scandalous, and defamatory publication. While the term defamatory may be sufficiently specific to afford a legal remedy, the other two terms would seem to be so vague as to thwart proper judicial application. In view of Justice Butler's view that libel laws in 1931 were inadequate to protect against defamations, one wonders what his reaction to the Sullivan-Hill-Gertz line of cases would have been.

[For more information on prior restraints on speech, see Casenote Law Outline on Constitutional Law, Chapter 12, § I, First Amendment Variables.]

QUICKNOTES

FREEDOM OF THE PRESS - The right to publish and publicly disseminate one's views.

PRIOR RESTRAINTS - A restriction placed on communication before it is made.

PUBLIC NUISANCE - An activity that unreasonably interferes with a right common to the overall public.

CONNICK v. MYERS
Employer (D) v. Employee (P)
461 U.S. 138 (1983).

NATURE OF CASE: Action challenging termination of employment on constitutional grounds.

FACT SUMMARY: Myers (P) alleged that her employment was wrongfully terminated because she had exercised her constitutionally protected right of free speech by preparing and circulating a questionnaire soliciting the views of fellow staff members concerning office transfer policy and related matters.

CONCISE RULE OF LAW: When an employee's speech contributes to his discharge, the court's task is to seek a balance between the interest of the employee, as a citizen, in commenting upon matters of public concern, and the interest of the state, as an employer, in promoting the efficiency of public services it performs through its employees.

FACTS: Myers (P), who had some opposition to her impending transfer to prosecute cases in another section of the criminal court, prepared a questionnaire soliciting the views of her fellow assistant district attorneys concerning office transfer policy, office morale, the need for a grievance committee, the level of confidence in supervisors, and whether employees felt pressured to work in political campaigns. She was told her distribution of the questionnaire was an act of insubordination and that she was terminated because of her refusal to accept the transfer. Myers (P) sued, alleging that her employment had been wrongfully terminated because she had exercised her right of free speech. The district court found that her distribution of the questionnaire was the actual reason for her termination and then held that the questionnaire involved matters of public concern and that the state had not "clearly demonstrated" that the survey "substantially interfered" with the operations of the District Attorney's office, as District Attorney Connick had claimed. The Fifth Circuit affirmed.

ISSUE: When faced with a situation in which an employee's speech contributes to his firing, should the court seek a balance between his interest as a citizen in commenting on matters of public concern, and the interest of the state, as an employer, in promoting the efficiency of the public services it performs through its employees?

HOLDING AND DECISION: (White, J.) Yes. When employee expression cannot be fairly considered as relating to any matter of political, social, or other concern to the community, governmental officials should enjoy a wide latitude in managing their offices, without intrusive oversight by the judiciary in the name of the First Amendment. Thus, if Myers' (P) questionnaire cannot be fairly characterized as constituting speech on a matter of public concern, it is unnecessary for this Court to scrutinize the reasons for her discharge. Whether an employee's speech addresses a matter of public concern must be determined by the content, form, and context of a given statement, as revealed by the whole record. In this case, with the exception of the question regarding being pressured to work in political campaigns, the questions Myers (P) posed to her coworkers do not fall under the rubric of matters of "public concern" but rather reflect her dissatisfaction with her transfer and an attempt to turn that displeasure into a cause celebre. Since one of the questions she touched on in her survey does, however, touch upon a matter of public concern and contributed to her discharge, the Court must determine whether Connick (D) was justified in discharging Myers (P). The district court erred in this phase by imposing an unduly onerous burden on the state to justify her discharge, making the government bear the burden of "clearly demonstrating" that the speech in question "substantially interfered" with official responsibilities. Yet, as the Pickering case unmistakably states, the state's burden in justifying a particular discharge varies depending upon the nature of the employee's expression. The Court must, in such cases, reach the most appropriate possible balance of the competing interests of the employee, a citizen, in commenting upon the matters of public concern and the interest of the state, as an employer, in promoting the efficiency of the public services it performs through its employees. When close working relationships are essential to the fulfilling of public responsibilities, a wide degree of deference to the employer's judgment is appropriate. It is not necessary for an employer to allow events to unfold to the extent that the disruption of the office and the destruction of working relationships is manifest before taking action. However, the Court cautions that a stronger showing may be necessary if the employee's speech more substantially involved matters of public concern. Also relevant is the manner, time, and place in which the questionnaire was distributed. Here, the questionnaire was prepared and distributed at the office, with the manner of distribution requiring not only Myers (P) but others to leave their work in order to tend to it. The fact that Myers (P) exercised her rights to speech at the office supports Connick's (D) fears that the functioning of his office was endangered, even if that potential outcome never actually came about. Finally, the context in which the dispute arose is significant; it came upon the heels of an unwelcome transfer notice. Although Myers' (P) survey touched upon matters of public concern in a most limited sense, it is most accurately characterized as an employee grievance concerning internal office policy. Thus, the limited First Amendment interest involved here does not require that Connick (D) tolerate action which he reasonably believed would disrupt the office, undermine his authority, and destroy close working relationships. Accordingly, his discharge of Myers (P) did not offend the First Amendment. Reversed.

DISSENT: (Brennan, J.) I believe that most of Myers' (P) questionnaire, and not just one question thereon, addressed matters of public concern because it discussed subjects that could reasonably be expected to be of interest to persons seeking

143

to develop informed opinions about the manner in which the Orleans Parish District Attorney, an elected official charged with managing a vital government agency, discharges his responsibilities. I also believe that the Court misapplied the Pickering test by effectively deciding, contrary to prior authority, that a public employer's mere apprehension that speech will be disruptive justifies suppression of that speech when all the objective evidence suggests that those fears are essentially unfounded.

EDITOR'S ANALYSIS: It was not until the 1950s and 1960s that the Court began to cast doubt on the theretofore unchallenged dogma that a public employee had no right to object to conditions placed upon the terms of employment — including those restricting his exercise of constitutional rights. While sitting on the Supreme Judicial Court of Massachusetts, Justice Holmes made the following statement expressing this position: "A policeman may have a constitutional right to talk politics, but he has no constitutional right to be a policeman." *McAuliffe v. Mayor of New Bedford,* 155 Mass. 216 (1892).

[For more information on the First Amendment protection of public employee speech and other activities, see Casenote Law Outline on Constitutional Law, Chapter 13, § II, Freedom of Association.]

QUICKNOTES

FIRST AMENDMENT - Prohibits Congress from enacting any law respecting an establishment of religion, prohibiting the free exercise of religion, abridging freedom of speech or the press, the right of peaceful assembly and the right to petition for a redress of grievances.

LIBEL - Speech published in order to defame a living person.

TIME, PLACE, AND MANNER RESTRICTION - Refers to certain types of regulations on speech that are permissible since they only restrict the time, place, and manner in which the speech is to occur.

WRONGFUL TERMINATION - Unlawful termination of an individual's employment.

NOTES:

NEW YORK TIMES CO. v. UNITED STATES

[The Pentagon Papers Case]
News publisher (D) v. Federal Government
403 U.S. 713 (1971).

NATURE OF CASE: Action seeking an injunction.

FACT SUMMARY: The U.S. (P) sought to enjoin the New York Times (D) and the Washington Post (D) from publishing the Pentagon Papers.

CONCISE RULE OF LAW: Any system of prior restraints of expression comes to the Court bearing a heavy presumption against its constitutional validity.

FACTS: The U.S. Government (P) sought to enjoin the New York Times (D) and the Washington Post (D) from publishing the contents of a classified study entitled, "History of U.S. Decision-Making Process on Vietnam Policy" (The Pentagon Papers).

ISSUE: Must one seeking a prior restraint on expression meet a heavy burden of showing justification for imposition of the restraint?

HOLDING AND DECISION: [Per curiam.] Yes. Any system of prior restraints of expression comes to the court bearing a heavy presumption against its constitutional validity. Here, the U.S. (P) carried a heavy burden of showing justification for the enforcement of such a restraint. It did not meet that burden. The denial of injunctive relief is affirmed.

CONCURRENCE: (Black, J.) The cases should have been dismissed and relief denied when they were first presented to the Court. Every moment's continuance of the injunctions against the newspapers amounts to a flagrant, indefensible violation of the First Amendment. To find that the President has "inherent power" to halt the publication of news by resort to the courts would wipe out the First Amendment.

CONCURRENCE: (Douglas, J.) The First Amendment leaves no room for government restraint on the press. Its dominant purpose was to prohibit the widespread practice of governmental suppression of embarrassing information.

CONCURRENCE: (Brennan, J.) The error that has pervaded these cases was the granting of any injunctive relief whatsoever since the entire thrust of the U.S. (P) claim was that publication of the material "could" or "might" or "may" prejudice the national interest. Only governmental allegation and proof that publication must inevitably, directly and immediately, cause the occurrence of an event kindred to imperilling the safety of a transport already at sea can support even the issuance of an interim restraining order. *already at sea?*

CONCURRENCE: (Stewart, J.) Since I cannot say that publication of this material will surely result in direct, immediate, and irreparable damage to the nation, the relief sought must be denied.

CONCURRENCE: (White, J.) While I do feel that publication will do substantial damage to public interests, I nevertheless agree that the U.S. (P) has not met its heavy burden. However, failure by the U.S. (P) to justify prior restraints does not measure its constitutional entitlement to a conviction for criminal publication. That the U.S. (P) mistakenly chose to proceed by injunction does not mean it could not successfully proceed in another way.

CONCURRENCE: (Marshall, J.) The issue in this case is whether this Court or Congress has the power to make law. Congress has specifically rejected passing legislation that would have clearly given the President the power he seeks here, and make the New York Times' (D) current activities unlawful. When Congress has specifically declined to make conduct unlawful it is not for this Court to redecide those issues — to overrule Congress. This Court has no authority to grant the requested relief.

Nixon's boy

DISSENT: (Burger, C.J.) The First Amendment is not an absolute. The record here is not a complete enough one for the Court to act upon. Its incompleteness is due to the fact that these cases have been conducted in unseemly haste. The course followed by the New York Times (D) precluded any possibility of an orderly litigation of the issues.

DISSENT: (Harlan, J.) The doctrine of prior restraints does not prevent the courts from maintaining the status quo long enough to act responsibly. The separation of powers requires that the judicial function in passing upon the activities of the executive in foreign affairs be narrowly restricted. Even if there is some room for the judiciary to override executive determinations of the probable impact of disclosure on national security, the scope of review must be very narrow. Here, the executive's conclusions were not given even the deference owing to an administrative agency, much less a coequal branch of the government.

DISSENT: (Blackmun, J.) The First Amendment is not absolute. There is a danger that publication would result in the death of soldiers, the destruction of alliances, the greatly increased difficulty of negotiation with our enemies, the prolongation of the war, and further delay in the freeing of U.S. prisoners.

EDITOR'S ANALYSIS: On June 13, 1971, the New York Times began publishing parts of the Pentagon Papers. On June 18, the Washington Post also began publishing parts of the papers. The government brought an action to restrain publication. Between June 15 and June 28, two district courts and two courts of appeals considered the case. On June 25, the Supreme Court granted certiorari. Restraining orders were continued in effect pending decision, which was handed down on June 30. Four Justices, Brennan, Marshall, Douglas, and Black dissented from the grants of certiorari, urging summary action and stating that they would not continue the restraint on the newspapers.

[For more information on prior restraint and national security interests, see Casenote Law Outline on Constitutional Law, Chapter 12, § I, First Amendment Variables.]

QUICKNOTES

PRIOR RESTRAINTS - A restriction placed on communication before it is made.

INJUNCTION - A court order requiring a person to do or prohibiting that person from doing a specific act.

FIRST AMENDMENT - Prohibits Congress from enacting any law respecting an establishment of religion, prohibiting the free exercise of religion, abridging freedom of speech or the press, the right of peaceful assembly and the right to petition for a redress of grievances.

CERTIORARI - A discretionary writ issued by a superior court to an inferior court in order to review the lower court's decisions; the Supreme Court's writ ordering such review.

NOTES:

CHAPTER 13
RIGHTS ANCILLARY TO FREEDOM OF SPEECH

QUICK REFERENCE RULES OF LAW

1. **Compelled Disclosure of Membership.** A state must demonstrate a controlling justification for the deterrent effect on the free enjoyment of the right to associate which disclosure of membership lists is likely to have. (NAACP v. Alabama)

   [For more information on the First Amendment freedom of association, see Casenote Law Outline on Constitutional Law, Chapter 13, § II, Freedom of Association.]

2. **Compelled Disclosure of Membership.** Even though a governmental purpose is legitimate and substantial, where a state statute interferes with associational freedom, it is invalid if the same basic purpose can be achieved by less drastic means. (Shelton v. Tucker)

   [For more information on the compelled disclosure of associations and other information as protected by the First Amendment, see Casenote Law Outline on Constitutional Law, Chapter 13, § II, Freedom of Association.]

3. **Compelled Disclosure of Membership.** While a state may properly investigate Communist infiltration of educational or other organizations, it may not demand of these groups disclosure of their membership if such disclosure will seriously impair or inhibit the exercise of constitutional rights. To compel disclosure, the state must show a crucial relationship between the lists and a proper governmental interest. (Gibson v. Florida Legislative Investigation Comm.)

   [For more information on legislative investigations of non-communist organizations, see Casenote Law Outline on Constitutional Law, Chapter 13, § II, Freedom of Association.]

4. **Restrictions on Organizational Activity.** It is well-settled that states have an inherent power to regulate the practice of law in their courts, but where solicitation and counseling activities by lawyers attain the status of political expression and association, free exercise of these rights may not be chilled by vague and overbroad bar regulations which lend themselves to selective enforcement against unpopular causes. (NAACP v. Button)

   [For more information on litigation as expression, see Casenote Law Outline on Constitutional Law, Chapter 13, § II, Freedom of Association.]

5. **Denial of Government Benefits Because of Association.** A law which attaches penalties to membership in certain organizations without requiring a showing of "specific intent" on the member's part to further any illegal aims of the organization infringes on the freedom of association protected by the U.S. Constitution. (Elfbrandt v. Russell)

   [For more information on loyalty oaths, see Casenote Law Outline on Constitutional Law, Chapter 13, § II, Freedom of Association.]

6. **Denial of Government Benefits Because of Association.** Legislation which prohibits mere knowing membership in an organization, without specific intent to further its unlawful goals, or inactive membership, violates constitutional rights of freedom of association. (Keyishian v. Board of Regents)

   [For more information on the compelled disavowal of association, see Casenote Law Outline on Constitutional Law, Chapter 13, § II, Freedom of Association.]

7. **Money and Political Campaigns.** Although "the First Amendment protects political association as well as political expression, a limitation upon the amount that any one person or group may contribute to (and associate with a) candidate or political committee entails only a marginal restriction on the contributor's ability to engage in free communication (and association)"; but, "a restriction on the amount of money a person or group can spend on political communication (as a whole) during a campaign (excessively) reduces the quantity of expression by restricting the number of issues discussed, the depth of their exploration, and the size of the audience reached." (Buckley v. Valeo)

   [For more information on money and political speech, see Casenote Law Outline on Constitutional Law, Chapter 13, § I, Free Speech in Special Contexts.]

8. **Governmental Demands for Information from the Press.** The First Amendment's freedom of press does not exempt a reporter from disclosing to a grand jury information that he has received in confidence. (Branzburg v. Hayes)

   [For more information on the absence of special press immunity from governmental inquiries, obligations, or processes, see Casenote Law Outline on Constitutional Law, Chapter 13, § III, Freedom of the Press.]

9. **Laws Discriminating Against the Press.** Differential taxation of the press places such a burden on the interests protected by the First Amendment that it cannot pass constitutional muster unless the state asserts a counterbalancing interest of compelling importance that cannot be achieved without differential taxation. (Minneapolis Star & Tribune Co. v. Minnesota Comm'r of Revenue)

   [For more information on differential taxation of the press, see Casenote Law Outline on Constitutional Law, Chapter 13, § III, Freedom of the Press.]

CPUSA — Dennis? ?
Jatka
Noto?
Scales?

NAACP v. ALABAMA
Association (D) v. State (P)
357 U.S. 449 (1958).

NATURE OF CASE: Appeal from conviction for contempt for failure to obey state court order to produce records.

FACT SUMMARY: The NAACP (D), in a hearing initiated by the State of Alabama (P) to oust it from the state for failure to comply with incorporation requirements, refused to obey a state court order to produce its membership lists.

CONCISE RULE OF LAW: A state must demonstrate a controlling justification for the deterrent effect on the free enjoyment of the right to associate which disclosure of membership lists is likely to have.

FACTS: Alabama (P) brought proceedings against the NAACP (D) to oust it from the state for failure to comply with a state statute setting forth requirements governing foreign corporations. The NAACP (D) claimed it was exempt. A state court issued an order restraining the NAACP (D) from continuing to engage in further activities or to attempt to qualify itself while the action was pending. Before the hearing began, the state moved for the production of the NAACP's (D) membership lists, alleging that the documents were necessary for adequate preparation for the hearing. The court granted the motion and issued an order to that effect. The NAACP (D) thereupon complied with the requirements of the statute but did not produce the lists. The NAACP (D) was held in civil contempt, fined, and prevented from obtaining a hearing on the merits of the ouster action until it produced the records.

ISSUE: May a state, consistent with the Due Process Clause of the Fourteenth Amendment, compel an organization to reveal to the state's Attorney General the names and addresses of all its state members and agents without demonstrating a controlling justification for the deterrent effect on free association disclosure would involve?

HOLDING AND DECISION: (Harlan, J.) No. Group association is an effective means to further advocacy of both public and private viewpoints. The fact that Alabama (P) has taken no direct steps to interfere with the Association's (D) freedom of association does not end the question for it may have engaged in more subtle intimidation. There is a vital relationship between the freedom to associate and privacy in one's associations. Here, there is a good possibility that disclosure would expose members to economic reprisal, loss of employment, and threat of physical coercion, thus having a deterrent effect on continued membership and discouraging others from joining. It is insufficient to answer that the pressure comes from the private community, and not the state for there is interplay between the two. Having found the potential for deterrence, the next inquiry is

whether the state was justified in seeking the lists. The disclosure of the lists has no substantial bearing on the issue of compliance with the state statute. This case differs substantially from an earlier Supreme Court decision involving the Ku Klux Klan and its failure to produce membership lists in violation of a New York law. There, the nature of the Ku Klux Klan, its violent tendencies which the Court took notice of, and its failure to comply with any conditions, unlike in the instant situation, distinguish the two groups. The judgment of civil contempt is reversed.

EDITOR'S ANALYSIS: At the same time that state investigations seeking public disclosure were prevailing over countervailing claims of First Amendment freedoms in other contexts, the Court, as evidenced in *NAACP v. Alabama* and *Shelton v. Tucker*, 364 U.S. 479, 81 S. Ct. 247, 5 L. Ed. 2d 231 (1960), required the state to produce a relevant justification for its probe and the collateral effect of disclosure on First Amendment freedoms. *NAACP v. Alabama* thus portends a shift in the Court's focus to greater scrutiny of reasons for state inquiries which have deterrent, or "chilling" effects, on freedom of speech, association, or expression. The new approach would gain wider application in the 1960's where the state's interest in seeking information was pitted against the individual's right to privacy.

[For more information on the First Amendment freedom of association, see Casenote Law Outline on Constitutional Law, Chapter 13, Freedom of Speech (III), § II, Freedom of Association.]

QUICKNOTES

CONTEMPT - An act of omission that interferes with a court's proper administration of justice.

CHILLING EFFECT - Resulting in the inhibition or restriction of an activity.

DUE PROCESS CLAUSE - Clauses found in the Fifth and Fourteenth Amendments to the United States Constitution providing that no person shall be deprived of "life, liberty, or property, without due process of law."

FREEDOM OF ASSOCIATION - The right to peaceably assemble.

RIGHT TO PRIVACY - The violation of an individual's right to be protected against unwarranted interference in his personal affairs, falling into one of four categories: (1) appropriating the individual's likeness or name for commercial benefit; (2) intrusion into the individual's seclusion; (3) public disclosure of private facts regarding the individual; and (4) disclosure of facts placing the individual in a false light.

SHELTON v. TUCKER
NAACP members (P) v. State (D)
364 U.S. 479 (1960).

NATURE OF CASE: Federal and state class actions to have statute requiring teachers to file membership lists declared unconstitutional.

FACT SUMMARY: Arkansas law required each public school teacher to file, as a condition of employment, a list of all organizations he has been a member of in the preceding five years.

CONCISE RULE OF LAW: Even though a governmental purpose is legitimate and substantial, where a state statute interferes with associational freedom, it is invalid if the same basic purpose can be achieved by less drastic means.

FACTS: Arkansas law required each public school teacher, as a condition of employment, to file annually an affidavit listing, without exception, every organization to which he has belonged or contributed regularly in the preceding five years. Shelton (P), a member of the NAACP, refused to do so and was fired from his position. Carr (P), a state university professor, listed only professional organizations, denied ever belonging to any subversive group, and offered to answer all questions relating to his professional qualifications. Gephardt (P), a teacher, did the same. Both Carr (P) and Gephardt (P) were advised that their contracts might not be renewed.

ISSUE: May a state comprehensively inquire into the membership affiliations of its public school teachers?

HOLDING AND DECISION: (Stewart, J.) No. The statute violates a teacher's associational right as protected and applied to the states by the Due Process Clause of the Fourteenth Amendment. While the state has a legitimate interest in checking the fitness and competence of its teachers, and the method here chosen is relevant, the individual's right to associate freely is also infringed upon. Requiring full disclosure poses the danger of public embarrassment, and attendant pressure on the teacher to avoid memberships which might displease his superiors. Because the scope of the statute is unlimited, a teacher is required to list memberships which have no possible bearing on his fitness or competence, and, therefore, the statute's sweep is too broad.

DISSENT: (Frankfurter, J.) The state is entitled to know whether the teacher, by joining too many organizations, is spreading himself too thin so that his work might suffer. Merely asking for the number of memberships, and the time involved, is insufficient since it is the quality and nature of the organizational work that is revealing. The issue the Court should have addressed is whether, in light of the particular kind of restriction placed upon

individual liberty, it is reasonable for the state to choose one form of regulation over another.

EDITOR'S ANALYSIS: The opinion in Shelton has been criticized for its failure to suggest what other narrower alternatives were available to the state. Consistent with this criticism, it has been suggested that the Court, by refusing to indicate alternatives, was attempting to ward off charges that it was "legislating."

[For more information on the compelled disclosure of associations and other information as protected by the First Amendment, see Casenote Law Outline on Constitutional Law, Chapter 13, § II, Freedom of Association.]

QUICKNOTES
AFFIDAVIT - A declaration of facts written and affirmed before a witness.

NOTES:

GIBSON v. FLORIDA LEGISLATIVE INVESTIGATION COMM.

NAACP member (D) v. State (P)

372 U.S. 539 (1963).

NATURE OF CASE: Appeal from conviction for contempt of state legislative committee.

FACT SUMMARY: Gibson (D), president of an NAACP branch, refused to bring membership and contribution lists with him when ordered to testify before a state legislative investigating committee.

CONCISE RULE OF LAW: While a state may properly investigate Communist infiltration of educational or other organizations, it may not demand of these groups disclosure of their membership if such disclosure will seriously impair or inhibit the exercise of constitutional rights. To compel disclosure, the state must show a crucial relationship between the lists and a proper governmental interest.

FACTS: The Florida Legislative Investigation Committee (P), which conducted inquiries into Communist infiltration in the field of race relations, ordered Gibson (D), the president of a local NAACP branch, to appear before it, and to bring membership and contribution lists with him. Gibson (D) refused to bring the lists, but did offer to answer any question on the basis of his own knowledge. Gibson (D) did testify that the names and photographs of 14 "known" Communists were not, in his knowledge, associated with the NAACP. Gibson (D) was convicted of contempt.

ISSUE: Must a state demonstrate a compelling government interest when investigating organizations not previously identified as subversive if the thrust of the investigation infringes upon rights protected by the First and Fourteenth Amendments?

HOLDING AND DECISION: (Goldberg, J.) Yes. No compelling state interest need be shown if: 1) the subject under investigation is the Communist Party (a subversive organization); and 2) the witness is questioned as to his own past or present membership in the party. Neither of these requirements is present here. First, the NAACP, as the record indicates, is against communism and certainly not subversive. Second, the inquiry was not directed at Gibson (D) himself, but at other members of the NAACP. Legitimate organizations do not forfeit their right to associational freedom simply because a legislative committee is investigating subversion or infiltration. There is no substantial evidence linking the NAACP to subversive activity or to the 14 individuals the Committee (P) identified as communists. Associational freedom must be particularly protected where, as here, an organization's beliefs are unpopular, and there is a danger of a "chilling" effect. The Committee (P) has laid no foundation.

DISSENT: (Harlan, J.) The "nexus" approach is wrong because: (1) it was only claimed that some of the NAACP's members were engaged in subversive activity; (2) there is no difference between Communist infiltration of and Communist activity by organizations; (3) an investigation cannot be reasonably expected to prove in advance the very thing it is trying to find out, and (4) the Committee (P) cannot defer to self-investigation by the NAACP. Finally, the scope of the inquiry here was limited.

EDITOR'S ANALYSIS: In *DeGregory v. New Hampshire Attorney General*, 383 U.S. 825 (1966), a state subversive activities investigation probed the past Communist membership of a witness who was no longer a member of the Party. In overturning a contempt conviction, the Court concluded that "the staleness of both the basis for the investigation and its subject matter makes indefensible such exposure of one's associational and political past the information being sought was historical, not current . . . and without relation to existing need."

[For more information on legislative investigations of non-communist organizations, see Casenote Law Outline on Constitutional Law, Chapter 13, § II, Freedom of Association.]

QUICKNOTES

CHILLING EFFECT - Resulting in the inhibition or restriction of an activity.

COMPELLING STATE INTEREST - Defense to an alleged Equal Protection Clause violation that a state action was necessary in order to protect an interest that the government is under a duty to protect.

CONTEMPT - An act of omission that interferes with a court's proper administration of justice.

NOTES:

NAACP v. BUTTON
Association (D) v. State (P)
371 U.S. 415 (1963).

NATURE OF CASE: Appeal of a finding of a violation of ABA Canons of Professional Ethics.

FACT SUMMARY: Virginia amended its bar regulations to ban the mass counseling and soliciting techniques of the NAACP.

CONCISE RULE OF LAW: It is well-settled that states have an inherent power to regulate the practice of law in their courts, but where solicitation and counseling activities by lawyers attain the status of political expression and association, free exercise of these rights may not be chilled by vague and overbroad bar regulations which lend themselves to selective enforcement against unpopular causes.

FACTS: As a part of their statewide school desegregation program, NAACP lawyers held regular meetings with Negro parents to explain legal steps necessary to achieve such desegregation. After such meetings, forms were provided to the parents authorizing the NAACP (D) to represent them. With such authorization, NAACP (D) attorneys would then commence action. In response to this practice, Virginia added a Chapter 33 to its code of conduct for lawyers which prohibited solicitation of legal action by agents of any organization which employs lawyers to carry out such actions. The Virginia Supreme Court of Appeals found the NAACP (D) in violation of this chapter as well as ABA Canons of Professional Ethics 35 (prohibiting the control of legal services by intermediary lay agencies) and 47 (prohibiting any lawyer from assisting such an intermediary lay agency). This appeal followed.

ISSUE: May a state statute regulating the practice of law constitutionally be used to prevent minority groups from associating to seek legal redress?

HOLDING AND DECISION: (Brennan, J.) No. It is well settled that states have an inherent power to regulate the practice of law in their courts, but where solicitation and counseling activities by lawyers attain the status of political expression and association, free exercise of these rights may not be chilled by vague and overbroad bar regulations which lend themselves to selective enforcement against unpopular causes. Virginia claims that solicitation, a crime, is outside the protections of the First Amendment, but First Amendment protection of vigorous advocacy may not be so inhibited by such labeling. Association for litigation (and thereby expression) may be the most effective way to protect minority rights. Proscribing it requires a compelling state interest which Virginia has failed to demonstrate here. Virginia claims that its interest in regulating the practice of law is sufficient. However, the purpose behind anti-solicitation rules has traditionally been to prevent improper private gain by attorneys. No such situation exists here. The ban is unconstitutional. Ruling is reversed.

DISSENT: (Harlan, J.) While the Court is correct in saying that association for litigation is a form of political expression and association, it should have balanced the state interests to reach a contrary outcome. Over and above the anti-private-gain purposes of the regulation of the bar, there is a deeper and more fundamental purpose of preventing outside interference with the attorney-client relationship. Here, even though the interests of the NAACP and the parents were identical, and the rights involved were fundamental, Virginia's attempt to so preserve the attorney-client relationship should have been upheld.

EDITOR'S ANALYSIS: This case points up the now generally recognized view that state regulation of the practice of law may not be used to interfere with any group's freedom of expression or association. This principle has been extended by the Court to cover associations less unpopular than the NAACP as well. In *Brotherhood of Railroad Trainmen v. Virginia* (1964), the Court held that a labor union had a right to set up a system of referrals of members to selected attorneys as a part of its freedom of association and expression in union-related activities. In *U.M.W. v. Illinois Bar* (1967), the court similarly held that a union had the right to hire a lawyer (on salary) to represent members before a state workmen's compensation board.

[For more information on litigation as expression, see Casenote Law Outline on Constitutional Law, Chapter 13, § II, Freedom of Association.]

QUICKNOTES

ATTORNEY-CLIENT RELATIONSHIP - The confidential relationship established when a lawyer enters into employment with a client.

COMPELLING STATE INTEREST - Defense to an alleged Equal Protection Clause violation that a state action was necessary in order to protect an interest that the government is under a duty to protect.

SOLICITATION - Contact initiated by an attorney for the purpose of obtaining employment.

VAGUENESS AND OVERBREADTH - Characteristics of a statute that make it difficult to identify the limits of the conduct being regulated.

ELFBRANDT v. RUSSELL
Teacher (P) v. State (D)
384 U.S. 11 (1966).

NATURE OF CASE: Declaratory judgment to have loyalty oath declared unconstitutional.

FACT SUMMARY: Anyone who took a loyalty oath required for state employment and "knowingly and willfully" joined the Communist Party or any organization dedicated to the overthrow of the government of Arizona was subject to prosecution for perjury and removal from office.

CONCISE RULE OF LAW: A law which attaches penalties to membership in certain organizations without requiring a showing of "specific intent" on the member's part to further any illegal aims of the organization infringes on the freedom of association protected by the U.S. Constitution.

FACTS: Arizona required that all state employees take a loyalty oath to uphold the U.S. Constitution, and the Constitution and laws of Arizona, and to defend them against all enemies. The state legislature had put a gloss on the oath by subjecting to prosecution for perjury and removal from public office anyone who took the oath and "knowingly and willfully" has membership in the Communist Party or "any other organization" having "for one of its purposes" the overthrow of the government of Arizona where the employee had knowledge of the unlawful purpose. Elfbrandt (P), a Quaker teacher, refused to take the oath, and claiming she did not know what the oath meant, sought a declaratory judgment.

ISSUE: Is mere membership in an organization without any showing of "specific intent" to further any illegal aim of the organization constitutionally sufficient to invoke penalties attached by the state?

HOLDING AND DECISION: (Douglas, J.) No. A blanket proscription of membership in a group having both legal and illegal goals may impair freedom of political expression and association. Nothing in the oath, or the statutory gloss put upon it attempts to exclude association by an employee who does not subscribe to the organization's unlawful ends. There is a danger that employees will be prosecuted for knowing but guiltless behavior. Juries may tend to label organizations they don't approve of as "Communist." There is no way the employee can get clearance in advance. If a member does not share the unlawful purpose of an organization or participate in its illegal activities, he poses no danger to the public. "Specific intent" must be proved: There can be no conclusive presumption based on mere membership. The statute violates the freedom of association protected by the First Amendment, and made applicable to the states through the Fourteenth Amendment; it discourages employees of integrity who are committed to intellectual freedom from becoming teachers. Where First Amendment freedoms are threatened, a statute must be narrowly drawn to punish only behavior which poses a "clear and present danger to a substantial interest of the state." The Act authorizing the loyalty oath here is unconstitutional.

DISSENT: (White, J.) "The crime provided by the Arizona law is not just the act of becoming a member of an organization, but it is that membership plus concurrent public employment." Since knowing membership in specified organizations is a valid disqualification, a government may also remove from office employees who engage in disqualifying acts.

EDITOR'S ANALYSIS: The obscurity of the Court's balancing test enunciated here has been criticized. Professor Israel has commented: "Opinions relying upon the 'overbroadness' rule often provide no more indication of the Court's analysis than a conclusionary statement that a particular aspect of the statutory infringement on speech was overly broad as it applied to the particular interest that the state advanced in that case. The majority opinion in Elfbrandt fits this pattern and, indeed, is more delinquent, since the Court failed in large part even to identify the state interest against which the legislation was balanced."

[For more information on loyalty oaths, see Casenote Law Outline on Constitutional Law, Chapter 13, § II, Freedom of Association.]

QUICKNOTES

DECLARATORY JUDGMENT - A judgment of the rights between opposing parties that is binding, but does not grant coercive relief (i.e. damages.)

PERJURY - The making of false statements under oath.

NOTES:

KEYISHIAN v. BOARD OF REGENTS

State university faculty member (P) v. State (D)

385 U.S. 589 (1967).

NATURE OF CASE: Action seeking declaratory and injunctive relief.

FACT SUMMARY: Keyishian (P) and other faculty members of a state university, who refused to sign certificates that they were not Communists, were notified that their refusal to sign would require their dismissal.

CONCISE RULE OF LAW: Legislation which prohibits mere knowing membership in an organization, without specific intent to further its unlawful goals, or inactive membership, violates constitutional rights of freedom of association.

FACTS: New York statutes provided that unreasonable or seditious utterances were grounds for dismissal from the public school system. The statutes also made membership in certain subversive organizations, among them the Communist Party, prima facie evidence of grounds for disqualification from any public school position. Keyishian (P) was a faculty member of a state university. He refused to sign a certificate that he was not a Communist. He was notified that his failure to sign would require his dismissal.

ISSUE: Is state legislation which makes membership in an organization advocating forceful overthrow of the government a ground for disqualification from public employment constitutional?

HOLDING AND DECISION: (Brennan, J.) No. Mere knowing membership without a specific intent to further the unlawful aims of an organization or inactive membership is not a constitutionally adequate basis for exclusion from public employment. Legislation proscribing such membership cannot be sustained. Measured against this standard, the New York statutes sweep overbroadly into association which may not be regulated. Proof of nonactive membership or a showing of the absence of intent to further unlawful aims will not rebut the presumption of disqualification raised by membership in certain organizations. Hence, the statutes suffered from impermissible overbreadth in that they sought to bar employment both for association which may be regulated and for association which may not be regulated without violating First Amendment rights. The statutes were invalid in so far as they sanction mere knowing membership without any showing of specific intent to further the unlawful aims of the Communist Party.

DISSENT: (Clark, J.) The majority has swept away our right of self-preservation. A state may provide that one who willfully and deliberately becomes a member of an organization that advocates that our government should be overthrown by force or violence or unlawful means, is prima facie disqualified from teaching in its university.

EDITOR'S ANALYSIS: The Warren Court often invoked the overbreadth principle to strike down legislation. Gunther states that the popularity of the overbreadth doctrine may be attributable to its relatively technical appearance. On its face, it does not, like many of the other techniques, deal explicitly with substantive values such as speech. It purports to be concerned with means to legitimate ends, rather than "ultimate quasi-legislative choices." As applied in the area of First Amendment rights, it still involves determining what expression is protected by the First Amendment, since to strike down an excessively broad statute because it impinges on an area of protected freedom presupposes, at least, an implicit judgment about what the contours of that area are.

[For more information on the compelled disavowal of association, see Casenote Law Outline on Constitutional Law, Chapter 13, § II, Freedom of Association.]

QUICKNOTES

DECLARATORY RELIEF - A judgment of the court establishing the rights of the parties.

FIRST AMENDMENT - Prohibits Congress from enacting any law respecting an establishment of religion, prohibiting the free exercise of religion, abridging freedom of speech or the press, the right of peaceful assembly and the right to petition for a redress of grievances.

INJUNCTIVE RELIEF - A court order issued as a remedy, requiring a person to do, or prohibiting that person from doing, a specific act.

NOTES:

BUCKLEY v. VALEO
Congressman (P) v. Federal government (D)
424 U.S. 1 (1976).

NATURE OF CASE: Action for declaration of unconstitutionality.

FACT SUMMARY: Senator Buckley (P) and others challenged the Federal Election Campaign Act's contribution and expenditure limitation, reporting and disclosure requirements, and public financing of presidential elections.

CONCISE RULE OF LAW: Although "the First Amendment protects political association as well as political expression . . . a limitation upon the amount that any one person or group may contribute to (and associate with a) candidate or political committee entails only a marginal restriction on the contributor's ability to engage in free communication (and association)"; but, "a restriction on the amount of money a person or group can spend on political communication (as a whole) during a campaign (excessively) reduces the quantity of expression by restricting the number of issues discussed, the depth of their exploration, and the size of the audience reached."

FACTS: In order to curtail political corruption, Congress in the Federal Election Campaign Act of 1971, as amended in 1974, developed an intricate statutory scheme for the regulation of federal political campaigns. Inter alia, Congress imposed a $1000 limitation on individual contributions "to a single candidate" in § 608 (b)(1), a $5000 limitation on "contributions" to a single candidate by political committees in § 608(b)(2), a $25,000 limitation on total "contributions" by any individual in one year to political candidates in § 608 (b)(3), a $1000 ceiling in "expenditures" relative to a known candidate in § 608 (e)(1), and similar ceilings on "expenditures" by the candidate and his family and on overall campaign "expenditures" § 608 (a) and (c). In addition, Congress required disclosure by candidates of all "contributions" greater than $10, and by individuals of all "contributions and expenditures" aggregating over $1000 — § 434 (e). In a separate action, Congress provided for federal financing of presidential elections. Senator Buckley (P) and others, pursuant to a special section in the Act of 1971, brought this action to have all the above mentioned sections declared an unconstitutional violation of their First Amendment rights of freedom of expression and association. This appeal followed.

ISSUE: Does the strong governmental interest in preventing election corruption justify imposition of substantial restrictions on the effective ability of any individual to express his political beliefs and engage in political association?

HOLDING AND DECISION: (Per Curiam) No. Although "the First Amendment protects political association as well as political expression . . . a limitation upon the amount that any one person or group may contribute to (and associate with) a candidate or a political committee entails only a marginal restriction on the contributor's

ability to engage in free communication (and association);" but, "a restriction on the amount of money a person or group can spend on political communication (as a whole) during a campaign (excessively) reduces the quantity of expression by restricting the number of issues discussed, the depth of their exploration, and the size of the audience reached." As such, the so-called "contribution" (i.e., to candidates) limitations here (§ 608(b)1-3) may be upheld as valid means for limiting political corruption by "fat cats." The so-called "expenditure" (on political expression) limitations (§ 608 a,c,e), however, places too broad a restriction on the individual's ability to speak out and must therefore be voided. As for the reporting and disclosure requirements, broad as they are, they are clearly upheld by the "compelling government interest" in deterring corruption by getting important information to the voters and providing records for enforcement of the law. finally, the challenge to the public financing of presidential elections is simply unfounded since it entails no abridgment of speech whatsoever.

CONCURRENCE AND DISSENT: (Burger, C.J.) The disclosure requirements for small contributions are unnecessarily broad intrusions into First Amendment rights since only large contributions are likely to cause the corruption the Act is supposed to remedy. The contribution limitations upheld by the Court place just as great a burden on political expression as expenditure limitations. Finally, there is no constitutional justification for the "incestuous" relationship between government and politics which the public financing law, upheld by the Court, creates.

CONCURRENCE AND DISSENT: (White, J.) Since the expenditure limitations, struck down by the Court, are neutral as to the content of speech, are not motivated by the fear of political expression and reflect the well-founded conclusion of Congress that regulation of campaign finances are essential to protect the integrity of the system, the First Amendment is not violated by them.

EDITOR'S ANALYSIS: In this case, the Court has identified one of the few "compelling governmental interests" which may be employed to justify congressional regulation of an area subject to strict judicial scrutiny. That interest is the interest in maintaining the integrity of the political process. Note, however, that even though the interest is held compelling, the Court does not automatically affirm its imposition. Note that the Court's decision left the Federal Election Campaign Act rife with loopholes. Perhaps the most exploited was that which permitted individuals to "expend" (i.e., separately from any candidate or his organization) large sums to endorse a vote for a particular candidate.

[For more information on money and political speech, see Casenote Law Outline on Constitutional Law, Chapter 13, § I, Free Speech in Special Contexts.]

QUICKNOTES
INTER ALIA - "Among other things."

BRANZBURG v. HAYES
News reporters (D) v. State and federal government (P)
408 U.S. 665 (1972).

NATURE OF CASE: Appeal from contempt citations for failure to testify before state and federal grand juries.

FACT SUMMARY: Newsmen refused to testify before state and federal grand juries, claiming that their news sources were confidential.

CONCISE RULE OF LAW: The First Amendment's freedom of press does not exempt a reporter from disclosing to a grand jury information that he has received in confidence.

FACTS: Branzburg (D), who had written articles for a newspaper about drug activities he had observed, refused to testify before a state grand jury regarding his information. Pappas (D), a television newsman, even though he wrote no story, refused to testify before a state grand jury on his experiences inside Black Panther headquarters. Caldwell (D), a reporter who had interviewed several Black Panther leaders, and written stories about the articles, refused to testify before a federal grand jury which was investigating violations of criminal statutes dealing with threats against the President and traveling interstate to incite a riot. Branzburg (D) and Pappas (D) were held in contempt.

ISSUE: Does the First Amendment protect a newsman from revealing his sources before a grand jury which has subpoenaed him to testify, even if the information is confidential?

HOLDING AND DECISION: (White, J.) No. The First Amendment's freedom of press does not exempt a reporter from disclosing to a grand jury information that he has received in confidence. The First Amendment does not invalidate every incidental burdening of the press that may result from the enforcement of civil or criminal statutes of general applicability. Newsmen cannot invoke a testimonial privilege not enjoined by other citizens. The Constitution should not shield criminals who wish to remain anonymous from prosecution through disclosure. Forcing newsmen to testify will not impede the flow of news. The newsman may never be called. Many political groups will still turn to the reporter because they are dependent on the media for exposure. Grand jury proceedings are secret and the police are experienced in protecting informants. More important, the public's interest in news flow does not override the public's interest in deterring crime. Here, the grand juries were not probing at will without relation to existing need; the information sought was necessary to the respective investigations. A grand jury is not restricted to seeking information from non-newsmen — it may choose the best method for its task. The contempt citations are affirmed.

CONCURRENCE: (Powell, J.) The newsman always has resort to the courts to quash subpoenas where his testimony bears only a remote and tenuous relationship to the subject of the investigation.

DISSENT: (Stewart, J.) The press should not be treated as an investigating tool of the government. Concrete evidence exists proving that fear of an unbridled subpoena power deters sources. The Court's inquiry should be: (1) whether there is a rational connection between the government's and the deterrence of First Amendment activity; and (2) whether the effect would occur with some regularity. The government has the burden of showing: (1) that the information sought is clearly relevant to a precisely defined subject of governmental inquiry; (2) it is reasonable to think the witness in question has that information; and (3) there is no other means of obtaining that information less destructive of First Amendment freedoms.

DISSENT: (Douglas, J.) A newsman has an absolute right not to appear before a grand jury so as to have absolute privacy in uncovering information in the course of testing his hunches. Effective government depends upon a free flow of opinion and reporting.

EDITOR'S ANALYSIS: Guidelines promulgated by the Attorney General for federal officials to follow when subpoenaing members of the press to testify before grand juries or at criminal trials included the following test for information: (1) whether there is "sufficient reason to believe that the information sought is essential to a successful investigation;" and (2) whether the information cannot be obtained from non-press sources. However, in "emergencies and other unusual situations, subpoenas which do not conform to the guidelines may be issued."

[For more information on the absence of special press immunity from governmental inquiries, obligations, or processes, see Casenote Law Outline on Constitutional Law, Chapter 13, § III, Freedom of the Press.]

QUICKNOTES

CONTEMPT - An act of omission that interferes with a court's proper administration of justice.

FREEDOM OF THE PRESS - The right to publish and publicly disseminate one's views.

GRAND JURY - A group summoned to investigate, inform, and accuse persons of crimes when sufficient evidence exists to do so.

SUBPOENA - A mandate issued by court to compel a witness to appear at trial.

MINNEAPOLIS STAR AND TRIBUNE CO. v. MINNESOTA COMM'R OF REVENUE

Newspaper publisher (P) v. State (D)

260 U.S. 575 (1983).

NATURE OF CASE: Action for a refund of use taxes paid.

FACT SUMMARY: The Minneapolis Star (P) contended that Minnesota had acted unconstitutionally in imposing a four percent use tax on the cost of ink and paper consumed in the production of any publication and then enacting an exemption that effectively resulted in only a few of the biggest newspapers having to pay any such use tax.

CONCISE RULE OF LAW: Differential taxation of the press places such a burden on the interests protected by the First Amendment that it cannot pass constitutional muster unless the state asserts a counterbalancing interest of compelling importance that cannot be achieved without differential taxation.

FACTS: Under the tax scheme set up by the Minnesota legislature, newspapers were exempt from the four percent sales tax. However, a four percent use tax on the costs of ink and paper consumed in the production of any publication was imposed. In addition, an exemption was provided for the first $100,000 worth of ink and paper consumed by a publication in any calendar year, which amounted to giving each publication an annual tax credit of $4,000. Only eleven papers, one of them the Tribune (P), used sufficient quantities of ink and paper to become liable for payment of use taxes beyond the amount of the tax credit in 1974. Only thirteen papers had to pay actual use tax in 1975. In challenging the constitutionality of the use tax and seeking a refund of the use taxes it had paid, the Tribune (P) argued that there had been a violation of the guarantees of freedom of the press and equal protection found in the First and Fourteenth Amendments. The Minnesota Supreme Court upheld the tax against this constitutional challenge.

ISSUE: In order to be constitutionally permissible, must any differential taxation of the press be necessary to the achieving of a state interest of compelling importance?

HOLDING AND DECISION: (O'Connor, J.) Yes. Because differential taxation of the press places such a burden on the interests protected by the First Amendment, it is not constitutionally permissible unless the state asserts a counterbalancing interest of compelling importance that cannot be achieved without differential taxation. By creating this special use tax, Minnesota singled out the press for special tax treatment. It justifies such by its need to raise revenue. Yet, that goal could be attained by taxing businesses generally, thus avoiding the censorial threat implicit in a tax that singles out the press. Minnesota offers the counter-argument that the use tax actually favors the press. However, the very selection of the press for special treatment threatens the press not only with the current differential treatment, but with the possibility of subsequent differentially more burdensome treatment. Thus, this Court would hesitate to fashion a rule that automatically allowed the state to single out the press for a different method of taxation as long as the effective burden on the press was lighter than that on other businesses. Such a rule should also be avoided because the courts as institutions are poorly equipped to evaluate with precision the relative burdens of various methods of taxation. Minnesota's ink and paper tax would not survive anyway because it violates the First Amendment for another reason other than its singling out of the press. It also violates the First Amendment because it targets a small group of newspapers. Recognizing a power in the state not only to single out the press but also to tailor the tax so that it singles out a few members of the press presents such a potential for abuse that no interest suggested by Minnesota can justify the scheme. When, as in this case, a tax exemption operates to select such a narrowly defined group to bear the full burden of the tax, the tax begins to resemble more a penalty for a few of the largest newspapers than an attempt to favor struggling smaller enterprises. There having been no satisfactory justification offered for this tax on the use of ink and paper, it must be held to violate the First Amendment. Reversed.

DISSENT: (Rehnquist, J.) The $1,224,747 the Tribune (P) actually paid in use taxes over the years in question is significantly less burdensome than the $3,685,092 that it would have had to pay were the sales of its newspapers subject to the sales tax. Thus the tax scheme, which allowed newspapers to pay a use tax in return for being free of sales tax actually benefitted, not burdened, the freedom of speech and the press. If there was no burden, there was no "abridgment" of these freedoms of speech and the press. Without such an "abridgement" there is no violation of the First Amendment.

EDITOR'S ANALYSIS: *Washington v. United States*, 460 U.S., (1983). There, the Court was dealing with a state tax that singled out federal contractors as a separate category. It did not evidence any reluctance in that case to assess the impact of the tax, finding it was not impermissibly discriminatory on the United States because it imposed a tax burden no greater than what the contractors would have had to otherwise pay in state taxes were they treated the same as everyone else.

[For more information on differential taxation of the press, see Casenote Law Outline on Constitutional Law, Chapter 13, § III, Freedom of the Press.]

QUICKNOTES

DIFFERENTIAL TAXATION - A marked disparity in tax rates between parties where such rates should be uniform.

CHAPTER 14
THE RELIGION CLAUSES: FREE EXERCISE AND ESTABLISHMENT

QUICK REFERENCE RULES OF LAW

1. **Laws Discriminating Against Religion.** If a law's object is to infringe upon or restrict religious practices, it must be justified by a compelling interest and be narrowly tailored to advance that interest. (Church of the Lukumi Babalu Aye v. City of Hialeah)

   [For more information on the free exercise of religion, see Casenotes Law Outline on Constitutional Law, Chapter 14, §II, Free Exercise of Religion.]

2. **Neutral Laws Adversely Affecting Religion.** It is an unconstitutional burden on a worker's free exercise of religion for a state to apply eligibility requirements for unemployment benefits so as to force a worker to abandon her religious principles respecting her religion's sabbath. (Sherbert v. Verner)

   [For more information on unemployment compensation eligibility requirements that burden the free exercise of religion, see Casenote Law Outline on Constitutional Law, Chapter 14, § III, Adjudication or Other Settlement of Religious Matters.]

3. **Neutral Laws Adversely Affecting Religion.** An individual's religious beliefs do not excuse noncompliance with an otherwise valid law prohibiting conduct that the state is free to regulate. (Employment Division, Dept. of Human Resources v. Smith)

   [For more information on the free exercise of religion, see Casenotes Law Outline on Constitutional Law, Chapter 14, § II, Free Exercise of Religion.]

4. **Enshrining Official Beliefs.** A religious released time program, which permits public school students to leave school to attend religious instruction and for which the schools do no more than accommodate their schedules, does not violate the First Amendment. (Zorach v. Clauson)

   [For more information on sectarian teaching during school hours off-premises, see Casenote Law Outline on Constitutional Law, Chapter 14, § I, The Establishment Clause.]

5. **Enshrining Official Beliefs.** Religious invocations and benedictions may not be given at a public primary or secondary school graduation ceremony. (Lee v. Weisman)

   [For more information on prayer in public schools, see Casenote Law Outline on Constitutional Law, Chapter 14, § I, The Establishment Clause.]

6. **Enshrining Official Beliefs.** Any statute requiring the teaching of a religious theory whenever a scientific theory is taught violates the Establishment Clause. (Edwards v. Aguillard)

   [For more information on state prohibition or promotion of teaching certain theories in order to protect or promote religion, see Casenote Law Outline or Constitutional Law, Chapter 14, Freedom of Religion, § I, The Establishment Clause.]

7. **Enshrining Official Beliefs.** The Establishment Clause does not prohibit a municipality from including a religious display in its annual Christmas display. (Lynch v. Donnelly)

   [For more information on governmental use of or association with religious symbols, see Casenote Law

Outline on Constitutional Law, Chapter 14, § I, The Establishment Clause.]

8. **Financial Aid to Religious Institutions.** The First Amendment forbids a state to exclude any of its citizens, because of their religious faith, or lack of it, from receiving the benefits of public welfare legislation. A statute authorizing the spending of tax-raised funds to pay the bus fares of parochial school children as part of a general program under which it pays the fares of children attending public and other schools is public welfare legislation. (Everson v. Board of Education)

> *[For more information on public aid to sectarian schools, see Casenote Law Outline on Constitutional Law, Chapter 14, § I, The Establishment Clause.]*

9. **Financial Aid to Religious Institutions.** The three-prong test for determining if a program aiding parochial schools violates the Establishment Clause is as follows: 1) does it have a secular purpose?; 2) does it have "the primary effect of advancing the sectarian aims of the nonpublic schools?"; and 3) does it "excessively entangle" the state in religion? (Mueller v. Allen)

> *[For more information on state tuition assistance to parents, see Casenote Law Outline on Constitutional Law, Chapter 14, § I, The Establishment Clause.]*

10. **Financial Aid to Religious Institutions.** A federally funded program providing supplemental, remedial instruction to disadvantaged children on a neutral basis is not invalid under the Establishment Clause when such instruction is given on the premises of sectarian schools by government employees pursuant to a program containing prescribed safeguards. (Agostini v. Felton)

> *[For more information on freedom of religion, see Casenote Law Outline on Constitutional Law, Chapter 14, § I, The Establishment Clause.]*

CHURCH OF THE LUKUMI BABALU AYE, INC. v. CITY OF HIALEAH

Church (P) v. Municipality (D)

508 U.S. 520, 113 S. Ct. 2217 (1993).

NATURE OF CASE: Review of decision upholding an ordinance prohibiting ritual animal sacrifice.

FACT SUMMARY: A church (P), which performed the sacrificial killing of animals as required by the Santeria religion, challenged various Hialeah (D) ordinances prohibiting such killings as a violation of the Free Exercise Clause of the First Amendment.

CONCISE RULE OF LAW: If a law's object is to infringe upon or restrict religious practices, it must be justified by a compelling interest and be narrowly tailored to advance that interest.

FACTS: The Church of the Lukumi Babalu Aye, (P) (Church) and its members practiced the religion of Santeria. An integral part of the religion was the sacrificial killing of animals for certain events. In 1987, the Church (P) leased land in the city of Hialeah (D) on which it planned to build various structures including a house of worship. Distressed by the Church's (P) plans, Hialeah (D) called an emergency public session during which it passed various ordinances that essentially prohibited the type of sacrifices required in Santeria. The Church (P) thereafter filed suit, arguing that the ordinances violated the Free Exercise Clause of the First Amendment by targeting its religious practices. The district court disagreed and upheld the ordinances with the court of appeals affirming. The U.S. Supreme Court granted review.

ISSUE: Must a law be justified by a compelling interest and be narrowly tailored to advance that interest if its object is to infringe upon or restrict religious practices?

HOLDING AND DECISION: (Kennedy, J.) Yes. If a law's object is to infringe upon or restrict religious practices, it must be justified by a compelling interest and be narrowly tailored to advance that interest. Neutral and generally applicable laws need not meet this higher level of scrutiny. The ordinances at issue, however, were not neutral and generally applicable. They restricted the practices because of their religious motivation. Though not evident on the face of the ordinances, their non-neutrality is clear from the expressed concerns of residents and citizens, the expressed motive of council members, and the ordinances' operation. Practically the only conduct prohibited by the ordinances is that exercised by Santeria church members. In addition, the ordinances in no way promoted the legitimate concerns of public morals, peace, or safety advanced in their support. Thus, since the ordinances were not neutral and were not narrowly tailored to serve compelling interests, they were unconstitutional. Reversed.

CONCURRENCE: (Scalia, J.) The ordinances violate the Free Exercise Clause simply because they prohibit the free exercise of religion, regardless of the good, bad, or nonexistent motive of the lawmakers.

CONCURRENCE: (Souter, J.) Though this case is correctly decided, the rule that neutral laws of general applicability are not subject to a higher level of scrutiny should be readdressed to prevent putting believers in religion to a choice between God and government.

CONCURRENCE: (Blackmun, J.) The rule that neutral laws of general applicability need not be justified by a compelling interest wrongly ignores the value of religious freedom as an individual liberty.

EDITOR'S ANALYSIS: Though a majority of the Court agrees that the correct result was reached, the concurring opinions evidence the hostility of many justices to the rule announced in *Employment Div., Dept. of Human Resources of Oregon v. Smith*, 494 U.S. 872 (1990) just three year earlier that neutral laws of general applicability are not subject to a high level of scrutiny. Thus, its continued viability is questionable as the makeup of the Court changes.

{For more information on the free exercise of religion, see Casenotes Law Outline on Constitutional Law, Chapter 14, §II, Free Exercise of Religion.}

QUICKNOTES

COMPELLING STATE INTEREST - Defense to an alleged Equal Protection Clause violation that a state action was necessary in order to protect an interest that the government is under a duty to protect.

FREE EXERCISE OF RELIGION - The right to practice one's religious beliefs free from governmental conduct or interference.

NOTES:

SHERBERT v. VERNER
Applicant for unemployment (P) v. Commission (D)
347 U.S. 398 (1963).

NATURE OF CASE: Action arising out of the Employment Security Commission's (D) denial of Sherbert's (P) claim for unemployment compensation benefits.

FACT SUMMARY: Sherbert (P) was discharged by her employer because she would not work on her religion's sabbath.

CONCISE RULE OF LAW: It is an unconstitutional burden on a worker's free exercise of religion for a state to apply eligibility requirements for unemployment benefits so as to force a worker to abandon her religious principles respecting her religion's sabbath.

FACTS: Sherbert (P) was discharged by her employer because she refused to work on Saturday, her religion's sabbath. The Employment Security Commission (D) found Sherbert (P) ineligible for benefits because her refusal to work on Saturday was failure without good cause to accept available work. The state law provides that no employee shall be required to work on Sunday.

ISSUE: Is it unconstitutional for a state to refuse unemployment benefits to a worker who was discharged because of her refusal to work on her religion's sabbath?

HOLDING AND DECISION: (Brennan, J.) Yes. It is an unconstitutional burden on a worker's free exercise of religion for a state to apply eligibility requirements for unemployment benefits so as to force a worker to abandon her religious principles respecting her religion's sabbath. Sherbert (P) was forced to choose between following her religion or obtaining unemployment benefits. Such a choice puts the same kind of burden on her free exercise of religion as would a fine imposed for Saturday worship. Further, by expressly providing that no one will be compelled to work on Sunday, the state saves the Sunday worshipper from having to make such a choice. The state has shown no compelling state interest to justify this burden on Sherbert's (P) free exercise of religion. Hence, the burden is unconstitutional. This case is distinguishable from *Braunfeld v. Brown*. There, the state showed a strong state interest in providing one uniform day of rest for all workers.

CONCURRENCE: (Stewart, J.) The cases dealing with the Establishment Clause have been wrongly decided, and this case is in conflict with them. They hold that the government must blind itself to differing religious traditions and beliefs. Yet, here the Court holds that because Sherbert's (P) refusal to work Saturdays is religiously motivated, she is entitled to unemployment benefits. Were she unable to work Saturdays due to indolence or lack of a babysitter, she would not be entitled to benefits. Also, this case is

in conflict with Braunfeld. The criminal statute involved there made the burden on religious freedom much greater than here. Braunfeld should be overruled.

DISSENT: (Harlan, J.) The purpose of unemployment benefits was to tide people over while work was unavailable. It was not to provide relief for those who for personal reasons became unavailable for work. Secondly, this decision is in conflict with and overrules Braunfeld.

EDITOR'S ANALYSIS: The Court has encountered many situations unlike Sherbert's, in which the individual's right to freedom of religious belief and practices is subordinated to other community interests. Freedom of religion is not absolute, and does not extend to situations where its practice would jeopardize public health, safety, or morals, or the rights of third persons. Hence, laws prohibiting polygamy and bigamy have been upheld, as well as those requiring compulsory vaccination and X-rays, in spite of allegations that such laws required action in violation of the Mormon and Christian Science religions. The conscientious objector's right to avoid military service has been said to rest upon legislative grace rather than constitutional right.

[For more information on unemployment compensation eligibility requirements that burden the free exercise of religion, see Casenote Law Outline on Constitutional Law, Chapter 14, § III, Adjudication or Other Settlement of Religious Matters.]

QUICKNOTES

COMPELLING STATE INTEREST - Defense to an alleged Equal Protection Clause violation that a state action was necessary in order to protect an interest that the government is under a duty to protect.

ESTABLISHMENT CLAUSE - The constitutional provision prohibiting the government from favoring any one religion over others, or engaging in religious activities or advocacy.

FREE EXERCISE OF RELIGION - The right to practice one's religious beliefs free from governmental conduct or interference.

EMPLOYMENT DIV., OREGON DEPT. OF HUMAN RESOURCES v. SMITH

State (P) v. Applicant for unemployment compensation (D)
494 U.S. 872 (1990).

NATURE OF CASE: Appeal from judgment declaring unconstitutional an Oregon statute prohibiting the sacramental use of peyote.

FACT SUMMARY: After Smith (D) ingested peyote during a ceremony of the Native American Church, he was terminated from his job as a drug counselor.

CONCISE RULE OF LAW: An individual's religious beliefs do not excuse noncompliance with an otherwise valid law prohibiting conduct that the state is free to regulate.

FACTS: Smith (D) was fired from his job with a private drug rehabilitation organization because he ingested peyote for sacramental purposes during a ceremony of the Native American Church. Oregon law classifies peyote as a controlled substance. Persons convicted of possessing peyote are guilty of a felony. Smith (D) was deemed ineligible for unemployment compensation benefits after it was determined he was discharged for "misconduct." The Oregon Court of Appeals and the Oregon Supreme Court reversed that determination on the basis that the Oregon prohibition of the sacramental use of peyote violated Smith's (D) free exercise of religion. The Supreme Court granted certiorari.

ISSUE: Do an individual's religious beliefs excuse noncompliance with an otherwise valid law prohibiting conduct that the state is free to regulate?

HOLDING AND DECISION: (Scalia, J.) No. An individual's religious beliefs do not excuse noncompliance with an otherwise valid law prohibiting conduct that the state is free to regulate. The free exercise of religion means the right to believe and profess whatever religious doctrine one desires. The exercise of religion often involves not only belief and profession but the performance of physical acts. A state would be prohibiting the free exercise if it seeks to ban acts that are only engaged in for religious reasons. Smith (D) contends that his religious motivation for using peyote places its use beyond the reach of a criminal law not specifically directed at religious practice even though the law is constitutional when applied against nonreligious use of a controlled substance. This Court's decisions have consistently held that the right of free exercise does not relieve an individual of the obligation to comply with a valid and neutral law of general applicability on the ground that the law proscribes conduct that his religion prescribes. Smith (D) contends that rejection of his claim for religious exemption for peyote use may only be justified by a balancing compelling state interest. The compelling state interest test is inapplicable to validate challenges to criminal prohibitions on a particular form of conduct. Application of the compelling interest standard in this context would open the prospect of constitutionally required religious exemptions from civic obligations of almost every conceivable kind — ranging from compulsory military service to the payment of taxes. Reversed.

CONCURRENCE: (O'Connor, J.) Oregon has a compelling state interest in regulating peyote use by its citizens, and accommodating Smith's (D) religiously motivated conduct will unduly interfere with the fulfillment of the government interest.

DISSENT: (Blackmun, J.) The critical question in this case is whether exempting Smith (D) from Oregon's general prohibition on peyote use will unduly interfere with fulfillment of the governmental interest. It is not Oregon's broad interest in fighting the critical war on drugs that must be weighed against Smith's (D) claim, but Oregon's narrow interest in refusing to make an exception for the religious, ceremonial use of peyote. The state's asserted interest amounts to the symbolic preservation of an unenforced prohibition. Almost half the states and the federal government have maintained an exemption for religious peyote use and have not found themselves overwhelmed by claims to other religious exemptions. Also, the courts should not turn a blind eye to the severe impact of a state's restrictions on the adherents of a minority religion. Oregon's interest in enforcing its drug laws against religious use of peyote is not sufficiently compelling to outweigh Smith's (D) right to the free exercise of religion.

EDITOR'S ANALYSIS: Selective service laws have traditionally exempted from military service conscientious objectors opposed to war in any form on religious grounds. However, the Court has traditionally held that the exemption is a product of the legislature rather than compelled by the constitutional prohibition on the free exercise of religion. See for example the Selective Draft Law Cases, 245 U.S. 366 (1918).

[For more information on the free exercise of religion, see Casenotes Law Outline on Constitutional Law, Chapter 14, § II, Free Exercise of Religion.]

QUICKNOTES

COMPELLING STATE INTEREST - Defense to an alleged Equal Protection Clause violation that a state action was necessary in order to protect an interest that the government is under a duty to protect.

FELONY - A criminal offense of greater seriousness than a misdemeanor; felonies are generally defined pursuant to statute as any crime that is punishable by death or by a term of imprisonment exceeding one year.

FREE EXERCISE OF RELIGION - The right to practice one's religious beliefs free from governmental conduct or interference.

SACRAMENTAL USE (referring to ingestion of peyote during church ceremonies - native Amer.) - Use pertaining to church ceremonies.

ZORACH v. CLAUSON
Parties not identified.
343 U.S. 306 (1952).

NATURE OF CASE: Taxpayer's suit challenging the constitutionality of a state statute.

FACT SUMMARY: A religious released time program allowed public schools to release students during the school day to attend religious classes.

CONCISE RULE OF LAW: A religious released time program, which permits public school students to leave school to attend religious instruction and for which the schools do no more than accommodate their schedules, does not violate the First Amendment.

FACTS: A religious released time program permitted public schools to release students during the school day so that they could leave the school grounds to attend religious instruction. Students who are not released remain in the classrooms. The religious groups reported to the school from which children were released but did not attend the religious instruction there. No use of public funds or buildings was involved. The religious groups bore all of the program's costs.

ISSUE: Does a religious released time program which releases public school children during the school day to attend religious instruction and for which the public schools do no more than accommodate their schedules, violate the First Amendment?

HOLDING AND DECISION: (Douglas, J.) No. The First Amendment does not say that in every and all respects there must be a separation of church and state. If it did, religion and state would be hostile to one another. Municipalities would not be allowed to render police or fire protection to religious institutions, and prayers in public meetings would have to be banned. This would not be in keeping with our heritage as a religious people. In *McCollum v. Board of Education*, a similar religious released time program was found to violate the First Amendment. However, there the public school classrooms were turned over to religious instructors. Here, the instruction occurs off school grounds, and the public schools do no more than accommodate their schedules to the program. No one is forced to attend. The program does not violate the First Amendment.

DISSENT: (Black, J.) New York is manipulating its compulsory education laws to help religious sects get students.

DISSENT: (Jackson, J.) First, the state compels students to yield a large part of their time for public secular education and, second, some of this time may be released to the students on the condition that they devote it to religious study. Simply shortening the school day would facilitate optional attendance at religious classes. It is objected that if the students are made free, they will not attend religious classes. Hence, they must be deprived of their freedom and allowed to choose between attending religious instruction or remaining at school, which serves as a temporary jail for the child who will not attend religious instruction.

EDITOR'S ANALYSIS: One of the few establishment cases that did not involve schools was *McGowan v. Maryland*, 366 U.S. 420, wherein the court rejected claims that Sunday closing laws violated the First Amendment. The Court stated, "The present purpose and effect of most of them is to provide a uniform day of rest for all citizens; the fact that this day is Sunday, a day of particular significance for the dominant Christian sects, does not bar the state from achieving its secular goals." *Epperson v. Arkansas*, 393 U.S. 97, which gained national notoriety in the Scopes trial, is one of the best known establishment controversies. There the Court held that a state law forbidding the teaching of evolution in public schools violated the First Amendment. "The overriding fact is that Arkansas law selects from the body of knowledge a particular segment which it proscribes for the sole reason that it is deemed to conflict with a particular religious doctrine." This was not religious neutrality.

[For more information on sectarian teaching during school hours off-premises, see Casenote Law Outline on Constitutional Law, Chapter 14, § I, The Establishment Clause.]

QUICKNOTES

ESTABLISHMENT CLAUSE - The constitutional provision prohibiting the government from favoring any one religion over others, or engaging in religious activities or advocacy.

NOTES:

LEE v. WEISMAN

School officials (D) v. Parent (P)

505 U.S. 577, 112 S. Ct. 2649 (1992).

NATURE OF CASE: Appeal of permanent injunction.

FACT SUMMARY: Daniel Weisman (P), father of student Deborah (P), sought a permanent injunction barring the Providence public school officials (D) from inviting clergy to deliver invocations and benedictions at graduation ceremonies.

CONCISE RULE OF LAW: Religious invocations and benedictions may not be given at a public primary or secondary school graduation ceremony.

FACTS: As allowed by the Providence School Committee (D), Principal Lee (D) invited Rabbi Gutterman to give the invocation and benediction at Lee's (D) middle school's graduation. Attendance at graduation exercises at Providence public schools is voluntary. Following school procedure, Lee (D) gave Rabbi Gutterman written guidelines for nonsectarian prayers. David Weisman (P), on behalf of himself and his daughter Deborah (P), sought a TRO against school officials (D) to prevent Rabbi Gutterman from delivering prayers at Deborah's (P) graduation. The TRO was denied, and Deborah (P) went through ceremonies. The students stood for a few minutes while Rabbi Gutterman delivered prayers. The Weismans' (P) suit continued since Deborah (P) was a student at a Providence public high school and would likely face the same situation at high school graduation. The district court held the prayers violated the Establishment Clause and permanently enjoined school officials (D) from inviting clergy to give invocations and benedictions at future graduations. The court of appeals affirmed.

ISSUE: May religious invocations and benedictions be given at a public primary or secondary school graduation ceremony?

HOLDING AND DECISION: (Kennedy, J.) No. Religious invocations and benedictions may not be given at a public primary or secondary school graduation ceremony. Here, state officials (D) directed the performance of a formal, explicit religious exercise at public school graduation. Principal Lee (D) decided which prayers should be given, selected the cleric, and gave written guidelines for the prayer. Even for students who objected to religious exercise, attendance and participation was in every practical sense obligatory. High school graduation is one of life's most significant occasions. To say that attendance is "voluntary" is formalistic in the extreme. Such prayers in public schools carry a particular risk of coercion. There is public and peer pressure on attending students to stand as a group, or maintain respectful silence. A dissenter is injured by his reasonable perception that others view his standing as approval, and that he is being forced by the state to pray. The First Amendment protects the objector from having to take unilateral, private action to avoid compromising religious principles at a state function. The fact that the prayer was "nonsectarian" does not make government involvement acceptable. Affirmed.

CONCURRENCE: (Blackmun, J.) The Establishment Clause not only prohibits government coercion, but also any government engagement in religious practices. The simple issue is whether the state placed a stamp of approval on a religious activity. Here, it did.

CONCURRENCE: (Souter, J.) The history of the First Amendment supports the settled principle that the Establishment Clause prohibits support for religion in general as much as support for a particular religion. A distinction between "sectarian" and "nonsectarian" prayers would involve courts in an unconstitutional inquiry as to whether particular prayers are ecumenical enough. A showing of coercion is not necessary to establish a violation of the Establishment Clause. Were coercion a requirement under the Establishment Clause, the Clause would be redundant. The Framers' writings and practices indicate a much broader reading than a mere ban on state coercion.

DISSENT: (Scalia, J.) Nonsectarian prayers at graduations and other public celebrations are a longstanding American tradition. From the Framers to our current President, Congress, and Supreme Court, government leaders have opened public functions with prayer. Deborah (P) was not forced to pray. Standing is not necessarily a sign of approval; more likely it is a sign of respect for religious beliefs of others, a civic virtue which our schools should cultivate. The Establishment Clause only bars state religious activity backed by threat of penalty for nonparticipation.

EDITOR'S ANALYSIS: The dissent claimed that the Court's failure to apply the three-part test of *Lemon v. Kurtzman*, 403 U.S. 602 (1971), means the test is no longer good law. However, Justice Kennedy in his opinion for the Court expressly declined to reconsider Lemon. Justices Kennedy and Souter both cited *Lemon* with approval, though they did not apply the test. Justice Blackmun's concurrence, joined by Justices Stevens and O'Connor, expressed the view that Lemon still applies in all Establishment Clause cases.

[For more information on prayer in public schools, see Casenote Law Outline on Constitutional Law, Chapter 14, § I, The Establishment Clause.]

QUICKNOTES

ESTABLISHMENT CLAUSE - The constitutional provision prohibiting the government from favoring any one religion over others, or engaging in religious activities or advocacy.

TRO - An order issued without notice or hearing used to preserve the status quo preventing specific activity from being conducted.

EDWARDS v. AGUILLARD
Parties not identified.
482 U.S. 578 (1987).

NATURE OF CASE: Appeal from invalidation of an education statute.

FACT SUMMARY: Louisiana (D) contended its statute, requiring the teaching of evolution and creationism together if either was taught, was constitutional.

CONCISE RULE OF LAW: Any statute requiring the teaching of a religious theory whenever a scientific theory is taught violates the Establishment Clause.

FACTS: Louisiana (D) enacted the Creationism Act which required the teaching of creationism if the theory of evolution was taught. The statute was challenged as contrary to the Establishment Clause. The state defended it, saying it promoted academic freedom. The trial court held the statute unconstitutional. The court of appeals affirmed and the Supreme Court granted certiorari.

ISSUE: Does the requirement that a religious theory be taught with scientific theory violate the Establishment Clause?

HOLDING AND DECISION: (Brennan, J.) Yes. Any statute requiring the teaching of religious theory along with scientific theory violates the Establishment Clause. This Act required public schools to advance a religious doctrine. It thus clearly had a nonsecular purpose and violated the Constitution. Affirmed.

CONCURRENCE: (Powell, J.) This Act was clearly passed to advance a religious purpose. It thus was invalid.

DISSENT: (Scalia, J.) There was no evidence this Act was primarily motivated by a desire to advance a particular religious theory.

EDITOR'S ANALYSIS: The Court pointed out that religious freedom was not advanced by this statute. Because this was the stated rationale for its passage, it could not survive. It was not promotive of freedom as it deterred the teaching of one theory by requiring the simultaneous teaching of the other.

[For more information on state prohibition or promotion of teaching certain theories in order to protect or promote religion, see Casenote Law Outline or Constitutional Law, Chapter 14, § I, The Establishment Clause.]

QUICKNOTES

ESTABLISHMENT CLAUSE - The constitutional provision prohibiting the government from favoring any one religion over others, or engaging in religious activities or advocacy.

NOTES:

LYNCH v. DONNELLY
Municipality (D) v. Union/residents (P)
465 U.S. 668 (1984).

NATURE OF CASE: Appeal from a judgment holding a public religious display unconstitutional.

FACT SUMMARY: The district court held that the City of Pawtucket's (D) display of nativity scene on public property violated the Establishment Clause.

CONCISE RULE OF LAW: The Establishment Clause does not prohibit a municipality from including a religious display in its annual Christmas display.

FACTS: The City of Pawtucket (D), Rhode Island included a nativity scene in its annual Christmas display. It had done so for over 40 years. The A.C.L.U. (P), and certain residents of Pawtucket, sued, contending the inclusion of the scene violated the Establishment Clause. The district court found for the A.C.L.U. (P), holding the scene conferred a substantial benefit on religion. The court of appeals affirmed, and the City (D) appealed.

ISSUE: Does the Establishment Clause prohibit a municipality from including a religious display in its annual Christmas display?

HOLDING AND DECISION: (Burger, C.J.) No. The Establishment Clause does not prohibit a municipality from including a religious display in its annual Christmas display. The Establishment Clause has historically not been interpreted in a strict manner. The inclusion of the nativity scene conferred no discernible advantage on religion that exceeded that resulting from the inclusion of "In God We Trust" on money and other permissible religious references. As a result, the display did not violate the Establishment Clause. Reversed.

CONCURRENCE: (O'Connor, J.) In this case there was no impermissible government entanglement in religion, and no municipal endorsement of religion. Therefore, it did not violate the Establishment Clause.

DISSENT: (Brennan, J.) This display is a recreation of an event which lies at the heart of the Christian religion. As a result, it promotes that religion and religion in general and violated the clause.

DISSENT: (Blackmun, J.) The Court ignored the established precedents in upholding the display.

EDITOR'S ANALYSIS: This case represents the trend in the Supreme Court's handling of Establishment Clause cases, instead of applying the set three-prong analysis used in many cases, such as *Larkin v. Grendel's Den, Inc.*, 459 U.S. 116 (1982), wherein a statute or other governmental action is evaluated for its effect on religion and government. In *Marsh v.* *Chambers*, 463 U.S. 783 (1983), the Court, again with Chief Justice Burger writing for the majority, failed to apply the three-prong analysis and upheld a government prayer observance valid.

[For more information on governmental use of or association with religious symbols, see Casenote Law Outline on Constitutional Law, Chapter 14, § I, The Establishment Clause.]

QUICKNOTES

ESTABLISHMENT CLAUSE - The constitutional provision prohibiting the government from favoring any one religion over others, or engaging in religious activities or advocacy.

NOTES:

EVERSON v. BOARD OF EDUCATION
Taxpayer (P) v. School board (D)
330 U.S. 1 (1947).

NATURE OF CASE: Taxpayer's suit challenging the constitutionality of a state statute.

FACT SUMMARY: Acting pursuant to a state statute authorizing local boards to make rules and contracts for the transportation of school children, a Board of Education (D) authorized the reimbursement to parents of money spent on their children's transportation to school, including parochial schools.

CONCISE RULE OF LAW: The First Amendment forbids a state to exclude any of its citizens, because of their religious faith, or lack of it, from receiving the benefits of public welfare legislation. A statute authorizing the spending of tax-raised funds to pay the bus fares of parochial school children as part of a general program under which it pays the fares of children attending public and other schools is public welfare legislation.

FACTS: A state statute authorizes local school boards to make rules and contracts for the transportation of school children. A Board of Education (D), acting pursuant to this statute, authorized reimbursement to parents of money spent on their children's transportation to school on the public transportation system. Part of this money was for the payment of transportation of children to Catholic parochial schools. At these schools, the children received religious instruction, as well as a secular education. Everson (P) brought this taxpayer's suit challenging the statute's constitutionality. He contended that the statute violated the First Amendment in that it forced its citizens to pay taxes to help support and maintain schools which taught the Catholic faith.

ISSUE: Does a state statute authorizing that parents be reimbursed for money spent on their children's transportation to parochial schools violate the First Amendment?

HOLDING AND DECISION: (Black, J.) No. The First Amendment, which is made applicable to the states by the Fourteenth Amendment, commands that a state shall make no law respecting an establishment of religion, or prohibiting the free exercise thereof. A state cannot, consistent with the First Amendment, contribute tax-raised funds to any institution which teaches the tenets and faith of any church. On the other hand, neither can a state hamper its citizens in the free exercise of their own religion. Hence, it cannot exclude members of any faith, because of their faith or lack of it, from receiving the benefits of public welfare legislation. State power is no more to be used so as to handicap religions than it is to favor them. Parents would be less willing to send their children to parochial schools if such children were not to be protected by police employed to protect them from traffic dangers, or if such schools were cut off from government services such as police and fire protection, sewage disposal, highways and sidewalks. Likewise, such parents might be less willing to permit their children to attend parochial schools if they were thereby cut off from state reimbursement for their children's school transportation. A statute authorizing the spending of tax-raised funds to pay the bus fares of parochial school children as a part of a general program under which it pays the fares of children attending public and other schools is public welfare legislation and does not violate the First Amendment.

DISSENT: (Jackson, J.) The test to be used is that money taken by taxation may not be used to support any religious training or belief. Here, the funds were raised by taxation and were given to religious institutions. The case is not comparable to one of furnishing fire or police protection or public highways, since those things are matters of common right and part of the general need for safety. There is no reason to require the state to pay for transportation to religious schools.

EDITOR'S ANALYSIS: The First Amendment guarantees that neither the federal nor any state government may establish an official religion and that every person is free to practice his faith as he chooses. The former involves the Establishment Clause, and the latter the Free Exercise Clause. These clauses protect overlapping values but they may exert conflicting pressures. Under the Establishment Clause, the Supreme Court has ruled against the giving of any state assistance to religious causes, even though it may be nondiscriminatory as between different faiths. Although the Court's attention to financial assistance involving religious groups is longstanding, it did not become intense and controversial until recently with the increasing demand for federal spending for education.

[For more information on public aid to sectarian schools, see Casenote Law Outline on Constitutional Law, Chapter 14, § I, The Establishment Clause.]

QUICKNOTES
ESTABLISHMENT CLAUSE - The constitutional provision prohibiting the government from favoring any one religion over others, or engaging in religious activities or advocacy.

FREE EXERCISE OF RELIGION - The right to practice one's religious beliefs free from governmental conduct or interference.

PAROCHIAL SCHOOLS - Schools affiliated with a parish or other religious body.

AGOSTINI v. FELTON

Parties not identified.

521 U.S. 203, 117 S. Ct. 1997 (1997).

NATURE OF CASE: Action seeking relief from permanent injunction banning remedial public instruction in parochial schools.

FACT SUMMARY: The New York City Board of Education (D) sought to overturn a prior Supreme Court decision holding that the Establishment Clause barred it from sending public school teachers into parochial schools to provide remedial education to disadvantaged children pursuant to a congressionally mandated program.

CONCISE RULE OF LAW: A federally funded program providing supplemental, remedial instruction to disadvantaged children on a neutral basis is not invalid under the Establishment Clause when such instruction is given on the premises of sectarian schools by government employees pursuant to a program containing prescribed safeguards.

FACTS: Title I of the Elementary and Secondary Education Act of 1965 provided funds to local educational agencies to provide remedial education, guidance, and job counseling to students failing or at risk of failing a state's student performance standards. Such funds were required to be made available to all eligible children, regardless of whether they attended public or private school. The New York City School Board (Board) (D) has since grappled with how to provide Title I services to the private school students within its jurisdiction since more than 90% of those private schools were religious. The Board (D) initially arranged to transport children to public schools for after-school Title I instruction, but attendance was poor, and a new plan was devised to allow Title I instruction on private school premises during school hours. The plan was specifically designed to ensure that teachers would work independently as Board (D) employees and would not introduce any religious matter into their teaching or become involved in any way with the religious activities of the private schools. In 1978, six federal taxpayers (P) sued the Board (D), arguing that the program required excessive entanglement of church and state. The district court granted summary judgment for the Board (D), but the court of appeals reversed. In Aquilar v. Felton, 473 U.S. 402 (1985), the Supreme Court affirmed the appellate court decision, finding that the Board's (D) Title I program did require excessive entanglement. It enjoined the Board (D) from employing public school teachers on the premises of private sectarian schools. The Board (D) then reverted to its prior practice of providing instruction at public school sites, at leased sites, and in mobile instructional units parked near the sectarian schools. In 1997, the Board (D) petitioned for relief from the earlier injunction under Federal Rule of Civil Procedure 60(b)(5) arguing that the Court's intervening Establishment Clause jurisprudence rendered its earlier decision invalid.

ISSUE: Is a federally funded program providing supplemental, remedial instruction to disadvantaged children on a neutral basis invalid under the Establishment Clause when such instruction is given on the premises of sectarian schools by government employees pursuant to a program containing prescribed safeguards?

HOLDING AND DECISION: (O'Connor, J.) No. A federally funded program providing supplemental, remedial instruction to disadvantaged children on a neutral basis is not invalid under the Establishment Clause when such instruction is given on the premises of sectarian schools by government employees pursuant to a program containing prescribed safeguards. Rule 60(b)(5) states that the court may relieve a party from a final judgment or order when it is no longer equitable that the judgment should have prospective application. The Supreme Court has held that it is appropriate to grant a Rule 60(b)(5) motion when the party seeking relief can show a significant change either in factual conditions or in law. Since the Aguilar decision, the Court has modified its approach to Establishment Clause challenges in two significant respects. First, the Court has abandoned the presumption that the placement of public employees on parochial school grounds inevitably results in the impermissible effect of state-sponsored indoctrination. Second, the Court has departed from the prior rule that all government aid that directly aids the educational function of religious schools is invalid. Furthermore, there is no basis for concluding that Title I services are an impermissible subsidy of religion when offered on-campus, but not when offered off-campus. Where aid is allocated on the basis of neutral, secular criteria that neither favor nor disfavor religion, and is made available to both religious and secular beneficiaries on a nondiscriminatory basis, the aid is less likely to have the effect of advancing religion. In sum, the Board's (D) Title I program does not result in governmental indoctrination, define its recipients by reference to religion, or create an excessive entanglement. Relief under Rule 60(b)(5) is granted. The judgment of the court of appeals is reversed and the case is remanded with instructions to vacate the 1985 order.

DISSENT: (Souter, J.) The Aguilar holding was a correct and sensible decision. The ban against governmental endorsement of religion is rooted in strong historical precedence. Any time the government assists a religious school, even in a remedial program, the school saves money and resources which it can then put back into its religious programs. While Title I sets worthy goals, constitutional lines must be drawn.

Continue on next page

DISSENT: (Ginsburg, J.) A proper application of the Rule 60(b)(5) would lead to the deferment of a reconsideration of Aguilar until the issue is presented in a more appropriate case.

EDITOR'S ANALYSIS: The dissenters, although admittedly moved by the well-intentioned nature of the Title I program at issue, believed that this still did not justify the rather unusual course of events represented by the history of this case. It seems only just that school boards be allowed as much leeway as possible in their efforts to provide an invaluable service to the disadvantaged youths the program targets. This case will certainly have a wide-reaching impact on thousands of schoolchildren throughout the country.

[For more information on freedom of religion, see Casenote Law Outline on Constitutional Law, Chapter 14, § I, The Establishment Clause.]

QUICKNOTES

ESTABLISHMENT CLAUSE - The constitutional provision prohibiting the government from favoring any one religion over others, or engaging in religious activities or advocacy.

FREEDOM OF RELIGION - The guarantee of the First Amendment to the United States Constitution prohibiting Congress from enacting laws regarding the establishment of religion or prohibiting the free exercise thereof.

NOTES:

MUELLER v. ALLEN
Taxpayer (P) v. State (D)
463 U.S. 388 (1983).

NATURE OF CASE: Action challenging the constitutionality of a state tax deduction law.

FACT SUMMARY: Mueller (P) instituted suit challenging the constitutionality of a Minnesota law allowing taxpayers, in computing their state income tax, to deduct certain expenses incurred in providing for their children's education, whether or not the children attended public schools or private parochial schools.

CONCISE RULE OF LAW: The three-prong test for determining if a program aiding parochial schools violates the Establishment Clause is as follows: 1) does it have a secular purpose?; 2) does it have "the primary effect of advancing the sectarian aims of the nonpublic schools?;" and 3) does it "excessively entangle" the state in religion?

FACTS: Minnesota passed a law allowing taxpayers, in figuring their state income tax, to deduct actual expenses incurred for the "tuition, textbooks and transportation" of dependents attending elementary or secondary schools, whether or not they are nonsectarian or sectarian. A maximum of $500 deduction for each dependent in grades K through six and $700 for each dependent in grades seven through twelve was permitted. Mueller (P) brought suit challenging the validity of the law under the Establishment Clause. The court of appeals held that the Clause was not offended by this argument.

ISSUE: In order to decide if a program aiding parochial schools (directly or indirectly) violates the Establishment Clause, must the following three-part test be applied: 1) does it have a secular purpose?; 2) does it have "the primary effect of advancing the sectarian aims of the nonpublic schools?"; and 3) does it "excessively entangle" the state in religion?

HOLDING AND DECISION: (Rehnquist, J.) Yes. A three-part test was laid down in the Lemon case and is the means by which it can be ascertained whether a particular program that in some manner aids parochial schools (either directly or indirectly) violates the Establishment Clause. The first part inquires whether the program has a secular purpose. In this case, the answer is yes. The tax deduction attempts to give parents an incentive to educate their children and this serves the secular purpose of ensuring a well-educated citizenry. The second part of the test asks the related question of whether the program has "the primary effect of advancing the sectarian aims of the nonpublic schools." Here, the answer is no. The deduction is available to all parents, including those sending their children to public schools and it channels whatever funds available to such schools only as a result of numerous, private choices of individual parents of school-age children. The third part of the test to which this program must be put inquires whether or not the program "excessively entangles" the state in religion. It does not. The only decision that might remotely involve state officials in state

surveillance of religious-type issues would be the decisions state officials have to make in determining whether particular textbooks qualify for the deduction. In making this decision, they must disallow deductions taken from "instructional materials used in the teaching of religious tenets, doctrines or worship, the purpose of which is to inculcate such tenets, doctrines or worship." Making this type of decision does not differ substantially from making the types of decisions approved in early opinions of this Court. Thus, the program at issue here must be considered constitutional, as it has passed the three parts of the appropriate test. Affirmed.

DISSENT: (Marshall, J.) As this Court requoted in Nyquist, indirect assistance in the form of financial aid to parents for tuition payments is impermissible because it is not "subject to . . . restrictions" which "guarantee the separation between secular and religious educational functions and ... ensure that state financial aid supports only the former." The Minnesota statute at hand here is little more than a subsidy of tuition masquerading as a subsidy of general education expenses. While tax deductions are ostensibly available to parents sending their children to public schools, most such parents have no tuition payments to make and would be able to deduct only what they pay for such things as gym clothes, pencils, notebooks, etc. These deductible expenses are de minimus in comparison to tuition expenses paid by most parents sending their children to parochial schools. Thus, the parochial schools are the ones benefitted. In this case, the Court for the first time approves a program providing financial support for religious schools without any reason at all to assume that the support will be restricted to the secular functions of those schools and will not be used to support religious instruction. This result is flatly at odds with the fundamental principle that a state may provide no financial support whatsoever to promote religion.

EDITOR'S ANALYSIS: In the previously decided Nyquist case, on which the constitutional challenge to this tax deduction program relied heavily, New York had passed a statute that gave the parents of children attending private schools thinly disguised "tax benefits" that actually amounted to tuition grants. This was found to violate the Establishment Clause. By simply providing in its tax deduction statute that all parents could take such tuition deductions, Minnesota kept its tax deduction scheme from being declared unconstitutional. Yet, it is really a change in form more than substance, for most public school parents do not have to pay tuition. So, giving them the opportunity to deduct tuition expenses is of little practical consequence and does little to change the effect of the program in providing indirect aid mostly to parochial schools.

[For more information on state tuition assistance to parents, see Casenote Law Outline on Constitutional Law, Chapter 14, § I, The Establishment Clause.]

QUICKNOTES

ESTABLISHMENT CLAUSE - The constitutional provision prohibiting the government from favoring any one religion over others, or engaging in religious activities or advocacy.

NOTES

Palm case - illegal to 'out' CIA agent.
    investigation to find who outed. Novak will know.
    2 journalists under contempt threats right now
      (Judith Miller).

Is J. Miller like Branzburg?
    distinction: here journalist is part of crime
      Branzburg: journalists
        only witnesses [+ still not exempted
                 from testimony]

Branzburg:

White doesn't want to get into
    balancing who gets 'newsman's privilege'

      note: common   priest-penitent   [time
         law privileges: MD - patient   immemorial
                   spousal

             could these
               be constitutionalized?
          priest - could make 1A free exercise
                         argument?

      returns to buyer in Belotty — refusal
                to reg. 'right of
                       press'
          doesn't
         want to into 'who is the press?'
              get
                (who is
                 priest, MD is
                    easier)

"A law of general
   applicability" → isn't this
             what white is
           saying?
    gen app?
    priest
    MD
    spouse

J White
↓
back
of
hand
master
↓
Bowers/
Hardwick
maj.,
↓
roe
dissent
+
Branzburg